HERITAGE *Picture History of*
CIVIL WAR

By the Editors of
AMERICAN HERITAGE
The Magazine of History

Editor in Charge
RICHARD M. KETCHUM

Narrative by
BRUCE CATTON

AMERICAN HERITAGE/WINGS BOOKS
NEW YORK/AVENEL, NEW JERSEY

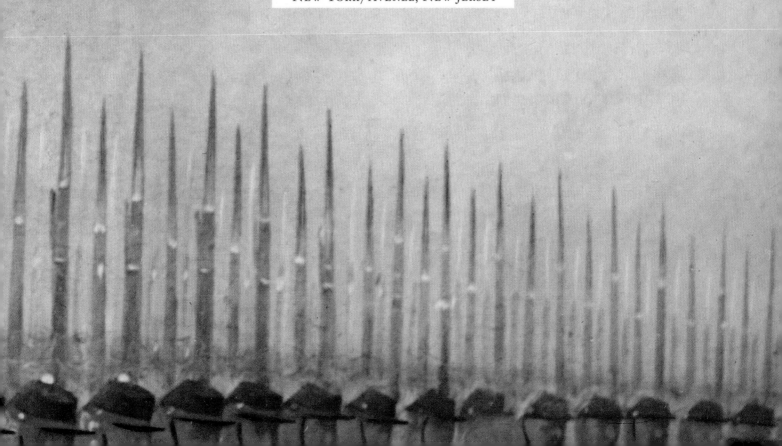

Staff for this Book

EDITOR
Richard M. Ketchum

ASSISTANT EDITOR
Stephen W. Sears

EDITORIAL ASSISTANTS
Joseph L. Gardner
Mary Sherman Parson

COPY EDITOR
Margaret Di Crocco
Assistant: Sally Dreyfus Carr

ART DIRECTOR
Irwin Glusker

DESIGNER
Elton S. Robinson

ORIGINAL MAPS
David Greenspan

This 1982 edition is published by Wings Books,
distributed by Outlet Book Company, Inc.,
a Random House Company, 40 Engelhard Avenue,
Avenel, New Jersey 07001, by arrangement with
American Heritage, a division of Forbes Inc.

Printed in the United States

Library of Congress Cataloging in Publication Data

Catton, Bruce, 1899–1978
   The American heritage picture history of the Civil War.

   Reprint. Originally published: New York:
American Heritage Pub. Co., 1960.
   Includes index.
   1. United States—History—Civil War, 1861–
1865.   I. Ketchum, Richard M., 1922–
II. American heritage.   III. Title.
E468.C284   1982   973.7   82–9603

ISBN: 0–517–385562

20   19   18   17   16   15   14

COOPER UNION MUSEUM

*A Union cavalryman, drawn
by Winslow Homer in 1863.*

The AMERICAN HERITAGE
Picture History of
THE CIVIL WAR

The AMERICAN

THE

Table of Contents

"Rainy Day in Camp" was painted by Winslow Homer, who first achieved fame as a Civil War combat artist.

Introduction

The war was over. The last Confederate army had surrendered, the victors had paraded down Pennsylvania Avenue in splendid review, and in New York an editor of *Harper's Weekly* began writing a tribute to a group of men whose services had gone largely unsung.

A "noble army of artists," he called them, and he went on to tell how they had set down an eyewitness story of four momentous years. They had portrayed it with pencil and sketch pad in the field, he said, recording it in the fading twilight with freezing or fevered fingers, making their sketches in ambulances and field hospitals, in trenches and on decks over which shells crashed and bullets whined. They had shared the fighting man's months of idleness and his moments of danger, accompanied him on all the long, weary marches across the shattered face of the land. And the result was apparent, even in 1865, to the *Harper's* man: in capturing what he termed the "glow of victory" and the "rage of defeat," they had

also made a lasting contribution to American history.

During the war those drawings were transformed into engravings and reproduced in *Harper's* or *Leslie's* or other popular magazines in what was the first large-scale use of what we call picture journalism. And all over the country, as a consequence, faces and events which the war made famous were tacked and pinned and pasted on the humblest walls, etched on the minds of the folks at home.

Yet the original sketches by the artists who worked for these illustrated weeklies had a freshness and often a ferocity which the engraver never caught when he redrew their work on wood blocks. In fact, the combat artists, knowing that their drawings were not much more than reference material for an engraver, frequently left their renderings unfinished and scrawled informative notes on them as instructions to the anonymous craftsman who would transfer them onto wood. In this book, in our effort to see the Civil War through the eyes of men who witnessed it, we have used wherever possible the vivid originals by such artists as Winslow Homer, Edwin Forbes, Alfred and William Waud, Henri Lovie, and Conrad Wise Chapman. Side by side with these pictures is the work of amateurs—of soldiers in the ranks who had some small knack with pen or pencil or brush, who whiled away the idle hours by setting down their impressions of war. Often these were mere marginal notes in a diary, sometimes they emphasized a point in a letter to the family back home, but whatever their function or quality, they have the great virtue of truth which came from seeing an event at firsthand.

It was, of course, almost impossible to paint a picture while a battle was going on, and the paintings which appear in these pages—many reproduced in color for the first time—fall into two general categories as a result. Some of them—water colors in particular—are the product of weeks and months of idleness in camp or prison. The oil paintings were usually done in the artist's studio, frequently from a sketch made in the field, sometimes on the basis of personal (but not always reliable) recollection.

Then there are photographs, the camera artistry of Mathew Brady, George Barnard, Alexander and James Gardner, George Cook, Timothy O'Sullivan, and the Main Street studio photographers of a score of American towns—pioneers in a field we now take for granted—who gave us the haunting likenesses of presidents and privates and showed us war's stark wreckage of man and nature. When the Civil War began, photography was only twenty-two years old; only twelve years had elapsed since the first photograph was made of a U.S. President in office; and only ten since the invention of the wet-plate process. But when it started, Mathew Brady recalled, "A spirit in my feet said, 'Go' and I went." And before it was over, he had spent $100,000 of his own money, and he and his assistants had traveled into virtually every theater of war to record history with their enormous, cumbersome cameras. At first Brady's ridiculous black mobile laboratory was such an oddity to men at the front that he called it his "What-is-it-wagon" as a result of their questions; later on the soldiers came to realize that wherever a battle was fought, the cameramen would be there, or not far behind.

Their cameras, suitable for studio work and not much else, were so slow that each exposure had to be a long one, which explains the fact that there are no real action shots. They would be set up near the black wagons, in position for the picture, and a photographer's assistant would rush out with an 8″ x 10″ glass plate which had been stored in a dust-proof box and then specially sensitized just before use. The plate would be exposed, rushed back to the wagon for developing, and if the weather was not just right, or the timing a little off, or the assistant a bit careless, the plate was spoiled, and the cameraman and his crew might have risked their lives for nothing. Even so, the Civil War was the first major conflict to be photographed in detail, and the men who accomplished it were artists no less than the men who worked with pen or pencil.

There is another dimension to be found in these pages. Of two and a half million Confederate and Union soldiers, all are gone. Only the scenes of their struggle remain: places called White Oak Swamp and Sharpsburg, Pittsburg Landing, Champion's Hill, and Stones River—names which meant very little to anyone before 1861, when they became the stage on which a nation's tragedy was acted out. Most of them have reverted to type now; pine and dogwood and grass have covered up the old scars. So there is a reason for the modern photographs which appear here. Beside the fact that they were taken at the same hour and season as some long-ago battle, they serve as reminders that these are places where present is also past, where we can learn a great deal about what it means to be a citizen of the United States.

Some scenes are recorded in still another fashion— in maps which show not only the terrain, but the ranks forming for battle, the movement of troops, reinforcements hurrying to the scene of action, and the swirling chaos of hand-to-hand combat. This is a new concept in map making. Naturally, it is not possible to indicate the actual number of soldiers engaged in a battle, and occasionally the artist has taken a certain license with perspective and distance in order to clarify his bird's-eye view of events. But what we are after here is understanding, and we have eliminated some of the trees in order to see the forest whole.

If we are able to catch a glimpse of the human courage and frailties which brought the Civil War to pass, it is because the participants left so much for us to see and remember. In addition to pictures they left words describing the events of four unforgettable years, and no man has succeeded in putting together their accounts and infusing life into the tale of their war in quite the same way, or with quite the same gift, as Bruce Catton. We publish his narrative here with a sense of privilege and pride.

This is the entire story of a war, told in words and in pictures, and above all in the hope of achieving a fuller knowledge of all that struggle meant to Americans a century ago, and what it means today. We have tried to produce what the unknown editor of *Harper's Weekly,* in speaking of the combat artists' work, called "a history quivering with life, faithful, terrible, romantic, the value of which will grow every year."

RICHARD M. KETCHUM

A HOUSE DIVIDED

THE AMERICAN people in 1860 believed that they were the happiest and luckiest people in all the world, and in a way they were right. Most of them lived on farms or in very small towns, they lived better than their fathers had lived, and they knew that their children would do still better. The landscape was predominantly rural, with unending sandy roads winding leisurely across a country which was both drowsy with enjoyment of the present and vibrant with eagerness to get into the future. The average American then was in fact what he has been since only in legend, an independent small farmer, and in 1860—for the last time in American history—the products of the nation's farms were worth more than the output of its factories.

This may or may not have been the end of America's golden age, but it was at least the final, haunted moment of its age of innocence. Most Americans then, difficult as the future might appear, supposed that this or something like it would go on and on, perhaps forever. Yet infinite change was beginning, and problems left unsolved too long would presently make the change explosive, so that the old landscape would be blown to bits forever, with a bewildered people left to salvage what they could. Six hundred thousand young Americans, alive when 1860 ended, would die of this explosion in the next four years.

At bottom the coming change simply meant that the infinite ferment of the industrial revolution was about to work its way with a tremendously energetic and restless people who had a virgin continent to exploit. One difficulty was that two very different societies had developed in America, one in the North and the other in the South, which would adjust themselves to the industrial age in very different ways. Another difficulty was that the differences between these two societies were most infernally complicated by the existence in the South of the institution of chattel slavery. Without slavery, the problems between the sections could probably have been worked out by the ordinary give-and-take of politics; with slavery, they became insoluble. So in 1861 the North and the South went to war, destroying one America and beginning the building of another which is not even yet complete.

In the beginning slavery was no great problem. It had existed all across colonial America, it died out in the North simply because it did not pay, and at the turn of the century most Americans, North and South alike, considered that eventually it would go out of existence everywhere. But in 1793 Yankee Eli Whitney had invented the cotton gin—a simple device which made it possible for textile mills to use the short-staple cotton which the Southern states could grow so abundantly—and in a very short time the whole

9

picture changed. The world just then was developing an almost limitless appetite for cotton, and in the deep South enormous quantities of cotton could be raised cheaply with slave labor. Export figures show what happened. In 1800 the United States had exported $5,000,000 worth of cotton—7 per cent of the nation's total exports. By 1810 this figure had tripled, by 1840 it had risen to $63,000,000, and by 1860 cotton exports were worth $191,000,000—57 per cent of the value of all American exports. The South had become a cotton empire, nearly four million slaves were employed, and slavery looked like an absolutely essential element in Southern prosperity.

But if slavery paid, it left men with uneasy consciences. This unease became most obvious in the North, where a man who demanded the abolition of slavery could comfort himself with the reflection that the financial loss which abolition would entail would, after all, be borne by somebody else—his neighbor to the south. In New England the fanatic William Lloyd Garrison opened a crusade, denouncing slavery as a sin and slaveowners as sinners. More effective work to organize antislavery sentiment was probably done by such Westerners as James G. Birney and Theodore Weld, but Garrison made the most noise—and, making it, helped to arouse most intense resentment in the South. Southerners liked being called sinners no better than anyone else. Also, they undeniably had a bear by the tail. By 1860 slave property was worth at least two billion dollars, and the abolitionists who insisted that this property be outlawed were not especially helpful in showing how this could be done without collapsing the whole Southern economy. In a natural reaction to all of this, Southerners closed ranks. It became first unhealthy and then impossible for anyone in the South to argue for the end of slavery; instead, the institution was increasingly justified as a positive good. Partly from economic pressure and partly in response to the shrill outcries of men like Garrison, the South bound itself emotionally to the institution of slavery.

Yet slavery (to repeat) was not the only source of discord. The two sections were very different, and they wanted different things from their national government.

In the North society was passing more rapidly than most men realized to an industrial base. Immigrants were arriving by the tens of thousands, there were vast areas in the West to be opened, men who were developing new industries demanded protection from cheap European imports, systems of transportation and finance were mushrooming in a fantastic manner—and, in short, this dynamic society was beginning to clamor for all sorts of aid and protection from

the Federal government at Washington.

In the South, by contrast, society was much more static. There was little immigration, there were not many cities, the factory system showed few signs of growth, and this cotton empire which sold in the world market wanted as many cheap European imports as it could get. To please the South, the national government must keep its hands off as many things as possible; for many years Southerners had feared that if the North ever won control in Washington it would pass legislation ruinous to Southern interests.

John C. Calhoun of South Carolina had seen this first and most clearly. Opposing secession, he argued that any state could protect its interests by nullifying, within its own borders, any act by the Federal government which it considered unconstitutional and oppressive. Always aware that the North was the faster-growing section, the South foresaw the day when the North would control the government. Then, Southerners believed, there would be legislation—a stiff high-tariff law, for instance—that would ruin the South. More and more, they developed the theory of states' rights as a matter of self-protection.

Although there were serious differences between the sections, all of them except slavery could have been settled through the democratic process. Slavery poisoned the whole situation. It was the issue that could not be compromised, the issue that made men so angry they did not want to compromise. It put a cutting edge on all arguments. It was not the only cause of the Civil War, but it was unquestionably the one cause without which the war would not have taken place. The antagonism between the sections came finally, and tragically, to express itself through the slavery issue.

Many attempts to compromise this issue had been made. All of them worked for a while; none of them lasted. Perhaps the most that can be said is that they postponed the conflict until the nation was strong enough—just barely so—to survive the shock of civil war.

There had been the Missouri Compromise, in 1820, when North and South argued whether slavery should be permitted in the land acquired by the Louisiana Purchase. Missouri was admitted as a slave state, but it was decreed that thereafter there should be no new slave states north of the parallel that marked Missouri's southern boundary. Men hoped that this would end the whole argument, although dour John Quincy Adams wrote that he considered the debate over the compromise nothing less than "a title-page to a great, tragic volume."

Then there was the Compromise of 1850, which

followed the war with Mexico. Immense new territory had been acquired, and Congressman David Wilmot of Pennsylvania introduced legislation stipulating that slavery would never be permitted in any of these lands. The Wilmot Proviso failed to pass, but it was argued furiously, in Congress and out of it, for years, and immense heat was generated. In the end the aging Henry Clay engineered a new compromise. California was to be admitted as a free state, the territories of New Mexico and Utah were created without reference to the Wilmot Proviso, the slave trade in the District of Columbia was abolished, and a much stiffer act to govern the return of fugitive slaves was adopted. Neither North nor South was entirely happy with this program, but both sections accepted it in the hope that the slavery issue was now settled for good.

This hope promptly exploded. Probably nothing did more to create anti-Southern, antislavery sentiment in the North than the Fugitive Slave Act. It had an effect precisely opposite to the intent of its backers: it aroused Northern sentiment in favor of the runaway slave, and probably caused a vast expansion in the activities of the Underground Railroad, the informal and all but unorganized system whereby Northern citizens helped Negro fugitives escape across the Canadian border. With this excitement at a high pitch, Harriet Beecher Stowe in 1852 brought out her novel *Uncle Tom's Cabin,* which sold three hundred thousand copies in its first year, won many converts to the antislavery position in the North, and, by contrast, aroused intense new resentment in the South.

On the heels of all of this, in 1854 Senator Stephen A. Douglas of Illinois introduced the fateful Kansas-Nebraska Act, which helped to put the whole controversy beyond hope of settlement.

Douglas was a Democrat, friendly to the South and well liked there. He cared little about slavery, one way or the other; what he wanted was to see the long argument settled so that the country could go about its business, which, as he saw it, included the development of the new Western country between the Missouri River and California. Specifically, Douglas wanted a transcontinental railroad, and he wanted its eastern terminus to be Chicago. Out of this desire came the Kansas-Nebraska Act.

Building the road would involve grants of public land. If the northerly route were adopted the country west of Iowa and Missouri must be surveyed and platted, and for this a proper territorial organization of the area was needed. But the South wanted the road to go to the Pacific coast by way of Texas and New Mexico. To get Southern support for his plan, the Illinois Senator had to find powerful bait.

He found it. When he brought in a bill to create the territories of Kansas and Nebraska he put in two special provisions. One embodied the idea of "popular sovereignty"—the concept that the people of each territory would decide for themselves, when time for statehood came, whether to permit or exclude slavery —and the other specifically repealed the Missouri Compromise. The South took the bait, the bill was passed—and the country moved a long stride nearer to war.

For the Kansas-Nebraska Act raised the argument over slavery to a desperate new intensity. The moderates could no longer be heard; the stage was set for the extremists, the fire-eaters, the men who invited violence with violent words. Many Northerners, previously friendly to the South, now came to feel that the "slave power" was dangerously aggressive, trying not merely to defend slavery where it already existed but to extend it all across the national domain. Worse yet, Kansas was thrown open for settlement under conditions which practically guaranteed bloodshed.

Settlers from the North were grimly determined to make Kansas free soil; Southern settlers were equally determined to win Kansas for slavery. Missouri sent over its Border Ruffians—hardfisted drifters who crossed the line to cast illegal votes, to intimidate free-soil settlers, now and then to raid an abolitionist town. New England shipped in boxes of rifles, known as Beecher's Bibles in derisive reference to the Reverend Henry Ward Beecher, the Brooklyn clergyman whose antislavery fervor had led him to say that there might be spots where a gun was more useful than a Bible. The North also sent down certain free-lance fanatics, among them a lantern-jawed character named John Brown.

By 1855 all of this was causing a great deal of trouble. Proslavery patrols clashed with antislavery patrols, and there were barn-burnings, horse-stealings, and sporadic shootings. The free-soil settlement of Lawrence was sacked by a proslavery mob; in retaliation, John Brown and his followers murdered five Southern settlers near Pottawatomie Creek. When elections were held, one side or the other would complain that the polls were unfairly rigged, would put on a boycott, and then would hold an election of its own; presently there were two territorial legislatures, of clouded legality, and when the question of a constitution arose there were more boycotts, so that no one was quite sure what the voters had done.

Far from Kansas, extremists on both sides whipped up fresh tensions. Senator Charles Sumner, the humorless, self-righteous abolitionist from Massachusetts, addressed the Senate on "the crime against Kansas," loosing such unmeasured invective on the head of Senator Andrew Butler of South Carolina that Congressman Preston Brooks, also of South Carolina, a relative of Senator Butler, caned him into insensibility on the Senate floor a few days afterward. Senator William H. Seward of New York spoke vaguely but ominously of an "irrepressible conflict" that was germinating. Senator Robert Toombs of Georgia predicted a vast extension of slavery and said that he would one day auction slaves on Boston Common itself. In Alabama the eloquent William Lowndes Yancey argued hotly that the South would never find happiness except by leaving the Union and setting up an independent nation.

Now the Supreme Court added its bit. It had before it the case of Dred Scott, a Negro slave whose master, an army surgeon, had kept him for some years in Illinois and Wisconsin, where there was no slavery. Scott sued for his freedom, and in 1857 Chief Justice Roger Taney delivered the Court's opinion. That Scott's plea for freedom was denied was no particular surprise, but the grounds on which the denial was based stirred the North afresh. A Negro of slave descent, said Taney, was an inferior sort of person who could not be a citizen of any state and hence could not sue anyone; furthermore, the act by which Congress had forbidden slavery in the Northern territories was invalid because the Constitution gave slavery ironclad protection. There was no legal way in which slavery could be excluded from any territory.

An intense political ferment was working. The old Whig Party had collapsed utterly, and the Democratic Party was showing signs of breaking into sectional wings. In the North there had risen the new Republican Party, an amalgamation of former Whigs, free-soilers, business leaders who wanted a central government that would protect industry, and ordinary folk who wanted a homestead act that would provide free farms in the West. The party had already polled an impressive number of votes in the Presidential campaign of 1856, and it was likely to do better in 1860. Seward of New York hoped to be its next Presidential nominee; so did Salmon P. Chase, prominent antislavery leader from Ohio; and so, also, did a lawyer and former congressman who was not nearly so well known as these two, Abraham Lincoln of Illinois.

In 1858 Lincoln ran for the Senate against Douglas. In a series of famous debates which drew national attention, the two argued the Kansas-Nebraska Act and the slavery issue up and down the state of Illinois. In the end Douglas won re-election, but he won on terms that may have cost him the Presidency two years later. Lincoln had pinned him down: Was there

any lawful way in which the people of a territory could exclude slavery? (In other words, could Douglas' "popular sovereignty" be made to jibe with the Supreme Court's finding in the Dred Scott case?) Douglas replied that the thing was easy. Slavery could not live a day unless it were supported by protective local legislation. In fact, if a territorial legislature simply refused to enact such legislation, slavery would not exist regardless of what the Supreme Court had said. The answer helped Douglas win re-election, but it mortally offended the South. The threatened split in the Democratic Party came measurably nearer, and such a split could mean nothing except victory for the Republicans.

The 1850's were the tormented decade in American history. Always the tension mounted, and no one seemed able to provide an easement. The Panic of 1857 left a severe business depression, and Northern pressure for higher tariff rates and a homestead act became stronger than ever. The depression had hardly touched the South, since world demand for cotton was unabated, and Southern leaders became more than ever convinced that their society and their economy were sounder and stronger than anything the North could show. There would be no tariff revision, and although Congress did pass a homestead act President James Buchanan, a Pennsylvanian but a strong friend of the South, promptly vetoed it. The administration, indeed, seemed unable to do anything. It could not even make a state out of Kansas, in which territory it was clear, by now, that a strong majority opposed slavery. The rising antagonism between the sections had almost brought paralysis to the Federal government.

And then old John Brown came out of the shadows to add the final touch.

With a mere handful of followers, Brown undertook, on the night of October 16, 1859, to seize the Federal arsenal at Harpers Ferry and with the weapons thus obtained to start a slave insurrection in the South. He managed to get possession of an enginehouse, which he held until the morning of the eighteenth; then a detachment of U.S. marines—temporarily led by Colonel Robert E. Lee of the U.S. Army—overpowered him and snuffed out his crackbrained conspiracy with bayonets and clubbed muskets. Brown was quickly tried, was convicted of treason, and early in December he was hanged. But what he had done had a most disastrous effect on men's minds. To people in the South, it seemed that Brown confirmed their worst fears: this was what the Yankee abolitionists really wanted—a servile insurrection, with unlimited bloodshed and pillage, from one end of the South to the other! The fact that some vocal persons in the North persisted in regarding Brown as a martyr simply made matters worse. After the John Brown raid the chance that the bitter sectional argument could be harmonized faded close to the vanishing point.

It was in this atmosphere that the 1860 election was held. The Republicans nominated Lincoln, partly because he was considered less of an extremist than either Seward or Chase; he was moderate on the slavery question, and agreed that the Federal government lacked power to interfere with the peculiar institution in the states. The Republican platform, however, did represent a threat to Southern interests. It embodied the political and economic program of the North—upward revision of the tariff, free farms in the West, railroad subsidies, and all the rest.

But by now a singular fatalism gripped the nation. The campaign could not be fought on the basis of these issues; men could talk only about slavery, and on that subject they could neither talk nor, for the most part, even think, with moderation. Although it faced a purely sectional opposition, the Democratic Party promptly split into halves. The Northern wing nominated Douglas, but the Southern wing flatly refused to accept the man because of his heresy in regard to slavery in the territories; it named John C. Breckinridge of Kentucky, while a fourth party, hoping desperately for compromise and conciliation, put forward John Bell of Tennessee.

The road led steadily downhill after this. The Republicans won the election, as they were bound to do under the circumstances. Lincoln got less than a majority of the popular votes, but a solid majority in the electoral college, and on March 4, 1861, he would become President of the United States . . . but not, it quickly developed, of all of the states. Fearing the worst, the legislature of South Carolina had remained in session until after the election had been held. Once it saw the returns it summoned a state convention, and this convention, in Charleston on December 20, voted unanimously that South Carolina should secede from the Union.

This was the final catalytic agent. It was obvious that one small state could not maintain its independence; equally obvious that if South Carolina should now be forced back into the Union no one in the South ever need talk again about secession. The cotton states, accordingly, followed suit. By February, South Carolina had been joined by Mississippi, Alabama, Georgia, Florida, Louisiana, and Texas, and on February 8 delegates from the seceding states met at Montgomery, Alabama, and set up a new nation, the Confederate States of America. A provisional constitution was adopted (to be replaced in due time by a permanent document, very much like the Constitution of the United States), and Jefferson Davis of Mississippi was elected President, with Alexander Stephens of Georgia as Vice-President.

Perhaps it still was not too late for an adjustment. A new nation had come into being, but its creation might simply be a means of forcing concessions from the Northern majority; no blood had been shed, and states which voluntarily left the old Union might voluntarily return if their terms were met. Leaders in Congress worked hard, that winter of 1861, to perfect a last-minute compromise, and a committee led by Senator John J. Crittenden of Kentucky worked one out. In effect, it would re-establish the old line of the Missouri Compromise, banning slavery in territories north of the line and protecting it south; it would let future states enter the Union on a popular sovereignty basis; it called for enforcement of the fugitive slave law, with Federal funds to compensate slaveowners whose slaves got away; and it provided that the Constitution could never be amended in such a way as to give Congress power over slavery in any of the states.

The Crittenden Compromise hung in the balance, and then collapsed when Lincoln refused to accept it. The sticking point with him was the inclusion of slavery in the territories; the rest of the program he could accept, but he wrote to a Republican associate to "entertain no proposition for a compromise in regard to the extension of slavery."

So the last chance to settle the business had gone, except for the things that might happen in the minds of two men—Abraham Lincoln and Jefferson Davis. They were strangers, very unlike each other, and yet there was an odd linkage. They were born not far apart in time or space; both came from Kentucky, near the Ohio River, and one man went south to become spokesman for the planter aristocracy, while the other went north to become representative of the best the frontier Northwest could produce. In the haunted decade that had just ended, neither man had been known as a radical. Abolitionists considered Lincoln too conservative, and Southern fire-eaters like South Carolina's Robert B. Rhett felt that Davis had been cold and unenthusiastic in regard to secession.

Now these two men faced one another, figuratively, across an ever-widening gulf, and between them they would say whether a nation already divided by mutual misunderstanding would be torn apart physically by war.

A Rural Image Hides the Industrial North

The Currier lithograph above unintentionally reveals the subtle transition to a market economy; in George Inness' painting (below) the solitary train-watcher seems unaware of the changes the chugging engines were already effecting on a rustic landscape.

SYRACUSE MUSEUM OF FINE ARTS

Mid-century America was still largely a rural land. In 1850 over five times as many people lived on farms as in towns and cities. During the following decade, however, a marked shift was taking place: while the farm population increased by only one-quarter, the figure for city dwellers jumped 75 per cent. In the North, particularly, the yeoman image was fading fast, as mechanization worked a revolution in agriculture. Cyrus McCormick demonstrated his amazing reaper in Virginia, but it was the North that took advantage of his invention. Wheat production rose an astonishing 75 per cent in the 1850's, corn 40 per cent.

Some 300,000 immigrants from Europe were flooding eastern seaports annually between 1844 and 1854—about 1,300,000 of them from Ireland, nearly a million from Germany. Many of these people, stranded by economic forces beyond their control, remained in eastern cities and provided the North with the cheap labor force needed for its industrial revolution. New York City, for example, closed a twenty-year period of expansion in 1860 with a population increase of half a million; its 800,000 residents made it the greatest metropolis of the western hemisphere.

By 1860 the total national product was nearly four billion dollars. That year—for the last time—the value of manufactured goods trailed agricultural products. The picture of the North remained one of rustic simplicity, but the reality beneath, scarcely perceived by contemporaries, was one of fundamental change.

Few nineteenth-century artists captured the image of the happy yeoman better than Eastman Johnson. As this 1860 painting of cornhusking indicates, his world was still an innocent, rural one.

OVERLEAF: *The jingle of harness bells can almost be heard in this crisp New England landscape of sleighs approaching a country church on Sunday, painted by genre artist George Henry Durrie.*
COLLECTION OF MR. & MRS. P. H. B. FRELINGHUYSEN

An 1851 jubilee on Boston Common celebrated the linking of Canada and America by rail. In W. C. Sharp's painting

President Millard Fillmore, on a black horse (right), tips his hat to the Canadian Governor-General in the carriage at left.

The Growing West
Adds New Strength to the North

ILLINOIS CENTRAL RAILROAD COMPANY
OFFER FOR SALE
ONE MILLION ACRES OF SUPERIOR FARMING LANDS,
IN FARMS OF
40, 80 & 160 acres and upwards at from $8 to $12 per acre.
THESE LANDS ARE
NOT SURPASSED BY ANY IN THE WORLD.
THEY LIE ALONG
THE WHOLE LINE OF THE CENTRAL ILLINOIS RAILROAD,
For Sale on LONG CREDIT, SHORT CREDIT and for CASH, they are situated near TOWNS, VILLAGES, SCHOOLS and CHURCHES.

Between 1837 and 1858 four lusty new states—Michigan, Iowa, Wisconsin, and Minnesota—joined the Union. With Ohio, Indiana, and Illinois, they formed a third major section of the nation; for by 1860 the population of this "Middle Border" region exceeded eight million—nearly equaling that of each of the older sections, Northeast and South. Senator Stephen A. Douglas had called this vigorous new area a "swelling power that will be able to speak the law to this nation . . ." Significantly, the people and resources of this vast, rich territory were swinging into commercial and industrial alignment with the Northeast. In the contest to come, the South would face not one, but two Norths.

Toll roads and canals had staked out the direction for migration from the East, but railroads made possible the astonishing growth of the Northwest. The Illinois Central was the first to use Federal land grants to lure settlers along the right of way. Western democracy had a flavor all its own, as evidenced by the Thomas Burnham painting (right) of Detroit's first election.

River traffic spurred St. Louis' growth in the 1850's, but that railroad on the far bank was to tie the city to the North and shatter the South's hopes of tapping northwestern markets via the Mississippi River.

Americans regarded themselves as a people with a special mission, and at mid-century the land teemed with causes and fads. An unknown artist satirized (counterclockwise from bottom left) free love, fugitive slaves, abolition, Jenny Lind's tour, the hapless

Collins steamships (top right), immigration, sea bathing, revivalists, real estate specula-
tion, railroad wrecks, temperance, medical quackery, and the Mormon exodus. At center
he dealt with political orators and the raggle-taggle militia companies of the period.

A Static South Lags Behind

Even more than the North, the antebellum South was dominated by agriculture. Cultivation was limited to a few huge cash crops which depleted the soil and made the grower almost completely dependent on a far-flung economic complex. The South sent its farm staples to England and to the northeastern United States, where humming factories were turning out manufactured products at an amazing clip. Because it lacked a substantial native industry, the South was forced to buy back the finished products it needed, under a credit financing system seemingly designed to keep the Southern farmer always in debt. Long before the war New York City had become—in the realm of banking at least—the Queen City of the South.

Below the Mason-Dixon Line thrived a civilization which, in many ways, was unrivaled for the ease and grace and luxury of its external symbols—the stately plantation, the proud lineage of Virginia's tidewater aristocracy, the Charleston town house, the treasured heirlooms and impressive family libraries handed down from generation to generation, the bustling cosmopolitanism of New Orleans. Yet this elegant façade too often concealed the other South of subsistence farmers and backwoods settlements. That dispassionate observer Frederick Law Olmsted, reporting for the New York *Times* in the 1850's, noted that "the proportion of the free white men who live as well in any respect as our working classes at the North, on an average, is small, and the citizens of the cotton states, as a whole, are poor." But at the time few Southerners seemed troubled by such disparity. Quite the contrary: "The wealth of the South is permanent and real, that of the North fugitive and fictitious," a Southern journalist crowed when his section emerged unscathed from the Panic of 1857. This all too hollow boast revealed a tragic ignorance and a fatal underestimation of the industrial revolution which had bypassed the South and was remaking the face of the states to the north.

Hyppolite Sebron painted the levees (left) at which New Orleans tapped the Mississippi Valley hinterland and eclipsed the commercial importance of Charleston. The latter city is shown above as it appeared in 1831.

OVERLEAF: *If the figures in Adrian Persac's painting of a Louisiana plantation look like fashion models, it is because the artist applied cutouts from current publications to his canvases and then painted over them.*

25

Giroux's idyllic painting of a cotton plantation, a self-sufficient world unto itself, is the stereotype generally accepted as representing the southern half of America. In reality, smaller farms far outnumbered the large slave-worked holdings.

The plantation system had reached a peak in colonial Virginia, where tobacco was the great cash crop, but before the end of the eighteenth century the Golden Age was badly tarnished, and the soil poor or exhausted. However, the institution of the plantation endured, as Augustus Köllner's 1845 sketch of a Virginia family indicates.

The South Concentrates on Cotton

Cotton culture was almost an afterthought in the development of the South's agricultural economy. The old colonial staples had been tobacco, rice, and indigo; and at the end of the Revolution only a few planters raised the long-staple sea-island cotton, which was limited largely to the Carolina coast. So long as this situation existed, thoughtful Southerners, Washington and Jefferson among them, regarded slavery as an evil which could and would be swept away eventually. As a French visitor wrote, "they are constantly talking of abolishing slavery, and of contriving some other means of cultivating their estates."

Then, in 1793, a Connecticut Yankee named Eli Whitney altered irrevocably the South's economy and its attitude toward slavery. His invention of a gin that separated the lint from the seeds of the upland, short-staple cotton gave immediate commercial value to that variety, and overnight cotton was being sown and harvested on an unprecedented scale. As the world's textile mills gobbled up everything they could produce, planters looked westward for new land, to the black prairies of Alabama and the loess soil of Mississippi. At the same time the value of black slaves to work the crop skyrocketed.

As long as virgin acreage was available there was no need, men thought, to practice careful tillage, and soon the eastern fields were worn out and eroded. By 1834 the Western states led in the production of cotton; by 1850 this area was the world's greatest cotton-growing region. Cotton was King—or so it seemed.

Big, rambling Eli Whitney, shown in a portrait by Charles B. King, invented a cotton gin which gave slavery a new lease on life. Ironically, his next idea, a system of practical interchangeable parts, brought the North technological superiority and the industrial strength which led to triumph in the Civil War.

Slavery Becomes a Necessity
in a One-Crop Economy

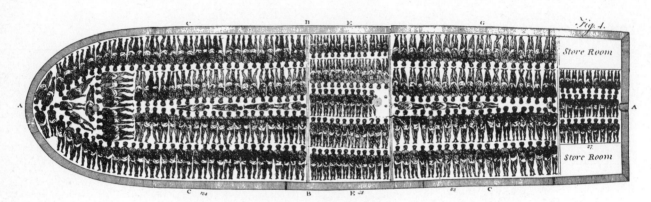

The slave trade was abolished in 1808, the date of the sectional drawing above, which shows how some 400 blacks crossed the Atlantic in a deck space measuring 25 by 100 feet. The water color below depicts a pitiful band of Virginia Negroes en route to a new owner in Tennessee. Their former master, his land exhausted, may have sold them to buy food for his remaining slaves.

In 1619 a Dutch trading vessel stopped at Jamestown, Virginia, to sell a few Negro slaves to tobacco planters. When the auction scene above was painted in 1852, slaves accounted for 40 per cent of the South's population. The photograph below, taken a decade later by a Union soldier in South Carolina, shows slaves still technically in bondage at a time when the institution was doomed.

To say that the South was committed to a one-crop cotton economy was also to say that it was committed to that "peculiar institution"—slavery. The back-breaking toil of raising the crop required a large, cheap labor force (of the 2,500,000 slaves engaged in agriculture in 1850, 75 per cent worked at cotton production). Concentration on cotton raising also led to centralization of slave ownership: of six million Southern whites, only 347,525 owned slaves in 1850; a scant 37,662 of that number had twenty or more. By the end of the 1850's the price of a prime field hand was $1,800, which meant that a slave force required a considerable cash investment. Cotton had saddled the South with a labor system that most impartial observers considered not only outdated, but uneconomical.

31

Replying to Hayne in 1830, Webster stated his credo: "Liberty and Union, now and forever, one and inseparable!"

Compromise Is Increasingly More Difficult

By 1819 the Union was equally divided, with eleven free states and eleven slave. But the vigor of American society, ever pushing westward, meant that this could not last. Missouri's petition for admission as a slave state that year raised the question of slavery's extension into the West. In 1820 Americans still considered it possible to draw a line that would serve as a permanent division between free and slave territory, and this Missouri Compromise stood for thirty years. When California requested admission as a free state in 1849, however, trouble was inevitable. One half of the nation thought its economic existence depended on slavery; the other half was generally opposed to the extension of slavery on economic and political grounds. Aging war horses joined battle: John C. Calhoun, less than a month away from death, had his last bitter attack on the North read by a fellow senator; Daniel Webster, risking his political reputation, spoke for conciliation; Henry Clay rallied for a final great effort at pacification. Yet the tortured Compromise of 1850 could accomplish little toward resolving a conflict that was now irreconcilable. Daniel Webster breathed a sigh of relief, saying "the Union stands firm"; but there were too many forces abroad in the land that would not be stilled for long.

Washington heat drove Henry Clay to the seashore during the debate on his Compromise of 1850. In late August he returned to prove that "his courage is of the sort that mounts with the occasion."

Abolitionist Senator William H. Seward (below, left) appealed beyond the Constitution to a "higher law"; John C. Calhoun (below, right) refused to be civil to him, saying he would "cut my throat."

Northern Extremists
Replace Moderates
in the Antislavery Movement

The venomous abolitionist attacks on slavery turned eventually to propaganda against the entire South. This illustration from the American Anti-Slavery Almanac *characterizes the region as a land where slaves were inhumanly treated, where lynchings, duels, cockfighting, and rough-and-tumble brawls were everyday affairs.*

Urged to write "something which would make this whole nation feel what an accursed thing slavery is," Harriet Beecher Stowe dashed off some powerful propaganda in novel form (right). Theodore Parker wrote the bitter placard at far right after a Negro runaway had been forcibly returned from Boston to Georgia.

Northern reaction to the Fugitive Slave Law, which was an integral part of the Compromise of 1850, was violent. Whittier scored Webster as a "fallen angel" for supporting it; Emerson called the statute a "filthy enactment." Once abolition had spoken with the calm voice of reason—Quaker Benjamin Lundy's *Genius of Universal Emancipation* in the 1820's; James G. Birney's policy of gradualism and colonization; modest Theodore Weld; his wife, Angelina Grimké, writing an open letter to Southern women; Angelina's sister Sarah, shyly addressing groups in parlors; Arthur and Lewis Tappan, supporting antislavery societies. But after 1850 the call grew shrill and strident. Boston's Wendell Phillips demanded division of the Union. William Lloyd Garrison took the extreme step of burning the Constitution publicly, after calling it "a covenant with death and an agreement with hell."

Inflexible William Lloyd Garrison fulminated against slavery for 35 years in the Liberator. *In 1865 he locked up the presses, convinced that his job was done.*

135,000 SETS, 270,000 VOLUMES SOLD.

UNCLE TOM'S CABIN

FOR SALE HERE.

AN EDITION FOR THE MILLION, COMPLETE IN 1 Vol., PRICE 37 1-2 CENTS.
"   "   IN GERMAN, IN 1 Vol., PRICE 50 CENTS.
"   "   IN 2 Vols,. CLOTH, 6 PLATES, PRICE $1.50.
SUPERB ILLUSTRATED EDITION, IN 1 Vol., WITH 153 ENGRAVINGS,
PRICES FROM $2.50 TO $5.00.

The Greatest Book of the Age.

CAUTION!!

COLORED PEOPLE

OF BOSTON, ONE & ALL,

You are hereby respectfully CAUTIONED and advised, to avoid conversing with the

Watchmen and Police Officers of Boston,

For since the recent ORDER OF THE MAYOR & ALDERMEN, they are empowered to act as

KIDNAPPERS

AND

Slave Catchers,

And they have already been actually employed in KIDNAPPING, CATCHING, AND KEEPING SLAVES. Therefore, if you value your LIBERTY, and the *Welfare of the Fugitives* among you, *Shun* them in every possible manner, as so many *HOUNDS* on the track of the most unfortunate of your race.

Keep a Sharp Look Out for KIDNAPPERS, and have TOP EYE open.

APRIL 24, 1851.

Southern Fire-Eaters Take the Lead

The defensive Southern image of slavery was perpetuated in such idyllic scenes as this Currier and Ives lithograph. Near their simple but snug cabin happy Negroes dance away the hours, secure in the knowledge that kindly master will take care of all earthly wants.

*William L. Yancey (above, left) died without seeing
the wreck of the Confederacy he had helped construct.
Robert Barnwell Rhett (above, right) lived until 1876,
still convinced of the right of Southern independence.*

There was a time when the South itself thought of abolition. Southern antislavery societies outnumbered Northern groups in 1827; prominent Southerners had emancipated their slaves and contributed to colonization efforts. In 1832 the Virginia legislature debated a proposal for gradual, compensatory emancipation that would have become effective in 1861—a year that was to see a tragically different outcome of the slavery controversy.

As Northern abolitionists became more virulent and intemperate in their attacks, however, the South first adopted a defensive attitude about its "peculiar institution," and then launched an offensive designed to prove that slavery, far from being an evil, was actually a positive good. The Bible was quoted, and Patrick Henry was parodied to read "Give us SLAVERY, *or* give us death!" Understanding between the North and South broke down, and rival sectionalism became a twisted dual nationalism. First the old Whig Party, then the Democrats, foundered on the slavery issue. Even church groups split in two. Twenty years before the Compromise of 1850, Calhoun had suffered defeat in the nullification controversy, and the Virginia dynasty in national affairs had come to an end. Now the South, beset with a nightmare fear of Northern hegemony, began to think of secession.

William L. Yancey of Alabama was the golden orator of the movement; patrician Robert Barnwell Rhett, editor of the Charleston *Mercury,* its most relentless proponent. A third secessionist spokesman was a peppery little agriculturist from Virginia, Edmund Ruffin, who would beat plowshares into swords. There were moderates in the South as in the North; but as the ranting abolitionist came to be the most vociferous voice in the Northern states, so the angry fire-eater, with his dialogue of disunity, was the man most frequently heard in the South.

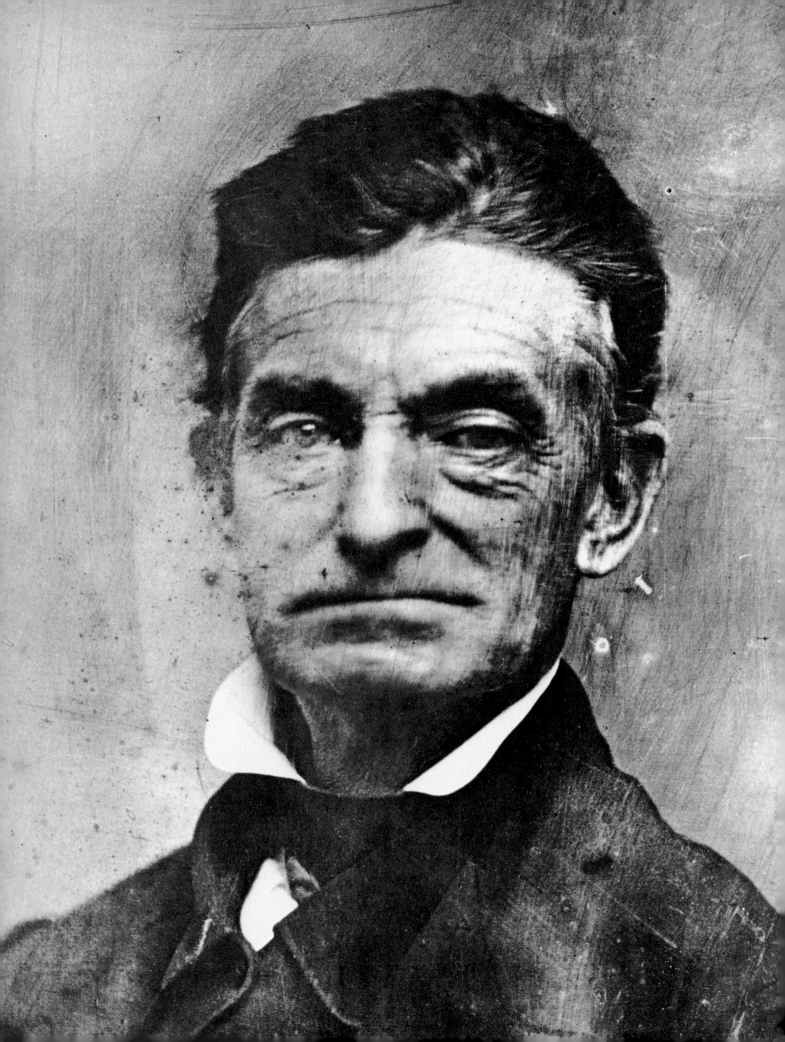

Passions Mount
in a
Week of Violence

Felix Darley drew these grimly resolute Border Ruffians invading Kansas.

Four years after the Compromise of 1850 had supposedly settled the question of slavery's extension into Western territory, the issue exploded anew. To Kansas, opened to settlement by the Kansas-Nebraska Act of 1854, came two diametrically opposed groups—Border Ruffians from Missouri bent on creating a new slave state, and abolitionists equally determined to make Kansas "the homestead of the free." Clashes were inevitable, and in the spring of 1856 came one climactic week of violence. In Washington on May 19 and 20, haughty Senator Charles Sumner of Massachusetts delivered an intemperate philippic on the "Crime Against Kansas." The following day a group of Border Ruffians rode into Lawrence, Kansas, and destroyed that Free State center. On May 22 Preston Brooks, a nephew of Senator Andrew Butler, whom Sumner had vilified in his speech, strode into the Senate and broke his gutta-percha cane over Sumner's head. Two days later the scene shifted back to Kansas. There John Brown, a fanatic abolitionist who had brought from Ohio his four sons and surplus artillery swords for just such a purpose, revenged the attack on Lawrence by hacking to death five proslavery settlers along Pottawatomie Creek. By 1856 America was a nation torn by hatred, bloodshed, and the lust for vengeance.

John Brown (left), photographed about 1856, bore a "touch of insanity about his glittering gray-blue eyes."

The Free State Hotel was a gutted ruin following the sack of Lawrence.

Charles Sumner was caned in the U.S. Senate by vengeful "Bully" Brooks.

Chief Justice Taney (above) manumitted his own slaves but denied freedom to Dred Scott (below), whose master freed him two months after the Supreme Court decision.

Taney and Buchanan Add Fuel to the Fire

James Buchanan of Pennsylvania, whose post as Minister to England removed him from the first Kansas controversy, had seemed a "safe" Democratic candidate in 1856. At his inauguration on March 4, 1857, he tried to reconcile the warring factions. Then, two days later, Chief Justice Roger B. Taney handed down the famous Supreme Court decision which refused freedom to Dred Scott, an illiterate Missouri Negro, and struck down the Missouri Compromise of 1820. With it collapsed the whole elaborate house of cards which was sectional compromise. Unhappily, Buchanan was weak, irresolute, and without convictions; and what he did now was hopelessly wrong. He failed to back up Robert J. Walker, his appointee as Kansas governor; then he submitted the proslavery Lecompton Constitution to Congress as the basis for Kansas' admission to the Union, thus losing the support of his party's leading figure, Stephen A. Douglas.

Above, a Kansas Free State battery, poised for action. Below, an 1856 caricature excoriates Democratic leaders for their failure in Kansas: Buchanan steals a watch from a corpse; a tipsy Franklin Pierce and Lewis Cass leer at the Fair Maid; while Stephen Douglas, in unaccustomed beard, scalps a victim.

LIBERTY, THE FAIR MAID OF KANSAS—IN THE HANDS OF THE "BORDER RUFFIANS".

Illinois Hears a

In the Kansas-Nebraska Act of 1854 Stephen A. Douglas had championed the principle of "popular sovereignty"—the right of settlers to determine their territory's future as a slave or free state. Over this issue he had finally clashed with his own Democratic Party, and when Buchanan threatened to run him out of the party, Douglas remained adamant. "I have taken a through ticket and checked all my baggage," he said. In 1858, when Douglas returned to Illinois to campaign for re-election to the Senate, he faced the most formidable opponent of his political career—a former Whig congressman and a rising figure in the new Republican Party, Abraham Lincoln.

Lincoln had accepted the Republican nomination for Douglas' seat with a ringing speech at Springfield in June: " 'A house divided against itself cannot stand.' I believe this government cannot endure permanently half slave and half free." In July Lincoln issued a quiet challenge to

"Senator Douglas is of world-wide renown. All the anxious politicians of his party . . . have been looking upon him . . . to be President," Lincoln said of his opponent (left). "Nobody has ever expected me to be President."

At Freeport, Lincoln asked Douglas the question which appears at right in his own handwriting. The wily Douglas eluded his opponent on this point and won the election, but only at the expense of Southern support.

Dramatic Debate

Douglas: "Will it be agreeable to you to make an arrangement for you and myself to divide time, and address the same audiences . . . ?" Douglas promptly accepted, although he had misgivings.

They appeared on the same platform seven times, once in each Congressional district except the two where they had both already appeared. The climax, however, was reached at the second debate. At Freeport, on August 27, Lincoln asked Douglas to reconcile "popular sovereignty" with the Dred Scott decision. Douglas replied that it mattered not what the Supreme Court decided as to whether or not slavery might go into a territory under the Constitution, for "slavery cannot exist a day or an hour anywhere, unless it is supported by local police regulations." This Freeport Doctrine helped Douglas win the election; but the debates themselves made Abraham Lincoln a towering new political figure on the Illinois plains.

Douglas described Lincoln, shown here in his first full-length portrait, as "the strong man of his party—full of wit, facts, dates—and the best stump speaker in the West . . . if I beat him, my victory will be hardly won."

"Can the people of a United States Territory, in any lawful way, against the wish of any citizen of the United States, exclude slavery from its limits prior to the formation of a State Constitution?"

John Brown Strikes at Harpers Ferry

At Harpers Ferry, John Brown stationed his force inside the engine house at left. Ten of his seventeen raiders, including two of Brown's sons, were killed or fatally wounded. Ironically, their first victim was a free Negro.

Within 36 hours of the raid Colonel Robert E. Lee ordered Lieutenant J. E. B. Stuart and a company of marines to storm the building where Brown was holding eleven hostages (left). A week later Brown was on trial for treason (below), rising from a pallet to proclaim "I did no wrong, but right." A. Berghaus sketched Brown being led from jail to ride to his execution on top of his coffin (bottom).

In February of 1857 John Brown placed an order in Connecticut for 1,000 pikes made from long-bladed Bowie knives fastened to six-foot poles. The following November he was back in Kansas, seeking volunteers for a secret mission. In May, 1858, he went to Canada, where he divulged his plan to liberate Southern slaves and set up a free Negro commonwealth in the mountains of Maryland and Virginia. The pikes were to arm the slaves who would rally to his cause. In December, 1858, he made a practice raid on Missouri, freed eleven slaves, and sent them to Canada. Then, on October 16, 1859, John Brown—bearded now, his hair flecked with white—struck at Harpers Ferry, Virginia. With little opposition he seized control of the two bridges into the sleepy town, the Federal armory and arsenal, and a rifle works nearby, then waited confidently for the slave uprising. It never came. Instead, the government sent troops to crush the incipient rebellion. John Brown was captured, tried, and executed for treason—a martyr to the North, a maniacal villain to the South.

The Republican challengers stare soberly out of this 1860 campaign poster.

A New Party Rises to Meet the Challenge

A British visitor painted this view of the "Wigwam," which Chicago—delighted by its choice as the Republican convention site—had hastily erected and billed as the country's largest auditorium.

The political parties were so divided over sectional issues by 1860 that it took Congress nine weeks and 44 ballots to transact the routine business of electing a Speaker of the House of Representatives. Six years earlier at Ripon, Wisconsin, a group of Whigs, Free-Soilers, and antislavery Democrats had called for the formation of a new political party dedicated to opposing slavery's extension into the territories. At Jackson, Michigan, on July 6, 1854, the name Republican was chosen for the new party. Purely sectional in its appeal, this fusionist organization lost its first national election in 1856 when John C. Frémont was defeated for the Presidency. In 1860, however, events were working in its favor; and in May of that year the party nominated Abraham Lincoln and Hannibal Hamlin as candidates. The split among the Democrats made the Republicans' prospects seem bright.

In 1860 Lincoln conducted a classic front-porch campaign at Springfield, where a reporter found him "not too proud to sit down upon his doorstep in his shirt sleeves and chat with his neighbors." Above, Lincoln (standing to right of doorway) appears at an August rally in his front yard.

The Democrats Collapse in 1860

When the Democratic nominating convention met in Charleston on April 23, 1860, Stephen A. Douglas was their leading candidate; but a coalition of Southern radicals and Buchanan's patronage holders was determined to block his nomination. After a week of bickering and bartering the Northern Democrats defeated a platform written by the Southerners, which advocated protection of slavery in the territories. In a dress rehearsal for secession, Alabama's thoroughly angered delegates walked out, followed by Mississippi, Louisiana, South Carolina, Florida, Texas, and scattered individuals from the remaining slave states. The following morning a decimated convention reassembled, and two days later, after 57 fruitless ballots, the Democrats adjourned without selecting a candidate.

On June 18 the convention reconvened in Baltimore, and when some of the Southern bolters applied for admission, they were rejected. This caused another walkout by sympathizers from Virginia, North Carolina, California, and Oregon. Finally Douglas was nominated by what remained of the Democratic convention. The seceders held a rump session across town in Baltimore, and chose John C. Breckinridge of Kentucky as their nominee. Meanwhile, an "old gentlemen's party" of ex-Whigs and Know-Nothings had named John Bell of Tennessee to head a Constitutional Union ticket.

The Republicans, in a tempestuous convention held in Chicago's new "Wigwam," unexpectedly nominated Lincoln instead of the favored William H. Seward. By late summer of 1860 it was apparent that the hopelessly divided Democrats would be unable to crack the preponderance of Northern votes which had rallied to the Republican cause. In the November 6 election Lincoln won the largest vote of any of the four candidates, even though he failed to obtain an absolute majority.

His electoral count was an overwhelming 180, against 72 for Breckinridge in the South, 39 for Bell from the border states, and a pathetic 12 for Douglas, who carried only Missouri and three New Jersey votes, although his popular vote was second only to Lincoln's.

"Ain't You Glad You Joined the Republicans?" sang perfervid companies of uniformed "Wide Awakes" as they stepped down New York's Broadway in the mammoth torchlight parade pictured above.

The Republican reform element was savagely mocked in the cartoon at left. Horace Greeley is shown carrying Lincoln on his famous rail into a lunatic asylum, followed by a motley group of eccentrics.

In the 1860 campaign Lincoln faced John C. Breckinridge, the States' Rights candidate; regular Democrat Stephen A. Douglas; and John Bell, a compromise entry, pictured at right on campaign buttons.

49

The United States Ceases to Exist

[Special Despatch to the Morning News.]

IMPORTANT FROM WASHINGTON!

Address of Senator Toombs to the People of Georgia.

PROPOSITIONS FOR NEW GURAN-TEES REJECTED!

THE SOUTH TREATED WITH DERISION AND CONTEMPT!

Senator Crittenden's Amendments Unani-mously Voted Down!

Secession the last and only Resort!

Washington, Dec. 23.—Senator Toombs telegraphs this morning the following, addressed to the people of Georgia:

Fellow-Citizens of Georgia:—I came here to secure your constitutional rights, or to demonstrate to you that you can get no guarantees for these rights from our Northern confederates.

The whole subject was referred to a Committee of thirteen in the Senate yesterday. I was appointed on the Committee and accepted the trust. I submitted propositions, which so far from receiving decided support from a single member of the Republican party on the Committee, they were all treated with either derision or contempt. The vote was then taken in Committee on the amendments to the Constitution proposed by Hon. J. J. Crittenden, of Kentucky, AND EACH AND ALL OF THEM WERE VOTED AGAINST UNANIMOUSLY BY THE BLACK REPUBLICAN MEMBERS OF THE COMMITTEE.

In addition to these facts, a majority of the Black Republican members of the Committee DECLARED DISTINCTLY THAT THEY HAD NO GUARANTEES TO OFFER, which was silently acquiesced in by the other members.

The Black Republican members of this Committee of Thirteen are representative men of their party and section, and, to the extent of my information, truly represent the Committee of Thirty-Three in the House, which on Tuesday adjourned for a week without coming to any vote, after solemnly pledging themselves to vote on all the propositions then before them on that date.

That Committee is controlled by Black Republicans, your enemies, who only seek to amuse you with delusive hope, until your election, in order that you may defeat the friends of secession. If you are deceived

Secession bred a new nationalism in the South, as reflected in the Georgia songsheet above (left). Disgusted by the failure of compromise, Robert Toombs sent this message (above, right) to his Georgia constituents.

The South Carolina legislature was sitting in Columbia when the election returns came in. "The tea has been thrown overboard," Rhett's *Mercury* proclaimed. "The revolution of 1860 has been initiated." A secession convention was called for December 17, was then adjourned to Charleston in the face of a threatened smallpox epidemic, and —at 1:30 P.M. on December 20—unanimously adopted an ordinance of secession. South Carolina had assumed "her position among the nations of the world."

Amidst bonfires, parades, and fireworks, one loyal Unionist barked: "South Carolina is too small for a republic and too big for a lunatic asylum." But commissioners from other cotton states, observing the secession festivities, were soon scurrying back to their homes. On January 9, 1861, Mississippi followed South Carolina out of the Union, and a chain reaction was set off—Florida seceded on January 10; Alabama, January 11; Georgia, January 19; Louisiana, January 26; and Texas, February 1.

The Alabama secession convention issued an invitation to other slaveholding states to meet in Montgomery on February 4 to consult "as to the most effectual mode of securing concerted and harmonious action in whatever measures may be deemed most desirable for our common peace and security." The new commonwealths did not prize their independence for long.

"Might as well attempt to control a tornado," one observer wrote of the secession sentiment of Charlestonians, pictured at left in a mass meeting.

South Carolina newspapers (opposite) trumpeted the dire news in what was surely the largest type available.

CHARLESTON

MERCURY

EXTRA:

Passed unanimously at 1.15 o'clock, P. M., December 20th, 1860.

AN ORDINANCE

To dissolve the Union between the State of South Carolina and other States united with her under the compact entitled " The Constitution of the United States of America."

We, the People of the State of South Carolina, in Convention assembled, do declare and ordain, and it is hereby declared and ordained,

That the Ordinance adopted by us in Convention, on the twenty-third day of May, in the year of our Lord one thousand seven hundred and eighty-eight, whereby the Constitution of the United States of America was ratified, and also, all Acts and parts of Acts of the General Assembly of this State, ratifying amendments of the said Constitution, are hereby repealed ; and that the union now subsisting between South Carolina and other States, under the name of " The United States of America," is hereby dissolved.

THE

UNION

IS

DISSOLVED!

The Confederacy Is Formed

Almost daily, Southern legislators in Washington announced their resignations from Congress as state followed state out of the Union. During the first week of February, 1861, many of these men, including some of the ablest political figures in the nation, converged on Montgomery, Alabama, a rough little frontier town of unpaved streets, inadequate hotel facilities, and a population of 8,000.

Delegates from six seceded states (the Texans were late in arriving) set about creating a new nation. By February 8 they had a new constitution, patterned generally after the old one. However, cabinet members were allowed to participate in legislative debates, the President was given power to disapprove specific appropriations in any bill he signed, and the "sovereign and independent character" of each state was reaffirmed. Although the external slave trade was prohibited, the central government was enjoined from passing any law denying the right to own slaves.

The following day the convention selected a Confederate President. Passing over the names of the rabid fire-eaters, the delegates picked Mississippi's respected Jefferson Davis, a former soldier, congressman, senator, and Secretary of War. Alexander H. Stephens of Georgia was named Vice-President.

Traveling from his Mississippi plantation to Montgomery, a distance of 100 miles, the President-elect may have paused to consider the logistics facing the new Confederacy. The most direct rail route between these points was via Chattanooga and Atlanta—a 600-mile trip.

Behind an erect military bearing, tall, slender Jefferson Davis concealed the physical suffering caused by frequent attacks of neuralgia. At right is his inauguration in Montgomery on February 18, 1861.

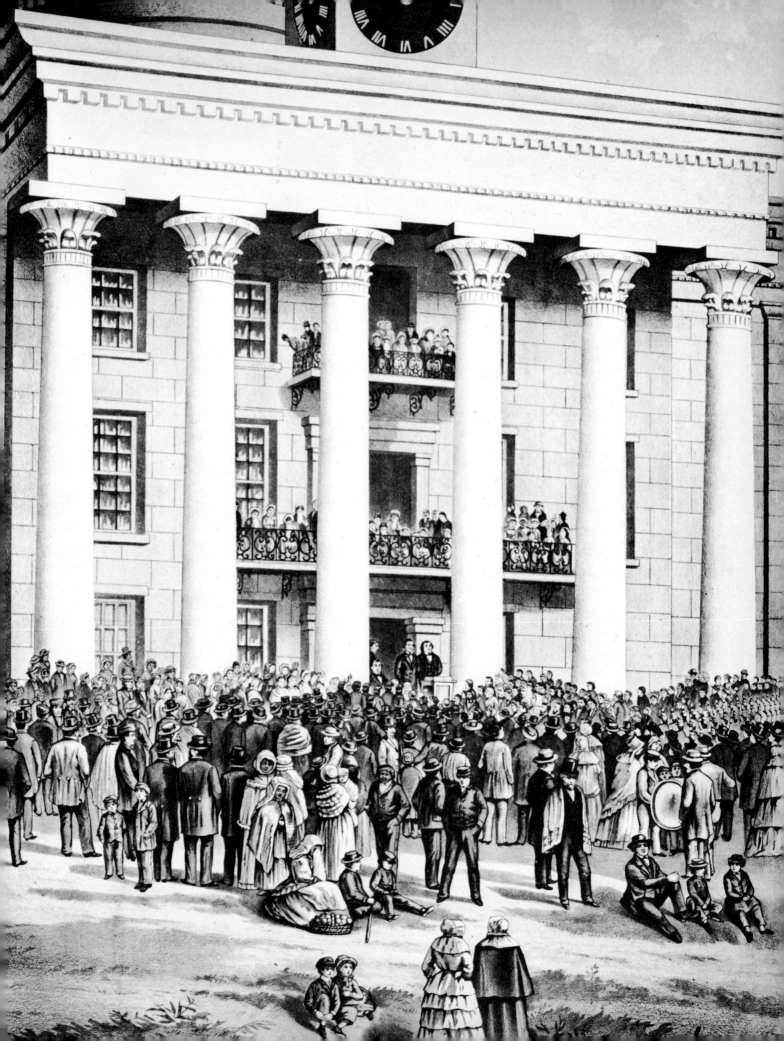

"No one not in my situation can appreciate my feeling of sadness at this parting," Lincoln said as he left Springfield. He never returned alive. Below, at Philadelphia's Independence Hall, he unfurled a new 34-star flag honoring admission of Kansas to the Union.

The President-Elect Makes a Long Journey from Springfield to Washington

This is how artist Thomas Nast imagined Lincoln changing trains in Baltimore. Actually, Lincoln's private car was drawn from one station to the other by horses.

With his own hands Abraham Lincoln tied up the family trunks, labeled them "Executive Mansion, Washington," and on February 11 he left Springfield for the capital. Throughout this twelve-day journey Lincoln attempted to maintain the dignified silence of his campaign, but he lapsed occasionally —as in his characterization of the secessionist view of the Union as "no regular marriage, but rather a sort of free-love arrangement, to be maintained on passional attraction." A nation unaccustomed to this humor thought his jokes crude. When he called out in a crowd to Grace Bedell, the girl who had suggested he grow a beard, many thought it indecorous. Finally, when detective Allan Pinkerton informed him that an attempt on his life might be made when he passed through Baltimore, Lincoln allowed himself to be spirited through that city at night, to arrive in Washington unannounced and accompanied by a single bodyguard. It was an inauspicious beginning.

Confederate caricaturist Adalbert John Volck acidly portrayed a frightened Lincoln (right) passing through Baltimore in a boxcar, disguised in a military cloak and a Scotch cap.

55

Lincoln Is Inaugurated

Sharpshooters were posted at the Capitol's windows, and a flying wedge of artillery was just out of sight at Lincoln's inauguration (above). A thoughtful Lincoln posed for Mathew Brady on February 23 (right).

March 4, 1861, dawned chill and cloudy, but by 12:30 P.M. the sun was shining when an open carriage pulled up in front of Willard's Hotel in Washington. President James Buchanan was come to escort Abraham Lincoln to his inauguration. Their route up cobblestoned Pennsylvania Avenue was gay with flags and bunting; bands and military units stepped by in colorful precision; white horses pulled a float with 34 pretty girls representing all 34 states.

However, crusty old General Winfield Scott was not thinking of parades this day. Anticipating violence, he had stationed riflemen on housetops along the parade route; platoons were posted every 100 yards; cavalry stood by in side streets.

Buchanan, grave and silent, sighed "audibly, and frequently," while Lincoln was calm, "impassive as an Indian martyr." Stepping onto the wooden platform erected at the Capitol's east portico, Lincoln looked awkwardly around for a place to put his new stovepipe hat. Generously, his old opponent Stephen A. Douglas took the hat and placed it on his knee. Lincoln put on a pair of steel-bowed spectacles and began reading his inaugural address in a clear, high-pitched voice that carried well out to the crowd of 25,000. The address was a document of inspired statesmanship. He reminded the South of his pledge not to interfere with slavery, but he firmly rejected secession—the Union was "unbroken." Finally he issued a grave warning: "In *your* hands, my dissatisfied fellow-countrymen, and not in *mine*, is the momentous issue of civil war. The government will not assail *you*. You can have, no conflict, without being yourselves the aggressors. *You* have no oath registered in Heaven to destroy the government, while *I* shall have the most solemn one to 'preserve, protect and defend' it." Abraham Lincoln was resolved to be President of the whole Union.

THE
OPENING
GUNS

THERE had been many woeful misunderstandings between North and South in the years that led up to the Civil War, but the most tragic misunderstanding of all was that neither side realized, until it was too late, that the other side was desperately in earnest. Not until the war had actually begun would men see that their rivals really meant to fight. By that time it was too late to do anything but go on fighting.

Southerners had been talking secession for many years, and most people in the North had come to look on such talk as a counter in the game of politics. You wanted something, and you threatened that dire things would happen if you did not get what you wanted; but you didn't necessarily mean to do what you were threatening to do, and there was no sense in taking brash words at their face value. America as a nation of poker players understood all about the business of calling bluffs. Not until the guns began to go off would the North realize that when men like Jefferson Davis talked about seceding from the Union they meant every word of it.

The same was true, in reverse, in the South. It seemed incomprehensible there that the Federal Union meant so much in the North that millions of people would be ready to make war to preserve it. The North seemed to dislike both slavery and slaveowners; to the average Southerner, it stood to reason that the North would be happy to get rid of both. Furthermore, it was not supposed that the North could fight even if it wanted to do so. It was a nation of mudsills and undigested immigrants, ruled by money-mad Yankees, and any army it raised would dissolve like the morning mists once it ran into real soldiers. The Southern orator who promised to wipe up, with his handkerchief, all of the blood that would be spilled because of secession was expressing a very common viewpoint.

For a while it looked as if the doubters on both sides might be right. Lincoln was inaugurated in Washington, and in his inaugural address he gave plain warning that he would do all in his power to "hold, occupy and possess" the property and places belonging to the Federal government which lay in Confederate territory. But after this speech was made nothing much seemed to happen, and the new Lincoln administration began to look strangely like that of the departed Buchanan.

When Lincoln said that he would hold all Federal property he referred chiefly to Fort Sumter, a pentagonal brick stronghold on an island near the mouth of Charleston Harbor. The commanding officer there was Major Robert Anderson, a regular army officer from Kentucky, and Anderson had sixty-eight soldiers, enough food to last a few more weeks, and a United States flag which he was determined to keep

A Rebel flag flies over Fort Sumter on April 14, 1861, after a long bombardment forced Union withdrawal.

flying until he was compelled to haul it down. The sight of that flag was an offense to South Carolinians, and through them to the entire Confederacy. An independent nation could not countenance the existence of a foreign fort in the middle of one of its most important harbors, and the Confederate authorities tried hard but unsuccessfully to induce Washington to evacuate the place. They also put some thousands of Southern troops in gun pits and encampments all around the harbor, planting batteries where they would do the most good. In the end, negotiations having failed, and Lincoln having sent word that he was going to run supplies into the beleaguered fort, a clear indication that he proposed to hold it indefinitely, Jefferson Davis gave the word to open fire and bombard the place into submission. The Confederate commander at Charleston was the flamboyant General P. G. T. Beauregard, and he obeyed orders promptly. Sumter was ringed with fire, and after a thirty-four-hour bombardment Anderson hauled down his flag, turned the fort over to the Confederacy, and embarked his men on a steamer for New York. And the war was on.

The bombardment of Fort Sumter was spectacular, momentous—and, somehow, anticlimactic. It was the visible symbol that the war had begun—the thunderous announcement, to America and to all nations, that the New World's experiment in democracy had taken a strange new turn—yet when the guns were fired they merely ratified decisions which Lincoln and Davis had already made. Both men had made up their minds to fight rather than to yield, and each man had come to see Fort Sumter as the place for the showdown. (Oddly enough, the long bombardment killed no one on either side, and the war which was to be so costly began with a bloodless battle. The only lives lost at Sumter were lost after the surrender, when Major Anderson was firing a last salute to his flag; a powder charge exploded and killed two men.

A hysterical wave of emotion swept across the country when the news of Fort Sumter came out. War actually seemed to be welcomed, as if a tension which had grown completely unendurable had at last been broken. Whatever might happen next, at least the years of drift and indecision were over. Grim knowledge of the reality of war would come quickly enough, but right at first an unsophisticated people surged out under waving flags with glad cries and with laughter, as if the thing that had happened called for rejoicing.

The first move was up to Lincoln, and he made it without delay. He announced to the nation that "combinations too powerful to be suppressed" by the ordinary machinery of peacetime government had assumed control of various Southern states; to restore order and suppress these combinations he called on the states to place 75,000 militia at the service of the Federal government. This call to arms brought a rush of enthusiastic recruiting all across the North, but at the same time it immediately put four more states into the Southern Confederacy. Virginia, North Carolina, Tennessee, and Arkansas had not yet left the Union; their sympathies were with the states which had seceded, but they had been clinging to the hope that the schism might yet be healed without bloodshed. Now they had to choose, and they chose promptly: all four left the Union and entered the Confederacy, and the Davis administration began to make arrangements to transfer the Confederate capital from Alabama to Richmond.

Neither North nor South was in the least ready for a war, and very few people in either section had any conception of the immense demands which the war was going to make. When the conflict began, the country's regular army consisted of no more than 16,000 men—barely enough to police the Indian country and the frontier and to man the coastal fortifications on a skeletonized basis. For whatever it might be worth, the army was at the disposal of the Federal government. It was obvious, however, that even if all of it could be massed in one spot (which was out of the question), it would not be nearly large enough for the job at hand. The load would have to be carried mainly by volunteers—which, at the beginning, meant state militia—and neither the weapons which the volunteers would use nor the uniforms they would wear, to say nothing of the officers who would lead them, as yet existed. Both sides were going to have to improvise.

The states did have their militia regiments, and these went to the colors at once. They were of uneven quality; none of them had ever had anything resembling combat training, and the best of them were drilled almost solely for parade-ground maneuvers. Even for parade, most units were poorly prepared. The average militia regiment was composed of one company from this town, another from that town, and so on, the ten companies scattered all across the state, and in many cases the individual companies had never been brought together to maneuver as a regiment. This was a serious handicap. By the military tactics of the 1860's, the ability of troops to maneuver as regiments or brigades was extremely important. To get from column into line—that is, from the formation in which they could march into the formation in which they could fight—called for a variety of highly intricate movements, for which incessant drill was required. A first-rate militia company which had never worked as part of a larger unit would be of little use on the battlefield until it had put in many hours of regimental and brigade drill.

Still, both sides were equally unready, and in both sections the work of preparation went on with excited haste if not with complete efficiency. All of these assorted military outfits went in for gaudy and impractical uniforms; most of them adopted flamboyant names, not realizing that the separate companies would quickly lose their identities as cogs in a larger machine. There were Frontier Guards, Rough-and-Ready Grays, Susquehanna Blues, and the like, and there were Game Cocks, Tigers, Invincibles, Fencibles, and Rangers beyond computation. (Some of the Blues, at this stage, were Southern, and some of the Grays were Northern; the adoption of recognizable national uniforms would come later, after a certain amount of battlefield confusion.) These separate companies were led by officers elected by the rank and file, which was also the case with most of the regiments. In most cases the officers owed their election to their talents as vote-getters, or simply to the fact that they were "leading citizens." Very few were chosen because they had any especial qualifications for military command. In time, field experience would weed out most of the misfits, but in the beginning the rival armies would consist of amateurs led by amateurs.

There were regular officers on hand, to be sure, but in the North the government did not quite know what to do with them. Lieutenant General Winfield Scott was general in chief; a fine soldier and an able strategist once, but very old now, physically all but helpless, perhaps touched with senility. He hoped to keep the regular army more or less intact, as the hard core around which the army of militiamen and volunteers would be built, and he did not want to see regular officers resign to take commissions with the amateurs. From the regulars, to be sure, would come the general officers—but not all of the general officers, at that, for the administration was going to make generals out of a certain number of political leaders, and some of these would be given very important commands. The army immediately in front of Washington, which would be known as the Army of the Potomac, was given to Brigadier General Irvin McDowell, a regular. An army which was being raised in Ohio, which presently would invade western Virginia, was led by Major General George B. McClellan, a brilliant young West Pointer who had served in the Mexican War and then had left the army to become a railroad president. In St. Louis command was held by another regular, Brigadier General William A. Harney; he would be replaced before long by Major General John Charles Frémont, who had served in the regular army and had won fame as "The Pathfinder" of Far Western exploration. He was no West Pointer, and his service had been with the topographical engineers rather than with the line. Many new brigadiers would be named, some of them West Pointers, others not. For some time to come the administration would feel its way toward its new command setup, with no fixed program.

The Confederacy was a little more systematic. Jefferson Davis was a West Pointer himself, with a good deal of field experience, and he had served as Secretary of War. He had a good understanding of the military arts, although he apparently believed that his talents in this field were a bit more extensive than was actually the case, and as far as possible he intended to use trained soldiers for his general officers. About a third of the West Pointers in the regular army had resigned to serve with the South; one of the Confederacy's assets lay in the fact that these included some of the most capable men on the army roster. There was Robert E. Lee, for instance, to whom at the outbreak of the war command of the Federals' principal field army had been offered. Lee had rejected the offer and had gone with his state, Virginia, and Davis would make him a full general. The Beauregard who had taken Fort Sumter, and who now commanded the chief Confederate army in Virginia, was a professional soldier, highly regarded. From the West was coming another West Pointer of substantial reputation, General Albert Sidney Johnston. Still another former regular who would play a prominent part was General Joseph E. Johnston, who had many talents, but who would prove utterly unable to get along with President Davis.

One oddity about the whole situation was the fact that the regular army before the war had been very small, with an officer corps whose members knew one another quite intimately. A Civil War general, as a result, was quite likely to be very well acquainted with the man who was commanding troops against him, knowing his strengths and his weaknesses. There would be times when this mutual knowledge would have a marked effect on strategic and tactical decisions.

The war aims of the two sides were very simple. The Confederacy would fight for independence, the North for re-establishment of the Union. So far, slavery itself was definitely not an issue. The North was far from unity on this point; it was vitally important for Lincoln to keep the support of Northern Democrats, most of whom had little or no objection to the continued existence of slavery in the South; and both he and the Congress itself were explicit in asserting that they wanted to restore the Union without interfering with the domestic institutions of any of the states. In addition, there were the border states, Maryland and Kentucky and Missouri, slave states where sentiment apparently was pro-Union by a rather narrow margin, but where most people had no use at all for abolitionists or the abolitionist cause. If these states should join the Confederacy, the Union cause was as good as lost; probably the most momentous single item on Lincoln's program was the determination to hold these states in the Union. If he could help it, Lincoln was not going to fight a straight Republican war.

War aims would govern war strategy. The Confederacy was a going concern: it had built a government, it was building an army, it considered itself an independent nation and it was functioning as such, and as far as Davis was concerned there would be no war at all unless the Lincoln administration forced one. The Confederacy, then, would act strictly on the defensive, and the opposite side of this coin was the fact that it was up to the North to be aggressive. Unless he could successfully take the offensive and keep at it until all of the "combinations too powerful to be suppressed" had been overthrown, Lincoln would have lost the war. In plain English, Northern armies had to invade the South and destroy the opposing government. This fact would go far to counterbalance the enormous advantages which the Federal government possessed in respect to manpower, riches, and the commercial and industrial strength that supports armies.

These advantages were impressive—so much so that Northern officers like William T. Sherman and James B. McPherson warned Southern friends at the outbreak of the war that the Confederacy was bound to fail. In the North there were over eighteen million people; the South had hardly more than nine million, of whom more than a third were Negro slaves. Nine-tenths of the country's manufacturing capacity was situated in the North, which also had two-thirds of the railway mileage, to say nothing of nearly all of the facilities for building rails, locomotives, and cars. The North contained most of the country's deposits of iron, coal, copper, and precious metals. It controlled the seas and had access to all of the factories of Europe; it was also producing a huge surplus of foodstuffs which Europe greatly needed, and these would pay for enormous quantities of munitions. Taken altogether, its latent advantages were simply overpowering.

They did not, however, mean that Northern victory would be automatic. For the North had to do the invading, and in any war the invader must have a substantial advantage in numbers. The Confederacy occupied an immense territory, and the supply lines of the invader would be long, immobilizing many troops for their protection. Although the North controlled the seas, the Confederacy's coast line was almost endless; to seal the Southland off from the outside world would require a navy far larger than anything the United States previously had dreamed of possessing. Finally, the terms on which the war would be fought meant that the average Southerner would always have a clearer, more emotionally stimulating picture of what he was fighting for than the average Northerner could hope to have. For the Southerner would see himself as fighting to protect the home place from the invader; the Northerner, on the other hand, was fighting for an abstraction, and the sacred cause of "the Union" might look very drab once real war weariness developed. To put it in its simplest terms, the North could lose the war if its people lost the desire to go on with the offensive; it could win only if it could destroy the Confederate people's *ability* to fight. In the end it would need every ounce of advantage it could get.

Old Winfield Scott had sketched in a plan. It would take time to raise, equip, and train armies big enough to beat the South; start, therefore, by blockading the seacoast, seal off the inland borders as well, then drive down the Mississippi, constricting the vitality out of the Confederacy—and, at last, send in armies of invasion to break the Southern nation into bits. As things worked out, this was not unlike the plan that was actually followed, but when it was first proposed—news of it leaked out immediately, Washington's ability to keep things secret being very limited—the newspapers derided it, calling it the "Anaconda Plan" and intimating that it was far too slow for any use. Very few men, either in the North or in the South, were ready to admit that the war would be a long one. The militia had been called into Federal service for just ninety days, the limit under existing law; it seemed reasonable to many people to suppose that before their term of service expired they ought to win the war.

Before the war could be won, however, the border states had to be secured, and to secure them the Lincoln administration used a strange combination of tactful delicacy and hardfisted ruthlessness.

Kentucky got the delicate handling. This state had a secessionist governor and a Unionist legislature, and in sheer desperation it was trying to sit the war out, having proclaimed its neutrality. For the time being both Lincoln and Davis were willing to respect this neutrality. They knew that it could not last, but the side that infringed it was apt to be the loser thereby, and until the situation elsewhere began to jell, both leaders were willing to leave Kentucky alone. (Both sides unofficially raised troops there, and there was a home guard organization which might turn out to be either Unionist or Confederate.)

If Kentucky got delicate handling, what Maryland and Missouri got was the back of the Federal government's hand.

Not long after Fort Sumter, the 6th Massachusetts Regiment was marching through Baltimore en route to Washington. There were many ardent Southerners in Baltimore, and these surrounded the marching column, jeering and catcalling. Inevitably, people began to shove and throw things, and finally the troops opened fire and there was a bloody fight in the streets. Soldiers and civilians were killed—more civilians than soldiers, as it happened—and although the 6th Regiment finally got to Washington, railroad connection via Baltimore was temporarily broken, and Lincoln took speedy action. Federal troops occupied Baltimore. Secessionist members of the legislature were thrown in jail, as were various city officials of Baltimore, and they were kept there until the Unionists got things firmly in hand. All of this, of course, was plainly illegal, but the Federal government was not going to let the secessionists cut Washington off from the rest of the North, no matter what it had to do to prevent it; with dissident legislators in jail, the Unionist governor of Maryland had little trouble holding the state in the Union.

What happened in Missouri was somewhat similar. The state had refused to secede, sentiment apparently being almost evenly divided, but like Kentucky it had a pro-Southern governor, and he maintained a camp of state troops on the edge of St. Louis. The presence of these troops worried the Federal commander, General Harney, not at all, but it worried other Unionists a great deal, the fear being that the state troops would seize the government arsenal in St. Louis. With the weapons taken there the governor could arm enough secessionist Missourians to take the state out of the Union. So Washington temporarily replaced General Harney with a fiery young regular, Captain Nathaniel S. Lyon—putting a captain in a brigadier's job was stretching things a bit, but not all of the old rules would be valid in this war—and Lyon took his soldiers out, arrested the state troops, disarmed them, and broke up their camp. As he marched his men back to barracks a street crowd collected; as in Baltimore there was jostling, shoving, name-calling, and a display of weapons; and at last the troops opened fire, killing more than a score of civilians. It may be instructive to note that the first fighting in the Civil War, after Fort Sumter, involved men in uniform shooting at men who were not in uniform—the classic pattern of a civil war.

Lyon was all flame and devotion, too impetuous by half. In an effort to keep some sort of peace in Missouri, Harney had worked out an informal truce with the governor of the state, the essence of it being that nobody would make any hostile moves until the situation had taken more definite shape. Lyon swiftly disavowed this truce, drove the governor away from the machinery of government, and marched his little army clear down into southwest Missouri in an effort to rid the state of all armed Confederates. He got into a sharp fight at Wilson's Creek and lost his life. His army had to retreat, and the Confederates continued to hold southwestern Missouri; and partly because of the bitterness growing out of Lyon's high-handed actions the unhappy state was plagued for the rest of the war by the most virulent sort of partisan warfare. But Missouri did not leave the Union, which was all that Washington cared about at the moment. Legally or otherwise, the Federal government was making the border secure.

Western Virginia also had to be dealt with, but that was easier.

The western counties of Virginia had long been antipathetic to the tidewater people, and when Virginia left the Union, the westerners began to talk about seceding from Virginia. Young General McClellan got an army over into the mountain country early in the war and without too great difficulty defeated a small Confederate force which he found there. With victorious Federal troops in their midst, the western Virginia Unionists perked up; in due course they would organize their own state of West Virginia, which the Federal government would hasten to admit to the Union; and although there might be a good deal to be said about the legal ins and outs of the business, the government had at least made certain that the Ohio River was not going to be the northern border of the Confederacy.

But if the border states had been held, the gain was negative. The South seemed unworried, and it was visibly building up its strength. Richmond now was the capital, new troops were pouring in for its defense, and cadets from the Virginia Military Institute were putting in busy days acting as drillmasters. (They had been led to Richmond by a blue-eyed, ungainly professor, a West Pointer who would soon be a Confederate general of renown, Thomas J. Jackson.) The North was never going to win the war by thwarting secessionist designs in Missouri and Maryland. It could win it only by moving south and giving battle; and as the summer of 1861 came on the time for such a move was at hand.

Major Anderson's Lonely Vigil Begins

Robert Anderson, Sumter's defender.

On November 15, 1860, Major Robert Anderson was posted to Charleston. Anderson, a loyal Kentuckian with a Georgia wife, was expected to protect the government's interests, particularly if South Carolina threatened the U.S. military installations in the harbor. The vulnerable position of Fort Moultrie on Sullivan's Island appalled him. Only recently sand had been removed from the sea wall to keep out stray cows, and even now hostile citizens could stroll in and out through gaps in the landward walls. As a good soldier, Anderson set out to rectify the situation. Square in the middle of the harbor entrance was Fort Sumter, a five-sided brick structure begun in 1829 and indifferently fortified in the intervening years. In 1860 Sumter was unoccupied except for workmen listlessly making repairs on the incomplete fortress. Anderson ordered this work expedited, and on December 26—six days after South Carolina's secession—he transferred the tiny garrison from Moultrie out into the harbor to begin a tense and lonely vigil.

As dawn lit the sky on April 12, 1861, Southern gun crews sighted their pieces on the dark shape of Fort Sumter (right) out in the middle of Charleston Harbor. Inside the fort Major Robert Anderson and a small garrison awaited reinforcements. At the left William Waud's wash drawing shows a gang of Negroes mounting a Rebel cannon on Morris Island before the bombardment.

South Carolina Fires the First Shot

Secessionist Edmund Ruffin.

The ineffectual and thoroughly frightened President, James Buchanan, was determined to sit out the remaining two months of his administration without making a decision on the Federal installations in Charleston Harbor. On March 4 he handed the burden over to Lincoln.

At first Lincoln did nothing either, wavering as his predecessor had over this crucial issue. Then, ignoring advice from his cabinet, he notified South Carolina on April 6 that an expedition was on its way to provision Sumter, where supplies were running low. Five days later South Carolina demanded the evacuation of the Union post. Major Anderson rejected the ultimatum, but he was forced to admit that "if you do not batter the fort to pieces . . . we shall be starved out in a few days." In November the Virginia fire-eater Edmund Ruffin had boarded a train for South Carolina, brandishing one of John Brown's pikes which he had obtained a year earlier at the execution. "As old as I am, I have come here to join you in [the] lead," he told his South Carolina friends. At 4:30 A.M. on April 12 Ruffin pulled the lanyard on a symbolic first shot of the new revolution. Under the direction of Anderson's former artillery student at West Point, P. G. T. Beauregard, the shelling continued through 34 hours and some 4,000 shells. Finally, at 2:30 P.M. on April 13, Major Anderson surrendered Fort Sumter.

Albert Bierstadt painted a beleaguered Fort Sumter (center) being fired upon from all sides. A signal from Fort Johnson (foreground) prompted Ruffin's shot from Cummings Point (right center), and guns at Fort Moultrie (left center) opened fire. Below is a Fort Sumter cannon, harmlessly aimed at modern Charleston.

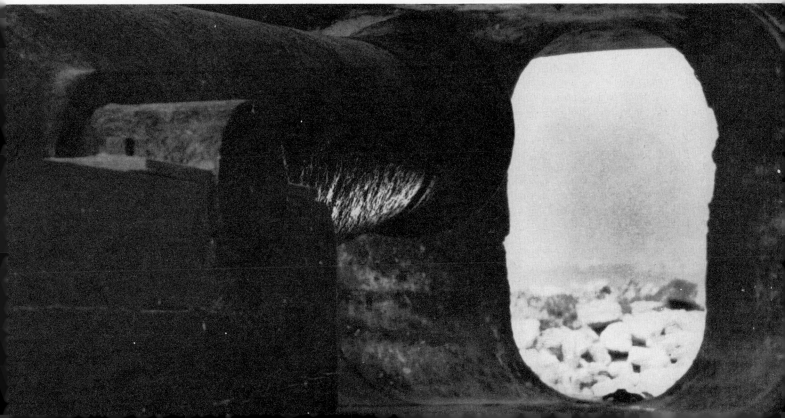

WILLIAM HENRY SEWARD coined the phrase "irrepressible conflict" as a Senator from New York in 1858, but by 1860 he was more moderate in his antislavery views. Disappointed at not receiving the Presidential bid himself, Seward hoped to dominate the administration as Lincoln's Secretary of State. In 1861 he suggested a diversionary foreign war to reunite the country.

NATIONAL ARCHIVES

SALMON PORTLAND CHASE, radical Republican Governor of Ohio, was another prima donna in Lincoln's cabinet. As Secretary of the Treasury, Chase was constantly at odds with Seward, and his backstairs political intriguing for the 1864 Presidential nomination led to his ouster from the administration. A forgiving Lincoln promptly appointed him Chief Justice.

NATIONAL ARCHIVES

GIDEON WELLES, a Connecticut journalist, was chosen by Lincoln to be Secretary of the Navy, to give New England representation in the cabinet. With his fluffy whiskers and fetching wig Welles presented a benign Father Neptune image. Surprisingly enough, he proved an able naval secretary, and his diaries provide an intimate picture of the administration.

LIBRARY OF CONGRESS

SIMON CAMERON of Pennsylvania went to the War Department in fulfillment of a convention bargain of which Lincoln had been unaware. So inept and corrupt was his handling of the office that within a year he was shipped off to be minister to Russia. His place was taken by Edwin M. Stanton, the staunch Ohio unionist who had served as Buchanan's last Attorney General.

COLLECTION OF MRS. FRANK J. COLEMAN

MONTGOMERY BLAIR of Maryland brought to the office of Postmaster General the prestige of a family prominent in national politics since Andrew Jackson's time. He alone advised provisioning Fort Sumter, and threatened to resign, within two weeks of taking office, if Lincoln failed to do so. He stayed on to institute many valuable postal reforms during his four years in office.

NATIONAL ARCHIVES

Union and Confederate

ROBERT TOOMBS, once a tireless champion of moderation, led Georgia out of the Union when the Republicans rejected the Crittenden Compromise in December, 1860. Bypassed for the Confederate Presidency, Toombs was further disappointed with his post as Secretary of State. In five months he had resigned to become commander of a Georgia brigade on the Virginia front.

COOK COLLECTION, VALENTINE MUSEUM

STEPHEN R. MALLORY served as Naval Affairs Committee chairman when he represented Florida in the Senate before the war. He did an admirable job as Secretary of the Navy, pioneering in ironclad construction, and was one of three original cabinet members (the others were Judah P. Benjamin and Postmaster General John Reagan) who lasted out the war.

COLLECTION OF FREDERICK HILL MESERVE

JUDAH P. BENJAMIN of Louisiana possessed perhaps the most brilliant legal mind in the South. First appointed Attorney General, he was shifted to the War Department in September, 1861, and then to the State Department in March, 1862. Benjamin bore calmly all political attacks, including those inspired by anti-Semitism, to become Jefferson Davis' indispensable adviser.

COLLECTION OF FREDERICK HILL MESERVE

LEROY P. WALKER of Alabama was named first Secretary of War as a matter of political expediency (six of the seven original Confederate states were represented in the cabinet, while Mississippi got the Presidency). Inadequate to the task, Walker resigned within seven months and was succeeded by Benjamin and four other war secretaries in the kaleidoscopic Davis cabinet.

COLLECTION OF FREDERICK HILL MESERVE

C. G. MEMMINGER, born in Germany, worked his way up from a Charleston orphanage to a position of prominence in ante-bellum South Carolina. As Secretary of the Treasury he followed a financial policy, based on paper money, which proved disastrous to the Confederacy. Often blamed for programs instituted by Congress, he was forced to resign his post in June, 1864.

COOK COLLECTION, VALENTINE MUSEUM

THE WAR.

Highly Important News from Washington.

Offensive War Measures of the Administration.

The President's Exposition of His Policy Towards the Confederate States.

A WAR PROCLAMATION.

Seventy-five Thousand Men Ordered Out.

Thirteen Thousand Required from New York.

Call for an Extra Session of Congress.

Preparations for the Defence of the National Capital.

The Great Free States Arming for the Conflict.

Thirty Thousand Troops to be Tendered from New York.

Strong Union Demonstrations in Baltimore.

THE BATTLE AT CHARLESTON.

EVACUATION OF FORT SUMTER.

Behind Lincoln's appeal for state militia was the sorry fact that the regular army in 1861 numbered only 16,000—a force scarcely adequate to keep peace among the Indians on the Western frontier. To the South his proclamation meant war, as the New York Herald headline above indicated. Colorful militia units like the Boston National Lancers, shown at top right in an 1855 print, responded eagerly to the call. Appeals were made to community pride, and the names of popular local leaders were often exploited, as in the stirring recruiting poster reproduced at the right.

70

To Arms!

COLLECTION OF MRS. JOHN NICHOLAS BROWN

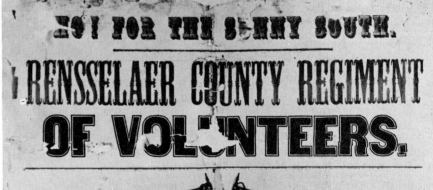

HO! FOR THE SUNNY SOUTH.

RENSSELAER COUNTY REGIMENT OF VOLUNTEERS.

REGIMENTAL HEADQUARTERS,  69 FIRST STREET, TROY, N. Y.

COL. W. T. WILLARD,

Having entered upon the duties and command of this Regiment, calls upon all Patriots and Lovers of their country to step forward at this most important crisis, in aid of their beloved country, in her efforts to

Preserve the UNION, Protect the CONSTITUTION,

With united efforts, ... shall soon be in the m...... .ender aid to crush Rebellion, and restore the Laws to their protecting influence, enabling the Citizens of this great Republic once more to meet on terms of harmony and friendship, banishing the demon Rebellion, and ambitious Traitors who have brought this evil day upon us.

Company Officers for Six Companies, are active in obtaining Volunteers at this moment, with flattering success. The other Companies will be organized immediately. YOUNG MEN of Character, Energy, and Capacity, are invited to come forward to fill up the unoccupied positions, and complete the organization. It is intended and desirable to pass the winter in a milder climate than our latitude affords. An early organization will do this, and enable the Regiment to participate in the operations now going on in the field of War.

Nov. 18, 1861.

W. T. WILLARD, Col. Com'g.

On April 15, 1861, Lincoln called for 75,000 men to be enlisted for 90 days. As a precedent for this proclamation, he reached back to a statute passed in Washington's time, which gave the President power to call the state militia into Federal service whenever the laws were resisted by "combinations too powerful to be suppressed."

The military organization called upon was an antiquated, creaking structure which dated back to the Revolution. Theoretically, all ablebodied men in a democratic society were always ready to rush to the defense of the fatherland. But the nation's standing militia was about as effective as might be expected of a theoretical organization. A little better were the uniformed volunteer companies composed of men who seemed at least to enjoy soldiering and took pride in their splendid and colorful military appearance.

GOD. OUR COUNTRY AND LIBERTY.!!

THE SPIRIT OF '61.

Up with the Standard and bear it on | Remember the deeds of Washington
Let its folds to the wind expand | And the flag of our native land.

Elmer Ephraim Ellsworth (above, arms folded) epitomized the prewar volunteer militiaman. His company of exotic Zouaves, patterned after the famous French fighting forces, thrilled the public with elaborate drills, but when these warriors went into battle they learned the hard way that their bizarre uniforms were not suited to combat. The dashing Ellsworth became one of the war's first victims. He was shot tearing down a secessionist flag the day Union troops entered Virginia. At left, a flamboyant "Spirit of '61" typified the delirious Northern response to Lincoln's call for volunteers.

The North Mobilizes Its Forces

Below is "Going to War," the opening scene in William Travis' 528 foot Civil War panorama celebrating the Federal Army of the Cumberland, which is here reproduced for the first time. Travis mounted his work on rollers and toured with it in the Midwest after the war

72

Above left is an eager company of New York militia in 1861. The belles (center) at the Pennsylvania Academy of the Fine Arts are sewing an outsize flag for the boys. Colonel Ambrose Burnside led the Detached Rhode Island Militia out of Providence, photographed at right.

Before nightfall on the day of Lincoln's proclamation Massachusetts regiments had orders to assemble on Boston Common. So great was the excitement there, Edward Everett observed, that the President might have called out 500,000 men. A crowd of 50,000 jammed New York's Union Square on April 20 to cheer an orator who beseeched them "to rally round the star-spangled banner so long as a single stripe can be discovered, or a single star shall shimmer from the surrounding darkness." The Governor of Iowa, at first worried about raising a whole regiment, in a few days was telegraphing Washington: "For God's sake send us arms. We have the men." How many men would Ohio furnish? "The largest number you will receive." Nathaniel Hawthorne said, "It was delightful to share in the heroic sentiment of the time, and to feel that I had a country—a consciousness which seemed to make me young again."

Southerners Flock to the Stars and Bars

These satirical sketches of Southern militia were drawn by Porte Crayon, pseudonym for David Hunter Strother, who toured the South for Harper's *in the years before the war.*

Virginia, which had been procrastinating on secession, was stunned by Lincoln's proclamation calling for 75,000 men to put down the insurrection. Secession was one thing; coercion of the secessionists quite another. On April 17, 1861, the Old Dominion voted itself out of the Union, to be followed by Arkansas (May 6), Tennessee (May 7), and North Carolina (May 20). With Virginia the Confederacy received its most illustrious soldier, Robert E. Lee. Rejecting Lincoln's offer of field command of the Union armies, Lee reluctantly resigned his commission to return to his native state, saying, "I cannot raise my hand against my birthplace, my home, my children." In Montgomery, Jefferson Davis announced that he already had 19,000 men under arms of the 100,000 authorized by the Confederate Congress in March "to repel invasion, maintain the rightful possession of the Confederate States, and to secure public tranquility and independence against threatened assault." The final scene of the prologue was completed when the Confederate capital was shifted to Richmond in June.

From now on, the focus of war in the eastern theater would be on the 100 miles separating Davis in Richmond from Lincoln in Washington.

Rallying proudly to their bonnie new flag in April, 1861, were these Georgians of the Sumter Light Guards. At first uniform details on both sides were largely a matter of local option. Only later would some standardization—blue and gray—be applied.

OVERLEAF: *New York's 7th Regiment, a crack parade unit, marched down Broadway on April 19, 1861. It was a sight Thomas Nast, who sketched it for* Harper's, *never forgot; eight years later he expanded his drawing into this famous oil painting.*

The Balance Sheet as War Began

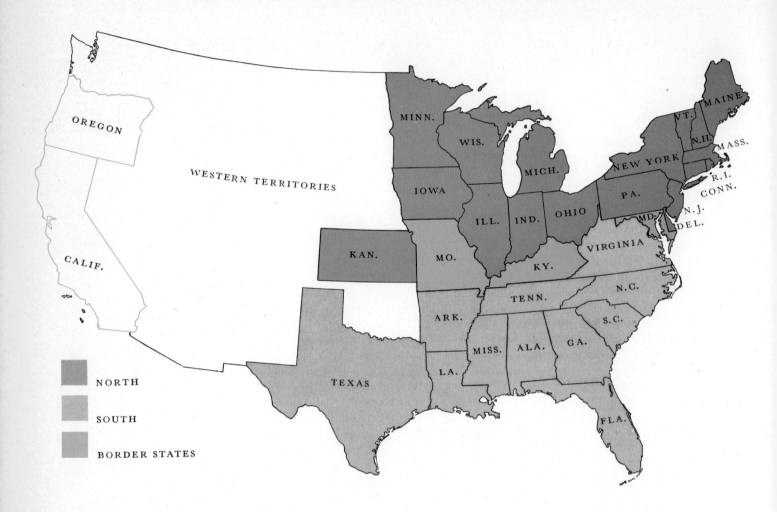

NORTH

SOUTH

BORDER STATES

The 34-star, prewar flag of 1861 symbolized an expanding Union. In the last decade the nation had leapfrogged over the prairies and mountains to admit California and Oregon; on the eve of Lincoln's inauguration Kansas came into the fold. Moreover, the Eighth Census, taken in 1860, revealed a country expanding in directions other than geographical. It showed a population increasing in almost geometric progression, a healthy agricultural boom, and an industry bursting at the seams. But a careful study of these statistics discloses a remarkable disproportion between the nation's two major sections—North and South.

In area there was little difference. The square mileage of eighteen Northern states (minus California and Oregon, which were too far distant to contribute much more than moral support to the coming conflict) was actually surpassed by the eleven Confederate states. Three brittle border states—Kentucky, Maryland, and Missouri—might swing either way; and, for this reason, they are shown in the graphs on the opposite page as a separate category.

In population (Graph 1) the North was double the size of the South, whose population was nearly 40 per cent slave. Of six leading agricultural products (Graph 2) the South

led in three; but of these, only one was an edible crop. The scales were not so heavily weighted in favor of the North in the livestock category (Graph 3).

Railroad mileage (Graph 4) must be interpreted in terms of total territory—the North had more than twice the mileage of the South for an almost equal area. The statistics for manufacturing and finance (Graphs 5 and 6) expose the basic shortcomings of an agricultural South in an industrial age.

This balance sheet of assets on the eve of war reveals a disparity that was far from apparent at the time to the two hostile factions.

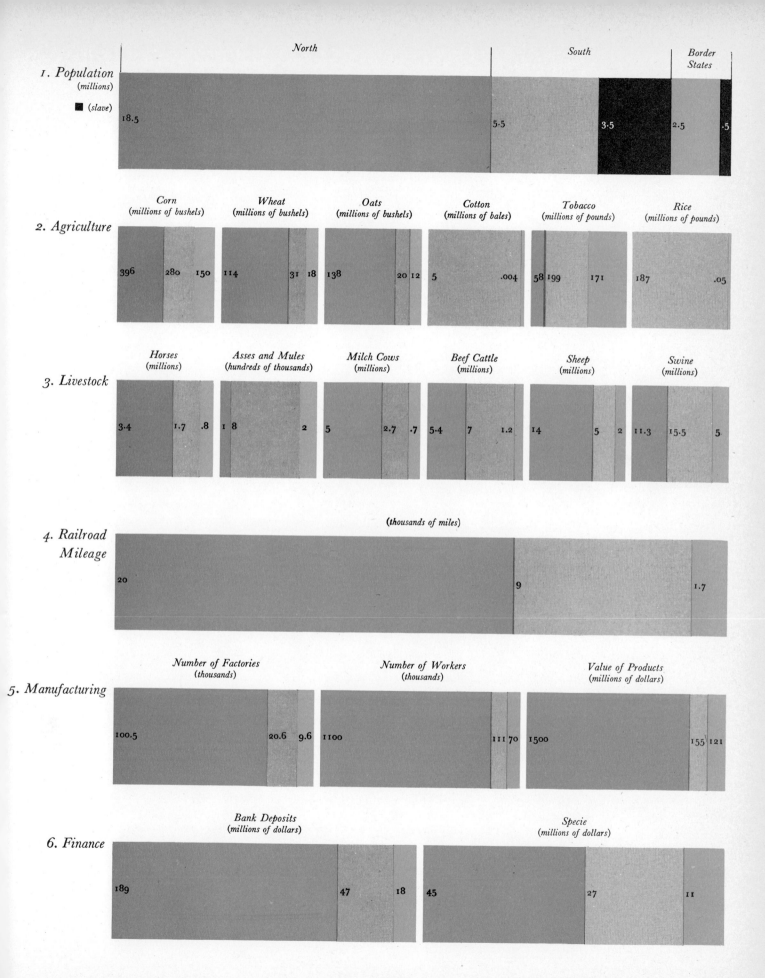

1. Population
(millions)

■ (slave)

North   South   Border States

18.5   5.5   3.5   2.5   .5

2. Agriculture

Corn (millions of bushels)	Wheat (millions of bushels)	Oats (millions of bushels)	Cotton (millions of bales)	Tobacco (millions of pounds)	Rice (millions of pounds)
396 280 150	114 31 18	138 20 12	5 .004	58 199 171	187 .05

3. Livestock

Horses (millions)	Asses and Mules (hundreds of thousands)	Milch Cows (millions)	Beef Cattle (millions)	Sheep (millions)	Swine (millions)
3.4 1.7 .8	1 8 2	5 2.7 .7	5.4 7 1.2	14 5 2	11.3 15.5 5

4. Railroad Mileage

(thousands of miles)

20   9   1.7

5. Manufacturing

Number of Factories (thousands)	Number of Workers (thousands)	Value of Products (millions of dollars)
100.5 20.6 9.6	1100 111 70	1500 155 121

6. Finance

Bank Deposits (millions of dollars)	Specie (millions of dollars)
189 47 18	45 27 11

West Point Classmates Are Divided

General Winfield Scott, shown above reviewing his troops at Mexico City, commanded such future Confederate generals as Braxton Bragg and Joseph E. Johnston during the Mexican campaigns. A national hero since the War of 1812, Scott was a dropsical 75—but still commanding general—at the beginning of the Civil War.

Ulysses S. Grant

COLLECTION OF LLOYD OSTENDORF

George B. McClellan

PRINCETON UNIVERSITY PRESS

George H. Thomas

COLLECTION OF MRS. FRANK J. COLEMAN

At the very outset of the Civil War divided allegiances split the exclusive club which was the officer corps of the U.S. Army. In the battles to come, men who had studied together at West Point and fought side by side in Mexico would be opponents, often thoroughly knowledgeable about one another's strengths and weaknesses.

At First Bull Run, P. G. T. Beauregard, second in the class of 1838, would face Irvin McDowell, twenty-third in the same class. Clever young George B. McClellan of the class of 1846 would find his quiet classmate, Thomas J. Jackson, known in the war as Stonewall, a deadly foe. Lovely young Ellen Marcy had once been forced to choose between two West Point graduates. She married McClellan; her rejected suitor, A. P. Hill, became her husband's enemy.

During the Mexican War of 1846–48 General Winfield Scott conducted what amounted to a postgraduate course in warfare for many officers who would be fighting one another. There Captain Robert E. Lee won Scott's admiration, and young Lieutenant Ulysses Grant, a regimental quartermaster, also saw combat.

In September, 1852, Lee, now a brevet colonel, became superintendent of West Point. An instructor of artillery there was another Virginian, George Thomas, who would remain loyal to the Union; graduating first in the class of 1853 was James B. McPherson, destined to be a brilliant Union general; while far down the class roster were two young men who would go separate ways—Philip Sheridan and John Bell Hood. The class of 1854, the last under Lee's supervision at West Point, took as its motto, "When Our Country Calls." The call was answered in different ways—with 23 men serving in the Union army, and 14 in the Confederate forces.

Robert E. Lee

COLLECTION OF MRS. FRANK J. COLEMAN

Braxton Bragg

COLLECTION OF MRS. FRANK J. COLEMAN

Joseph E. Johnston

COLLECTION OF MRS. FRANK J. COLEMAN

Thomas J. Jackson

NATIONAL ARCHIVES

Benjamin F. Butler

Northern Political Generals

Lincoln was almost constantly under pressure to make military appointments on the basis of political considerations—to reward loyal Republicans, woo prominent War Democrats, and appease the constituents of powerful legislators. The Civil War, primarily a political struggle, was to have its military strategy directed not only by the politicians who held office but also by such political generals.

Some of these figures were to cause the administration great embarrassment. Walruslike Ben Butler of Massachusetts became the center of every conceivable controversy; New York's Dan Sickles was the target of criticism both military and political, public and personal. On the other hand, some of these politician-soldiers performed essential services: Franz Sigel was instrumental in rallying German-Americans to the Union cause; John A. McClernand, a mediocre general with delusions of grandeur, personally recruited thousands of soldiers in the Mississippi Valley. Moreover, a few of the politicians in uniform became good soldiers. Francis Preston Blair, Jr. (brother of the Postmaster General) won the admiration of both Sherman and Grant. John A. Logan of Illinois won rapid promotion, earned a fine reputation as a combat soldier, but was relieved because of his contempt for adequate logistical preparation. The Civil War was to be an amateurs' war and a professionals' war; both had their good men and bad.

Francis Preston Blair, Jr.

John A. McClernand

Franz Sigel

Daniel E. Sickles

John A. Logan

83

Four infantrymen were killed, 36 wounded, when a Baltimore mob attacked Massachusetts troops being pulled in train cars through the city's streets on April 19.

A chastened Baltimore watched Massachusetts troops return amidst a violent thunderstorm on May 12 to take possession of the city, sketched below by Frank Schell.

An actual sketch, made on the spot by one of the Special Artists of Frank Leslie's Illustrated Newspaper.

Mr. Leslie holds the copyright and right of publication.

The First Threat to Washington

The Crittenden family epitomized Kentucky's division. When the compromise efforts of Senator John J. Crittenden (right) failed, one son, Thomas (left), became a Union general, while another, George (center), joined the Confederate army against his father's wishes.

While an exultant North rushed to arms, Lincoln worried about undefended Washington, surrounded by hostile slave territory. Six companies of regulars, fifteen of volunteers, and a handful of marines at the navy yard were the only forces which could be mustered to protect the national capital against any Confederate threat.

On April 18 the first troops arrived in response to Lincoln's call —some 500 boys of "unlicked patriotism . . . poured ragged and unarmed out of Pennsylvania." But the following day the 6th Massachusetts Regiment, en route to Washington, was met in Baltimore with stones and bullets from Southern sympathizers. That evening they limped into Washington, bearing their wounded on stretchers, to take up quarters in the Senate chamber. A harried Lincoln complained: "I don't believe there is any North! The Seventh [New York] Regiment is a myth! Rhode Island is not known in our geography any longer!"

From a second-floor window in the White House the President could see through his spyglass a Confederate flag flying over Arlington Heights, Virginia; and at night the campfires of gathering enemy forces flickered in the darkness south of the Potomac. To the north, Maryland focused attention on the special problems represented by the border states. While Lincoln's native Kentucky wavered between a secessionist governor and a legislature largely Union in sympathy, the situation was reversed in Maryland. There a loyal but weak governor was intimidated by a secession-minded legislature, and the state's fealty to the Union was in doubt. Railroad bridges north of Baltimore were out, telegraph wires through that city had been cut, and Washington seemed isolated.

At noon on April 25 a locomotive whistle alerted Washington to the arrival of New York's 7th Regiment, which had laid rails and rebuilt bridges to reach the city. Other Northern regiments soon followed; and by early May Washington had a defending force of 10,000, Maryland had been pacified, and the capital was temporarily saved.

More Trouble in the West

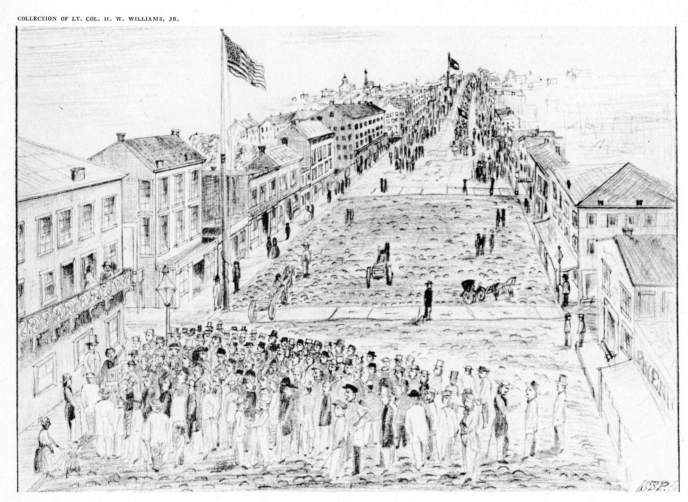

At divided Knoxville, Tennessee, rival Union and Confederate meetings drew equal crowds in 1861.

Lincoln regretted having to take firm action against Maryland, but the lines of communication between the North and Washington had to be protected. Kentucky, which proclaimed its neutrality in mid-May, received a kid-glove treatment that temporarily made it safe for the Union. But when Tennessee's Andrew Johnson, sole remaining senator from the seceded states, pleaded in Washington for Union protection of his loyal eastern mountain people, nothing could be done.

Out beyond the Mississippi River the state of Missouri was also tottering. Lincoln's call for troops had been characterized by Governor Claiborne Jackson as "illegal, unconstitutional, [and] revolutionary." Despite a large German population loyal to the Union, St. Louis was controlled by secessionists; and Governor Jackson began arming the state militia, encamped nearby.

In February, Captain Nathaniel Lyon had been assigned to the St. Louis arsenal, with its 60,000 stand of arms which Jackson's militia was now eyeing covetously. With the backing of Francis Preston Blair, Jr., Lyon obtained command of the arsenal and on April 25 he spirited most of the arms across the Mississippi into Illinois. Then, on May 10, he raided the pro-Southern camp, forced the Rebels to surrender, and paraded his captives through the streets of St. Louis. Someone in a crowd threw a stone, and Lyon's forces began firing. Before the clash ended, 28 persons had been killed or fatally injured. Missouri, though it would remain in the Union, had entered a period of bitter partisan warfare.

A month after Lyon's raid on the militia camp, a volunteer company of loyal Germans—called Hessians by indignant pro-Southern St. Louisans—was attacked in the center of the city. In the painting above, by William Streeter, the volunteers are directing their fire at the second story of an engine house from which they claimed the first shot had come. The Recorder's Court, meeting in a room just off the balcony, was understandably disrupted.

Fighting at
Wilson's Creek

Nathaniel Lyon

Infuriated by bloodshed in St. Louis, the Missouri legislature in Jefferson City took war measures, and Governor Jackson appointed Sterling Price commander of the state's forces. A temporary truce was arranged by Federal General W. A. Harney, but Blair soon had Nathaniel Lyon put in his place. Lyon drove Jackson out of his capital and headed southwest, hoping to pierce Arkansas. He got within 50 miles of the border before realizing that he was 120 miles from his railroad base and was outnumbered two to one by Price's 12,000 Confederates. Hoping to strike one blow before he was forced to retreat, Lyon staged a pretentious little battle at Wilson's Creek on August 10. Franz Sigel's surprise attack on the Confederate rear ended in rout, and at the Union front the red-bearded Lyon was waving his hat to rally the men when a bullet knocked him dead from his horse. The Union troops fled, and southwestern Missouri remained in Confederate control.

AN actual sketch, made on the spot by one of the Special Artists of Frank Leslie's Illustrated Newspaper.

Mr. Leslie holds the copyright and reserves the exclusive right of publication.

Leslie's *gave its combat artists sketch pads with a copyright notice printed*

them (lower left). This drawing of Lyon's death has artist Henri Lovie's instructions to the engravers at top.

THE CLASH OF AMATEUR ARMIES

THE WAY General Scott had planned it, the first year of the war would be spent, mostly, in getting ready. The old general had a poor opinion of volunteer troops—like most West Pointers, he felt that they had behaved badly in the Mexican War—and he believed that it would take a long time to prepare them for field service. It would also take a long time to get the supply service organized, so that boots and pants and coats and tents and muskets and all of the other things the new armies would need could be produced in adequate quantities. It would be absurd to start offensive operations until properly trained armies, fully supplied and equipped, were ready to move.

In all of this General Scott was quite correct, by the standards of military logic. Unfortunately, however, military logic was not going to be controlling in this war. What was going on between North and South was a violent extension of a political contest, and the rules and axioms of formalized warfare were not going to mean much.

By those rules and axioms, for instance, Mr. Davis' Confederacy was in hopeless shape. Some of the best manpower any soldier ever saw was flocking to the colors—lean, sinewy men used to handling weapons and to outdoor life, men who could get along very

well on poor rations and skimpy equipment, violent men who had a positive taste for fighting—but much of this manpower could not be used because there were no arms. At the beginning of the war the U.S. government arsenals held more than 500,000 small arms, and 135,000 of these were in the South. These, of course, the Confederacy had promptly seized, but it needed a great many more, and anyway only 10,000 of the confiscated guns were modern rifles. The rest were old-fashioned smoothbores, many of them flintlocks little different from the Brown Bess of Revolutionary War days. Frantic state governors had tried to collect weapons from their backwoods owners—shotguns, country rifles, and whatnot—but very little could be done with these; their use would complicate the ammunition supply pattern beyond solution.

To make things worse, the Confederate government had made a miscalculation in respect to cotton which would have a permanently crippling effect.

The Northern blockade was not yet effective, and it would be many months before it would be. The markets of Europe were open, and all of the munitions which the South so desperately needed were for sale in them. Furthermore, they could very easily be paid for with cotton, of which the South had millions of bales. Energetic action in the first few months of

War was still an adventure to these ardent Southerners, striking a truculent pose before First Bull Run.

the war could have solved all of the Confederacy's problems of equipment.

But the Southern leaders had chanted "Cotton is King" so long that they had come to believe it. If England and France, and most particularly England, could not get the cotton which their mills needed, it was believed, they would presently intervene in this war, break the Union blockade (which did not yet really exist), and underwrite the Confederacy's independence in order to insure their own supply of cotton. Consequently, the Confederate government in its wisdom refused to export cotton, in order to make certain that England and France would feel the pressure. In effect, it made the Federal blockade effective until such time as the Federal navy could handle the job unaided; and what it had failed to figure on was that because there had been heavy cotton crops during the years just before the war began, there was a substantial carry-over on the world market in 1861. England and France could get along nicely for months to come; so nicely that even in 1862 England was actually shipping some of its cotton back to New England.

Because of all this the Confederacy was not getting the weapons it wanted at the time when it needed them most, and when it could unquestionably have got them without the slightest difficulty. So it could not arm all of the men who were clamoring to get into the army, and the ones who were armed were armed most imperfectly. In time, this problem of weapons would be adjusted. Meager as its industrial facilities were, the South would do wonders with what was available and would produce artillery, small arms, powder, and bullets; it would eventually import European goods in spite of the tightening blockade; and from first to last it would capture a great deal of war material from the Yankees. But in 1861 it was in dire straits, with untrained armies, inadequate in size and very poorly outfitted. By military logic it was little better than helpless.

But the North was not a great deal better off. To be sure, it had more weapons than the South had, and its means of adding to its supply were much broader. Washington by now was ringed with camps, very martial-looking, with some of the new three-year volunteer regiments mingling with the ninety-day militia units, and to Northern editors and politicians it seemed that it was high time for a little action. That the generals who would control these formless levies had never handled large bodies of troops before, that the soldiers themselves were mere civilians in arms with very little discipline and no understanding of the need for any, that what was believed to be an army was simply a collection of independent companies and regiments hopelessly unready to maneuver or fight as a coherent mass—of all of these things few people had any comprehension. The pressure for an immediate advance on the new Confederate capital at Richmond became stronger. Horace Greeley, the forceful but eccentric editor of the powerful New York *Tribune,* was sounding off with his "Forward to Richmond!" war-cry; and although General McDowell, commander of the troops around Washington, knew perfectly well that it would be a long time before his men were ready for a battle, there was nothing he could do about it. Ready or not, he was going to have to move.

Events in western Virginia in June and early July seemed to show that the time for a big offensive campaign was at hand.

General McClellan had taken some 20,000 men across the Ohio River and was moving east from Parkersburg along the line of the Baltimore and Ohio Railroad. With a portion of his army he surprised and routed a small contingent of Confederates at the town of Philippi, winning a very small victory which a jubilant press enlarged into a major achievement. With other troops he made an advance to Beverly, on the turnpike that led via Staunton to the upper end of the Shenandoah Valley, and at Rich Mountain, near Beverly, he routed a Confederate army of 4,500 men. Western Virginia apparently was safe for the Union now, and McClellan's dispatches spoke enthusiastically of the way his men had "annihilated two armies . . . intrenched in mountain fastnesses fortified at their leisure." To a country hungry for good news this was most welcome. Furthermore, McClellan's troops were no better trained than McDowell's. If they could campaign in rough mountain country, annihilating their foes and storming lofty passes, it seemed reasonable to suppose that McDowell's men could do as well in the more open country between Washington and Richmond. Early in July, McDowell was directed to organize and launch a thrust at the principal Confederate army, which lay at and around Manassas Junction, some twenty-five miles from Washington, behind a meandering little river known as Bull Run.

The military situation in Virginia was slightly complicated.

Federal troops under one of the newly created political generals, Ben Butler of Massachusetts, occupied Fort Monroe, at the tip of the Virginia Peninsula. Butler had essayed a mild advance up the Peninsula but had given it up when his advance guard lost a sharp little skirmish at a place known as Big Bethel. He would be inactive, his force not large enough to require more than a small Confederate contingent to watch it.

Up the Potomac River, in the vicinity of Harpers Ferry, there were 16,000 Federal troops commanded by an aged regular, Major General Robert Patterson. Patterson meant well, but he was far past his prime and would very shortly demonstrate that he was much too infirm for field command. Facing him were perhaps 9,000 Confederates under the canny Joe Johnston.

Behind Bull Run there were approximately 20,000 Confederates under Beauregard. Johnston outranked Beauregard, but while Johnston remained in the Shenandoah Valley, Beauregard was virtually independent. Since Beauregard had the biggest force, and since he lay squarely across the line of the Orange and Alexandria Railroad, which looked like the best way for a Federal army to approach Richmond, Beauregard's army was the chosen target.

McDowell, therefore, would march down overland to make his attack. He noted that a railway line ran from Manassas Junction to the Shenandoah Valley, within convenient range of Johnston's men; if Johnston could give Patterson the slip he could quite easily move his troops down to the Bull Run area and reinforce Beauregard. Patterson, accordingly, was instructed to keep pressure on Johnston so that he could not detach any troops. McDowell, whose army would total about 35,000 men, thus would have what ought to be a decisive numerical advantage when he made his fight. On the afternoon of July 16 his troops started out.

There is nothing in American military history quite like the story of Bull Run. It was the momentous fight of the amateurs, the battle where everything went wrong, the great day of awakening for the whole nation, North and South together. It marked the end of the ninety-day militia, and it also ended the rosy time in which men could dream that the war would be short, glorious, and bloodless. After Bull Run the nation got down to business.

When it set out from Washington, McDowell's army was at least brilliant to look at. The militia regiments wore a variety of uniforms. Many of the contingents were dressed in gray. Others wore gaudy clothing patterned after the French Zouaves—baggy red breeches, short blue coats, yellow or scarlet sashes about the waist, turbans or fezzes for the head. There was a New York regiment which called itself the Highlanders, and it had kilts for dress parade, although on this campaign the men seem to have worn ordinary pants. Regimental flags were of varicolored silk, all new and unstained. Baggage trains, which were somewhat tardy, were immense. A regiment at that time had as many wagons as a brigade would have a little later. From McDowell on down no one knew anything about the mechanics of handling a large army on the march, and logistics were badly fouled up. The fact that most of the soldiers would break ranks as the mood took them—to wander into a field to pick blackberries, to visit a well for drinking water, or simply to take a breather in the shade—did not help matters much. No more informal, individualistic collection of men in uniform ever tried to make a cross-country march. The weather was hot, and great clouds of dust settled over the fancy uniforms.

Beauregard, at Manassas Junction, knew that the Yankees were coming. He had a good intelligence service, with spies in Washington who kept him posted, and in any case there was nothing secret about this move; half of the country knew about it, and Beauregard had ample time to make preparations. He was an able soldier, this Beauregard, but rather on the flashy side, given to the construction of elaborate plans, and he considered that he would smite this invading host by a clever flank attack without waiting for it to assault him. His troops were in line along eight miles of Bull Run, covering the bridges and the fords, and Beauregard planned to swing his right over the stream and strike the Union left before McDowell was ready. Oddly enough, McDowell was planning a somewhat similar move himself—to demonstrate before the Confederate center, cross the bulk of his troops a few miles upstream, and come down hard on the Confederate left.

McDowell's army moved very slowly—which, considering everything, is hardly surprising—and contact with the Confederates was not made until July 18. On this day a Union division prowled forward to Blackburn's Ford, near the center of the line, to make a demonstration; it prowled too far, and was driven back with losses, and the Confederates were mightily encouraged.

Meanwhile, in the Shenandoah Valley, Joe Johnston had given Patterson the slip. He had moved for-

93

ward and had made menacing gestures, which led Patterson to believe that he was about to be attacked; then, while the old Federal took thought for his defenses, Johnston got most of his men away and took the cars for Manassas. His men would arrive at Bull Run just in time. Johnston himself, ranking Beauregard, would be in command of the united armies, although this was a point that Beauregard never quite seemed to understand.

In any case, the great battle finally took place on July 21, 1861. This was the day on which Beauregard was to make his flank attack, modeled, he proudly remarked, on Napoleon's battle plan at Austerlitz. (Most professional soldiers then had the Napoleon complex, and of all armies that of the French was the most respected.) Beauregard's move, however, was a complete fiasco. Like McDowell, he had no staff worthy of the name, and routine staff work in consequence never got done. Orders went astray, those that did reach their destination were not understood or followed, and the advance of the Confederate right amounted to nothing more than a series of convulsive twitches by a few brigades.

All in all, this was a lucky break for the Confederates. The Rebel army at Bull Run was in no better shape than the Federal army, but when the showdown came it was able to fight on the defensive—which, as numerous battles in this war would show, was infinitely easier for untrained troops. For McDowell's flank move was actually made, and although it was inordinately slow and confused, it did at last put a solid segment of the Union army across Bull Run at a place called Sudley Church, in position to march down and hit the Confederates' left flank. A doughty Confederate brigadier commanding troops at the Stone Bridge, where the main road to Washington crossed Bull Run, saw the Yankees coming and fought a stout delaying action which held them off until Johnston and Beauregard could form a new line, on the wooded plateau near the Henry House, to receive the attack. McDowell sent forward two excellent regular army batteries, and the battle was on.

For men who had never fought before, and who had been given no training of any real consequence, the Northerners and Southerners who collided here did a great deal better than anyone had a right to expect. A good many men ran away, to be sure, but most of them stayed and fought, and the struggle was a hot one. For a time it seemed that the Confederate line would be broken and that the "Forward to Richmond" motif would come to a triumphant crescendo. The two regular batteries that had been doing such good work were advanced to the crest of Henry House Hill, infantry came surging along with them, and a number of the Confederate units weakened and began to drift to the rear.

Then came one of those moments of dramatic inspiration that men remember. Brigadier General Barnard Bee sought to rally some of the wavering Confederate regiments. Not far away he saw a Virginia brigade of Johnston's troops, standing fast and delivering a sharp fire: a brigade led by that former V.M.I. professor, Brigadier General T. J. Jackson.

"There is Jackson standing like a stone wall!" cried Bee, gesturing with his sword. "Rally behind the Virginians!"

So a great name was born. From that moment on the man would be Stonewall Jackson.

Bee's troops rallied. Fresh Confederate troops, just off the train from the Valley, kept coming in on their flank. The two pestiferous Union batteries, placed too far forward to get proper support from their own infantry, were taken by a sudden Confederate counterattack—the Rebels here wore blue uniforms, and the gunners held their fire until too late, supposing the attacking wave to be Unionists coming up to help—and suddenly the Union offensive, which had come so near to success, collapsed, all the heart gone out of it, and the soldiers who had been involved in it turned and headed for the rear.

There was no rout here. The Union attack had failed and the men were withdrawing, but there was no panic. One trouble apparently lay in the fact that the tactical maneuver by which troops fighting in line would form column and go to the rear was very complicated, and most of these green Union troops did not have it down pat; a withdrawal under fire was bound to become disordered and finally uncontrollable, not because the men had lost their courage but simply because they had not had enough drill. McDowell saw that nothing more could be done here and passed the word for a retreat to his advanced base at Centreville, four or five miles nearer Washington.

It was after the beaten army had crossed Bull Run that the real trouble came, and the fault lies less with the soldiers than with the reckless Washington civilians who had supposed that the edge of a battlefield would be an ideal place for a picnic.

For hundreds of Washingtonians had come out to see the show that day. They came in carriages, wagons, buggies, and on horseback, they brought hampers of food and drink with them, and they were spread all over the slanting fields east of Bull Run, listening to the clangor of the guns, watching the smoke clouds billowing up to the July sky, and in general making a holiday out of it. Now, as Union wagon trains, ambulances, reserve artillery, and knots of disorganized stragglers began to take the road back to Washington, all of these civilians decided that it was high time for them to get out of there. They got into their conveyances and went swarming out onto the highway which the army wanted to use, creating the father and mother of all traffic jams; and just as things were at their worst a stray Confederate shell came arching over and upset a wagon on a bridge over a little stream called Cub Run, blocking the road completely.

After this there was unadulterated turmoil, growing worse every moment, with disorganized troops and panicky civilians trying to force their way through a horrible tangle of wheeled vehicles, mounted men riding around and past them, bodies of troops trying in vain to march where they had been told to march; a new surge of fear rising every now and then when someone would shout that Confederate cavalry was coming on the scene. In the weeks before the battle, imaginative newspaper and magazine writers had written extensively about the "black horse cavalry" which the Confederates had developed, and what they said had stuck in men's minds. In the dust and confusion of this disorganized retreat, frightened individuals began to shout that the black horse cavalry was upon them, and outright panic developed, with bewildered thousands dropping their weapons and starting to run, communicating their fears to others by the simple act of running. Before dark there was complete and unregimented chaos spilling all over the landscape, and hardly anyone who could move at all stopped moving until he had reached the Potomac River. For the time being most of McDowell's army had simply fallen apart. The bits and pieces of it might be useful later on, but right now they were nothing more than elements in a universal runaway.

The Confederates might have pursued, but did not.

Jefferson Davis had reached the scene, and he conferred extensively with Johnston and Beauregard, almost ordered a pursuit, finally did not; and, as a matter of fact, the Confederate army was almost as disorganized by its victory as the Union army was by its defeat. In the end it stayed in camp, sending cavalry patrols to pick up Yankee stragglers and gleaning the field of an immense quantity of military loot, including many stands of small arms which soldiers had thrown away. Stonewall Jackson, it is said, muttered that with 5,000 men he could destroy what remained of the Yankee army, but Stonewall was not yet a man to whom everybody listened. The Confederate high command was content. It had won a shattering victory, and men believed that night that Confederate independence might be a reality before much longer.

It seemed at the time that the casualty lists were fearful, although by the standards of later Civil War battles they would look moderate. The Federals had lost 2,896 men in killed, wounded, and missing, and Confederate losses came to 1,982. For an unmilitary country which had been subconsciously expecting that the war would not really be very costly, these figures were shocking. People began to see that beneath the romance which had been glimpsed in the bright uniforms, the gay flags, and the lilting tunes played by the military bands, there would be a deep and lasting grimness. Holiday time was over. No one was going to play at war any longer. The militia units could go home now; it was time to get ready for the long pull.

For Bull Run was what awakened the North to reality. (It may have had an opposite effect in the South; the victory looked so overwhelming that many Southerners considered the Yankees poor fighters, and expected a speedy final triumph.) Before there could be another campaign, a real army would have to be put together, and expert attention would have to be given to matters of organization, training, and discipline. To attend to this job, President Lincoln plucked victorious George B. McClellan out of the western Virginia mountains and put him in command of the Army of the Potomac.

An unidentified "special artist" for **Leslie's** sketched McClellan's advance on the heights near Philippi (above). Although this drawing was never reproduced, other sketches by the same man, including the one below, were published as an eyewitness record of the campaign.

In the picture below, from **Leslie's**, Union troops catch up with the Confederate rear guard retreating from Rich Mountain. The 7th Indiana crossed Carrick's Ford in a driving rain to flank the Rebel position, visible in the center background, forcing its evacuation.

Action Begins in the Hills of Western Virginia

In the spring of 1861 George Brinton McClellan, a distinguished veteran of the Mexican War, lately a railroad executive, and now, at 34, a major general commanding Ohio volunteers, found himself playing a brisk opening role in the Northern war effort. Ordered to clear western Virginia of Rebel forces, he marched his Ohio and Indiana recruits eastward into the Alleghenies, and defeated a handful of Confederates at Philippi in a night attack on June 3. On July 11 a flanking march over an obscure wagon road dislodged the Confederates from the passes at Rich Mountain and Laurel Mountain, and drove them back toward the Shenandoah Valley. The Rebel toll in casualties and prisoners came to about 700, including the commanding general, Robert S. Garnett, who was killed in a rear-guard skirmish.

McClellan had proclaimed: "No prospect of a brilliant victory shall induce me to depart from my intention of gaining success by maneuvering rather than by fighting." And in this tidy little month-and-a-half campaign the idea worked. Later on, this reluctance to commit his forces to battle would seriously impair his effectiveness, but just now he could do no wrong, and enthusiastic Northerners began calling him the man of the hour, a young Napoleon.

The final blow to Confederate hopes in western Virginia was delivered by General William S. Rosecrans in the Kanawha Valley Campaign in September of 1861. This sketch of a Federal column in a tangled mountain defile is by Corporal Nep Roesler of the 47th Ohio.

97

On to Richmond

In July the war entered its third month, and the North was more and more indignant over the sight of a Rebel army insolently encamped at Manassas Junction, just 25 miles from Washington. Horace Greeley, who daily ran "The Nation's War-Cry" (below) on the masthead of his influential *Tribune,* magnified the hue and cry for action. Aside from political pressures, Lincoln was faced with the problem of three-month enlistments which were running out. So orders were issued: ready or not, the Federal army should attack. Its commander, General Irvin McDowell, wanted more time to organize his raw levies, but Lincoln replied, "You are green, it is true; but they are green also. You are all green alike." As McDowell's ponderous advance began, a reporter shrilled, "Our brave army moves toward Manassas, and thence—we hope, without delay —to RICHMOND! The fever's up, and our bold troops ask only·to be led, and listen earnestly for the thrilling order—'forward!'"

New-York Daily Tribune.

SUNDAY, JUNE 30, 1861.

THE NATION'S WAR-CRY.

Forward to Richmond! Forward to Richmond! The Rebel Congress must not be allowed to meet there on the 20th of July! BY THAT DATE THE PLACE MUST BE HELD BY THE NATIONAL ARMY!

An unknown artist, basing his work on an 1861 drawing by Thomas Nast, painted the Army of the Potomac marching in unending ranks down Pennsylvania Avenue in Washington.
COLLECTION OF ALEXANDER MC COOK CRAIGHEAD

Two Armies Meet at Bull Run

Shortly after noon on July 18 a Federal artillery shell arched up over the northern Virginia landscape and plopped unceremoniously into the chimney of the house near Manassas Junction where Pierre Gustave Toutant Beauregard was having dinner. Only ten days earlier the Confederate general, hero of Fort Sumter, had confidently written "If I could only get the enemy to attack me . . . I would stake my reputation on the handsomest victory that could be hoped for." Now Beauregard's West Point classmate, Irvin McDowell, with 35,000 men, was preparing to give him that very chance.

McDowell's march, which began as a brilliant procession trailed by carriages of Congressmen and ladies, gradually disintegrated into a disorderly stream of stragglers as his untrained men succumbed to heat, dust, and sore feet. It took him two days to cover twenty miles, while Beauregard strengthened his lines along Bull Run. On July 20 General Joseph E. Johnston, the top-ranking Confederate, arrived at Manassas Junction in response to an order from Jefferson Davis, and his force of 9,000, added to Beauregard's, gave the Rebels about 30,000 men at Manassas. July 21, 1861, Beauregard wrote, was to be a day "bearing the fate of the new-born Confederacy."

Burnside's novice Rhode Islanders, as sketched here by A. R. Waud, led the attack against Rebel batteries at Bull Run.

Vintage guns pulled by heavy draft animals made up this Confederate "Bull Battery," sketched by an unknown artist prior to First Bull Run; artillery batteries were normally pulled into battle by horses. At Manassas Southern artillery distinguished itself in combat with superior Federal guns.

Brigadier General Irvin McDowell

Brigadier General P. G. T. Beauregard

McDowell's intricate attack took an untried Union army across Bull Run, the torpid, muddy little stream pictured above. The first Rebel defenders fell at Matthews Hill (below).

McDowell's
Army Attacks

Rousing his exhausted men from sleep at 2 A.M., Irvin McDowell launched an elaborate offensive on Sunday morning, July 21. Two feints at the strong Confederate line were initiated—one at the Stone Bridge where the Warrenton pike crossed Bull Run, the other at Blackburn's Ford, some four miles downstream. McDowell himself led two divisions to Sudley Springs Ford, roughly three miles above the Stone Bridge, to envelop the exposed Rebel left flank.

Beauregard, meanwhile, had won approval from Joe Johnston for his plan to strike with the Rebel right at Blackburn's Ford, exactly where the first Union feint would be put in motion. However, the initially successful Union flanking movement soon forced him to cancel his offensive. About 2 P.M. the Northern tide swept up the Henry House Hill toward a line which had just been formed by Thomas J. Jackson, and impending collapse of the Confederate defense forced Beauregard and Johnston to leave their observation post, which had been set up to overlook the battle they had planned and not the one which was now being fought. Near the front Johnston found a motionless Alabama regiment in perfect alignment at order arms; none of its officers was alive to direct movements, and Johnston himself gave the order that sent it into action.

Jackson's line held, Confederate reinforcements arrived, and the Union assault petered out. The green troops just were not up to a sustained attack, and by late afternoon McDowell was forced to pull his men back across Bull Run. The Confederates had won, but their efforts, Johnston complained, left them "more disorganized by victory than [the Union army was] by defeat."

Through the afternoon of July 21 heavy fighting raged across the Henry House Hill, photographed above. Toward sunset the Union forces began to withdraw, leaving the South in command of the field.

FIRST BULL RUN
July 21, 1861

N

Sudley
Springs
Ford

②

SUDLEY
CHURCH

MANASSAS-SUDLEY ROAD

MATTHEWS
HOUSE

③

MATTHEWS HILL

STONE
HOUSE

YOUNG'S B...

WARRENTON TURNPIKE

⑧

⑦

BALD HIL

CHINN
HOUSE

David Greenspan

Washington

Chantilly

Fairfax C.H.

CUB RUN

CUB RUN
BRIDGE

Centreville

⑨

BULL RUN

①

④

STONE
BRIDGE

ROBINSON
HOUSE

⑤

HENRY
HOUSE

HENRY HOUSE HILL

⑥

FIRST BULL RUN (or Manassas): A predawn Union feint is made at the Stone Bridge (1), as McDowell takes two divisions on a circuitous route to strike at Sudley Springs Ford (2). The Confederates are forced to swing their defense from Bull Run to Matthews Hill (3), where the day's first heavy fighting occurs. Colonel William T. Sherman moves his brigade across a ford (4) to strike at the new Rebel right, but the initial impetus of the Federal drive has been slowed. On the Henry House Hill the Southerners rally around T. J. Jackson's brigade (5). Union batteries near the Henry House hold their fire, and a Confederate regiment clothed in blue captures the position (6). Kirby Smith, leading the last of Johnston's troops to arrive at Manassas from the Shenandoah Valley, reaches the battlefield about 4 P.M.—in time to reinforce the Rebel line (7); and Jubal Early drives up from the southwest (8) to force a Union retirement. McDowell's withdrawal turns into a rout when an overturned wagon on Cub Run Bridge holds up the retreat (9). Afterward, the disorganized Union troops can scarcely be stopped short of Washington (in the distance at the upper right), some 25 miles away.

Confederate General Barnard Bee, painted by Conrad Chapman.

Retreat to Washington

William Russell, the correspondent of the London *Times,* watched with horror as McDowell's army was driven off the Bull Run battlefield. "What is all this about?" he asked imperiously of a breathless Federal officer. "Why it means we are pretty badly whipped, that's the truth," the man replied. Disgusted, Russell rode back to Washington's safety. Congressman Alfred Ely of New York, another spectator, ended the day in a Richmond prison.

Many of McDowell's soldiers were three-month volunteers, and the battle coincided with the end of their enlistments. Was the entire army in retreat, a straggler was asked? "That's more than I know," he said. "I know I'm going home. I've had enough of fighting to last my lifetime."

The Bull Run rout, depicted above in a period engraving, was a great disaster in the minds of those Northerners intent on a one-stroke victory over the South.

Jackson's statue, at right, guards the lonely eminence of Henry House Hill, where Bee rallied his men to the cry: "There is Jackson standing like a stone wall!"

The Union Takes Stock

As usual on Sunday afternoon, President Lincoln had gone for a carriage ride on July 21. Toward evening he returned to the White House, learned the bad news, and walked over to army headquarters to read the latest dispatch: "The day is lost. Save Washington and the remnants of this army. The routed troops will not re-form."

Through that gloomy Sunday night and on into a drenching Monday morning the bedraggled Union army stumbled back across the Potomac's Long Bridge. Loyal women rushed from houses to feed the weary men; many of the soldiers collapsed on doorsteps; the President lay sleepless on a lounge in the cabinet room. "But the hour, the day, the night pass'd, and whatever returns, an hour, a day, a night like that can never again return," wrote Walt Whitman. It was, he added, Abraham Lincoln's "crucifixion day."

On July 23 Lincoln penciled a program for action. The blockade was to be maintained; Baltimore would be held; volunteer troops would be properly disciplined—and those who refused to stay were to be replaced with long-term enlistees. Congress passed a resolution defining the war as a struggle "to defend and maintain the supremacy of the Constitution, and to preserve the dignity, equality, and rights of the several States unimpaired." Once this was accomplished, it was felt, the war would end.

Historian John Lothrop Motley, in Washington to receive his appointment as minister to Austria, thought differently. To his wife he wrote, "A grim winter is before us. Gather you rosebuds while you may. The war is to be a long one."

The young Union warrior in Winslow Homer's poignant oil sketch at left reveals the shy uncertainty of a boy suddenly thrust into a man's world.

At an evacuated Rebel post near Centreville, Union patrols found this "Quaker gun"—a "derisive log, painted black, frowning upon the Federal army." This gag photograph resulted.

Soon after Bull Run army camps ringed Washington, and dust clouds rose over newly cut fields as raw regiments, like the Pennsylvanians below, learned the mysteries of drill.

McClellan Takes Command

"Barring guard and fatigue duty and the deprivation of female society," a soldier's life suited boys on both sides. Above is a Confederate's happy impression of camp.

In S. R. Gifford's 1862 painting below, a Union sentinel guards Baltimore at Fort McHenry, where Francis Scott Key saw a "Star-Spangled Banner" 48 years earlier.

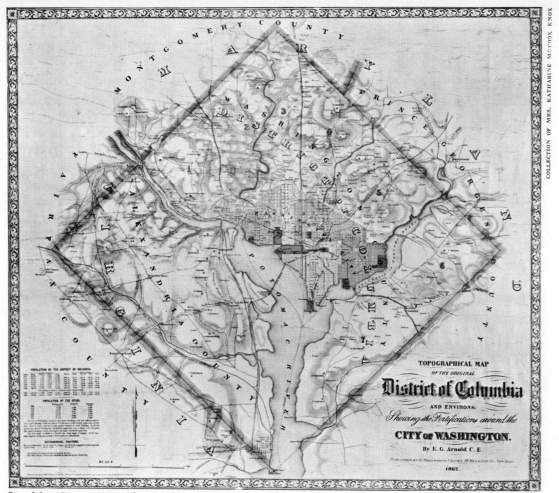

In this 1862 map each red dot represents a Union fort in Washington's circle of defenses.

The day after First Bull Run, Lincoln sent for George B. McClellan, the hero of western Virginia; and on July 27 Little Mac took over command of troops in the Washington area. To his wife the confident McClellan wrote, "I find myself in a new and strange position here: President, cabinet, Gen. Scott, and all deferring to me. By some strange operation of magic I seem to have become the power of the land."

Almost daily new Northern regiments were reaching Washington. Soon herds of cattle en route to commissary butchers were familiar sights in the city streets, and mountains of provisions rose in warehouses. Within two months McClellan's Army of the Potomac had swelled to a staggering force of 168,000, four times the size of the enemy beyond Manassas.

111

REAL
WARFARE
BEGINS

OR THE time being there was an uneasy breathing space. The victory at Bull Run left the Confederate command feeling that the next move was pretty largely up to the Yankees, and the Yankees would not be ready to make another move for months to come. The Confederate army around Manassas built extensive lines of entrenchments, and in many redoubts General Johnston mounted wooden guns, which looked like the real thing from a distance but which would never kill any Yankees if a fight developed. He also edged patrols forward to the hills on the south bank of the Potomac and erected batteries downstream so that during the summer and fall the water approach to Washington was fairly effectively blockaded. To the Shenandoah Valley, Johnston sent Stonewall Jackson with a division of infantry and a handful of undisciplined but highly effective partisan cavalry led by a minor genius named Turner Ashby.

In Washington glamorous young General McClellan applied himself to the creation of a new army. It would be a national army—the ninety-day militia regiments were sent home and demobilized—and except for a small contingent of regular troops this army would be composed of volunteer regiments enlisted for a three-year term. Yet although these were Federal troops, the states' rights tradition was still powerful, and the new volunteer regiments were recruited and officered by the governors of the separate states. In effect, each governor was a separate and largely independent war department. Washington told him how many regiments he was to provide, but the raising and organizing of these troops were entirely up to him. Only after a regiment was fully up to strength, with its proper complement of officers, was it transferred from state to Federal control. The system was cumbersome, and because the appointment of officers provided a governor with a handy form of political patronage, it made impossible the creation of any effective system of replacements for battle-worn regiments. When new men were needed, it was politically profitable for a governor to raise whole new regiments rather than to recruit men to strengthen outfits that already existed. However, in the summer of 1861 the system worked well enough, and scores of new units came down to the chain of camps around Washington.

McClellan was an exceptionally able organizer. Camps were laid out in formal military pattern, the service of supply was reorganized so that food, munitions, and equipment were properly distributed, and there was an unending program of drill. At frequent intervals there would be reviews, with McClellan himself riding the lines to inspect the newly organized brigades and divisions, and the men were taught to cheer lustily whenever the general appeared. They needed very little urging. McClellan made them feel

Federal ordnance build-up at Yorktown, Virginia, for McClellan's Peninsular Campaign against Richmond.

113

like soldiers, and they responded by giving him their complete confidence and a deep, undying affection. As summer drew on into fall the Washington scene was completely transformed. The army was beginning to be an army, and the slapdash informality of the old militia days was gone. The capital took heart.

But it was clear that there would be no major campaign in the Virginia area for some time to come. McClellan was going to do what the luckless McDowell had not been allowed to do—get everything ready before he moved—and in addition he was excessively cautious—cautious, his detractors finally would complain, to the point of outright timidity. He had put Allan Pinkerton, already famous as a detective, in charge of military intelligence, and Pinkerton was sadly out of his depth: through a series of fantastic miscalculations he consistently estimated Confederate numbers at double or treble their actual strength, and McClellan trusted him implicitly. On top of all this, the disaster at Ball's Bluff served as a powerful deterrent to hasty action.

Ball's Bluff was a wooded hill on the south bank of the Potomac, thirty-odd miles upstream from Washington. Confederate infantry was camped in the area, and in October McClellan ordered a subordinate to make a reconnaissance in force and see what the Rebels were doing. Several regiments crossed the river, inexpertly led, blundered into a more expertly handled force of Confederates, and were routed with substantial losses. The whole affair had little military significance, but Congress made an issue of it—Colonel Edward D. Baker, a prominent member of the Senate, was among the killed—and the subsequently notorious Joint Committee on the Conduct of the War was set up to look into the doings of the generals. All in all, enough fuss was raised to make it clear that any general who stumbled into defeat might be in for a rough time in Washington.

Still, for the time being McClellan's star was rising. In November Winfield Scott resigned, age and physical infirmities making it impossible for him to continue in active command, and Lincoln made McClellan general in chief of all the armies. McClellan had boundless self-confidence, this fall, and when Lincoln feared that the load of command might be too heavy, McClellan replied jauntily: "I can do it all." He would control military operations all across the board, but he would remain with the Army of the Potomac and would make it his first concern.

Yet the war really began to get into high gear a long way from Virginia. Then and now, what happened in Virginia took the eye. The two capitals were only a hundred miles apart, the armies which defended and attacked them got the biggest head-

lines, but the war actually took shape in the West. Before McClellan got the Army of the Potomac into action, battles of lasting consequence had been fought in the Mississippi Valley.

To begin with, early in September Kentucky ceased to be neutral and reluctantly but effectively cast its lot with the North. The Federals had a concentration of troops at Cairo, Illinois, where the Ohio River joins the Mississippi, and these troops obviously would invade the Southland sooner or later, either via the Mississippi or up the channels of the Tennessee and the Cumberland. General Frémont, commanding for the Federals in the western area, lacked competence and would presently be replaced, but he had done two things of prime importance: he had started construction of a fleet of gunboats, and he had put a remarkably capable, although then little known, brigadier general named U. S. Grant in command at Cairo.

Top man for the Confederacy in western Tennessee was Major General Leonidas Polk, a classmate of Jefferson Davis at West Point, who had resigned from the army years ago to take holy orders and had become a bishop in the Episcopal Church. When the war began, he returned to military service, and this fall he rightly concluded that the Yankees would soon be occupying Kentucky. He beat them to it, moving troops up to seize and fortify the bluffs at the town of Columbus, on the Mississippi, northern terminus of the Mobile and Ohio Railroad. Grant countered by seizing Paducah, which controlled the mouths of the Tennessee and Cumberland rivers, and Kentucky was squarely in the war.

Davis sent out a new man to take over-all command in the West: a highly regarded regular army officer, General Albert Sidney Johnston, who was thought to be perhaps the ablest of all the professional soldiers who had joined the Confederacy. Johnston was woefully handicapped by a shortage of manpower and equipment, but he did his best with the materials at hand. He made a strong point out of Columbus, mounting heavy guns to control the river and establishing a garrison of some 20,000 troops there. The rest of his line extended eastward through Kentucky, with 25,000 men or more in and around Bowling Green, and with a smaller contingent anchoring the eastern end of the line in the mountainous country along the Tennessee border near the upper reaches of the Cumberland River. Rising in the Kentucky mountains, the Cumberland makes a long loop into Tennessee, passing the state capital, Nashville, and then turning north to flow into the Ohio. Just below the Kentucky-Tennessee line it flows more or less parallel with the Tennessee, twelve miles to the west.

These two rivers offered a military highway of

prime importance. The Cumberland led to Nashville, and the Tennessee led all the way to northern Mississippi and Alabama. With the powerful works at Columbus blocking the way down the Mississippi, a Federal invasion was almost certain to follow the line of these two rivers, and just below the Kentucky line the Confederates had built two forts to bar the way—Fort Henry on the Tennessee and Fort Donelson on the Cumberland. These forts drew Federal attention as the year 1862 began.

Federal command in the West was divided. Frémont had been replaced by Major General Henry Wager Halleck, a professional soldier who possessed vast book knowledge of war, had certain talents as an administrator, and was known, somewhat irreverently, in the old army as Old Brains. Halleck's control, however, extended only to the Cumberland. East of that, Federal forces in Kentucky were commanded by Brigadier General Don Carlos Buell, a close friend of McClellan and a cautious type who shared McClellan's reluctance to move until every preparation had been made. Between them, Halleck and Buell commanded many more men than Johnston could bring to oppose them, but neither man had real driving force, and it seemed to be very hard for them to co-operate effectively. McClellan, who could give orders to both of them, was too far away to enforce real co-ordination, and most of his attention was centered on Virginia.

In any case, as the new year began these armies started to move. The first action came at the eastern end of the line, where Johnston's right wing, under Major General George B. Crittenden, crossed the Cumberland and began an advance toward central Kentucky. Buell's left was led by Virginia-born Brigadier General George H. Thomas, and Thomas fell on Crittenden's little force near the hamlet of Mill Springs and completely routed it. The eastern anchor of Johnston's defensive line was to all intents and purposes annihilated.

Shortly afterward, Halleck ordered Grant to move on Fort Henry. Grant took 15,000 men and a squadron of new ironclad gunboats commanded by Flag Officer Andrew Foote, and by February 6 he got boats and men up to this bastion. Fort Henry proved unexpectedly weak: built on low ground, it was partly under water, the Tennessee being almost at flood stage then, and Foote's gunboats pounded it into surrender before the infantry could get into position to make the attack. Grant promptly turned east, marching his troops cross-country to attack Fort Donelson, on the Cumberland, and sending Foote around to join him by water, and a week after Fort Henry had fallen, the Federals opened their attack.

Donelson was a tougher nut to crack. The fall of Fort Henry made Johnston see that the whole center of his line was in peril, and he evacuated Bowling Green, sending 15,000 men to defend Fort Donelson and taking the rest back to Nashville. Donelson held out for three days, but Grant got strong reinforcements and shelled the place into submission. It surrendered on February 16, and Grant suddenly found himself famous—not only had he captured 15,000 Confederates, but his note demanding capitulation had struck a chord that stirred Northern emotions powerfully: "No terms except an immediate and unconditional surrender can be accepted."

Now the Confederates were in serious trouble. Johnston could do nothing but retreat, posthaste, and this he did without delay. Nashville could not be held, and it was evacuated, with substantial military stores falling into Union hands. Even the fortress at Columbus had to be given up. Beauregard, so unhappy in Virginia, had been sent west to be second in command to Johnston, and he led the Columbus garrison south: he and Johnston, if the Federals let them, would reunite their forces at Corinth, Mississippi, just below the Tennessee line. Here the vital railway line which led east from Memphis, connecting the western part of the Confederacy with Virginia, crossed the north-south line of the Mobile and Ohio. Richmond was scraping the seacoast garrisons to provide reinforcements, and if Johnston could reassemble his forces he would perhaps have 50,000 men. Halleck and Buell, between them, could send 70,000 against him if they managed things properly.

Really effective management was not forthcoming. As a reward for victory, Halleck had been given top command in the West and Grant had been made a major general, and under Halleck's orders Grant was moving up the Tennessee with approximately 45,000 men while Buell was marching down from Nashville with 25,000 more. But Halleck had his columns moving slowly; both Grant and Foote wanted to press the beaten foe with vigor, but one delay succeeded another, and Johnston and Beauregard were given just time to regroup and reorganize their troops at Corinth. There Johnston realized that the Federals would before long bring overpowering numbers against him. Grant had put his army on the western bank of the Tennessee at Pittsburg Landing, with most of the men in camp near a country meetinghouse known as Shiloh Church, a little more than twenty miles from Corinth. Johnston concluded that his only hope was to strike Grant before Buell could arrive, and in the first days of April the Confederate army marched up from Corinth to give battle.

The result was the bewildering and bloody Battle of Shiloh, fought on April 6 and 7, 1862. Grant was caught off guard, and in the first day's fight his army was almost pushed into the Tennessee River. It rallied just in time, Johnston was killed in action, and at dark Buell's troops began to arrive and one of Grant's divisions which had been delayed in reaching the field got to the scene. On the second day the Federals reversed the tide, and by midafternoon Beauregard had to admit defeat. He drew his badly battered army back toward Corinth, and the Federals, equally battered, made no more than a gesture at pursuit. The greatest battle ever fought on the American continent, up to that date, was over. The Federals had lost 13,000 men, the Confederates, 10,000. The troops had fought with impressive valor, but they had been poorly handled, especially on the Union side.

But although the terrible casualty list and the fact that Grant had let himself be taken unawares stirred violent criticism in the North, the battle nevertheless had been of decisive importance. At Shiloh the Confederacy made its supreme bid to regain western Tennessee. It failed, and after that the Confederate path in the West went downhill all the way. Nor was Shiloh the only disaster, that spring. At Pea Ridge, Arkansas, a Union army under Brigadier General Samuel Curtis defeated a Confederate army led by Major General Earl Van Dorn. Other Union forces came down the Mississippi itself, taking New Madrid, Missouri, and capturing a powerful fort at Island Number Ten. Union gunboats came down and destroyed a Confederate river fleet at Memphis, and two months after Shiloh, Memphis itself had to be abandoned. Halleck assembled an army of substantially more than 100,000 men near Pittsburg Landing and moved slowly down to take Corinth—moved with excessive caution, for Beauregard had not half of Halleck's numbers and dared not stay to give battle, but Halleck was the most deliberate of generals. In the end Beauregard left Corinth and retreated toward central Mississippi, the Federals held all of western Tennessee and were in a fair way to reclaim the entire Mississippi Valley, and in the West the Southern cause was well on the way to defeat.

But in Virginia everything was very different.

Like Halleck, McClellan moved with deliberation. He also suffered from a handicap which never afflicted Halleck: he had aroused the active distrust and hostility of the radical Republican leaders in Washington, including the Secretary of War, Edwin M. Stanton. These men had come to distrust McClellan's will to fight. Some of them even believed he was pro-Confederate at heart, and they suggested openly that he was potentially a traitor, willing to let the enemy win the war. What McClellan did in the spring of 1862 cannot be appraised fairly unless this bitter hostility and suspicion are taken into account. If McClellan moved later than he said he would move (which was usually the case), he was certain to be accused of sabotaging the war effort; if a battle went against him, there were sure to be grandstand critics in Washington who would proclaim that he might easily have won if he had really wanted to win.

The first result of all of this was that in the middle of March McClellan lost his job as general in chief of all the armies and was limited to command of the Army of the Potomac. The second result was that when he finally made his move he made it under great difficulties, some of them self-inflicted.

McClellan had given up the idea of moving on Richmond via Manassas. Instead he wanted to go down to Fort Monroe by steamboat and then advance up the Virginia Peninsula, with rivers to protect his flanks and a secure line of communications. President Lincoln and Secretary Stanton agreed to this very reluctantly. A Union army moving overland toward Richmond would always stand between Washington and the main Confederate army; but it seemed to these men that under McClellan's plan the capital would be dangerously open to capture by a sudden Confederate thrust. As a soldier, McClellan considered this highly unlikely; as politicians, Lincoln and Stanton were bound to realize that if Washington should be captured the Union cause was irretrievably lost, and they refused to take chances. They let McClellan make his move, therefore, on condition that he leave enough troops in Washington (which by now was strongly fortified) to make it safe beyond question. McClellan agreed to this, but apparently he did not take the business very seriously. After he and the army had taken off for the Peninsula, the President and the Secretary of War began counting heads and discovered that the numbers McClellan had promised to leave behind just were not there. Accordingly, they removed an entire army corps from his command—it was commanded by the General McDowell who had had such bad luck at Bull Run—and ordered it to cover the area between Washington and Fredericksburg. Simultaneously, they created a separate command in the Shenandoah Valley, entrusting it to a political major general from Massachusetts, the distinguished, if unmilitary, Nathaniel P. Banks. As a final step they called General Frémont back from retirement and put him in command in western Virginia, with instructions to begin moving east.

So McClellan started up the Peninsula with only 90,000 men instead of the 130,000 he had expected to have. His troubles immediately began to multiply.

Joe Johnston had long since evacuated Manassas,

but he had not yet got all of his men down to the Peninsula. At Yorktown he had a chain of earthworks and some 15,000 soldiers under Major General John Bankhead Magruder. In the old army Magruder had been famous as an amateur actor, and he used all of his talents now to bemuse McClellan. As the Yankees approached the Yorktown lines Magruder marched his troops up hill and down dale, safely out of range but plainly visible, and he did it so well that the Unionists concluded that he had a very substantial army. McClellan took alarm, erected works facing the Yorktown lines, and prepared to lay siege. He could certainly have overwhelmed Magruder with one push, and even after Johnston got the rest of his army to the scene the Confederate works could probably have been stormed; but McClellan played it safe, and as a result he lost an entire month. Johnston evacuated Yorktown on May 4—McClellan had his big guns in position, and was going to open a crushing bombardment next day—and the long move up the Peninsula began. The Confederates fought a brisk delaying action at Williamsburg the next day, but they did not try to make a real stand until they had reached the very outskirts of Richmond.

Meanwhile, other things had been happening which would have a marked effect on McClellan's campaign. The canny Confederates quickly discovered the extreme sensitivity of Lincoln and Stanton about the safety of Washington and made cruel use of it. In the Shenandoah Valley, Stonewall Jackson with 8,000 men faced Banks, who had nearly twice that number; and Frémont was beginning to edge in through the western mountains with as many more. Jackson was given reinforcements, nearly doubling his numbers; then he set out on one of the war's most dazzling campaigns. A quick march west of Staunton knocked back Frémont's advance; then Jackson swept down the Valley, completely deceiving Banks as to his whereabouts, breaking his supply line and forcing him to retreat, and then striking him viciously while he was retreating and turning his withdrawal into a rout. Banks had to go clear north of the Potomac River, and Jackson's quick movements convinced Secretary Stanton that a major invasion of the North was beginning. McDowell had been under orders to march down and join McClellan, who had drawn his lines astride of the Chickahominy River no more than half a dozen miles from Richmond: these orders were canceled, and McDowell had to send troops posthaste to the Shenandoah to break up Jackson's game. Jackson coolly waited until the Federal panic was at its height, then withdrew up the Valley, bloodied the noses of two pursuing Federal columns—and then slipped swiftly down to Richmond to take a hand in the coming fight with McClellan's Army of the Potomac.

All in all, the Federal government had been utterly bamboozled. By skillful use of his 17,000 men Jackson had immobilized more than 50,000 Yankee troops. When the Confederacy fought to defend its capital, it would not have to face nearly as many men as might easily have been sent against it.

Joe Johnston would not be in command in this fight. At the end of May his troops had fought a hard two-day battle with McClellan's left wing at Fair Oaks—an indecisive struggle that left both sides about where they had been before—and Johnston had been seriously wounded. To replace him, Davis called on Robert E. Lee, who would command the most famous of all Confederate levies, the Army of Northern Virginia, until the end of the war.

Lee's part in the war thus far had been onerous and not particularly happy. He had tried to direct Confederate operations in western Virginia, but the situation there had been hopeless and the area had been lost. He had helped fortify the Southern seacoast, and then he had served Davis as military adviser, in a post which carried heavy responsibility but no genuine authority. (If Jackson had executed the Valley Campaign, the underlying idea was largely Lee's.) Now he was taking an active field command, and within a few weeks he would prove that he was the ideal man for the job.

Because of the success of the Valley Campaign, McClellan's army lay on both sides of the Chickahominy River with substantially less strength than McClellan had expected to have when he took that position. It contained, as June drew to a close, more than 100,000 soldiers, of whom 25,000 were north of the Chickahominy. Lee, his army reinforced to a strength of nearly 85,000, left a few divisions to hold the lines immediately in front of Richmond, marched some 65,000 men to the north bank of the Chickahominy, and struck savagely at the exposed Federal flank.

There followed the famous Seven Days' battles—Mechanicsville, Gaines' Mill, Savage's Station, Frayser's Farm, Malvern Hill, and a host of lesser fights and skirmishes in between—and at the end of all of this McClellan's army had been roundly beaten and compelled to retreat to Harrison's Landing on the James River, badly shattered and greatly in need of a refit. McClellan's stock at the War Department was lower than ever, his army was effectively out of action as an offensive unit for some time to come, and the way was open for Lee to take the offensive and give some substance to President Lincoln's fears for the safety of Washington. This General Lee would very quickly do; and as he did it the Southern cause would reach its brief, tragic high-water mark for the war.

Opening Guns in the West

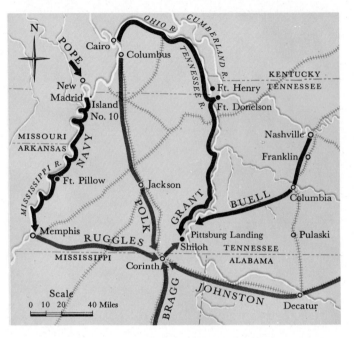

Grant would give his prewar army friend Simon Buckner (above) no terms but the unconditional surrender of Fort Donelson. In Alexander Simplot's sketch below, Flag Officer Foote's fleet of gunboats and armored transports shells Fort Henry into submission at almost point-blank range.

The map above indicates, in black, the initial Federal thrusts in 1862, aimed at seizing the Mississippi Valley, and the South's countermoves. Included are the capture of Forts Henry and Donelson, the Battle of Shiloh, and the reduction of Southern strong points which opened the Mississippi as far south as Memphis, Tennessee.

In the West, as the year 1862 began, military strategy centered on the Mississippi and its tributaries. Control of the Cumberland and Tennessee rivers would give the North much of Kentucky and western Tennessee; and to this end Brigadier General U. S. Grant and Flag Officer Andrew Foote moved against Forts Henry and Donelson, which guarded these rivers. Fort Henry fell easily to Foote's gunboats before Grant even arrived; but Donelson promised to be far more difficult.

Albert Sidney Johnston, the Southern commander in the West, had heavily reinforced the garrison. The Union plan called for Foote to steam up the Cumberland while Grant closed in; but in the attack Foote was badly wounded, and his gunboats were repulsed. Then, in quick succession, Grant was reinforced, and the Confederates bungled a breakout attempt. No choice but surrender remained. On February 16 an unhappy Simon Bolivar Buckner turned over the fort and 15,000 troops to Grant. It was the North's first major victory.

Hemmed in by Grant, the Confederates tried to fight their way out of Fort Donelson on February 15. They were close to success when the division of C. F. Smith (above, mounted at right) stormed the other end of their line; turning to meet this assault, they lost their last chance to escape. The photograph below was taken from the cellar beneath the fort.

The Battle of Pea Ridge

With the border state Kentucky safely in the Northern column after the capture of Forts Henry and Donelson, the war suddenly swirled off to the southwest. In Missouri Brigadier General Samuel Curtis, with 11,000 troops, chased the Rebels from the state into northwestern Arkansas. To meet this threat, the dashing Mississipian Earl Van Dorn assembled his scattered forces and moved north. Curtis, a ramrod-stiff old ex-regular, was outnumbered and prudently dug in, in front of a rocky eminence known as Pea Ridge.

On March 7 Van Dorn executed a "double envelopment"—half his army stole behind Pea Ridge, marched around three-fourths of Curtis' force, and struck his left rear near Elkhorn Tavern; the other half attacked the right rear. Curtis countered by ordering his force about-face. The fighting was severest near the tavern, where a stubborn defense by a tough regular, Colonel Eugene Carr, absorbed repeated Confederate attacks.

Van Dorn's fancy tactics had put the enemy between him and his supply train, and now his men were hungry and almost out of ammunition. The next day Curtis sent Franz Sigel's unblooded troops against them. Sigel had one of his rare good days of the war, and the shattered Rebels were sent flying in all directions. For three more years guerrilla warfare would ravage the state, but the Union grip on Missouri was now secure.

At left, Brigadier General Samuel R. Curtis. At right is Confederate artillerist Hunt Wilson's painting of his battery in the Rebel line at Elkhorn Tavern, under attack in the second day's action at Pea Ridge.

Johnston Prepares
a Surprise Attack

This photograph of Confederate Albert Sidney Johnston was taken before the war. Hit in the leg during the Peach Orchard assault, he was carried to the blossom-filled ravine below, where he bled to death before his staff physician, treating Federal wounded, reached him.

In March, 1862, Major General Henry W. Halleck was put in command of all Federal forces in the Mississippi Valley, and he initiated a slow advance which sent his two armies south along the Tennessee River. By early April Grant had some 37,000 men near Shiloh Church and Pittsburg Landing, close to the Tennessee-Mississippi border, and off to the east Don Carlos Buell's 25,000 were on their way from Nashville to join him. Meanwhile, Albert Sidney Johnston was desperately assembling all the Confederate troops he could find at Corinth, Mississippi. He had more men than Grant, but he would have to strike before Buell arrived.

The Union position was a reasonably strong one, but Grant and his division commanders felt it would be bad for morale to have the men entrench. General C. F. Smith told Grant, "By God, I want nothing better than to have the Rebels . . . attack us! We can whip them to hell. Our men suppose we have come here to fight, and if we begin to spade, it will make them think we fear the enemy." In the Federal camps a peach orchard was in glorious bloom, and war and killing seemed remote.

But just 25 miles to the south Johnston was pushing his raw levies onto the roads. Like most of Grant's men, these Confederates were as green as grass. They ambled along, whooping and shouting, firing their guns just to see if they would work, driving their officers into a frenzy. P. G. T. Beauregard, second in command, urged that the attack be called off, but Johnston was adamant: "I would fight them if they were a million." He ordered an assault for dawn on Sunday, April 6.

The Federal camp was blissfully unaware of Johnston's approach. When a nervous colonel of the 53rd Ohio warned William T. Sherman of activity on his front, Sherman snapped, "Take your damn regiment back to Ohio. There is no enemy nearer than Corinth."

BOTH: BERN KEATING, BLACK STAR

A Rebel at Shiloh recalled "How the cannon bellowed, and their shells plunged and bounded, and flew with screeching hisses over us!" Nearly a hundred Aprils later those silent guns, wreathed in dogwood, dot the battlefield park. The picture below recalls Johnston's boast before the battle: "Tonight we will water our horses in the Tennessee River."

Shiloh:
The First Day

At 6 A.M., as the massed Confederates, three battle lines deep, came booming out of the woods, a Union officer dashed off to report, "The Rebels are out there thicker than fleas on a dog's back," and the astounded Yankees dropped their Sunday breakfasts and grabbed their muskets. Johnston hoped to drive through the Union left to cut Grant off from support arriving via Pittsburg Landing, but the fighting soon became one massive push against the entire Union line, and thousands of frightened boys trickled to the rear of both armies in the chaos of noise and smoke.

After the first panic caused by the attack on the Union right, the divisions of Sherman and John McClernand steadied, then gave way slowly. Over in the Peach Orchard bullets clipped the blossoms, causing a rain of pink petals (spring's offering to the heroic dead, Captain Daniel McCook called it). In the center Benjamin Prentiss' Federals laid down such a killing fire from a sunken road that the Rebels dubbed it the Hornet's Nest. Here Johnston was mortally wounded, and Grant, seeing his right and left wings falling back, ordered Prentiss to hold "at all hazards."

This chromolithograph, issued by the McCormick Harvester people in 1885, prominently features their reaper (left), reassuringly impervious to shot and shell. Loosely based on a now-lost Shiloh panorama painting, it shows the Hornet's Nest at center, Grant and his staff at right.

SHILOH·APRIL 6ᵗʰ 1862·

S COME VICTORIOUSLY OUT OF EVERY CONTEST, AND WITHOUT A SCRATCH.

COMPLIMENTS OF McCORMICK HARVESTING MACHINE COMPANY

COPIED BY SPECIAL PERMISSION
From The
·PANORAMA PAINTING·
ON EXHIBITION IN CHICAGO

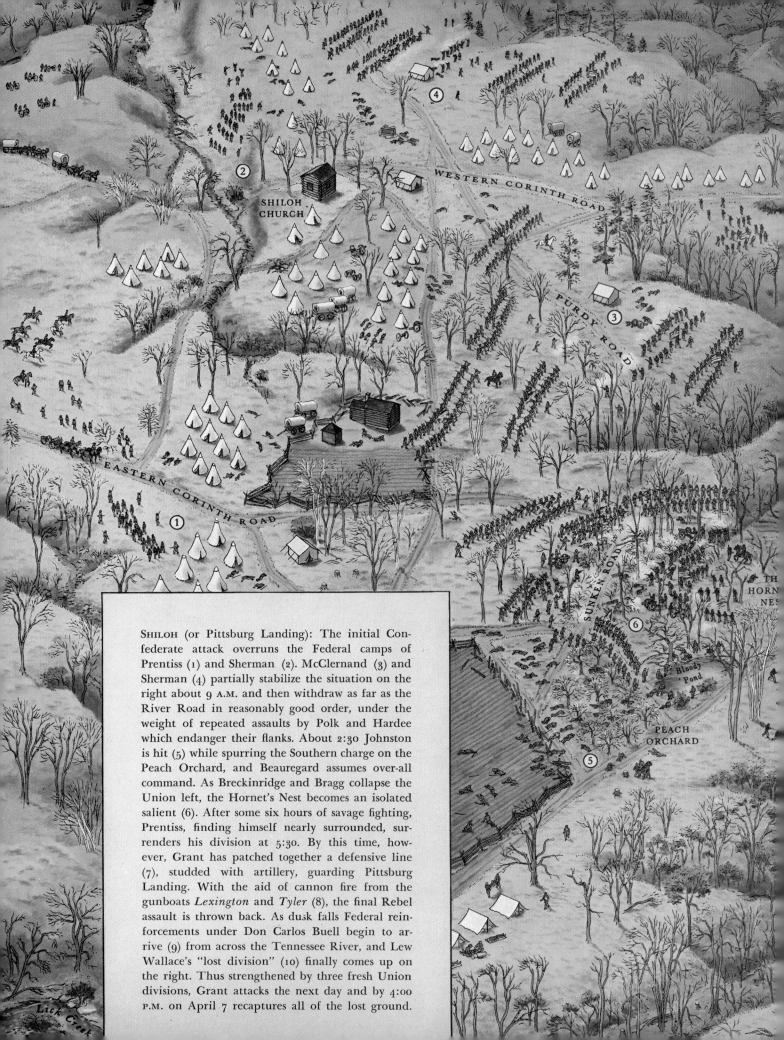

WESTERN CORINTH ROAD

SHILOH CHURCH

PURDY ROAD

EASTERN CORINTH ROAD

SUNKEN ROAD

TH
HORN
NES

Bloody
Pond

PEACH
ORCHARD

Lick Creek

SHILOH (or Pittsburg Landing): The initial Confederate attack overruns the Federal camps of Prentiss (1) and Sherman (2). McClernand (3) and Sherman (4) partially stabilize the situation on the right about 9 A.M. and then withdraw as far as the River Road in reasonably good order, under the weight of repeated assaults by Polk and Hardee which endanger their flanks. About 2:30 Johnston is hit (5) while spurring the Southern charge on the Peach Orchard, and Beauregard assumes over-all command. As Breckinridge and Bragg collapse the Union left, the Hornet's Nest becomes an isolated salient (6). After some six hours of savage fighting, Prentiss, finding himself nearly surrounded, surrenders his division at 5:30. By this time, however, Grant has patched together a defensive line (7), studded with artillery, guarding Pittsburg Landing. With the aid of cannon fire from the gunboats *Lexington* and *Tyler* (8), the final Rebel assault is thrown back. As dusk falls Federal reinforcements under Don Carlos Buell begin to arrive (9) from across the Tennessee River, and Lew Wallace's "lost division" (10) finally comes up on the right. Thus strengthened by three fresh Union divisions, Grant attacks the next day and by 4:00 P.M. on April 7 recaptures all of the lost ground.

OWL CREEK

CREEK

⑩

River Road

N

SHILOH

First Day: April 6, 1862

⑦

Pittsburg
Landing

⑨

⑧

LEXINGTON

TENNESSEE RIVER

David Greenspan

Crisis in the Hornet's Nest

Henri Lovie's vivid sketch shows the tangle of troops, guns, and wagons at Pittsburg Landing as Grant's last-ditch line, braced by some 50 cannon commanded by J. D. Webster, repulses the final assault at dusk on April 6.

Grant galloped all over the shot-torn field, "paying no more attention to the missiles than if they had been paper wads," working hard to build a defensive line strong enough to hold until Lew Wallace's division and Buell's advance guard reached him. Everything depended on Prentiss' men in the Hornet's Nest.

Prentiss and General W. H. L. Wallace were taking a terrific pounding; an Illinois soldier wrote, "From right to left, everywhere, it was one never-ending, terrible roar, with no prospect of stopping." They repulsed some twelve assaults, but were flanked on both sides. Instead of continuing to advance on a wide front, almost the entire Confederate army concentrated its firepower on the Hornet's Nest, and Rebel artillerist Dan Ruggles wheeled 62 guns into line to rake the position at close range. At 5:30, having given Grant the time he needed, Prentiss surrendered the remnant of his command —2,200 men, half his original force.

Grant's final line, supported by heavy siege guns, guarded Pittsburg Landing, with the extreme right under Sherman holding the road by which Wallace was expected. The fought-out Confederates made a last feeble charge, but with two wooden gunboats pitching 20-pound shells and the siege guns roaring, they were beaten back. Buell's men began to arrive, ferried by steamboat from the east bank of the Tennessee. The Illinois private quoted above remembered, "Never to me was the sight of reinforcing legions so . . . welcome as on that Sunday evening when the rays of the descending sun were flashed back from the bayonets of Buell's advance column as it deployed on the bluffs of Pittsburg Landing." When Wallace arrived at last, having floundered around on back roads all day, Grant began to lay plans to recoup his losses.

Wounded of both armies drank side by side at this shallow pool, called Bloody Pond, near the Hornet's Nest.

129

Shiloh: The Second Day

Henri Lovie sketched Buell's troops crossing the Tennessee River on steamers to support Grant at Pittsburg Landing. The Union gunboats Tyler *and* Lexington *can be seen in the middle distance.*

The peculiar horror of Shiloh—the biggest battle in the nation's history up to that time—lay in the fact that it was simply a fight between two untrained mobs of armed boys. It is estimated that fully 80 per cent of the 77,000 men engaged had never before heard a gun fired in anger; a sizable number did not even know how to work their rifles. One Union private, a veteran of Fort Donelson, had walked up and down behind the firing line, showing the recruits how to load and fire, telling them, "It's just like shooting squirrels, only these squirrels have guns, that's all." In one ghastly day these young men had had to learn their trade, and now Grant was preparing to resume the struggle.

That night he received more than 25,000 fresh troops, and on the morning of April 7 threw his whole army forward. The Confederates fell back under the pressure; and Johnston's successor, Beauregard, who had telegraphed Richmond of "a complete victory, driving the enemy from every position," barely managed to rally his men at the Peach Orchard and around Shiloh Church. They held there, but he knew it was only a matter of time before the positions would be breached.

Despairing of receiving expected reinforcements, Beauregard conducted an orderly retreat, and when Sherman made a stab at pursuit, Bedford Forrest's cavalry threw him back.

The casualty lists staggered North and South. Some 23,000 men had been shot or captured. Whole units had disintegrated; Pat Cleburne's Rebel brigade, for instance, had suffered over a thousand casualties. In proportion to the number engaged, that Sunday's fighting was the costliest day of the war. Grant was severely criticized for the defenseless condition of his camps; but, for all that, he had won a decisive victory. Any hope the South had of destroying him was gone now, and along with it western Tennessee.

The North still had the initiative, but it was largely dissipated when "Old Brains" Halleck, who believed in making war by the book, hustled down to Shiloh to take charge. By April 30 he had assembled over 100,000 men and began to move on Beauregard at Corinth, but his glacierlike offensive took four weeks to cover 20 miles. The outnumbered Beauregard evacuated Corinth, but Halleck proceeded to scatter his huge army all over the landscape, assigning men to garrison duty and the rebuilding of railroads.

The Union division under Lew Wallace (below), which might have turned the tide of Sunday's fighting, did not arrive until the battle was over.

During the action thousands of stragglers huddled in the thickets (above) along the river. Below is one of the country lanes by which Wallace finally reached the battlefield.

Confederate Strongholds
Begin to Crumble

In the scene above, from a Civil War panorama by Thomas C. Gordon, raiders led by James Andrews steal a Rebel train, intending to cut a Georgia railroad line. After the "Great Locomotive Chase" of April, 1862, Andrews and seven of his men were hanged as spies.

While Grant campaigned in Tennessee, other Federal land and naval forces were loosening the Confederate grip on the Mississippi River. A month after Grant's advance forced the Rebels to evacuate their "Gibraltar of the West" at Columbus, Kentucky, the strong points at New Madrid and Island No. 10, 60 miles downriver, were in Union hands, seized in dramatic fashion by General John Pope, working in cooperation with gunboats.

A little Confederate fleet briefly halted this advance by ramming and sinking two Federal ironclads, but revenge was quick and sweet. On June 6 a squadron challenged these Rebel craft, and as thousands watched from the Memphis bluffs the Federals made short work of them. Two fast new rams designed by Charles Ellet knocked out three Rebel gunboats, the heavy Dahlgren cannon of the Union fleet scored repeatedly, and seven of the eight Confederate ships were sunk, burned, or captured. Memphis then surrendered.

Union mortar scows fruitlessly tried to shell Island No. 10 into submission, as painted above by William Jorgerson; then the batteries were run by two ironclads. Under their guns Pope's army crossed the Mississippi on transports, and succeeded in capturing the Rebel post.

Commanded by Henry Walke, Federal gunboat Caron-delet *(above) ran the Island No. 10 guns on the night of April 4; three nights later the* Pittsburgh *followed. One of eight ironclads built in 100 days by James B. Eads, the* Carondelet *saw action at Forts Henry and Donelson.*

Below is Alexander Simplot's painting of the brief, savage naval battle at Memphis. In the foreground the Union ram Monarch *strikes and cripples the* General Beauregard. *Of the eight lightly armed and armored Confederate craft, only one, the* Van Dorn, *escaped.*

The Fall of New Orleans

Rear Admiral David G. Farragut

In April, 1862, the deep-water navy added its weight to the Union drive to open the Mississippi. David G. Farragut, with an imposing squadron of warships and 19 mortar schooners, headed for New Orleans, the South's greatest seaport. Ninety miles downstream were Forts Jackson and St. Philip, the city's chief defense; and after the mortars had poured almost 17,000 rounds into them with little effect, Farragut determined to run their batteries. "Conquer or be conquered," he told his officers.

At 2 A.M. on April 24 he steamed upriver. The ensuing cannonade seemed like "all the earthquakes in the world, and all the thunder and lightnings . . . going off at once." The forts were successfully passed, although Farragut's flagship was grounded briefly and set ablaze by a fire raft. A gallant sortie by the Rebel side-wheeler ram *Governor Moore* sank the *Varuna*, but the *Moore* and her consorts were soon wrecked or scattered. New Orleans surrendered, then Baton Rouge and Natchez. By midsummer the South's hold on the Mississippi was limited to the frowning citadels of Vicksburg and Port Hudson.

William Waud sketched Farragut's mortar schooners (below), their masts camouflaged with branches, moving upriver toward Forts St. Philip and Jackson.

The Confederate forts guarding New Orleans are shown here, in a photograph taken from the Mississippi, as they must have looked to Farragut's squadron anchored downstream. The sun is setting behind Fort St. Philip; Fort Jackson is hidden by the headland at left.

135

Forts in the Delta Jungle

Forts Jackson and St. Philip are now nearly hidden by rank subtropical jungle. Fort Jackson (facing page and above, top left) is viewed from its flooded, hyacinth-choked parade ground. The remaining pictures show Fort St. Philip, half buried in silt.

OVERLEAF: *In J. Joffray's colorful canvas, Farragut runs the fiery gantlet between Forts Jackson (left) and St. Philip. The leading Federal ships fire on a small Rebel fleet (background).*

FARRAGUT APRIL
J. JOFFRAY, P

Federal troops, jaunty and eager for action, stream onto the Peninsula from their transports in Hampton Roads.

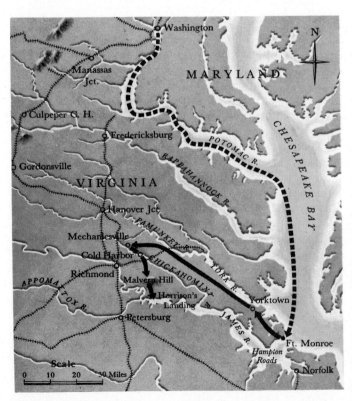

Winslow Homer's study of a Yankee sharpshooter stationed in a tree near Yorktown (above) was painted in 1862. The map at right traces McClellan's water-borne advance down Chesapeake Bay, his campaign on the Peninsula, and his subsequent withdrawal to Harrison's Landing on the James.

140

The Peninsular Campaign Begins

Young George McClellan was increasingly disenchanted with his exalted position as general in chief of the Union armies as the winter of 1861–62 wore on. He was under pressure from all sides to take the offensive; to break the hold of Joe Johnston's Confederate army on the lower reaches of the Potomac River; and, above all, to capture Richmond.

Unfortunately, McClellan never quite got it through his head that the politicians would have as much to say about how a civil war was conducted as professional soldiers would. He ignored Lincoln's efforts to make him see this unhappy fact; instead, he wrote his wife that "the necessity for delay has not been my fault. I have a set of men to deal with unscrupulous and false."

The general planned to outflank Johnston by an amphibious landing at Urbana on the Rappahannock River, directly east of Richmond, but when the wily Johnston pulled back, McClellan decided to switch his objective southward to the James River peninsula.

By April 2 he had 58,000 men—over half his army—at Fort Monroe, preparing to move up the Peninsula against Richmond, some 70 miles away. At Lincoln's insistence General McDowell's 38,000 troops remained near Washington, although McClellan counted on this force coming to his support as he closed on Richmond. What he did not know was that Northern politicians and Stonewall Jackson would prevent this from happening.

Major General George B. McClellan

141

The Siege of Yorktown

Robert E. Lee, military adviser to President Davis, had more than George McClellan's invasion to worry about that April. The Confederate Congress passed the first conscription law in American history, which meant that the entire Confederate army had to be reorganized. (Secretary of War Stanton, showing far less foresight, had closed Union recruiting stations.)

The South needed time, and "Prince John" Magruder supplied it by some fancy maneuvering of his sparse forces, which convinced McClellan that Magruder's line was "one of the most extensive known to modern times." As the astounded Joe Johnston commented to Lee, "no one but McClellan could have hesitated to attack." When the Young Napoleon set up his huge mortars, capable of blasting the Yorktown defenses with 400 tons of shells a day, Johnston realized that his soldiers could not resist an onslaught of such magnitude, and on May 4 he pulled back.

As the Federals set out in pursuit both armies found the Peninsula a highly undesirable place to make war. Steady rains turned each narrow road into a morass, and men fought and died in sodden fields and gloomy, dripping thickets.

The generals labored to hasten both retreat and pursuit: Johnston helped to haul free a gun which was hub-deep in a mud hole; Federal Phil Kearny forced his column through a stalled wagon train, thundering at the teamsters to "set the torch to your goddamned cowardly wagons!" There was a vicious rearguard fight near Williamsburg on May 5, as James Longstreet and D. H. Hill held off McClellan's advance; then the two armies resumed their plodding progress toward Richmond.

Brigadier General Philip Kearny

Portions of the Confederate lines at Yorktown, superimposed on Cornwallis' old Revolutionary War defenses, still survive today.

James Gibson's photograph above shows one of the Federal mortar batteries near Yorktown. Mc-Clellan had 44 of these huge mortars in place, but the Rebels withdrew before they fired a shot.

In Alfred R. Waud's wash drawing below, Philip Kearny leads his division against the Confederate rear guard at Williamsburg. Kearny told his corps commander, "I can make men follow me to hell!"

In many areas of the Peninsula the tangled, vine-choked undergrowth which hampered the movements of the armies of 1862 remains virtually unchanged today.

Slow Progress Toward Richmond

For two weeks after the scrap at Williamsburg, Johnston continued to fall back toward lines being prepared near Richmond. McClellan followed slowly on the wretched roads, complaining that "the weather is infamous." By May 15 his army was on the Pamunkey River, where he received supplies by water.

In spite of his progress George McClellan was a very worried general. He accepted as gospel the intelligence reports of private detective Allan Pinkerton—fantastic estimates giving Johnston close to 120,000 troops, when he actually had about half of that number. To McClellan it seemed increasingly vital that he have the support of McDowell's divisions.

McClellan canters ahead of his staff in the foreground of James Hope's panoramic painting (above) of the Federal camp at Cumberland Landing on the Pamunkey River. Below is James Gibson's contemporary photograph of the same camp.

The Battle of Fair Oaks

Above, the charge of the New York Excelsior Brigade at Fair Oaks, as sketched by Waud. Below, T. S. C. Lowe's Federal observation balloon Intrepid *being inflated; and ascending to reconnoiter the battlefield.*

To get at Richmond, McClellan had to cross what he called "the confounded Chickahominy" River, and by May 28 the main body of his army was on the north side of the stream, while Brigadier General Erasmus Keyes and the IV Corps had crossed and were isolated on the opposite shore at Fair Oaks. The river was at flood stage, making it extremely difficult for McClellan to reinforce Keyes, and Johnston saw his chance to strike the exposed IV Corps. His plan called for the 23 brigades of Longstreet, D. H. Hill, and Benjamin Huger to advance over three roads converging on Fair Oaks and to knock Keyes and any reinforcements into the Chickahominy.

In this campaign, however, the Confederates were plagued with bad staff work. Longstreet's men snarled traffic, and the battle began at 1 P.M. on May 31 instead of dawn. At that Longstreet was late, and Huger's troops never got into action at all. D. H. Hill did most of the fighting.

Hill pushed Keyes back, and Gustavus Smith aimed a blow at the Federals' exposed flank. General Edwin Sumner, an old regular called "The Bull of the Woods" because of his thundering voice, was ordered to support Keyes, but the engineers told him that the Chickahominy bridges were unsafe. Sumner snapped: "Impossible? Sir, I tell you I *can* cross! I am ordered!" Cross he did, and one of his divisions was in time to blunt Smith's assault. The chaotic battle was a draw, as was the brief action the next day. The fight for Richmond would go on, it seemed, longer than either side expected.

Major General Gustavus W. Smith

Below, another Waud drawing shows the grisly aftermath of war: burying dead soldiers and burning dead horses after the Battle of Fair Oaks.

Arlington, Lee's neoclassic home across from Washington, was occupied in 1861 by Federal troops, who posed before its columns (above). The mansion was sold in 1863 for nonpayment of taxes.

The anonymous painting below of Davis and his generals was probably done at the time of Bull Run, before Lee's emergence. Left to right: Beauregard, Jackson, Davis, Stuart, and Johnston.

Robert E. Lee Takes Command

The Battle of Fair Oaks was inconclusive, but one of the 11,000 casualties affected profoundly the story of the Confederate States of America. Joseph E. Johnston took a bullet in the shoulder and a shell fragment in the chest, knocking him out of the war for months, and in his place Davis appointed Robert E. Lee.

Johnston himself pinpointed a fact of supreme importance about this man Lee: "The shot that struck me down is the very best that has been fired for the Southern cause yet. For I possess in no degree the confidence of our government, and now they have in my place one who does possess it." Not only did Lee have the trust and loyalty of President Davis, he had the capacity to mold into a smoothly functioning fighting unit what was probably the most eccentric, touchy, individualistic—and talented—group of general officers ever assembled in an American army. They were men such as acid-tongued D. H. Hill; impetuous A. P. Hill; James Longstreet, ponderous but wholly capable; the incredibly flamboyant Jeb Stuart; "Old Bald Head" Dick Ewell, birdlike and sickly; and the strangest of them all, Stonewall Jackson, a man of brimstone and fire straight out of the Old Testament.

The Peninsular Campaign was the crucible from which Lee's newly christened Army of Northern Virginia would be cast.

At right, Lee wearing his military sash and dress sword, photographed in 1864 by J. Vannerson of Richmond.

Lee Turns
to Jackson

Three Union commanders who faced Jackson in the Shenandoah Valley: Major Generals John C. Frémont (above, left) and Nathaniel Banks (above, right), and Brigadier General Robert Milroy (below).

The outcome of the Peninsular Campaign, as both Lee and McClellan knew, would depend on whether the promised Union reinforcements—some 55,000 troops under McDowell and Nathaniel Banks—arrived. If this force fell on Richmond from the north, the Confederate capital was as good as lost. Even before assuming command of the Rebel army at Richmond, Lee gave Stonewall Jackson, operating in the Shenandoah Valley, the job of blocking these reinforcements.

Jackson, "a particularly seedy, sleepy-looking old fellow, whose uniform and cap were very dirty," was ideally suited for such an independent command. Despite a passion for keeping his own counsel (Dick Ewell once exploded, "Dammit, Jackson is driving us mad. He don't say a word . . . no order, no hint of where we're going"), Stonewall conducted as remarkable a campaign as the Civil War produced.

He started off inauspiciously, losing a battle at Kernstown on March 23 to a vastly superior force led by James Shields. Unwilling to believe that 4,200 men constituted Jackson's entire army—which in fact they did—Washington braced for a Confederate invasion of the North. Banks and McDowell were withheld, and an entire division was detached from McClellan to protect the Valley.

Although he had ironically achieved Lee's objective by suffering a defeat, Jackson, now reinforced, soon resumed the offensive. His soldiers, noting how his blue eyes blazed in the heat of battle, took to calling him Old Blue Light.

150

The grim Stonewall Jackson, photographed in 1863, two weeks before his fatal wounding at Chancellorsville.

THE SHENANDOAH VALLEY: This lovely region of rich farms nestled amid blue-shadowed mountains played a crucial role in the war. During most of the conflict it served the Confederacy as a vital source of food and forage. Beyond that, geography made it an important military highway, a great "covered way" for the Southern forces. Shielded on the east by the Blue Ridge Mountains, whose gaps were easily screened from prying eyes by cavalry, a Rebel army could march straight down toward the Northern heartland. Conversely, any Union army marching up the Valley would be headed away from Richmond. In 1862 it was the scene of Jackson's great campaign; in 1864 the North's high command decided on a policy of total war and ordered General Philip Sheridan to put the South's granary to the torch. When he finished, the Valley was a scene of blackened desolation.

ALLEGHENY MOUNTAINS

SHENANDOAH M

Moorefield

Franklin

Mt. Jackso

McDowell

New
Market

VALLEY TURNPIKE

Harrisonburg

Cross Keys

VIRGINIA CENTRAL R. R.

Staunton

Port
Republic

Swift Run
Gap

Brown's
Gap

Waynesboro

Rockfish
Gap

BLUE RIDGE MOUNTAINS

Charlottesville

David Greenspan

Cumberland

Romney

SOUTH BRANCH OF POTOMAC

POTOMAC RIVER

BALTIMORE & OHIO R.R.

Williamsport

Martinsburg

Sharpsburg

Shepherdstown

Cedar Creek

Strasburg

Fisher's
Hill

Winchester

Kernstown

Harpers Ferry

SHENANDOAH RIVER

NORTH FORK

MASSANUTTEN MOUNTAIN

Ashby's
Gap

Front
Royal

Manassas
Gap

SOUTH FORK

MANASSAS GAP R.R.

Thornton's
Gap

Carter
Gap

BULL RUN MOUNTAINS

ray

Thoroughfare
Gap

Centreville

Bull Run

er's
ap

ORANGE & ALEXANDRIA R.R.

Manassas
Junction

Culpeper

N

THE VALLEY

RAPIDAN RIVER

RAPPAHANNOCK RIV

donsville

Jackson's Valley Campaign

A ll Old Jackson gave us was a musket, a hundred rounds, and a
gum blanket, and he druv us like
hell," remarked a Rebel prisoner,
neatly summarizing Stonewall's mode
of operation.

With Ewell's division bringing his
strength to 17,000, he withdrew up
the Valley, then swung west to rout
Frémont's lieutenant, Robert Milroy,
at McDowell (*see* map, pages 152–53).
Moving north again on the Valley
Turnpike, he crossed Massanutten
Mountain, destroyed the Front Royal
garrison, and crushed Banks on May
25 at Winchester, chasing him all the
way to the Potomac.

Thoroughly alarmed, Lincoln and
Stanton hoped to trap Jackson between the converging columns of Frémont and Shields, totaling 50,000
troops. But despite a seven-mile-long,
double-column train of booty-filled
wagons, Jackson slipped between
them, whipped Frémont at Cross
Keys and Shields at Port Republic,
and joined Lee in late June. "God
has been our shield," Jackson said.

*Jackson's control of the crossings of South Fork (above) at
Port Republic prevented Frémont and Shields from combining
against him. Below is Alfred Waud's sketch of the Federal
charge on a stone wall held by the 37th Virginia at Kernstown.*

Resorting to one of his famous forced marches, Jackson caught Banks at Winchester on May 24, and in the next day's foggy dawn (above) routed him. Banks fled from the Valley, leaving immense stores behind, which led the Rebels to dub him "Commissary."

In the haze-shrouded mountains near McDowell (left), Jackson won his first Valley victory. Massanutten Mountain (right), a long ridge running down the center of the Valley, played an integral part in Jackson's deadly game of hide-and-seek.

Lee Takes
the Offensive

"McClellan will make this a battle of posts . . . under cover of his heavy guns and we cannot get at him," Lee wrote as the Federal army moved south of the Chickahominy to within sight of Richmond. Lee's eye was caught, however, by Fitz-John Porter's V Corps, stationed north of the river to guard the Union supply line. To find Porter's exact position, he called on Jeb Stuart.

Stuart delighted in gaudy trappings—yellow sash, scarlet-lined cape, plumed hat, jack boots, gauntlets—but not without reason: "We must substitute *esprit* for numbers," he said. "Therefore I strive to inculcate in my men the spirit of the chase." In mid-June Stuart's 1,200 troopers successfully rode completely around the Federal army, pursued by Stuart's father-in-law, cavalryman Philip St. George Cooke. (When Cooke went North in 1861, Stuart's acid comment had been: "He will regret it but once, and that will be continuously.")

Armed with the information that Porter was vulnerable, Lee summoned Jackson from the Valley and shifted 47,000 troops to strike the 25,000-man V Corps. It was risky leaving Magruder with only 25,000 before Richmond, but Magruder rose to the occasion, repeating with effect his Yorktown histrionics and again hoodwinking McClellan. On June 26 Lee hit Porter at Mechanicsville, northeast of Richmond. Although this first major battle of the Seven Days was a failure—Porter repulsed A. P. Hill at Beaver Dam Creek, and Jackson arrived too late to drive in the Union flank—Lee planned to resume his attack on the Federal right the next day.

The muddy Chickahominy River (above) was at its highest level in twenty years during the Peninsula fighting. Lee lost nearly 1,500 men at Mechanicsville, mainly at Beaver Dam Creek (below), now a quiet little stream meandering through a pleasant grove.

YOICHI OKAMOTO

rigadier General J. E. B. Stuart

157

Breakthrough at Gaines' Mill

Major General Fitz-John Porter

Waud's fine drawing above shows Confederates overrunning a disabled Federal battery at Gaines' Mill. The aftermath of the battle is pictured below in another Waud sketch: McClellan, ordering a "change of base," blows his supply dumps and retreats toward the James River.

McClellan ordered Porter to fall back from Mechanicsville to a new line near Gaines' Mill, rejecting any notion of a lunge through the weakened Richmond defenses. Porter's new position was very strong, with lines of infantry ranged across a slope, artillery massed on the plateau behind them, and swampy ground forming a virtual moat between them and the Rebels.

A. P. Hill opened the Battle of Gaines' Mill at noon on June 27, fruitlessly attacking the Union center. Again, as at Mechanicsville, Jackson was late coming up on the flank; and when D. H. Hill's division finally struck the Union right, Hill's old West Point roommate, George Sykes, hurled him back. Throughout the afternoon Porter's troops shattered the piecemeal Confederate charges.

Finally, as shadows lengthened across the fire-torn field, Lee ordered a massive, three-mile-wide assault. Hood's Texans broke through the Federal center, and when a gallant, doomed charge by the 5th U.S. Cavalry failed to close the gap, Porter had to withdraw across the Chickahominy. Having cut McClellan's supply line, Lee wrote Davis, "We sleep on the field and shall renew the contest in the morning."

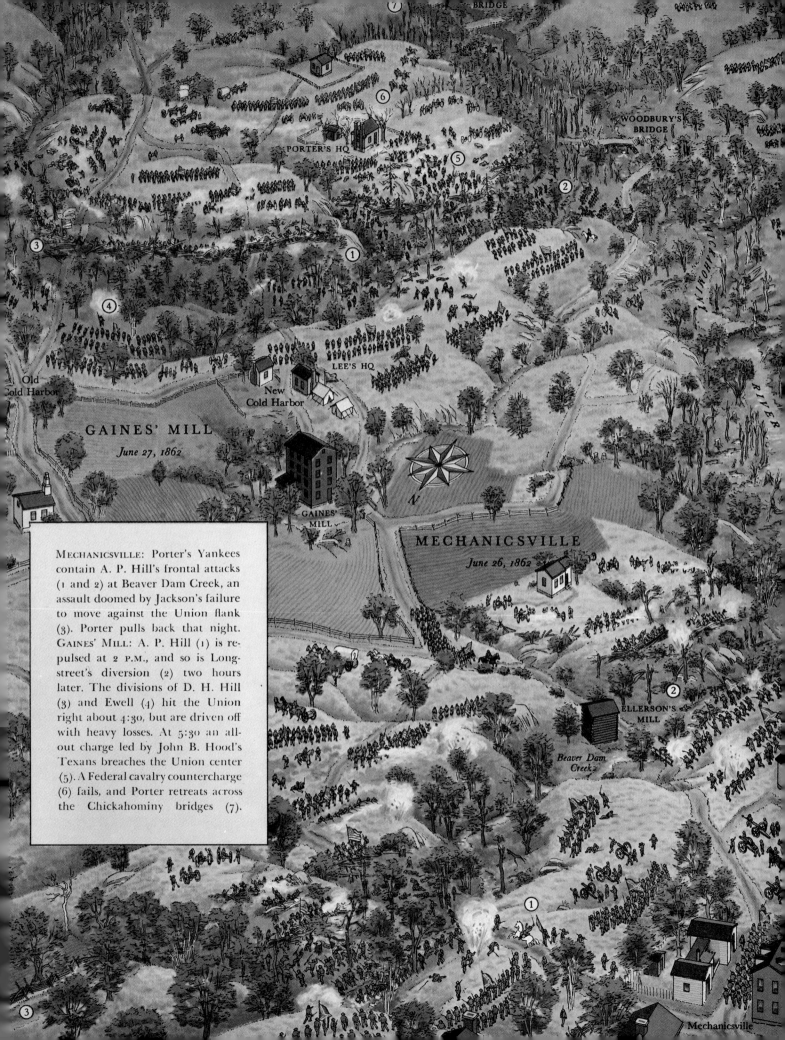

WOODBURY'S
BRIDGE

PORTER'S HQ

CHICKAHOMINY RIVER

LEE'S HQ

Old Cold Harbor

New Cold Harbor

GAINES' MILL

June 27, 1862

GAINES' MILL

N

MECHANICSVILLE

June 26, 1862

ELLERSON'S MILL

Beaver Dam Creek

Mechanicsville

MECHANICSVILLE: Porter's Yankees contain A. P. Hill's frontal attacks (1 and 2) at Beaver Dam Creek, an assault doomed by Jackson's failure to move against the Union flank (3). Porter pulls back that night. GAINES' MILL: A. P. Hill (1) is repulsed at 2 P.M., and so is Longstreet's diversion (2) two hours later. The divisions of D. H. Hill (3) and Ewell (4) hit the Union right about 4:30, but are driven off with heavy losses. At 5:30 an allout charge led by John B. Hood's Texans breaches the Union center (5). A Federal cavalry countercharge (6) fails, and Porter retreats across the Chickahominy bridges (7).

The Retreat to the James

In the contemporary lithograph below, McClellan's vast train—4,300 wagons and ambulances—fords Bear Creek near Savage's Station on the retreat from Richmond. In the foreground an officer prods laggard troops.

McClellan's withdrawal was so hasty that 2,500 sick and wounded Federals in the field hospital at Savage's Station, shown in James Gibson's photograph at right, had to be abandoned to the pursuing Confederates.

When Lee realized that McClellan was giving up the Richmond siege, he set about hastening the Federals along. To reach a new supply base at Harrison's Landing on the James River, McClellan had to march south across White Oak Swamp, and the confused fighting that followed resulted from Lee's effort to cut the Union column while it straddled this morass.

At Savage's Station on June 29 Magruder struck McClellan's rear guard, but had to break off the action when Jackson failed to come to his support. On June 30 Lee planned to hit the Federal column south of White Oak Swamp, near Glendale: two-thirds of his army would converge on McClellan's flank; Jackson, with the remaining third, would slash at his rear.

But again the chance was bungled. The flank attack at Frayser's Farm was made by only two divisions, and their vicious hand-to-hand struggle was to no avail—the huge Yankee supply and artillery train had passed this spot en route to safety some five hours before.

Most disappointing to Lee, however, was the performance of Jackson, who failed for the fourth time in a row to act effectively. Quite possibly the man was completely exhausted by his strenuous Valley Campaign, for a Rebel gunner noted that he "appeared worn down to the lowest point of flesh consistent with active service."

McClellan dug in on Malvern Hill and telegraphed Washington, "I shall do my best to save the army. Send more gunboats."

OVERLEAF: *Civil War photographer Alexander Gardner wrote of White Oak Swamp: "The air seemed to be suffocating with stagnation . . . beneath the pall of mist." This is the swamp today, pictured in the rain.*

YOICHI OKAMOTO

161

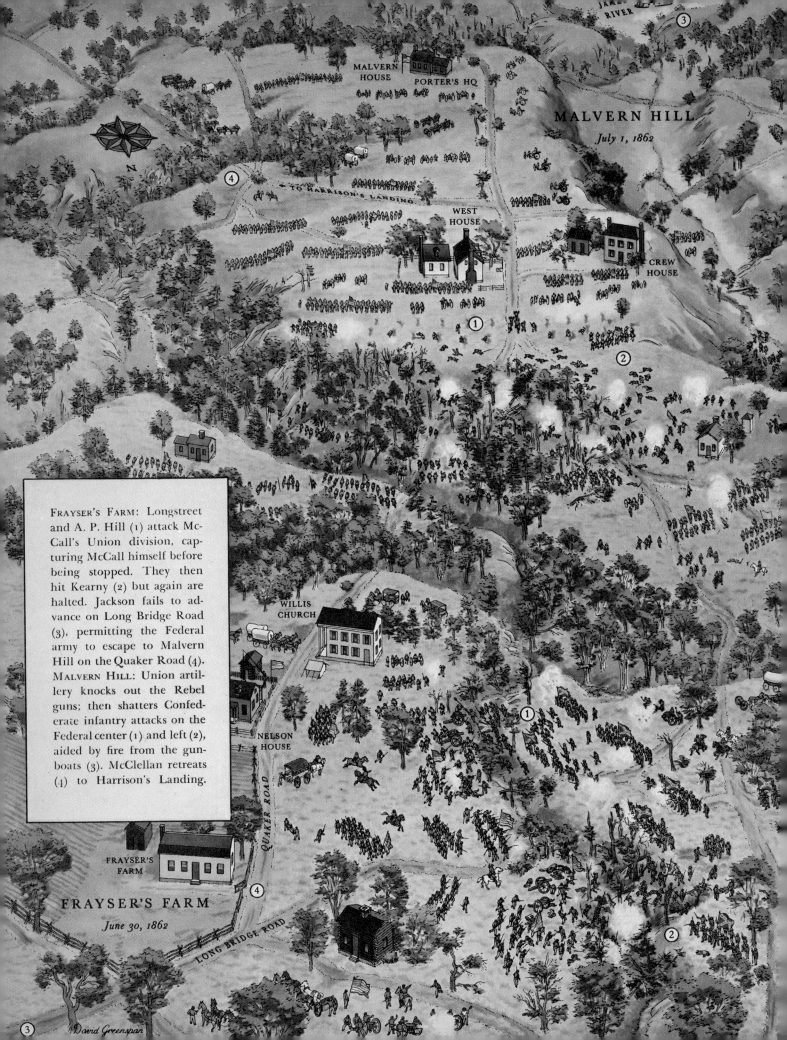

MALVERN HILL

July 1, 1862

MALVERN HOUSE

PORTER'S HQ

N

TO HARRISON'S LANDING

WEST HOUSE

CREW HOUSE

①

②

FRAYSER'S FARM: Longstreet and A. P. Hill (1) attack McCall's Union division, capturing McCall himself before being stopped. They then hit Kearny (2) but again are halted. Jackson fails to advance on Long Bridge Road (3), permitting the Federal army to escape to Malvern Hill on the Quaker Road (4). MALVERN HILL: Union artillery knocks out the Rebel guns; then shatters Confederate infantry attacks on the Federal center (1) and left (2), aided by fire from the gunboats (3). McClellan retreats (4) to Harrison's Landing.

WILLIS CHURCH

NELSON HOUSE

QUAKER ROAD

①

FRAYSER'S FARM

June 30, 1862

LONG BRIDGE ROAD

②

③

David Greenspan

Last of the Seven Days' Battles

A Union gun fires over two Federal battle lines at the Rebels charging Malvern Hill, as drawn by Alfred Waud.

It seemed to Robert E. Lee that one more push might be all the Federal army could take. But Fitz-John Porter, who had the task of holding the 150-foot-high eminence known as Malvern Hill which lay on the route to Harrison's Landing, made Lee's assumption a bloody mistake.

Porter had plenty of infantry in place and in reserve, but more important, he had plenty of fieldpieces —over 100 of them, parked hub-to-hub—plus the support of long-range siege guns and the heavy batteries of gunboats on the James.

Longstreet placed the Rebel cannon so as to take Porter's guns in cross fire. After silencing them, he thought, the Confederate infantry would repeat its brilliant Gaines' Mill charge and drive Porter off his perch. D. H. Hill, surveying the massed Federal guns, did not share Longstreet's optimism. "If General McClellan is there in strength," he felt, "we had better let him alone." Union artillery was to prove itself again and again during the war, but at Malvern Hill it probably achieved its highest measure of superiority. In a short time every Southern battery within range had been silenced.

Another mix-up in Lee's orders caused the troops of Magruder, Huger, and D. H. Hill to make gallant but suicidal charges into the massed fire of Porter's guns. As Hill remarked later, "It was not war, it was murder." Some 5,500 Confederates fell on the slopes of Malvern Hill on July 1, 1862, the seventh of the Seven Days, and the next morning, when a horrified Union officer looked at the body-strewn hill, "A third of them were dead or dying, but enough of them were alive and moving to give the field a singular crawling effect."

McClellan marched the eight miles from Malvern Hill to Harrison's Landing to rest and refit his mangled army. Lee fell back to Richmond for the same purpose; he had suffered 20,000 casualties to McClellan's 16,000.

In spite of repeated failures to bring McClellan to bay, Lee, by daring and by keeping a tight hold on the initiative, had lifted the siege of Richmond, driving a superior force before him. No matter how skillful a retreat he had conducted, George McClellan had been outthought and outfought.

Aftermath
of Battle

Below are Lieutenant George A. Custer (right) and his Confederate prisoner, former West Point classmate James Washington. After the Seven Days the two armies returned to the routine of camp life, captured at left in Winslow Homer's ironic "Home, Sweet Home."

A haunting face from a truly lost generation: Georgia private Edwin Jennison, killed at Malvern Hill.

THE NAVIES

WHILE the rival armies swayed back and forth over the landscape, wreathing the countryside in smoke and visiting the dread and sorrow of long casualty lists on people of the North and the South, a profound intangible was slowly beginning to tilt the balance against the Confederacy. On the ocean, in the coastal sounds, and up and down the inland rivers the great force of sea power was making itself felt. By itself it could never decide the issue of the war; taken in conjunction with the work of the Federal armies, it would ultimately be decisive. In no single area of the war was the overwhelming advantage possessed by the Federal government so ruinous to Southern hopes.

The Civil War came while one revolution in naval affairs was under way, and it hastened the commencement of another. The world's navies were in the act of adjusting themselves to the transition from sail to steam when the war began; by the time it ended, the transition from wooden ships to ironclads was well along. Taken together, the two revolutions were far-reaching. The era of what is now thought of as "modern" warfare was foreshadowed by what happened on land; it actually began on the water, and by 1865 naval warfare would resemble the twentieth century much more than it resembled anything Lord Nelson or John Paul Jones had known.

At the start of the war the South had no navy at all, and the North had one which, although it was good enough for an ordinary combat with an overseas enemy, was almost wholly unadapted for the job which it had to do now. Both sides had to improvise, and in the improvisation the South displayed fully as much ingenuity and resourcefulness as the North. The great difference was that the North had so much more to improvise with. The South was compelled to enter a contest which it had no chance to win.

When the flag came down on Fort Sumter in April, 1861, the Federal government possessed some ninety warships. More than half of these were sailing vessels —models of their class a generation earlier, obsolete now. About forty ships were steam-driven, and a great number of these were tied up at various navy-yard docks, out of commission—"in ordinary," as the expression then went. Some of them were badly in need of repair. Of the steamers that were in commission, many were scattered on foreign stations, and it would take time to get them back into home waters.

Pride of the navy was its set of five steam frigates. They were powerful wooden vessels, ship-rigged, with adequate power plants and exceptionally heavy armament—forty 9-inch rifles on the gun decks, and a few larger weapons mounted on the spar decks. They were probably as powerful as any ships then afloat. All of these were out of commission.

In the climactic naval duel of the war, the **U.S.S.** *Kearsarge sinks the Rebel raider* **Alabama** *off the French coast.*

A Northern recruiting poster, calling for seamen.

The map at right illustrates the slow, strangling effect of the Northern blockade in closing Confederate ports. Dates indicate Union seizure of various points along the coast line.

Sails augmented steam in such vessels as the Pensacola, pride of the prewar Union fleet.

Then there were five first-class screw sloops, smaller and less formidable than the steam frigates but sturdy fighting craft all the same. There were four side-wheelers, dating back to the navy's first experiments with steam power: they were practically obsolete, because machinery and boilers were largely above the water line, but they could still be used. There were eight lighter screw sloops and half a dozen of third-class rating, along with a handful of tugs and assorted harbor craft. That was about the lot.

With this navy the United States had to blockade more than 3,500 miles of Confederate coast line. It had, also, to control such rivers as the Mississippi and the Tennessee, to say nothing of the extensive sounds along the Atlantic coast. Furthermore, it had to be prepared to strike at Southern seaports, most of them substantially fortified, and to join with the army in amphibious offensives all the way from Cape Hatteras to the Rio Grande. To do all of these things it did not have nearly enough ships, and most of the ones it did have were of the wrong kind. The powerful frigates and sloops were designed for combat on the high seas or for commerce raiding, not for blockade duty. They drew too much water to operate in shallow sounds and rivers. For war with a European power they would have been excellent, once they were all repaired and commissioned; for war with the Confederacy they were not quite what the navy needed.

At the very beginning of the war Lincoln proclaimed a blockade of all Southern ports. This, as he soon discovered, was a serious tactical error. A nation "blockaded" the ports of a foreign power; when it dealt with an internal insurrection or rebellion it simply closed its ports. The proclamation of blockade almost amounted to recognition of the Confederacy's independent existence, and European powers promptly recognized the Southland's belligerent rights. On top of this, foreign nations were not obliged to respect a blockade unless it were genuinely effective. A paper blockade would do no good: unless the navy could make it really dangerous for merchant ships to trade with Confederate ports, the blockade would have no standing in international law. So the navy's first problem was to find, somewhere and somehow, at any expense but in a great hurry, enough ships to make the paper blockade a real one.

The job was done, but it cost a great deal of money and resulted in the creation of one of the most heterogeneous fleets ever seen on the waters of the globe. Anything that would float and carry a gun or two would serve, for most of these blockaders would never have to fight; they were simply cops on the beat, creating most of their effect just by being on the scene. Vessels of every conceivable variety were brought into service, armed, after a fashion, and sent steaming down to take station off Southern harbors: ferryboats,

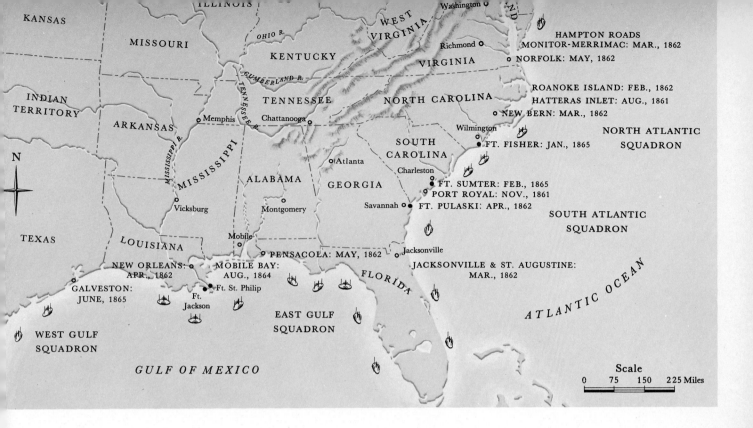

KANSAS
MISSOURI
INDIAN TERRITORY
ARKANSAS
TEXAS
LOUISIANA
ILLINOIS
OHIO R.
KENTUCKY
TENNESSEE
Memphis
Chattanooga
MISSISSIPPI
ALABAMA
Vicksburg
Montgomery
Mobile
NEW ORLEANS: APR., 1862
GALVESTON: JUNE, 1865
Ft. Jackson
Ft. St. Philip
MOBILE BAY: AUG., 1864
PENSACOLA: MAY, 1862
WEST GULF SQUADRON
EAST GULF SQUADRON
GULF OF MEXICO

WEST VIRGINIA
Washington
Richmond
VIRGINIA
HAMPTON ROADS
MONITOR-MERRIMAC: MAR., 1862
NORFOLK: MAY, 1862
NORTH CAROLINA
ROANOKE ISLAND: FEB., 1862
HATTERAS INLET: AUG., 1861
NEW BERN: MAR., 1862
Wilmington
FT. FISHER: JAN., 1865
NORTH ATLANTIC SQUADRON
SOUTH CAROLINA
Atlanta
GEORGIA
Charleston
FT. SUMTER: FEB., 1865
PORT ROYAL: NOV., 1861
Savannah
FT. PULASKI: APR., 1862
SOUTH ATLANTIC SQUADRON
Jacksonville
JACKSONVILLE & ST. AUGUSTINE: MAR., 1862
FLORIDA
ATLANTIC OCEAN

Scale
0   75   150   225 Miles

excursion steamers, whalers, tugs, fishing schooners, superannuated clippers—a weird and wonderful collection of maritime oddities, which in the end gave more useful service than anyone had a right to expect. They made the blockade legally effective, and their work was aided by the Confederate government's folly in withholding cotton from the overseas market. At the very least they gave the navy time to build some new vessels specially designed for the job.

These included two dozen 500-ton gunboats, steam powered, of shallow draft and moderate armament— "ninety-day gunboats," they were called, because it took just three months from keel-laying to final commissioning. Deep-sea cruisers to run down Confederate commerce destroyers were built, along with forty-seven double-enders—unique, canoe-shaped side-wheelers, with rudders and pilot houses at each end, for use in the narrow rivers that fed into the coastal sounds where there was no room to turn around. The double-enders could change course simply by reversing their engines.

In the end the blockade was made highly effective, and by the final year of the war its effect was fatally constrictive. It was never airtight, and as long as a Southern port remained open, daring merchant skippers would slip in and out with priceless cargoes of contraband; but the measure of its effectiveness was not the percentage of blockade-runners which got

through the net, but the increasing quantity of goods which the Confederacy had to do without. Under the blockade the Confederacy was doomed to slow strangulation.

For offensive operations the Federal navy was in much better shape, and the war was not very old before offensive operations got under way. Late in August, 1861, a squadron of warships commanded by Flag Officer Silas Stringham, accompanied by transports bearing infantry under Ben Butler, dropped down the coast for an assault on the Confederate forts which guarded Hatteras Inlet, North Carolina, principal entrance to the vast reaches of Pamlico Sound. Stringham had two of the huge steam frigates with him, and his bombardment pounded the unprepared forts into submission. The government apparently had not done its advance planning very carefully, and for the time being neither the army nor the navy was prepared to do anything but hold the captured position. However, the operation did set a pattern, and important results would grow from it.

In November a much stronger expedition, the naval part of it commanded by Flag Officer Samuel F. Du Pont, broke into the waters of South Carolina, shelling Forts Walker and Beauregard into surrender and occupying Port Royal, which became a secure base for the blockading fleet. Early in 1862 Flag Officer Louis M. Goldsborough and Brigadier General Am-

171

A Union tar, in familiar bell-bottomed pants.

brose E. Burnside led an amphibious foray into the North Carolina sounds from Hatteras Inlet. Roanoke Island was seized, Elizabeth City and New Bern were captured, and powerful Fort Macon, commanding the approach to Beaufort, was taken. In effect, this action gave the Unionists control of nearly all of the North Carolina coast line and made the task of the blockading fleet much easier; it also added appreciably to Jefferson Davis' problems by posing the constant threat of an invasion between Richmond and Charleston. Simultaneously, another army-navy expedition took Fort Pulaski, at the mouth of the Savannah River.

Most important of all was the blow at New Orleans, largest city in the Confederacy. This was entrusted to an elderly but still spry officer named David Glasgow Farragut, who had a strong fleet of fighting craft and a flotilla of mortar vessels—converted schooners, each mounting a tub-shaped mortar that could lob a 13-inch shell high into the air and drop it inside a fort with surprising accuracy. Farragut got his vessels into the mouth of the Mississippi and in mid-April opened a prolonged bombardment of Forts Jackson and St. Philip, which guarded the approach to New Orleans. The mortar boats, commanded by Captain David Dixon Porter, tossed shells into the forts for a week; then, in the blackness of two in the morning on April 24, Farragut's ships went steaming up the river to run past the forts.

The Confederates sent fire rafts downstream, but these were dodged. A collection of armed river vessels put up as much of a fight as they could, and the big guns in the forts flailed away in the darkness, Farragut's broadsides replying, the river all covered with heavy smoke lit by the red flares from the burning rafts and the sharp flashes of the guns—and suddenly most of Farragut's ships were past the forts with only moderate damage, the Confederate vessels were sunk or driven ashore, and Farragut went plowing on to occupy New Orleans. Hopelessly cut off, the forts presently surrendered, Ben Butler came in with troops to take possession of the forts and the city, and the mouth of the great river was in Federal hands.

The capture of New Orleans strikingly illustrated the immense value of unchallenged sea power. The Federals could strike when and where they pleased, and all the Southern coast was vulnerable. The Confederates had known that New Orleans was in danger, but they had supposed that the real peril lay upriver, where Shiloh had just been lost and where the Federal gunboats were hammering their way down to Memphis: coming up through the mouth of the river, Farragut had, so to speak, entered by the back door. The loss of New Orleans was one of the genuine disasters to the Southern cause, and it proved irretrievable.

Yet if the Lincoln government had the enormous

The hardened veterans of Admiral Du Pont's flagship, Wabash, *were hand-picked, perhaps for the musical talents displayed in this photograph.*

Mere boys served as powder monkeys.

advantage that goes with control of the sea, the Confederacy made valiant attempts to redress the balance. The South lacked a merchant marine and a seafaring population, and it had very little in the way of shipyards and the industrial plant that could build machinery and armament for warships, but it had vast ingenuity and much energy, and its naval authorities, working with very little, accomplished much more than anyone had a right to expect. Not even the Yankees were any more inventive: the chief difference was that it was easier for the Yankees to turn an invention into a working reality.

The famous case of the *Merrimac* offers an interesting example.

Merrimac was one of the Federal navy's great steam frigates. Her engines were in bad order, and when the war began she was laid up in the Norfolk navy yard, out of commission. Situated in an ardently pro-Confederate community, the navy yard was quickly lost; and by seizing it on April 20, 1861, the Confederates acquired not only the physical plant but more than a thousand powerful cannon, which served to arm Confederate forts all along the seacoast.

When the Federals were driven from the yard they set fire to *Merrimac* and scuttled her, but Confederate engineers had little trouble raising the hulk, and on inspection it was found sound, only the upper works having been destroyed by fire. The imaginative Southerners thereupon proceeded to construct a fighting ship the likes of which no one had ever seen.

Merrimac's hull was cut down to the berth deck, and a citadel with slanting sides was built on the midships section, with ports for ten guns. The walls of this citadel were made of pitch pine and oak two feet thick, and on this was laid an iron sheathing four inches thick. An open grating covered the top of this citadel, admitting light and air to the gun deck. An armored pilothouse was forward, and a four-foot iron beak was fastened to the bow. When she left the dry dock, *Merrimac*, rechristened *Virginia*, looked like nothing so much as a barn gone adrift and submerged to the eaves. The decks forward and aft of the citadel were just awash. *Merrimac*'s engines, defective to begin with, had not been improved by the fact that they had spent weeks under water, but somehow the engineers got them into running order, and the ship could move. She could not move very fast, and she was one of the unhandiest brutes to steer that was ever put afloat; but in all the navies of the world there were not more than two ships that could have given her a fight. (The French had one ironclad frigate, and the British had another; all the rest of the world's warships were of wood.)

It should be pointed out that since warships had never worn armor, no one had ever bothered to create an armor-piercing shell, and *Merrimac*'s iron sides—

173

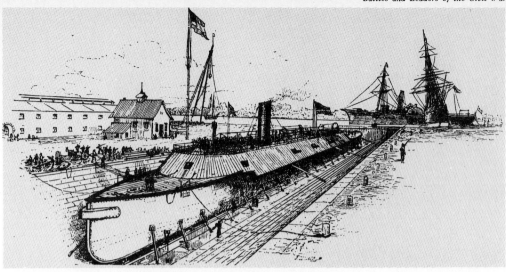

The resurrected Merrimac, *being outfitted by the Rebels at Norfolk as the ironclad* Virginia.

very thinly armored, by later standards—were impervious to anything the ordinary warship would fire at her. It developed, as the war wore along, that the only way to deal with an ironclad was to fire solid shot from the largest smoothbore cannon available—15-inch, if possible—at the closest possible range. These would not exactly pierce good iron sheathing, but repeated blows might crack it so that other projectiles could pierce it. This worked sometimes, and sometimes it did not; but when *Merrimac* left the Elizabeth River, on March 8, 1862, and chugged laboriously out into the open waters of Hampton Roads, none of the Federal warships in sight mounted guns that could do her any particular damage.

On her first day in action *Merrimac* created a sensation and put the Lincoln administration—especially Secretary of War Stanton—into something like a panic. She destroyed two of the navy's wooden warships, *Congress* and *Cumberland,* drove the big steam frigate *Minnesota* aground, and was herself so little damaged by the shot which the Union warships threw at her that it almost looked as if she could whip the entire Federal navy. When evening came *Merrimac* went back into her harbor, planning to return in the morning, destroy *Minnesota,* and sink any other ships that cared to stick around and fight.

The next day, March 9, brought what was certainly the most dramatic naval battle of the war—the fa-

mous engagement between *Merrimac* and *Monitor.*

It had taken the Confederates many months to design and construct their pioneer ironclad, and word of what they were doing quickly got North—very few military secrets were really kept, in that war—and the Federal Navy Department had to get an ironclad of its own. It went to the redoubtable Swedish-American inventor John Ericsson for a design, getting a craft which in its own way was every bit as odd-looking as the rebuilt *Merrimac.* Ericsson built a long, flat hull with no more than a foot or two of freeboard, putting amidships a revolving iron turret mounting two 11-inch guns. A smoke pipe came up aft of this, and forward there was a stubby iron pilothouse; people who saw *Monitor* afloat said she looked like a tin can on a shingle. This craft was finished just in the nick of time, came down to the Chesapeake from New York in tow of a tug, almost foundering en route—neither of these great ironclads was very seaworthy—and steamed in past the Virginia capes late in the afternoon of March 8, just as *Merrimac* was completing her day's chores. Next day the two ships met in open combat.

The fight was singularly indecisive. Each ship took a sound hammering, but neither one was badly damaged. Although *Merrimac,* in the end, retired to a safe spot in the Elizabeth River, *Monitor* did not try to follow her, nor did the Federal craft ever attempt

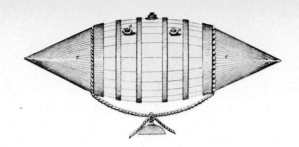

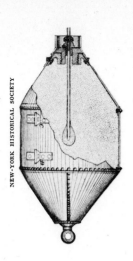

Ingenious Confederate inventors devised these mines. Above, a converted beer keg; at left, an electric model, triggered from shore.

Wide-open fighting decks of the age of sail were replaced with covered decks such as this on a Union gunboat, sketched by Alex Simplot.

to force a finish fight. *Merrimac* destroyed no more Union warships, but she remained afloat until May 10, effectively keeping the Federals out of the James River; indeed, her continued existence was one of the reasons why McClellan was so very slow in moving up the Virginia Peninsula. She was lost, finally, when the Federals occupied Norfolk, which left her without a home port. She drew too much water to go up the James to Richmond, and she was far too unseaworthy to go out into the open ocean, and her crew had no recourse but to scuttle her. But by any standard she had been a success, she had helped to create a revolution in naval warfare, and her design and construction proved that Southern engineers were quite as ready as Yankees to move into the new mechanical age.

If the South had had Northern industrial facilities, the story of the war at sea might have been very different. A number of ironclads on the *Merrimac* pattern were built, and most of them were highly serviceable. There was *Arkansas*, built in Memphis, Tennessee, which ran straight through a fleet of Yankee gunboats above Vicksburg, outfought the best the Yankees could send against her, and was destroyed by her own crew when her engines failed and sent her hopelessly aground near Baton Rouge. There was *Albemarle*, which shook Federal control of the North Carolina sounds until young Lieutenant William Cushing sank her with a torpedo; and there was *Ten-*

nessee, which singlehanded fought Farragut's entire fleet at Mobile Bay in the summer of 1864, surrendering only after having survived one of the most onesided contests in naval history. As a matter of fact, a Confederate ironclad almost saved the day at New Orleans. A very heavily armored vessel named *Louisiana* was built to hold the lower river, but Farragut came along before she was quite ready: her engines were not serviceable, and her gun ports needed to be enlarged so that her guns could train properly, and she was tied to the bank, virtually useless, when the Federal fleet steamed by. When the forts surrendered, *Louisiana* was blown up.

The marvel in all of this is not that the Confederacy did so poorly with its navy, but that it did so well. Almost uniformly, her ironclads gave the Federal navy much trouble, and it is worth recording that most of them finally failed not because they were poorly designed, but because the industrial facilities that could put them into first-class shape and keep them there did not exist. The South was painfully short of mechanics, short of metal, short of fabricating plants; there was never any chance that she could create a fleet solid enough to go out and challenge the Federal navy, and what was done had to be done on a bits-and-pieces basis. All things considered, the Confederate Navy Department acquitted itself very well.

Confederate commerce raiders drew a great deal of

The attempt of makeshift Union vessels to stop blockade-runners is lampooned in this lithograph.

attention during the war and in the generations that followed, but although they were a most expensive nuisance to the North, they could never have had a decisive effect on the course of the war. The best of them, like *Alabama* and *Shenandoah,* were built in England: ably commanded, they roamed the seven seas almost at will, helping to drive the American merchant fleet out from under the American flag but ultimately having only a minor bearing on the war itself. Toward the close of the war English yards did undertake the construction of a number of ironclad rams for the Confederacy, ships meant for close combat rather than for commerce destroying, and if these had been delivered they might have changed everything. But their construction and intended destination became known, the United States government plainly meant to go to war with Great Britain if they were actually delivered, and in the end the British government saw to it that they were kept at home.

Far more important to the Southern cause than the commerce destroyers were the blockade-runners. Most of these were built abroad for private account—long, lean, shallow-draft side-wheelers, for the most part, capable of high speeds, painted slate gray to decrease their visibility, and burning anthracite coal so that smoke from their funnels would not betray them to the blockading fleets. In the usual course of things, goods meant for the Confederacy were shipped from England (or from a port on the Continent) to Nassau, in the Bahamas—a little port that enjoyed a regular Klondike boom while the war lasted. There the cargoes were transferred to the blockade-runners, which would make a dash for it through the Federal cruisers to some such Southern seaport as Wilmington, North Carolina. Many of these were caught, to be sure, but many of them got through, and profits were so remarkable that if a ship made one or two successful voyages her owners were money ahead, even if thereafter she were captured. On the return trip, of course, the blockade-runners took out cotton.

Not all of the material imported via these vessels was for military use. It paid to bring in luxuries, and so luxuries were brought in, to be sold at fantastic prices; and eventually the Confederate government took a hand, outlawing the importation of some luxuries entirely and stipulating that one-half of the space on every ship must be reserved for government goods. Tightly as the Federal squadrons might draw their patrols, they were never able to stop blockade-running entirely; it ceased, at last, only when the last of the Confederate ports was occupied. But if the traffic could not be entirely stopped, it was increasingly restricted, and the very fact that the blockade-runners could make such outlandish profits testified to the Southland's desperate shortage of goods from the outside world.

176

A SPECIAL PICTURE PORTFOLIO

On her first sortie the *Merrimac* burned the *Congress,* sank the *Cumberland,* and drove the *Minnesota* aground.

O n March 8, 1862, a Federal naval officer aboard the warship *Congress* peered through his spyglass at a squat black shape which had just emerged from the Elizabeth River into Hampton Roads. "That *Thing* is coming down!" he shouted. News of the *Merrimac,* an ironclad the Rebels were building at Norfolk, had long since reached the North, but it is doubtful if many people realized that this "Thing" was the embodiment of an astonishing revolution in naval warfare.

The story of that naval revolution in the Civil War, encompassing far more than the *Monitor* and the *Merrimac,* is presented in this special picture portfolio. In some instances—notably, in the capture of New Orleans—the war on the waters was an integrated part of military strategy on the land; and these aspects are treated elsewhere in proper chronology. But the isolated and often unrelated naval engagements—the landing at Hatteras Inlet, the siege of Charleston, the blockade and the blockade-runners, and finally the duel of the *Alabama* and the *Kearsarge* off the coast of France—are discussed in this chronicle of the navies in the Civil War.

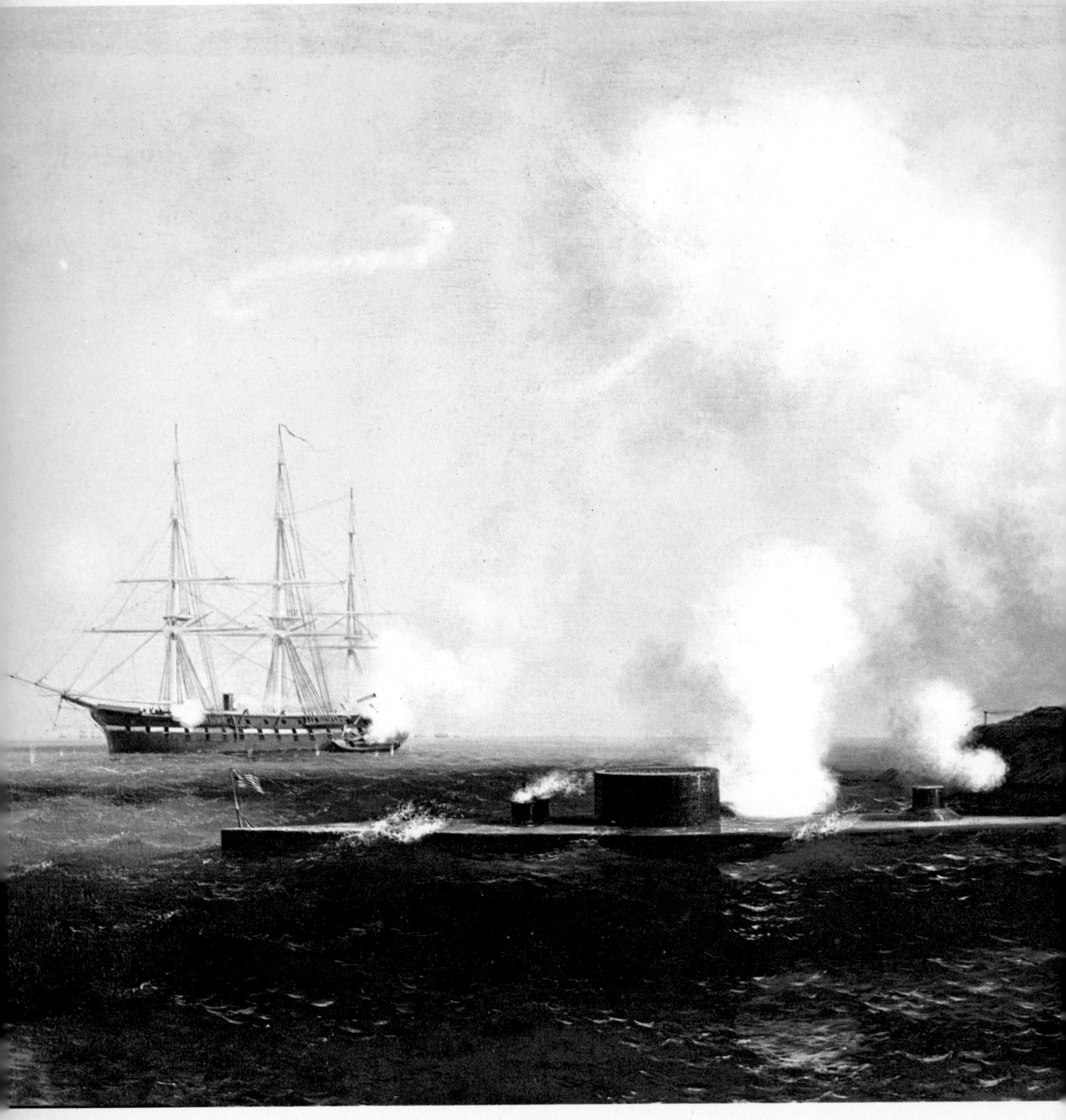

Monitor versus Merrimac

In September, 1861, a brilliant, cantankerous Swedish immigrant, John Ericsson, submitted to the Navy Department a proposal for a Union ironclad to meet the challenge of the *Merrimac,* which was known to be under construction. After studying Ericsson's curious model, a naval officer handed it back: "Take it home and worship it," he said. "It will not be idolatry. It is the image of nothing in the heavens above, or the earth beneath, or the waters under the earth." Despite this skepticism Ericsson received a contract from Secretary of the Navy Gideon Welles and feverishly set about building his armor-plated raft with a revolving gun turret. On January 30, 1862, the *Monitor* was launched in New York and, astonishingly, was en route to Hampton Roads the very day the *Merrimac* left her lair.

When news of the destruction wrought by the Confederate ironclad on March 8 reached Washington the following morning, the administration was thrown into turmoil. Lincoln went repeatedly to White House windows to see if the *Merrimac* was approaching up the Potomac. Welles, although alarmed himself, found "something inexpressibly ludicrous in the wild, frantic talk, action and rage of [Secretary of War] Stanton." That evening, however, a reassuring message arrived from Hampton Roads. Early on the morning of March 9 the *Monitor* had engaged the *Merrimac* in battle. "These two ironclad vessels," the report read, "fought part of the time touching each other, from 8 A.M. to noon, when the *Merrimac* retired. . . . The *Monitor* is uninjured and ready at any moment to repel another attack." The challenge had been met.

Xanthus Smith painted the naval duel between *Monitor* (left) and *Merrimac.*

1

Men Who Made a Revolution

3

4

5

Although its navy was small and outmoded, the North had a clear superiority over the South in the industrial resources and manpower that would make a naval revolution possible. The Union had all but two of the nation's shipyards, and it also had three men whose ideas and plans kept shipbuilders and ordnance factories busy throughout the war.

James Buchanan Eads, a self-educated steamboat engineer, told Lincoln that a fleet of armor-plated, steam-propelled gunboats was needed on the Mississippi River. Told to build such a fleet, Eads returned to St. Louis, set 4,000 men to working around the clock, and had the first boat ready 45 days later. John A. Dahlgren had spent ten prewar years in the Ordnance Bureau, perfecting the 11-inch gun which bore his name as standard naval equipment. And John Ericsson, when the *Monitor* brought him fame, turned his patents over to the government. It was, he said, his "contribution to the glorious Union cause."

(1) Specializing in boilers and engines for river steamers, New York's Novelty Iron Works improvised in turning out the revolving gun turret for the *Monitor*. The shop is pictured here in an 1850 advertising lithograph. (2) The *Cairo,* one of Eads' ironclads, was the first victim of yet another Civil War innovation, the torpedo. (3) John A. Dahlgren left his Ordnance Bureau desk to command the South Atlantic Blockading Squadron. (4) James B. Eads sent his fleet into action at Fort Henry when the boats were still technically in his ownership. (5) John Ericsson was a testy genius who preferred to work alone in the secluded privacy of his New York home.

OVERLEAF: Rather more sophisticated than the *Monitor* was the ironclad *Keokuk,* built at New York in 1862.

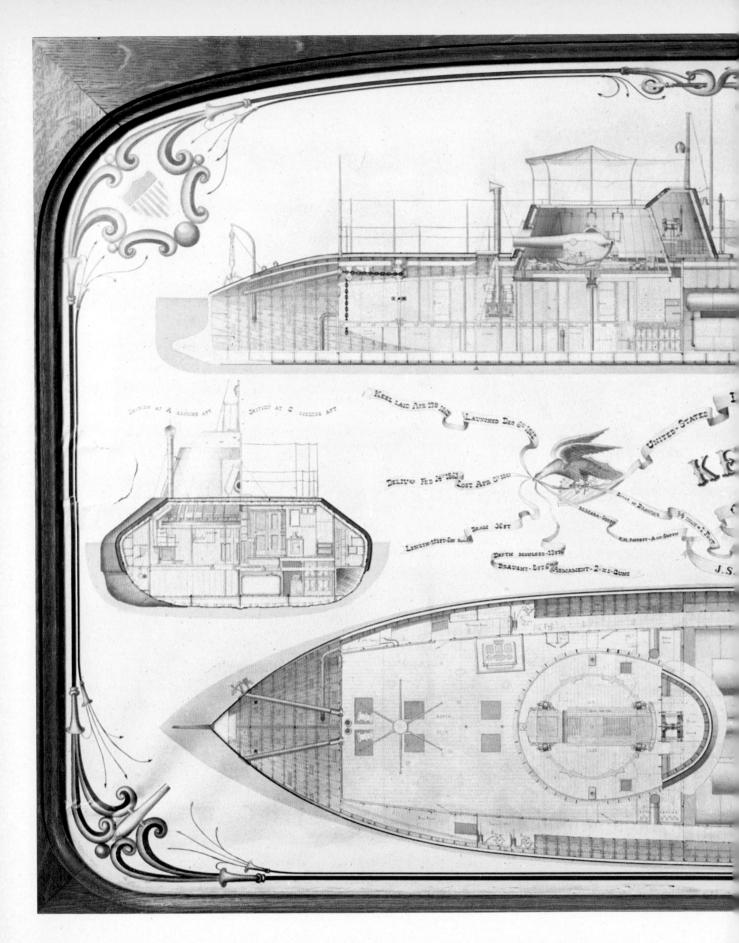

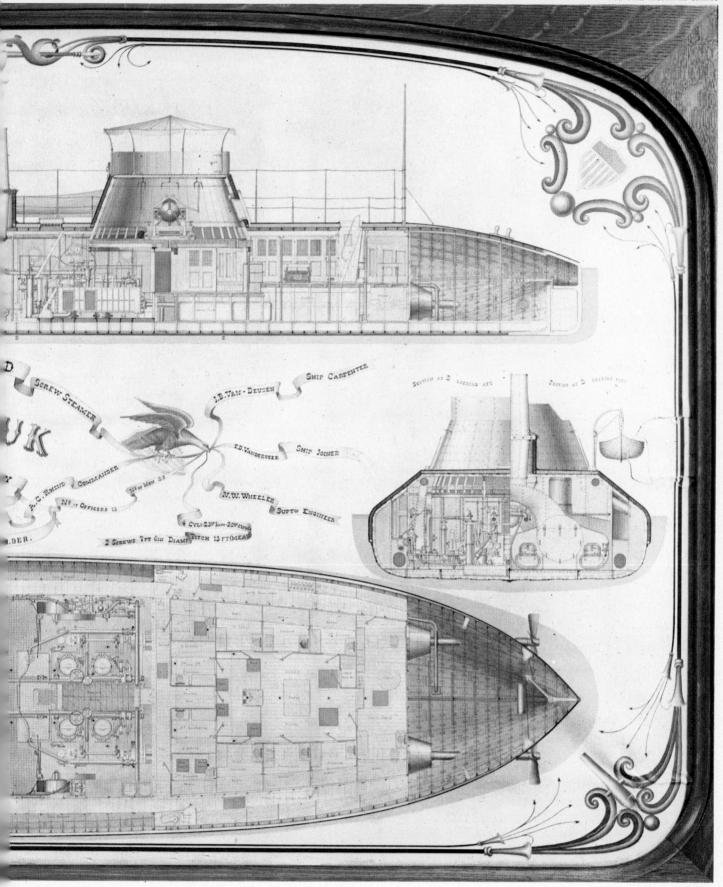

1

2

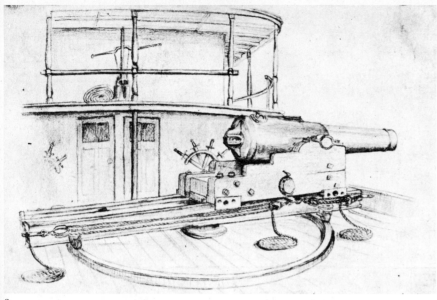

3

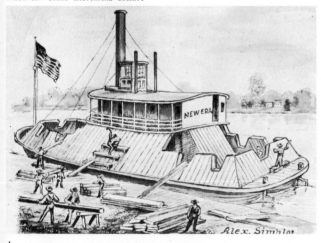

4

Welles labored unceasingly to build a new navy. The number of workers in government navy yards increased, early in 1862, from 4,000 to 17,000. Over 200 vessels were built, and some 400 others were purchased as the Union navy grew from a pathetic 90 ships in 1861 to the 671 noted in Welles' report to Congress in December, 1864. Throughout, Welles was under constant attack—from the press, from greedy contractors, from Congressional critics, and from rivals in the cabinet—"But I have no reason to complain when I look at results," he confided to his diary early in 1865. "Others could have done better, perhaps . . . yet, reviewing hastily, I see very little to regret in my administration of the Navy."

(1) After examining the *Monitor,* Admiral Porter heartily endorsed the building of the twin-turreted *Kickapoo,* which saw action at Mobile Bay and survived to the end of the war. (2) William Hoel, the pilot who took the *Carondelet* past Island No. 10, kept a notebook in which he entered these recognition flags of every boat in the Union's Mississippi Squadron. (3) A prewar Mississippi River sidewheeler, the Confederate gunboat *General Bragg* was sunk by the Union navy in 1862. Later it was raised, outfitted with this 32-pound pivot gun sketched by F. A. Castle, and reconverted into a Federal gunboat, still impudently bearing the Rebel name. (4) Alex Simplot sketched the metamorphosis of the ferryboat *New Era* into a light-draft gunboat in 1861. (5) To extricate his flotilla of ironclads and gunboats trapped in the shallows of the Red River, Admiral Porter had wing dams built at Alexandria, Louisiana, in May, 1864. This painting, by James Madison Alden, shows the steamer *Lexington* riding the crest of the broken dam, to be followed to safety by the other vessels.

5

1

2

Rebel Innovations

3

Inequality of numbers may be compensated by invulnerability," Confederate Secretary of the Navy Stephen Mallory pronounced in 1861. "Thus not only does economy, but naval success, dictate the wisdom and expediency of fighting with iron against wood, without regard to cost." The *Merrimac*, two months after her spectacular debut, had to be burned when the Rebels abandoned Norfolk; but until the end of the war the Confederates continued experimenting with ironclads, mines (called torpedoes), and even a submarine.

David Bushnell had introduced his one-man submarine, the *Turtle*, in the Revolution; later Robert Fulton had experimented with an underwater vessel. But when Horace L. Hunley loaded his frail, cigar-shaped iron boiler on a flatcar and brought it to Charleston in the summer of 1863, no submarine had ever sunk a ship in combat. After several disastrous trials in which over 20 men, including Hunley, perished, the submarine—appropriately named the *Hunley*—was ready to strike. Only a phosphorescent glow marked the silent underwater passage of the tiny vessel as it sliced through the waters of Charleston Harbor on the moonlit night of February 17, 1864. A terrific explosion sent the Union sloop *Housatonic* to the bottom, and with her the *Hunley* and her crew of nine. Submarine warfare was feasible.

(1) Conrad Chapman painted the tiny sub *Hunley*, docked at Charleston. (2) Eight men, operating hand cranks, propelled the *Hunley* at a speed of four miles an hour. Basing his drawing on rumor, a Union artist overpopulated the submarine and failed to link the drive shaft to the propeller. (3) The Rebel ram *Albemarle*, built in North Carolina, challenged the Union blockade until sunk by daredevil Lt. William B. Cushing.

187

1

The North's Amphibious Warfare

3

In order to make its audacious blockade effective, the North first had to gain toe holds along the 3,500-mile Confederate coast. In August, 1861, a small army-navy force secured a beachhead at Hatteras Inlet on the narrow sandspit protecting Pamlico Sound, then serving as a haven for blockade-runners. Not until the following February did the Union press its advantage with additional landings, to make the North Carolina coast safe, but in the meantime a 12,000 man amphibious force under Samuel F. Du Pont had stormed Port Royal, South Carolina, on November 7, 1861. Du Pont's warships loosed a barrage after which, a reporter noted, "the rising of the dust on shore in perpendicular columns looked as if we had suddenly raised . . . a grove of poplars." The best vessels the Rebels could bring against Du Pont were three river steamers, commanded by an officer of the old navy, who sadly dipped his pennants to his former messmates and scuttled for safety. On shore Confederate General Thomas F. Drayton, whose brother, Percival, commanded one of the attacking ships, bitterly watched the "magnificent armada" as it advanced "to vomit forth its iron hail, with all the spiteful energy of long-suppressed rage and conscious strength." Within four hours the enemy was shelled into submission. To the end of the war Port Royal remained a valuable Union coaling base, supply depot, and repair yard.

(1) Alfred Waud sketched Union troops landing at Hatteras Inlet. (2) Theodor Kaufmann made this pencil and water-color rendering of the Rebel capitulation at Hatteras. (3) This 1862 lithograph gives a bird's-eye view of Du Pont's Port Royal battle plan. Moving in circles, the vessels shelled, in turn, Forts Beauregard (right) and Walker (left).

189

CONFEDERATE MUSE

2

CONFEDERATE MUSEUM

Both as the birthplace of secession and as a strategic port, Charleston was an important objective of the Union blockading fleet. In the North, Admiral Du Pont's chief of staff wrote, "the desire was general to punish that city by all the rigors of war." On April 7, 1863, Du Pont sent eight ironclads into the harbor. As the flotilla advanced the guns of Fort Sumter boomed out: "Sublime, infernal, it seemed as if the fires of hell were turned upon the Union fleet," an eyewitness said. The *Keokuk* (*see* pages 182–83), "riddled like a colander," went down, and the harbor proved "a circle of fire not to be passed." That summer Du Pont was relieved by tough, ambitious Rear Admiral John A. Dahlgren.

On August 17 Dahlgren's ships began pounding Sumter into rubble; but when its last gun was destroyed, Confederate infantry replaced the weary artillery defenders. Fort Sumter endured, a proud Southerner wrote, having "at last tired out, and in this way silenced, the great guns that once had silenced it."

(1) Castle Pinckney is at right in Conrad Wise Chapman's view of Charleston. Seven scenes executed by the Southern artist in 1863–64 appear here and on the following two pages. (2) Battery Simkins is pictured during a heavy Union artillery barrage. (3) The Rebels' White Point Battery was on the Charleston Promenade. (4) Palmettos graced Battery Marion. (5) Battery Bee protected the main ship channel for blockade-runners. (6) Chapman painted the interior of Fort Sumter before Union artillery had turned it into "a shapeless pile of shattered walls and casements . . ."

OVERLEAF: The tattered flag of Sumter was a proud, defiant symbol of Southern independence. Not until February, 1865, was it hauled down.

1

2

Two More Gaps Are Closed

3

At 5:45 A.M. on August 5, 1864, with the wooden ships of his fleet lashed together in pairs, David Glasgow Farragut prepared to steam past the twin Confederate forts guarding the narrow entrance to Mobile Bay. Shot after shot crashed into the admiral's flagship *Hartford,* "mowing down the men, deluging the decks with blood, and scattering mangled fragments of humanity so thickly that it was difficult to stand on the deck . . ." When the lead vessel faltered, Farragut moved ahead, ignoring Rebel mines. By 8:35 the *Hartford* was well into the bay, and Farragut had breakfast served to the crew.

Then doughty Franklin Buchanan, first superintendent of Annapolis in the prewar navy, brought up his Rebel ironclad *Tennessee.* "I did not think old Buck was such a fool," Farragut said as he returned to the fight. With two other Federal vessels the *Hartford* began ramming the hapless *Tennessee* at five-minute intervals. When one of the Union ships got in his way, Farragut angrily asked if "For God's sake" could be transmitted by signal. If it could, thundered the admiral, "say to the *Lackawanna,* 'For God's sake get out of our way and anchor.' " At 10 A.M. the *Tennessee* surrendered. Mobile Bay was closed to the Confederacy.

(1) The last gap in the blockade was plugged on January 15, 1865, when an army-navy team took Fort Fisher, North Carolina, thus bottling up Wilmington, the South's principal port for blockade-runners. Frank Vizetelly painted the Rebel defenses. (2) The Union attack on Fort Fisher. (3) A Federal vessel firing on the Confederate ram *Tennessee* at Mobile Bay.

OVERLEAF: Farragut, who was lashed to the rigging during the Battle of Mobile Bay, here fearlessly watches the *Tennessee* brush past the *Hartford.*

The "Iona" and "Flora" anchored near the Spit Light.

Running the Blockade

"The blockade-runners are doing a great business," wrote the British consul at Charleston in 1862, "and no one seems to think there is the slightest risk . . ." Risks there were, but these were easily outweighed by the enormous rewards. It took only two successful trips to realize a profit above the initial investment in ship and cargo—exported cotton being exchanged in Europe for goods commanding swollen prices in the South. A net return of $150,000 each way was not uncommon. On a single voyage in 1861 one runner brought in 400 barrels of powder, 10,000 rifles, 1,000,000 cartridges, and 2,000,000 percussion caps. All the South's needs, it appeared, might be supplied by blockade-runners.

(1) The blockade-runners *Iona* and *Flora* are shown quietly anchored at Cork. Six of a series of 36 water colors by an unknown artist, depicting blockade-runners in the Irish port, are reproduced here for the first time.
(2) This sun-bleached skeleton off Charleston, South Carolina, served as a bleak warning of the risks that were inevitable in blockade-running.
(3) The *Lizzie*, built in Scotland.
(4) Ten days out from Wilmington, the *Gibraltar*, flying the British merchant flag, put into Cork on December 5, 1863. After a coaling stop she proceeded to Liverpool with her cargo.
(5) The *Flamingo*, en route from Glasgow, was at Cork in July, 1864.
(6) The *Mars*, her sails unfurled, left Cork for Nassau in November, 1863.
(7) The optimistically named *Alliance* left Ireland in September, 1863. The following April she was grounded and captured in the Savannah River.

OVERLEAF: St. George, Bermuda, enjoyed a wartime boom. Here and at Nassau cargoes from Europe were transferred to fleet blockade-runners for the final dash to Rebel ports.

A Pipeline to the South

2

3

Along the 3,500-mile Confederate coast line there were some 189 harbors or inlets in which the swift blockade-runner could find a haven. Painted the color of a Hatteras fog and burning smokeless anthracite coal, the long, low, converted side-wheeler could lose herself against a wooded shore line and wait for night-fall to make the final dash for a pro-tective harbor. If cornered, the cap-tain of a blockade-runner often ran his ship aground rather than surren-der. Thus at least some of his valu-able cargo might be salvaged.

An estimated 8,000 round trips were made by a fleet of 1,650 vessels; and 600,000 small arms were brought into the Confederacy. Yet, as the Northern blockade tightened, the Richmond government became in-creasingly irritated over the traffic in luxury goods. Finally, in February, 1864, the Confederate Congress passed a law requiring a permit for blockade-running and limiting im-ports to necessities. "No more wa-tered silks and satins; no more Yan-kee and European gewgaws; nothing but Confederate sackcloth!" lament-ed a Richmond newspaper. On Janu-ary 12, 1865, Lee telegraphed the commandant of Fort Fisher, guard-ing Wilmington: "If Fort Fisher falls, I shall have to evacuate Richmond." Three days later it surrendered. Blockade-running, like all its other hopes, at last failed the Confederacy.

(1) Many blockade-runners also served as commerce raiders, with commis-sions giving them a status one step above privateers. Here the *Nashville* burns a captured merchant vessel. (2) Rakish John N. Maffitt ran the raider *Florida* from the Gulf of Mex-ico to New York and back to the equator, capturing 55 merchant ships. (3) The Earl of Dunmore made this water color sketch of the *Nashville* running the blockade in April, 1862.

1

2

Commerce Raiders

Confederate commerce raiders carried the Civil War far beyond the continental U. S. Their instructions, one captain noted, were "brief and to the point, leaving much to the discretion, but more to the torch." The most notorious commerce destroyer was the English-built *Alabama,* commanded with ruthless dedication by Raphael Semmes.

On June 11, 1864, the *Alabama*—having destroyed 58 vessels valued at $6,547,000 during her two-year career—put into Cherbourg, France, for repairs. When the Federal sloop *Kearsarge* appeared three days later, Semmes challenged her to a duel. At 10:57 A.M. on June 19 the two ships, moving in concentric circles, began firing broadsides at each other. Although the vessels were equally classed as to size, speed, and armament, the unpracticed gunners of the *Alabama* were no match for Captain John A. Winslow's well-drilled Yankees. The raider's victories had been over unarmed merchantmen, and her crew had been denied practice ammunition. Of 370 shots fired by the *Alabama,* only 28 hit the mark, and these did little damage and wounded only three men. Shortly after noon, with 40 casualties on his sinking ship, Semmes hoisted the white flag, dropped his sword into the sea, and jumped overboard.

(1) In June, 1865, the famous raider *Shenandoah* was still destroying Yankee whalers in the Bering Sea, unaware that the war had ended in April. (2) Captain Winslow (third from left) posed with his officers on board the *Kearsarge* after sinking the *Alabama.* (3) Raphael Semmes was saved by an English yacht when the *Alabama* sank.

OVERLEAF: "Graceful even in her death," wrote a sailor on the *Alabama.* In Xanthus Smith's painting the *Kearsarge* stands off at a distance.

CONFEDERATE HIGH-WATER MARK

Toward the end of the summer of 1862 the mirage of final Southern independence looked briefly and dazzlingly like an imminent reality. In April the Confederacy had been on the defensive everywhere—New Orleans lost, McClellan approaching the gates of Richmond, Halleck coming in on Corinth as slowly and as irresistibly as a glacier, Missouri gone and the whole Mississippi Valley apparently about to follow it. But by August the Southern nation had gone on the offensive, and for a few weeks it looked as if the gates were about to open. Never before or afterward was the Confederacy so near to victory as it was in the middle of September, 1862.

There was a tremendous vitality to the Southern cause, and it was aided this summer by fumbling military leadership on the part of the North. For a time the Federals had no over-all military commander except for the President and the Secretary of War, who were men who knew exactly what they wanted but who did not quite know how to get it. Then, in July, Lincoln called General Halleck to Washington and made him general in chief of the Union armies.

On form, the choice looked good. The great successes had been won in Halleck's territory, the West, and as far as anyone in Washington could tell, he was fully entitled to take the credit. Except for continuing guerrilla activity, Kentucky and Missouri had been swept clear of armed Confederates, western Tennessee had been reclaimed, there was a Yankee army in Cumberland Gap, another one was approaching Chattanooga, and a third was sprawled out from Memphis to Corinth, preparing to slice down through Mississippi and touch hands with the Union occupation forces in Baton Rouge and New Orleans. If any Northern general was entitled to promotion, that general certainly appeared to be Halleck.

Halleck was a bookish sort of soldier, a headquarters operator who could handle all of the routine chores of military housekeeping with competence, but who somehow lacked the vital quality which such Confederates as Lee and Jackson possessed in abundance—the driving, restless spirit of war. The impulse to crowd a failing foe into a corner and compel submission simply was not in him, nor did he have the knack of evoking that spirit in his subordinates. His grasp of the theories of strategy was excellent, but at heart he was a shuffler of papers.

He came east to repair disaster. McClellan had been beaten in front of Richmond, and his army was in camp on the bank of the James River—still close enough to the Confederate capital, and still strong

Dead Rebel gunners and the debris of their battery at the Dunker Church, after bloody Antietam.

enough to resume the offensive on short notice, yet temporarily out of circulation for all that. (Like Halleck, McClellan was not especially aggressive.) In northern Virginia the Federal government had put together a new army, 50,000 men or thereabouts, troops who might have gone down to help McClellan in the spring, but who had been held back because of Jackson's game in the Shenandoah Valley. This army had been entrusted to one of Halleck's old subordinates, John Pope, who had taken Island Number Ten and New Madrid, and who seemed to have a good deal of energy and a desire to fight. Pope was moving down toward Richmond along the line of the Orange and Alexandria Railroad, and the general notion was that Robert E. Lee could not possibly fend off both Pope and McClellan.

The general notion was good enough, but Lee had accurately appraised the generals he was fighting. He suspected that McClellan would be inactive for some time to come, so while he held the bulk of his own army in the defensive lines around Richmond, he detached Stonewall Jackson with 25,000 men and sent him north to deal with Pope. (Pope was given to bluster and loud talk, and Lee held him in contempt: he told Jackson he wanted Pope "suppressed," as if the man were a brawling disturber of the peace rather than a general commanding an army of invasion.)

Arriving in Washington, Halleck could see that the Union military situation in Virginia was potentially dangerous. Pope and McClellan together outnumbered Lee substantially, but they were far apart, and communication between them was slow and imperfect. Lee was squarely between them, and unless both armies advanced resolutely he might easily concentrate on one, put it out of action, and then deal with the other at his leisure. Halleck went down to the James to see McClellan and find out if he could immediately move on Richmond.

This McClellan could not quite do. He needed reinforcements, material, time, and he had no confidence that Pope was going to do anything important anyway. Convinced that the Army of the Potomac would not advance, Halleck ordered it to leave the Peninsula and come back to Washington. It seemed to him that the sensible thing was to unite both armies and then resume the drive on the Confederate capital. Protesting bitterly, McClellan prepared to obey. But it would take a long time to get all of his troops back to the Washington area, and the move presented Lee with a free gift of time to attend to General Pope.

Of this gift Lee took immediate advantage.

It began on August 9, when Jackson advanced, met a detachment of Pope's army at Cedar Mountain, not far from Culpeper, and drove it in retreat after a sharp battle. This Confederate victory gained very little, since Pope's main body was not far away and Jackson soon had to withdraw, but it was a forecast of things to come. Concentrating his troops in front of Pope, and leaving only detachments to see McClellan off, Lee began a series of maneuvers which caused Pope to retreat to the north side of the upper Rappahannock River. Pope held the river crossings and, for the time at least, seemed quite secure. McClellan's troops were coming north, some of them marching west from Fredericksburg and others going by boat to Alexandria, across the Potomac from Washington; with Halleck's blessing, Pope proposed to stay where he was until these troops joined him. Then the Federal offensive could begin in earnest.

Lee could see as clearly as anyone that time was on the side of the Federals. If McClellan and Pope finally got together, their strength would be overwhelming; Lee's only hope was to beat Pope before this happened. With consummate skill he set about this task, although he was compelled to take some hair-raising risks in the process.

According to the military textbooks, no general should ever divide his forces in the presence of the enemy. This is a very sound rule in most cases, but it is a rule that was made to be broken now and then, and Lee was the man to break it. He was in the immediate presence of John Pope's army, with the shallow Rappahannock River between; and now he divided his army, sending half of it, under Stonewall Jackson, on a long hike to the northwest, and holding the remainder, with Major General James Longstreet in immediate command, to keep Pope occupied. Jackson swung off behind the Bull Run Mountains, came swiftly east through Thoroughfare Gap, and pounced suddenly on the Federal army's base of supplies at Manassas Junction, twenty miles or more in Pope's rear. Pope turned to attend to Jackson, and Lee and Longstreet then followed Jackson's route, to join him somewhere east of the Bull Run Mountains.

Seldom has a general been more completely confused than Pope was now. He had vast energy, and he set his troops to marching back and forth to surround and destroy Jackson, but he could not quite find where Jackson was. With his 25,000 men, Stonewall had left Manassas Junction before the Federals got there—destroying such Federal supplies as could not be carried away—and took position, concealed by woods and hills, on the old battlefield of Bull Run. Pope wore out his infantry and his cavalry looking for him, blundered into him at last, and gathered his men for a headlong assault. There was a hard, wearing fight on August 29, in which Jackson's men held their ground with great difficulty; on the morning of August 30 Pope believed he had won a great victory, and he sent word to Washington that the enemy was in retreat and that he was about to pursue.

No general ever tripped over his own words more ingloriously than Pope did. Unknown to him, Lee and Longstreet had regained contact with Jackson on the afternoon of August 29, and on August 30, when Pope was beginning what he considered his victorious pursuit, they struck him furiously in the flank while Jackson kept him busy in front. Pope's army was crushed, driven north of Bull Run in disorder, and by twilight of August 30 the Confederates had won a sensational victory. Pope had lost the field, his reputation, and about 15,000 men. The Confederate casualty list had been heavy, but in every other respect they had won decisively.

Lee had acted just in time. Some of McClellan's divisions had joined Pope and had taken part in the battle, and the rest of McClellan's army was not far off. Two or three days more would have made the Union force safe: the big point about Lee was that he was always mindful of the difference that two or three days might make.

By any standard, Lee's achievements this summer had been remarkable. He had taken command of the Army of Northern Virginia in June, almost in the suburbs of Richmond, badly outnumbered by an enemy which had thousands upon thousands of additional troops not far away. By the end of August he had whipped the army that faced him, had whipped the army that came to its relief, and had transferred the war from the neighborhood of Richmond to the neighborhood of Washington. (After the Bull Run defeat the Federals withdrew to the fortifications of Washington, leaving practically all of Virginia to the Confederates.) Now Lee was about to invade the North.

In the spring the Federal War Department had been so confident that it had closed the recruiting stations. Now Secretary Stanton was frantically appealing to the Northern governors for more troops, and President Lincoln—to the great joy of the soldiers—was reinstating McClellan in command of the Army of the Potomac, with which Pope's troops were incorporated.

Technically, McClellan had never actually been removed from that command. His army had simply been taken away from him, division by division, and when the Second Battle of Bull Run was fought, McClellan was in Alexandria, forwarding his men to Manassas but unable to go with them. After the battle, speedy reorganization was imperative, and Lincoln could see what Stanton and the Republican radicals could not see—that the only man who could do the job was McClellan. Such men as Stanton, Secretary of the Treasury Salmon P. Chase, and Senators Ben Wade and Zachariah Chandler believed that McClellan had sent his men forward slowly, hoping that Pope would be beaten; Lincoln had his own doubts, but he knew that the dispirited soldiers had full confidence in Mc-Clellan and that it was above all things necessary to get those soldiers back into a fighting mood. So Pope was relieved and sent off to Minnesota to fight the Indians, a task which was well within his capacities; and McClellan sorted out the broken fragments of what had been two separate armies, reconstituted the Army of the Potomac, manned the Washington fortifications, and early in September marched northwest from Washington with 95,000 men to find General Lee, who had taken the Army of Northern Virginia across the Potomac into western Maryland on September 5.

Lee seemed bent on getting into Pennsylvania. He had gone to Frederick, Maryland, forty miles from Washington, and then he went off on the old National Road in the direction of Hagerstown, vanishing from sight behind the long barrier of South Mountain, whose gaps he held with Jeb Stuart's cavalry. Following him, McClellan did not know where Lee was or what he was up to, and until he found out, he was in trouble: to lunge straight through the gaps with his massed force would be to risk letting Lee slip past him on either flank and seize Washington itself. A real advance was impossible until he had better information, the news that was coming out of western Maryland was confused, contradictory, and of no value to anyone . . . and if Lee was not quickly caught, fought, and driven below the Potomac, the Northern cause was lost forever.

It was not only in Maryland that the Federals were in trouble. In the western area, where everything had looked so prosperous, there had been a similar reversal of fortune. At the beginning of the summer a sweeping Federal triumph west of the Alleghenies looked inevitable; by mid-September the situation there looked almost as bad as it did in the East, one measure of the crisis being the fact that Cincinnati had called out the home guard lest the city be seized by invading Rebels.

Several things had gone wrong in the West, but the root of the trouble was General Halleck's fondness for making war by the book. The book said that in a war it was advisable to occupy enemy territory, and after the capture of Corinth, Halleck had set out to do that. He had had, in front of Corinth, well over 100,000 men, and with that army he could have gone anywhere in the South and beaten anything the Davis government could have sent against him. But instead of continuing with the offensive under circumstances which guaranteed victory, Halleck had split his army into detachments. Grant was given the task of holding Memphis and western Tennessee. Buell was sent eastward to occupy Chattanooga, rebuilding and protecting railway lines as he moved—a task that took so much of his time and energy that he never did get to Chattanooga. Other troops were sent to other duties, and by August the war had come to a standstill. Halleck was in Washington by now, and Grant and Buell were independent commanders.

The principal Confederate army in the West, the Army of Tennessee, was commanded now by General Braxton Bragg—a dour, pessimistic martinet of a man, who had an excellent grasp of strategy and a seemingly incurable habit of losing his grip on things in the moment of climax. (Beauregard, this army's former commander, had been relieved, the victim of ill-health and inability to get along with President Davis.) Bragg had his men, 30,000 strong, in Chattanooga; Major General Edmund Kirby Smith was in Knoxville with 20,000 more; and in August these generals moved northward in a campaign that anticipated nothing less than the reoccupation of western Tennessee and the conquest—or liberation, depending on the point of view—of all of Kentucky.

The small Union force at Cumberland Gap beat a hasty retreat all the way to the Ohio River. Buell, outmaneuvered, gave up railroad-building and turned to follow Bragg, who had slipped clear past him. Grant was obliged to send all the troops he could spare to join Buell; and to keep him additionally occupied, the Confederates brought troops from across the Mississippi and formed an army of between 20,000 and 25,000 men in northern Mississippi under Earl Van Dorn. By late September, Bragg had swept aside the hastily assembled levies with which the Federals tried to bar his path and was heading straight for the Ohio River, Buell marching desperately to overtake him, Kirby Smith near at hand. It looked very much as if Bragg's ambitious plan might succeed, and if Van Dorn could defeat or evade Grant and reach Kentucky too the Union situation in the West would be almost hopeless.

Never had military events better illustrated the folly of surrendering the initiative in war. In both the East and West the Federals had a strong advantage in numbers; but in each area an inability to make use of that advantage in a vigorous, unceasing offensive, and a desire to protect territory rather than to compel the enemy's army to fight, had caused the Federals to lose control of the situation. Now, in Maryland, in Kentucky, and in Tennessee, the North was fighting a defensive war, and the Confederates were calling the tune. (To use an analogy from football, the North had lost the ball and was deep in its own territory.)

This was the authentic high-water mark of the Confederacy. Never again was the South so near victory; never again did the South hold the initiative in every major theater of war. Overseas, the British were on the verge of granting outright recognition—which, as things stood then, would almost automatically have meant Southern independence. Cautious British statesmen would wait just a little longer, to see how this General Lee made out with his invasion of the North. If he made out well, recognition would come, and there would be a new member in the world's family of nations.

Then, within weeks, the tide began to ebb.

Preparing to move into Pennsylvania, Lee wanted to maintain some sort of line of communications with Virginia. At Harpers Ferry the Federals had a garrison of 12,000 men, and these soldiers were almost on Lee's communications. It seemed to the Confederate commander that it would be well to capture Harpers Ferry and its garrison before he went on into the Northern heartland. He knew that McClellan was very cautious and deliberate, and he believed the man would be even more so now because he had to reorganize his army. So it looked as if the Army of Northern Virginia could safely pause to sweep up Harpers Ferry: with the South Mountain gaps held, McClellan could be kept in the dark until it was too late for him to do anything about it.

So Lee once more divided his army. The advance, under Longstreet, was at Hagerstown, Maryland, not far from the Pennsylvania border. One division, under Major General D. H. Hill, was sent back to Turner's Gap in South Mountain, to make certain that no inquisitive Federals got through. The rest, split into three wings but all under the general control of Jackson, went down to surround and capture Harpers Ferry.

Now sheer, unadulterated chance took a hand, and changed the course of American history.

Some Confederate officer lost a copy of the orders which prescribed all of these movements. Two Union enlisted men found the order, and it got to McClellan's headquarters, where there was an officer who could identify the handwriting of Lee's assistant adjutant general and so convince McClellan that the thing was genuine. Now McClellan had the game in his hands: Lee's army was split into separate fragments, and McClellan was closer to the fragments than they were to each other. If he moved fast, McClellan could destroy the Army of Northern Virginia.

McClellan moved, although not quite fast enough. He broke through the gap in South Mountain, compelling Lee to concentrate his scattered forces. Lee ordered his troops to assemble at Sharpsburg, on Antietam Creek, near the Potomac. At that point Jackson, who had had just time to capture Harpers Ferry, rejoined him; and there, on September 17, McClellan and Lee fought the great Battle of Antietam.

Tactically, the battle was a draw. The Federals attacked savagely all day long, forcing the Confederates to give ground but never quite compelling the army to retreat, and when Lee's battered army held its position next day, McClellan did not renew the attack. But on the night of September 18 Lee took his worn-out army back to Virginia. Strategically, the battle had been a Northern victory of surpassing importance. The Southern campaign of invasion had failed. The Federals had regained the initiative. Europe's statesmen, watching, relaxed: the time to extend recognition had not arrived, after all.

Antietam was not only strategically decisive: it has the melancholy distinction of having seen the bloodiest single day's fighting in the entire Civil War. The Union army lost over 12,000 men, and the Confederate loss was nearly as great. Never before or after in all the war were so many men shot on one day.

In the West, too, the Confederate offensive collapsed. Until he actually arrived in Kentucky, Bragg had handled his campaign with vast skill. Now, however, he became irresolute, and his grasp of strategic principles weakened. It had been supposed that the people of Kentucky, crushed under the heel of Northern despots, would rise in welcome once they were liberated by Confederate armies, and whole wagon-loads of weapons were carried along by the Confederates to arm the new recruits. The anticipated welcome did not develop, however, recruits were very few in number, and Bragg's swift drive became slower. He lost time by going to Frankfort to see that a secessionist state government was formally installed—it would fall apart, once his troops left—and Buell was just able to get his own army between Bragg's Confederates and the Ohio River.

Buell managed to bring Bragg to battle at Perryville, Kentucky, on October 8. Only parts of the two armies were engaged, and the fight was pretty much a standoff; but afterward the mercurial Bragg concluded, for some reason, that his whole campaign had been a failure, and he and Kirby Smith drew off into eastern Tennessee. Buell pursued with such lack of spirit that the administration removed him and put William S. Rosecrans in his place, and Rosecrans got his army into camp just below Nashville, Tennessee, and awaited further developments. Meanwhile, in northern Mississippi, a part of Grant's army, then led by Rosecrans, had beaten a detachment from Van Dorn's at Iuka on September 19 and 20, and early in October defeated the entire force in a hard-fought engagement at Corinth. Van Dorn retreated toward central Mississippi, and Grant began to make plans for a campaign against Vicksburg.

So by the middle of October the situation had changed once more. The one great, co-ordinated counteroffensive which the Confederacy was ever able to mount had been beaten back. In the East the Federals would begin a new campaign aimed at Richmond; in the West they would resume the advance on Chattanooga and would continue with the drive to open the whole Mississippi Valley. They would have many troubles with all of these campaigns, but they had at least got away from the defensive. The danger of immediate and final Northern defeat was gone.

Lincoln Summons New Commanders

Major General Henry Halleck

Major General John Pope

With McClellan beaten on the Peninsula, the President shuffled his command, appointing Henry Halleck general in chief and making John Pope head of the new Army of Virginia. That these two were no match for Lee and Jackson was soon painfully evident. Pope issued a pompous address to his troops and headed south toward Gordonsville, whereupon Jackson fought his advance units under Nathaniel Banks at Cedar Mountain. Pope withdrew north of the Rappahannock to await reinforcements from McClellan, but Lee, who had no intention of allowing a junction of the Union armies, planned a surprise for John Pope.

On August 9 Banks hit Jackson's left flank at Cedar Mountain, drawn above by Edwin Forbes. A. P. Hill's arrival and a counterattack by the Stonewall Brigade routed Banks, inflicting casualties of 30 per cent.

As Pope withdrew northeast to the Rappahannock after the Cedar Mountain repulse, his army was followed by Virginia Negroes fleeing from slavery. Below, a pathetic refugee family crosses the river into the Northern lines.

Dejected Yankees survey boxcars burned to their trucks by Jackson in his raid on Pope's base at Manassas Junction.

The Confederates Bait the Trap

Lee's first move sent Jeb Stuart to tear things up in the Federal rear. Stuart had lost his favorite plumed hat in a skirmish a few days before and intended "to make the Yankees pay for that hat." He raided Pope's headquarters (the general was out), seized $350,000 in cash, Pope's dress coat, and his dispatch book, which gave the disposition of Federal forces.

Armed with this information, Lee took the offensive.

Jackson swung far to the left, his "foot cavalry" marching 62 miles in 48 hours, and fell upon the Union supply depot at Manassas Junction. After cutting Pope's lifeline, the Orange and Alexandria Railroad, Jackson's men took the depot apart. "To see a starving man eating lob-

ster-salad and drinking Rhine wine, bare-footed and in tatters, was curious," a Rebel lieutenant wrote.

Pope spun about to find his tormentor, crowing, "We shall bag the whole crowd," but Jackson's 25,000 troops were digging in on the old Bull Run battlefield, and Lee and James Longstreet were moving to close the door on Pope.

Edwin Forbes sketched Pope's men plodding through drenching rain on August 28 in pursuit of the elusive Jackson.

SECOND BULL RUN
CAMPAIGN

*Evening, August 28 —
Dawn, August 29, 1862*

CAMPAIGN OF SECOND BULL RUN: After pillaging Pope's stores at Manassas Junction (1) on August 26, Jackson moves toward Centreville (2), pursued by Heintzelman and Reno (3). Jackson slips away and digs in (4) near Grove- ton on August 28. That evening he attacks King (5), revealing his position. Sigel (6) countermarches, followed by Porter (7). As the various Federal columns converge on Groveton, Longstreet (8) advances to join Jackson.

Second Bull Run: The First Day

Stonewall Jackson selected his position with care—an unfinished railroad embankment north of the Warrenton Turnpike, convenient to Thoroughfare Gap, through which Longstreet was expected. He had been there some five hours when Rufus King's unsuspecting Union column appeared on the turnpike, marching east to join Pope. Deciding it was time to let Pope sniff the bait, Jackson attacked. The Battle of Groveton, a vicious stand-up fight in the deepening twilight, ended in a draw. It was the baptism of fire for John Gibbon's Iron Brigade, one-third of whose men were shot.

The next day, August 29, Pope had 62,000 troops at Groveton, but wasted this strength in a series of un-co-ordinated assaults which Jackson fought off. The Federals came closest against the Confederate left, where Phil Kearny led the attack. "Kearny was pitiless," wrote a Confederate who saw Maxcy Gregg's South Carolinians pushed back step by step, their ammunition running low. Gregg prepared to hold his position with the bayonet; then Rebel reinforcements arrived, and Kearny pulled back.

Undetected, Longstreet's 30,000 men forced lightly guarded Thoroughfare Gap and took position squarely on the Union left flank, but Old Pete fussed cautiously with placement and alignment and took no part in the day's fighting. Fitz-John Porter had been ordered to hit Jackson's right, but demurred when he discovered that to do so he would have to march directly across the front of a very large number of Rebel troops—the first inkling that Longstreet had arrived. Pope refused to believe him, and Porter was later made the scapegoat of defeat and cashiered from the army.

The Rebels had not been budged, and the pious Jackson remarked that the day had been won "by nothing but the blessing and protection of Providence." As for Pope, he was convinced that the enemy was retreating. He seems to have ignored all reports of Longstreet's presence.

218

Forbes' panoramic view of the Bull Run battlefield looks west from Bald Hill. Fig. 1 is Thoroughfare Gap; Fig. 2, the Confederate lines; the
Stone House (4) was used as a Union hospital.

The Dogan House in Groveton (above) was the
scene of heavy fighting during the two-day battle. At left, the railroad embankment, where Jackson's defensive line was posted, as it looks today.

219

Major General James Longstreet

Second Bull Run: The Second Day

Not until 2 P.M. on August 30 was Pope ready to launch his "pursuit." The long wait was impatiently endured by the Confederate high command, which wanted very badly to be attacked. Finally it came, a massive effort on a two-mile front. Jackson's line was stretched to the breaking point, his men hurling rocks at the attackers when their ammunition ran out. Longstreet waited until Pope committed his reserves, then went into action. A terrific artillery barrage halted the Federals; then, screaming the Rebel yell "like demons emerging from the earth," Longstreet's five divisions rolled forward to crush the Federal left flank.

John Bell Hood's Texans spearheaded Longstreet's attack on the Union flank. In Forbes' sketch below they surge out of the woods in late afternoon, overwhelming two New York regiments in their path.

Today only the foundation remains of the spacious Chinn House, which stood in the way of Longstreet's divisions.

SECOND BULL RUN

Second Day: August 30, 1862

JACKSON'S HQ

N

GROVETON — SUDLEY ROAD

SUDLEY CHURCH

UNFINISHED RAILROAD

①

⑥

MANASSAS — SUDLEY ROAD

MATTHEWS HILL

MATTHEWS HOUSE

Groveton

③

WARRENTON TURNPIKE

POPE'S HQ

STONE HOUSE

YOUNG'S BRANCH

②

ROBINSON HOUSE

HENRY HOUSE HILL

TO CENTREVIL

HENRY HOUSE

STC BRI

⑤

④

BALD HILL

CHINN HOUSE

BULL RUN

David Greenspan

SECOND BULL RUN (or Manassas): Pope begins the second day's action with an assault (1) on Jackson. Then Longstreet's artillery (2) stuns the Union left, followed by a flank attack (3 and 4) which captures Bald Hill. As the Federals form a new defensive line (5) on the Henry House Hill, Jackson strikes their right wing (6). This patchwork line holds long enough for the rest of the Federal army to escape via the Stone Bridge to Centreville.

Final Defeat at Bull Run

*In Alfred Waud's pencil sketch a Union battery,
firing canister at point-blank range, tries to check
the charge against the Union left wing while a
mounted officer attempts to rally his fleeing men.*

A thin line of Federals resisted Longstreet's onslaught, fighting desperately to give Pope time to bring up reinforcements. And they succeeded, at terrible cost: one New York Zouave regiment had 124 of 490 men killed, the highest percentage of deaths in a Federal regiment in any Civil War battle. A Virginia private described a wild melee around a Union battery: "There was a frenzied struggle in the semi-darkness around the guns, so violent and tempestuous, so mad and brain-reeling that to recall it is like fixing the memory of a horrible, blood-curdling dream. Everyone was wild with uncontrollable delirium."

As Pope tried to stem the tide on the left Jackson hit him on the right, bending the whole Union line into a horseshoe. A handful of Yankees under John Gibbon managed a gallant stand on the Henry House Hill, allowing the rest of the army to escape across Bull Run to Centreville, and as dusk fell Phil Kearny rode up to Gibbon, furious at the rout: "Reno . . . is not stampeded. I am not stampeded. You are not stampeded. That is about all, sir, my God, that's about all!"

Lee kept up the pressure, attacking the next day at Chantilly and killing the brilliant Kearny, whom Winfield Scott had once called "the bravest man I ever saw . . . a perfect soldier."

The Federals had suffered about 15,000 casualties, the Rebels, 9,000, and a Northern corps historian summed it up: John Pope "had been kicked, cuffed, hustled about, knocked down, run over, and trodden upon as rarely happens in the history of war." Pope pulled back to Washington and was fired, and McClellan got his badly used army back.

Lee's Army
Invades the North
for the
First Time

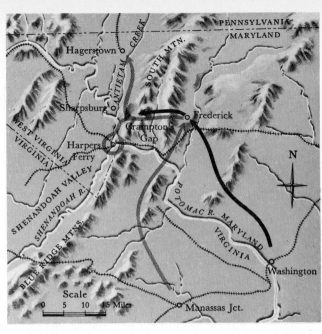

The Army of Northern Virginia headed north into Maryland early in September. Alfred Waud's sketch (below) shows Federal pickets observing Lee's crossing of the Potomac River on a bright moonlit night.

Lee's invasion (gray lines), screened by Stuart's cavalry, led to Frederick, then behind South Mountain, where he divided his forces to take Harpers Ferry. McClellan's pursuit is indicated in black.

Artist Waud, "detained within the enemy lines," made this pencil drawing of the 1st Virginia Cavalry. "Their carbines," he noted, "were mostly captured from our own cavalry, for whom they expressed utter contempt."

If George McClellan had his faults as a field commander, he nevertheless had two qualities the North very badly needed after Second Bull Run. He was an able organizer, and he had the unquestioning loyalty of the Federal foot soldier. When the word came that he had replaced Pope, one soldier recalled "such a hurrah as the Army . . . had never heard before . . . The effect of this man's presence upon the Army of the Potomac—in sunshine or rain, in darkness or in daylight, in victory or defeat—was electrical." McClellan, always aware of the hand of destiny, wrote his wife: "Again I have been called upon to save the country."

It was Robert E. Lee's hope that an advance into Maryland would encourage foreign intervention, and perhaps bring that border state into the Confederacy. His men were fresh from an overwhelming victory, his enemy, he thought, demoralized. "We cannot afford to be idle," he wrote President Davis, "and though weaker than our opponents . . . must endeavor to harass them if we cannot destroy them." And so he led 50,000 tough fighting men, the very cream of his army, across the Potomac into Maryland. An eyewitness watched the Army of Northern Virginia march by: "They were the dirtiest men I ever saw, a most ragged, lean, and hungry set of wolves. . . . Yet there was a dash about them that the northern men lacked. . . . They were profane beyond belief and talked incessantly," he observed.

The first blow to Lee was his cool reception in Maryland, where so many ardent secessionists were supposedly waiting to rise. Possibly that ardor dimmed with the sight of the hungry Rebel soldiers, many of whom were also barefoot. The second blow was nearly catastrophic, for a copy of Lee's orders was lost and picked up by Yankee soldiers. McClellan had been following blindly, but now he knew the exact positions of Lee's divided army. Here was a dazzling opportunity, and McClellan jubilantly waved the lost orders before the eyes of General Gibbon, exclaiming, "Here is a paper with which, if I cannot whip Bobby Lee, I will be willing to go home."

225

Harpers Ferry (above, painted by William McLeod) was doomed when the Rebels seized commanding Maryland Heights (foreground). The Potomac is at right, the Shenandoah River at left.

In the lithograph at left two Ohio regiments capture a stone and rail fence at Turner's Gap on South Mountain. Lt. Col. Rutherford B. Hayes (left, above wagons) was a Union casualty.

Jackson's spoils from Harpers Ferry included 13,000 small arms and 73 cannon. In 1861 the Confederates had blown the railroad bridge (right) and removed the machinery from the arsenal there.

226

The Prelude
to Antietam

Lee's apparent object was the vital Northern rail center of Harrisburg, Pennsylvania. Once there, circumstances and the position of the Army of the Potomac would dictate his next move. Threatening his supply line, however, was the 12,000-man garrison at Harpers Ferry. He sent Jackson and half the army to attend to that; the other half was to concentrate in the vicinity of Hagerstown, Maryland, twenty miles to the north. Only Stuart's cavalry and D. H. Hill's division were left on McClellan's front. Although Lee's lost Order No. 191 revealed most of this to McClellan, the Confederate general, thanks to the ubiquitous Stuart, knew within 24 hours that McClellan had it. Immediately he began to pull together his scattered army. Meantime, McClellan, who wired Lincoln that "Lee has made a gross mistake," sat and mulled things over for sixteen mortal hours. He seems to have been haunted by intelligence reports of a Rebel army of 120,000, well over twice its actual strength. On September 14, when he tried to force South Mountain at Crampton's and Turner's gaps, D. H. Hill, with a last-minute assist from Longstreet, fought stubbornly to buy Lee another precious day. On the fifteenth Jackson gobbled up the Harpers Ferry garrison and moved to join Lee, who was then just north of the Potomac at the little hamlet of Sharpsburg, seventeen miles from Harpers Ferry. Although all his fine plans had gone awry, Lee nevertheless intended to turn and fight.

227

Calm Before the Storm

Federal gunnery at Antietam was particularly effective, due in part to artillery spotters like those above, whose signal tower on Elk Mountain had a commanding view of Rebel positions.

Lee's 18,000 troops arrived in Sharpsburg on September 15 and took position—not a particularly strong one—on a ridge overlooking Antietam Creek. At their backs was the Potomac, with only one usable ford. Later that day McClellan's host, some 87,000 men, began appearing on the opposite side of the Antietam. McClellan's reports to Washington were enthusiastic, and Lincoln wired him, "God bless you and all with you. Destroy the rebel army if possible."

On the sixteenth McClellan labored over his plans, wanting everything to be just right. By nightfall Lee's force was doubled by Jackson's arrival, and A. P. Hill's division, still at Harpers Ferry, was ordered up on the double. Looking over at the massed Federals, Longstreet admitted that it was "an awe-inspiring sight."

McClellan's battle plan was a perfectly good one: three full army corps would smash the Confederate left flank; a fourth would keep Lee busy by attacking his right, aiming for Sharpsburg and the Potomac crossing. A reserve in the center would pitch in as the Rebel left was rolled up. September 17, 1862, dawned foggy and gray, and the very existence of the Army of Northern Virginia seemed to hang in the balance.

The Bloody Struggle

for Farmer Miller's

Cornfield

Lee's left, under Jackson, straddled the Hagerstown Turnpike and ran from one patch of woods through a farmer's field into another patch of woods. History has given these commonplace features names etched in blood—the West Wood, the Cornfield, the East Wood.

With the first light of dawn "Fighting Joe" Hooker's I Corps came bowling down the turnpike against this line, and the Cornfield became a 40-acre holocaust, with rifle and artillery fire slashing the ripe corn, knocking men down in rows. Hooker's men were driving toward key ground around a whitewashed Dunker Church when a savage counterattack by John B. Hood's Texas Brigade —furious because its first hot meal in days had been interrupted—sent them reeling back through the Cornfield. Its fire, wrote a survivor, was "like a scythe running through our line." The Federals rallied in the Miller barnyard, by a six-gun battery which tore the charging Texans apart with double-shotted canister at a range of twenty yards. White-haired old General Mansfield sent his corps through the East Wood and it recaptured the Cornfield, but Mansfield was killed, and there was a terrific fight at the rail fence along the turnpike. A Federal spearhead managed to seize part of the area around the Dunker Church; but it was stranded there, with no reinforcements at hand.

The Rebel left still held by a thread as both sides paused to reckon the carnage. Hood said that his division was "Dead on the field." The 2nd Wisconsin counted only nineteen men present for duty.

At left is the infamous Cornfield as it looks now; the East Wood is in the background. Hooker noted: "every stalk . . . was cut as closely as could have been done with a knife."

Above is Alexander Gardner's photograph of Southern dead by the fence bordering the Cornfield.

Major General Joseph Hooker

Major General Joseph K. F. Mansfield

The Yankee Attack Falls Apart

Major General Edwin V. Sumner

A fatal flaw in McClellan's grand scheme was now becoming apparent: the high command was having a bad day even for the Army of the Potomac. The trouble began with McClellan's orders, which were both vague and late, with the result that his commanders had not had time to reconnoiter the terrain. Then Mansfield was killed and Hooker shot in the foot. Edwin Sumner's II Corps was held back too long to support the main assault on the Confederate left, and when it did arrive it was in the wrong place. The leading division of 5,000 men marched in close order straight into the fire of Jeb Stuart's horse artillery, which plagued the Federals all morning, and then into a murderous cross fire. No Federal attacks had gotten under way elsewhere on the field, and Lee was able to hit Sumner's men with a varied collection of troops under Lafayette McLaws, John Walker, and Jubal Early. It was a slaughter, and when Sumner shouted, "My God, we must get out of here," his men fled. Nearly half of the division had been shot.

In the print above, after a painting by James Hope of the 2nd Vermont, Sumner's troops move toward the Dunker Church and the West Wood (left). Stephen D. Lee's Rebel battery (foreground) contests the advance.

A portion of the West Wood (below) still remains, part of the Antietam battlefield park. The Confederate left flank was anchored in this area, making it the target for Federal attacks early in the battle.

ANTIETAM

September 17, 1862

TO POTOMAC RIVER

LEE'S HQ

TO HARPERS FERRY

Sharpsburg

8

ANTIETAM CREEK

6

BURNSIDE'S
BRIDGE

7

David Greenspan

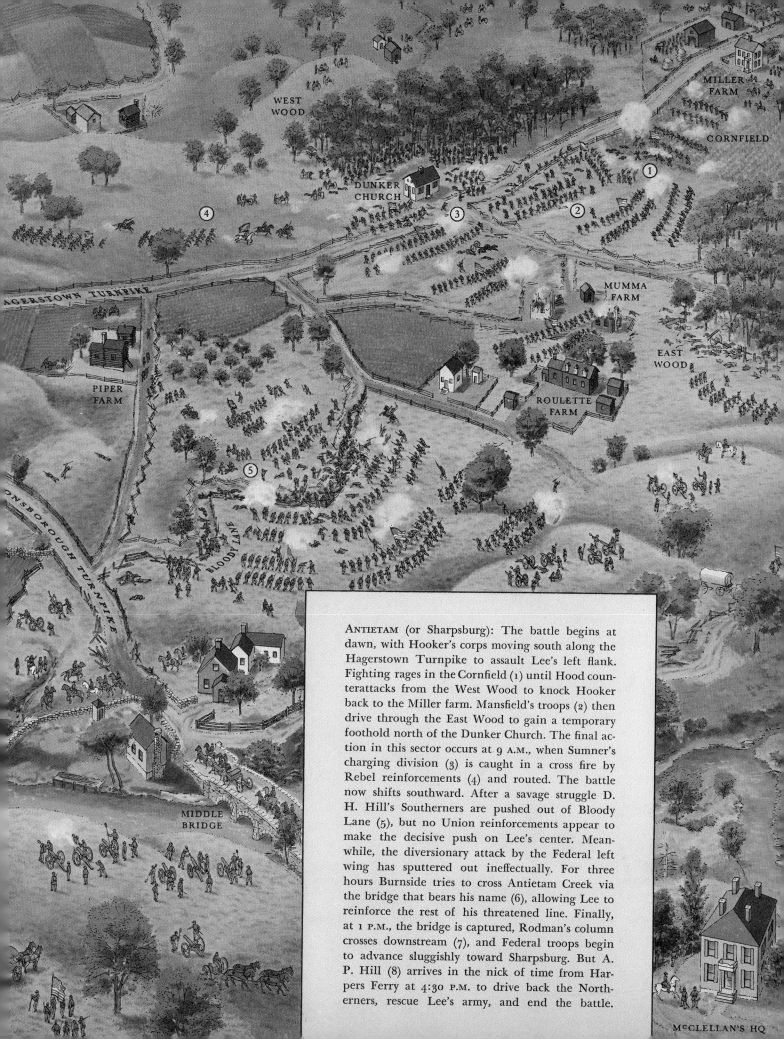

WEST
WOOD

MILLER
FARM

CORNFIELD

① ② ③ ④

DUNKER
CHURCH

MUMMA
FARM

HAGERSTOWN TURNPIKE

EAST
WOOD

PIPER
FARM

ROULETTE
FARM

⑤

BLOODY LANE

ONSBOROUGH TURNPIKE

MIDDLE
BRIDGE

ANTIETAM (or Sharpsburg): The battle begins at
dawn, with Hooker's corps moving south along the
Hagerstown Turnpike to assault Lee's left flank.
Fighting rages in the Cornfield (1) until Hood counterattacks from the West Wood to knock Hooker
back to the Miller farm. Mansfield's troops (2) then
drive through the East Wood to gain a temporary
foothold north of the Dunker Church. The final action in this sector occurs at 9 A.M., when Sumner's
charging division (3) is caught in a cross fire by
Rebel reinforcements (4) and routed. The battle
now shifts southward. After a savage struggle D.
H. Hill's Southerners are pushed out of Bloody
Lane (5), but no Union reinforcements appear to
make the decisive push on Lee's center. Meanwhile, the diversionary attack by the Federal left
wing has sputtered out ineffectually. For three
hours Burnside tries to cross Antietam Creek via
the bridge that bears his name (6), allowing Lee to
reinforce the rest of his threatened line. Finally,
at 1 P.M., the bridge is captured, Rodman's column
crosses downstream (7), and Federal troops begin
to advance sluggishly toward Sharpsburg. But A.
P. Hill (8) arrives in the nick of time from Harpers Ferry at 4:30 P.M. to drive back the Northerners, rescue Lee's army, and end the battle.

McCLELLAN'S HQ

Bloody Lane today (facing page) shows little sign of the bitter struggle that raged there. The view is east, toward the battlefield observation tower. Above, the 7th Maine crosses the human wreckage in Bloody Lane, only to be held off by a last-ditch Confederate line. The road at the right leads to Sharpsburg.

McClellan Assaults the Rebel Center

Major General D. H. Hill

A s the firing died down around the Dunker Church the focus of action shifted to the Confederate center. This second phase of the Battle of Antietam began by accident. Sumner's misdirected second and third divisions slanted off to the left, advancing through the Mumma and Roulette farmyards. (A Rebel shell smashed Mr. Roulette's beehives, and the angry bees took a heavy toll of the 132nd Pennsylvania.) As the Yankees came under the fire of D. H. Hill's men, posted in an eroded farm lane, they charged. A Southerner remembered the scene: "With flags flying and the long unfaltering lines rising and falling as they crossed the rolling fields, it looked as though nothing could stop them." But Hill's fast-firing soldiers did just that.

General Israel Richardson then sent his division in, spearheaded by the rugged Irish Brigade, and Richardson was mortally wounded in the furious fighting. Rebel guns came under withering counterfire, and in desperation Longstreet and his staff manned two of the pieces.

Suddenly a Southern brigade, misunderstanding an order, withdrew from part of the sunken road—remembered, simply, as Bloody Lane—and the Federals seized it, to pour a dreadful enfilading fire into the remaining defenders. They finally fled, but the Union troops were too spent to exploit the opening. Lee's center was gone, and he had nothing with which to patch it. But McClellan, with an entire army corps in reserve, muffed his chance.

Major General Israel Richardson

237

Antietam Creek, placid and shimmering, photographed at a point near Burnside's Bridge.

Ambrose Burnside and His Bridge

Above, Edwin Forbes' sketch of the capture of Burnside's Bridge. The Union troops fanned out to capture the heights in the background. Below, the bridge as it appears now, seen from the Rebel positions.

Along the banks of Antietam Creek, southeast of Sharpsburg, a day-long series of Federal blunders reached a tragic climax. Ambrose Burnside was to have assaulted Lee's right flank while Hooker hit the left, but somehow Burnside could not get this notion through his head. Shallow Antietam Creek, which he had to cross, could be waded in most places, but General Burnside was mesmerized by a stone bridge directly in his front.

Early in the day McClellan was pleading with Burnside to attack, but each time he tried to storm the narrow bridge his men were thrown back with severe loss. This went on all morning, and Lee was able to pull men out of this line to defend his hard-pressed left and center. At last, early in the afternoon, Burnside's troops took the bridge in one quick thrust. One of his divisions, under Isaac Rodman, forded the creek farther south.

Robert Toombs, commanding a few thin regiments of Georgia troops, found himself facing four full Union divisions, some 12,000 men. Still Burnside did not mount his attack, despite McClellan's demands to "advance . . . at all hazards and at any cost." It was not until 3 P.M. that his men had their ammunition replenished and began to roll forward. It was slow, hard work, for the Confederates fell back stubbornly, making a stand behind every fence and stone wall. Lee had no reserves for a counterattack, and the Yankee battle flags moved gradually nearer to Sharpsburg. Viewed from Northern headquarters, it "was one of the most brilliant and exciting exhibitions of the day," as the proud Army of Northern Virginia teetered on the brink of total defeat.

A. P. Hill was a tower of strength to Lee and Jackson; his name was on both men's lips as they died.

A. P. Hill Rescues Lee

About the time the Battle of Antietam was getting under way, Ambrose Powell Hill, at Harpers Ferry, received Lee's order to get his crack Light Division to Sharpsburg without delay. A. P. Hill was an impetuous, driving fighter, and within an hour he had his men on the march. They had seventeen hot, dusty miles to go, and Hill pushed them hard; nearly half the 5,000 men fell by the wayside exhausted. But the rest reached the battlefield at precisely the moment when they were needed most.

Hill had on his red battle shirt that day, and without hesitation he sent his tired soldiers crashing into the exposed left flank of the Federals advancing on Sharpsburg. The Yankees were further confused by the fact that many of Hill's men wore blue uniforms captured at Harpers Ferry, and the whole Union left wing was knocked back to the heights along Antietam Creek.

The battle and the long day were over. A Confederate soldier remembered that "The sun seemed almost to go backwards, and it appeared as if night would never come." About 23,500 men had fallen, and the blasted landscape around Sharpsburg smoldered and smoked, filled with the pitiful cries of thousands of wounded men.

The Northern troops had fought fully as gallantly as their Southern counterparts, but their generals had failed badly. McClellan, with 25,000 fresh troops in reserve, could not bring himself to make one final all-out attack. As one of his veterans wrote after the war, he "never realized the metal that was in his grand Army of the Potomac." Audaciously, Lee held his battered lines the next day, inviting an attack that never came, and on the night of September 18 withdrew across the Potomac, his invasion at an end.

In Forbes' drawing the 9th New York Zouaves force the withdrawal of Rebel batteries toward Sharpsburg about 3:30 P.M., shortly before A. P. Hill's flank attack.

241

Buell's troops cross the flooded Big Barren River near Bowling Green, Kentucky, in pursuit of Bragg's Confederates.

The Confederate Invasion in the West

In the West, too, the Confederates were driving northward in the late summer of 1862. Braxton Bragg, planning "rapid movements and vigorous blows," had as his goal the key border state of Kentucky, and came a good deal closer to realizing his objective than Lee did in the East.

Surveying the scattered Union forces in his theater, Bragg sent Kirby Smith bucketing northward from Knoxville in the middle of August. By the end of the month Smith had 12,000 troops in Lexington, Kentucky, and controlled the central part of the state. Bragg then moved out of Chattanooga with the main Rebel army to join him.

The Union commander in Tennessee, Don Carlos Buell, discovered ruefully that his opponent had side-stepped right around him, and his hasty pursuit was too late to save a 4,200-man Union garrison at Munfordville, which surrendered on September 17—the day of Antietam.

At this point the Confederate invasion began to lose headway. Bragg was north of Buell, astride the latter's supply line to Louisville. He was outnumbered, however, because he and Smith failed to join forces. Bragg had to give up his advantageous position and swing east toward Lexington, leaving the Federals a clear path to Louisville.

As Lee had discovered in Maryland, the border states were unenthusiastic about being liberated. Smith said, "The Kentuckians are slow and backward in rallying to our standard. Their hearts are evidently with us, but their blue-grass and fat cattle are against us."

As the armies tramped across Kentucky two hard fights had occurred at Iuka and Corinth in northeastern Mississippi. A Confederate striking force, intended to keep U. S. Grant tied down and then to give Bragg a hand in Kentucky, failed in its objective. Grant and William S. Rosecrans were able to blunt the attack and still send troops to Buell's aid.

Major General Don Carlos Buell   *Major General Edmund Kirby Smith*

Union soldiers guarding the Green River crossing at Munfordville repulsed Bragg's advance guard, as sketched below by Leslie's *artist Henri Lovie. However, Bragg countered by surrounding and taking the post.*

These two unique paintings of the Battle of Perryville are from the William Travis Civil War panorama. In the scene above, a Federal counterattack is made to regain a farm lot on the Union left. Below, a Yankee

The Standoff Battle of Perryville

officer rallies his men, as reinforcements move up to meet the assault of Benjamin Cheatham's Rebel division.

The Battle of Perryville, on October 8, 1862, was a curious anticlimax to Bragg's invasion of Kentucky. Neither commanding general intended to fight there, and neither exerted forceful control when the armies blundered into each other. In fact, Buell was not even aware that a fight was going on until it was almost over.

Buell had moved eastward from Louisville, intending to catch Bragg before he could join up with Kirby Smith. The leading Federal column, under a new brigadier named Philip Sheridan, got into a skirmish with Rebels at Doctor's Creek near Perryville on October 8. Kentucky was then in the grip of a persistent drought, both armies were thirsty, and Sheridan's boys had a tough time winning water rights to the creek.

Later that day Bragg, unaware that he was outnumbered three to one, punched hard at the Union left. The divisions of Benjamin Cheatham and Simon Buckner had a brief initial success, but finally the situation was stabilized, thanks largely to Sheridan, who was proving himself to be a good fighting man. Half of Buell's army took no part in the battle.

Neither side could claim much from this inept action, but Bragg, concluding gloomily that he had done all he could in Kentucky, withdrew. Buell let him go unmolested, much to the ire of the War Department, which replaced him with William Rosecrans. Before the month was out, both armies were back in Tennessee.

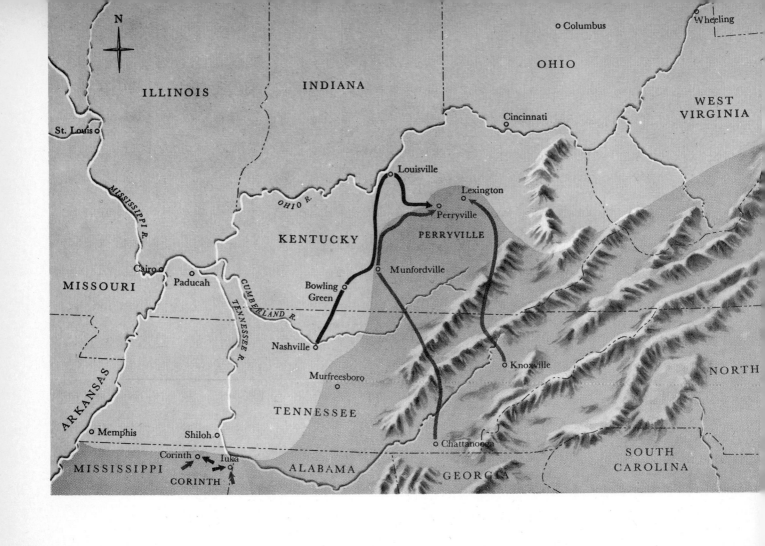

Aftermath of the South's Two Invasions

The gray arrows on the map indicate the Rebel invasion routes in the East and West in the fall of 1862; the Union pursuit is in black. The high tide of the Confederacy is shown in the portion shaded gray. In Alexander Gardner's photograph, Lincoln inspects the headquarters of the Army of the Potomac on October 1. General McClellan is the short man (sixth from left). A month later the President removed him from command.

In purely military terms the battles of Antietam and Perryville were inconclusive. Neither North nor South had won what could be called a decisive victory, and in that narrow view the 31,000 men who fell in the two encounters would seem to have been sacrificed to no purpose.

Yet in the broader view—and with the benefit of hindsight—the battles were as decisive as any fought in the Civil War. The concerted Confederate offensives mounted by Lee and Bragg had failed completely. The South had lost the initiative and would never regain it to the degree achieved during those fateful months of autumn, 1862. The genius of Lee gave the Confederacy an edge in the East for nearly a year after Antietam, but in the West a series of barren victories and costly defeats sent the Rebel cause into an irretrievable downhill slide.

Following Antietam and Perryville a new kind of war began to emerge, a war of ruthless, grinding attrition, in which the catchwords like honor and glory did not quite fit any more. Lincoln's Emancipation Proclamation committed the Union to crushing slavery by force and sealed off the Confederacy from the outside world. Union generals like McClellan and Buell were gone, and tenacious fighters like Grant and Sherman and Sheridan were moving toward the top. After October, 1862, chances for a negotiated peace flickered out. The war could end only when the armies—and the civilians—of North or South were beaten to their knees.

Confederate Nathan Bedford Forrest once remarked that "war means fighting and fighting means killing," and Federal William Tecumseh Sherman said, "War at best is barbarism." The country was now to know the full meaning of their words.

247

A SEARCH FOR ALLIES

IN SPITE of all of its material handicaps, the South during the first eighteen months of the war did have one great advantage which probably would have proved decisive if it had continued. Its war aims were perfectly clear and definite, and every Southerner could understand them both with his mind and with his heart. The South wanted its independence: its people, struggling for their freedom, were fighting off invaders. The ordinary Confederate soldier might understand little and care less about the intricacies of the states' rights argument, but he did feel that he was protecting the home place against people who wanted to despoil it, and that was enough for him.

By contrast, the Federal government seemed to be fighting for an abstraction. The call to make war for the Union did indeed arouse deep feelings of patriotism, but as the hard months passed and the casualty lists grew longer and longer this rallying call did not seem quite adequate. Much blood was being shed for it, but by itself it seemed bloodless. The deep principle that was involved in it became hard to see through the thick layers of battle smoke. Simply to defend the *status quo* against a revolutionary upheaval offers little nourishment for the blood and muscles and spirit when war weariness sets in. In plain terms, the Union

cause was not quite broad enough to support a war of this magnitude.

All of this had a direct bearing on the United States' foreign relations.

The relations that were most important were those with the two dominant powers of Europe, England and France. Each country was a monarchy, and a monarchy does not ordinarily like to see a rebellion succeed in any land. (The example may prove contagious.) Yet the war had not progressed very far before it was clear that the ruling classes in each of these two countries sympathized strongly with the Confederacy—so strongly that with just a little prodding they might be moved to intervene and bring about Southern independence by force of arms. The South was, after all, an aristocracy, and the fact that it had a broad democratic base was easily overlooked at a distance of three thousand miles. Europe's aristocracies had never been happy about the prodigious success of the Yankee democracy. If the nation now broke into halves, proving that democracy did not contain the stuff of survival, the rulers of Europe would be well pleased.

To be sure, the Southern nation was based on the institution of chattel slavery—a completely repugnant anachronism by the middle of the nineteenth century.

249

Distinguished, highly respected Charles Francis Adams faithfully served the Union as Minister to Great Britain.

Neither the British nor the French people would go along with any policy that involved fighting to preserve slavery. But up to the fall of 1862 slavery was not an issue in the war. The Federal government had explicitly declared that it was fighting solely to save the Union. If a Southern emissary wanted to convince Europeans that they could aid the South without thereby aiding slavery, he could prove his case by citing the words of the Federal President and Congress. As far as Europe was concerned, no moral issue was involved; the game of power politics could be played with a clear conscience.

So it *was* played, and the threat of European intervention was real and immediate. Outright war with England nearly took place in the fall of 1861, when a hot-headed U.S. naval officer, Captain Charles Wilkes, undertook to twist the lion's tail and got more of a reaction than anyone was prepared for.

Jefferson Davis had named two distinguished Southerners, James M. Mason of Virginia and John Slidell of Louisiana, as commissioners to represent Confederate interests abroad, Mason in England and Slidell in France. They got out of Charleston, South Carolina, on a blockade-runner at the beginning of October and went via Nassau to Havana, where they took passage for England on the British mail steamer *Trent*.

Precisely at this time U.S.S. *San Jacinto* was returning to the United States from a long tour of duty along the African coast. She put in at a Cuban port, looking for news of Confederate commerce raiders which were reported to be active in that vicinity, and there her commander, Captain Wilkes, heard about Mason and Slidell. He now worked out a novel interpretation of international law. A nation at war (it was generally agreed) had a right to stop and search a neutral merchant ship if it suspected that ship of carrying the enemy's dispatches. Mason and Slidell, Wilkes reasoned, were in effect Confederate dispatches, and he had a right to remove them. So on November 8, 1861, he steamed out into the Bahama Channel, fired twice across *Trent*'s bows, sent a boat's crew aboard, collared the Confederate commissioners, and bore them off in triumph to the United States, where they were lodged in Fort Warren, in Boston Harbor. Wilkes was hailed as a national hero. Congress voted him its thanks, and Secretary of the Navy Gideon Welles, ordinarily a most cautious mortal, warmly commended him.

But in England there was an uproar which almost brought on a war. The mere notion that Americans could halt a British ship on the high seas and remove lawful passengers was intolerable. Eleven thousand regular troops were sent to Canada, the British fleet was put on a war footing, and a sharp note was dispatched to the United States, demanding surrender of the prisoners and a prompt apology.

If the general tempo of things had not been so feverish just then, experts on international law might have amused themselves by pointing out that the American and British governments had precisely reversed their traditional policies. In the Napoleonic wars British warships had exercised the right of search and seizure without restraint, stopping American merchant ships on the high seas to remove persons whom they suspected of being British subjects—doing, in fact, exactly what Wilkes had done with a slightly different object. The United States government had protested that this was improper and illegal, and the whole business had helped bring on the War of 1812. Now an American naval officer had done what British naval officers had done half a century earlier, and the British government was protesting in the same way the earlier American government had done. If anyone cared to make anything of it, the situation was somewhat ironic.

It was touch and go for a while, because a good many brash Yankees were quite willing to fight the British, and the seizure of the Confederate commissioners had somehow seemed like a great victory. But Lincoln stuck to the policy of one war at a time, and after due deliberation the apology was made and the prisoners were released. The *Trent* incident was forgotten, and the final note was strangely anticlimactic. The transports bearing the British troops to Canada arrived off the American coast just after the release and apology. Secretary of State Seward offered, a little too graciously, to let the soldiers disembark on American soil for rapid transportation across Maine, but the British coldly rejected this unnecessary courtesy.

The *Trent* affair had been symptomatic. The war had put a heavy strain on relations between the United States and Great Britain, and there would always be danger that some unexpected occurrence would bring on a war. Yet the two countries were fortunate in the character of their diplomats. The American Minister in London was Charles Francis Adams, and the British Minister in Washington was Lord Lyons, and these two had done all they could, in the absence of instructions from their governments, to keep the *Trent* business from getting out of hand. Even Secretary of State Seward, who earlier had shown a politician's weakness for making votes in America by defying the British, proved supple enough to retreat with good grace from an untenable position; and Earl Russell, the British Foreign Secretary, who had sent a very stiff note, nevertheless phrased it carefully so that Seward could make his retreat without too great difficulty.

Much more serious was the situation that developed late in the summer of 1862. At that time, as far as any European could see, the Confederacy was beginning to look very much like a winner—a point which James Mason insistently pressed home with British officialdom. The Northern attempt to capture the Confederate capital had failed, Virginia's soil had been cleared of invaders, and in the East and West alike the Confederates were on the offensive. Minister Adams warned Seward that the British government might very soon offer to mediate the difficulty between North and South, which would be a polite but effective way of intimating that in the opinion of Great Britain the quarrel had gone on long enough and ought to be ended—by giving the South what it wanted. Adams knew what he was talking about. Earl Russell had given Mason no encouragement whatever, but after news of the Second Battle of Bull Run reached London, he and Lord Palmerston, the Prime Minister, agreed that along in late September or thereabouts there should be a cabinet meeting at which Prime Minister and Foreign Secretary would ask approval of the mediation proposal. (Implicit in all of this was the idea that if the Northern government should refuse to accept mediation, Britain would go ahead and recognize the Confederacy.) With a saving note of caution, Russell and Palmerston concluded not to bring the plan before the cabinet until they got further word about Lee's invasion of the North. If the Federals were beaten, then the proposal would go through; if Lee failed, then it might be well to wait a little longer before taking any action.

On October 7 the Chancellor of the Exchequer, William E. Gladstone, made a notable speech at Newcastle in which he remarked that no matter what one's opinion of slavery might be, facts had to be faced: "There is no doubt that Jefferson Davis and other leaders of the South have made an army; they are making, it appears, a navy; and they have made what is more than either—they have made a nation." He added, "We may anticipate with certainty the success of the Southern States so far as regards their separation from the North."

Naturally enough, this raised a sensation. Gladstone explained that he had simply been expressing his own opinion rather than that of the government, and when Earl Russell saw the speech, he wrote Gladstone that he "went beyond the latitude which all speakers must be allowed." His lordship went on to say that he did not think the cabinet was prepared for recognition, but that it would meet very soon to discuss the project.

In all of this there was less of actual hostility toward the North than is usually supposed. Palmerston and Russell were prepared to accept an accomplished fact, when and if such a fact became visible; if the Confederacy was definitely going to win, the fact ought to be admitted and the war ought to be ended. But they were not prepared to go further than that. Gladstone might commit his calculated indiscretion, the upper class might continue to hold the Confederates as sentimental favorites, and the London *Times* might thunder at intervals against the Northern government; but the British government itself tried to be scrupulously correct, and long before the war ended, ardent Southerners were complaining that the government's attitude had been consistently hostile to the Confederacy. Even the business of the British-built cruisers and ironclad rams did not alter this situation. Legally, vessels like the *Alabama* were simply fast merchant ships, given arms and a warlike character only after they had left English waters, and the government had no legal ground to prevent their construction and delivery. The famous rams themselves were technically built for French purchasers, and even though it was an open secret that they would ultimately go into the Confederate navy, there was never anything solid for the British authorities to put their teeth into. When the British government finally halted the deal and forced the builders to sell the rams to the British navy, it actually stretched the law very substantially. That it did this under a plain threat of war from the United States did not alter the fact that in the end the Confederacy could not get what it desperately wanted from Great Britain.

Nor was the United States without active friends in England. Such reformers as John Bright and Richard Cobden spoke up vigorously in support of the Lincoln government, and even when the cotton shortage threw thousands of textile workers out of employment, the British working class remained consistently opposed to the Confederacy. But the decisive factor, in the fall of 1862 and increasingly thereafter, was the Battle of Antietam and what grew out of it.

Antietam by itself showed that Lee's invasion was

not going to bring that final, conclusive Confederate triumph which had been anticipated. The swift recession of the high Confederate tide was as visible in England as in America, and as the autumn wore away Palmerston and Russell concluded that it would not be advisable to bring the mediation-recognition program before the cabinet.

Far more significant than Antietam, however, was the Emancipation Proclamation, which turned out to be one of the strangest and most important state papers ever issued by an American President.

During the late spring and early summer of 1862 Lincoln had come to see that he must broaden the base of the war. Union itself was not enough; the undying vitality and drive of Northern antislavery men must be brought into full, vigorous support of the war effort, and to bring this about the Northern government must officially declare itself against slavery. Lincoln was preparing such a declaration even before McClellan's army left the Virginia Peninsula, but he could not issue it until the North had won a victory. (Seward pointed out that to issue it on the heels of a string of Northern defeats would make it look as if the government were despairingly crying for help rather than making a statement of principle.) Antietam gave Lincoln the victory he had to have, and on September 22 he issued the famous proclamation, the gist of which was that on January 1, 1863, all slaves held in a state or a part of a state which was in rebellion should be "then, thenceforward and forever free."

Technically, the proclamation was almost absurd. It proclaimed freedom for all slaves in precisely those areas where the United States could not make its authority effective, and allowed slavery to continue in slave states which remained under Federal control. It was a statement of intent rather than a valid statute, and it was of doubtful legality; Lincoln had issued it as a war measure, basing it on his belief that the President's undefined "war powers" permitted him to do just about anything he chose to do in order to win the war, but the courts might not agree with him. Abolitionists felt that it did not go nearly far enough, and border-state people and many Northern Democrats felt that it went altogether too far. But in the end it changed the whole character of the war and, more than any other single thing, doomed the Confederacy to defeat.

The Northern government now was committed to a broader cause, with deep, mystic overtones; it was fighting for union and for human freedom as well, and the very nature of the Union for which it was fighting would be permanently deepened and enriched. A new meaning was given to Daniel Webster's famous "Liberty *and* Union, now and forever, one and inseparable"; the great Battle Hymn now rang out as an American Marseillaise, and Northerners who had wondered whether the war was quite worth its terrible cost heard, at last, the notes of the bugle that would never call retreat. A war goal with emotional power as direct and enduring as the Confederacy's own had at last been erected for all men to see.

And in Europe the American Civil War had become something in which no western government dared to intervene. The government of Britain, France, or any other nation could play power politics as it chose, as long as the war meant nothing more than a government's attempt to put down a rebellion; but no government that had to pay the least attention to the sentiment of its own people could take sides against a government which was trying to destroy slavery. The British cabinet was never asked to consider the proposition which Palmerston and Russell had been talking about, and after 1862 the chance that Great Britain would decide in favor of the Confederacy became smaller and smaller and presently vanished entirely. The Emancipation Proclamation had locked the Confederates in an anachronism which could not survive in the modern world.

Along with this there went a much more prosaic material factor. Europe had had several years of short grain crops, and during the Civil War the North exported thousands of tons of grain—grain which could be produced in increasing quantities, despite the wartime manpower shortage, because the new reapers and binders were boosting farm productivity so sharply. Much as Great Britain needed American cotton, just now she needed American wheat even more. In a showdown she was not likely to do anything that would cut off that source of food.

All of this did not mean that Secretary Seward had no more problems in his dealings with the world abroad. The recurring headache growing out of the British habit of building ships for the Confederate navy has already been noted. There was also Napoleon III, Emperor of the French, who was a problem all by himself.

Napoleon's government in many ways was quite cordial to the Confederates, and in the fall of 1862 Napoleon talked with Slidell and then proposed that France, England, and Russia join in trying to bring about a six-month armistice. To Slidell the Emperor remarked that if the Northern government rejected this proposal, that might give good reason for recognition and perhaps even for active intervention. Neither Britain nor Russia would go along with him, but early in 1863 Napoleon had the French Minister at Washington suggest to Seward that there ought to be a meeting of Northern and Southern representatives to see whether the war might not be brought to a close. Seward politely but firmly rejected this suggestion, and the Congress, much less politely, formally resolved that any foreign government which made such proposals was thereby committing an unfriendly act. Whether Napoleon really expected anything to come of his suggestion is a question; probably he strongly wanted a Southern victory but was afraid to do anything definite without British support. His real interest was in Mexico, where he took advantage of the war to create a French puppet state, installing the Hapsburg Maximilian as Emperor of Mexico in direct violation of the Monroe Doctrine. Propped up by French troops, Maximilian managed to hang on to his shaky throne for several years, and if his control over the country had been firmer, Napoleon would probably have given the Confederacy, from that base, more active support. Shortly after Appomattox the Federal government sent Phil Sheridan and 50,000 veterans to the Mexican border in blunt warning, Seward filed a formal protest against the occupation, and Napoleon withdrew his soldiers. When the French troops left, the Mexicans regained control, and Maximilian was deposed and executed.

Singularly enough, the one European country which showed a definite friendship for the Northern government was Czarist Russia. In the fall of 1863 two Russian fleets entered American waters, one in the Atlantic and one in the Pacific. They put into New York and San Francisco harbors and spent the winter there, and the average Northerner expressed both surprise and delight over the visit, assuming that the Russian Czar was taking this means of warning England and France that if they made war in support of the South, he would help the North. Since pure altruism is seldom or never visible in any country's foreign relations, the business was not quite that simple. Russia at the time was in some danger of getting into a war with England and France, for reasons totally unconnected with the Civil War in America; to avoid the risk of having his fleets ice-bound in Russian ports, the Czar simply had them winter in American harbors. If war should come, they would be admirably placed to raid British and French commerce. For many years most Americans believed that for some inexplicable reason of his own the Czar had sent the fleets simply to show his friendship for America.

Considering the course of the war as a whole, it must be said that Northern diplomacy was highly successful and that Southern diplomacy was a flat failure. At the time, most Northerners bitterly resented what they considered the unfriendly attitude of Britain and France, but neither country did much that would give the South any real nourishment. The British commerce raiders were indeed expensive nuisances to the North, and the famous "*Alabama* claims" after the war were prosecuted with vigor; but cruisers like the *Alabama* might have ranged the seas for a generation without ever compelling the North to give up the struggle. The open recognition, the active aid, the material and financial support which the South needed so greatly were never forthcoming. Europe refused to take a hand in America's quarrel. North and South were left to fight it out between themselves.

The lithograph above presents John Bull's dilemma in being forced to choose between cotton and the abolition of slavery. Napoleon III of France (at left in the caricature below) followed Queen Victoria's England in issuing a proclamation of neutrality, despite Confederate overtures.

War with England Looms

Without firing a gun, without drawing a sword, should they make war on us we could bring the whole world to our feet. . . ." It was March 4, 1858, and South Carolina's James H. Hammond was addressing the Senate: "No, you dare not make war on cotton. No power on earth dares to make war upon it. Cotton is king." Three years later the South went off to war, supremely confident that the European powers, led by cotton-hungry England, would not only grant it diplomatic recognition but also supply it with the arms and treasure needed to win independence.

In proclaiming the blockade on April 19, 1861, Lincoln committed a grave blunder. According to the usages of international law, a blockade implies a state of belligerency. In its Proclamation of Neutrality issued on May 13 England took note of this belligerency—and few doubted that recognition would be the next step. That very day Charles Francis Adams, the new American Minister, arrived at Liverpool. A week later Secretary of State Seward instructed him to shun the British should they enter into negotiations with the Rebels. Adams was following the footsteps of his father, John Quincy Adams, and his grandfather, John Adams, in representing America in Britain during times of trial, but he was pessimistic about his chances of success.

That fall the Union navy's seizure of two Confederate envoys, James M. Mason and John Slidell, from the British steamer *Trent*, created a sensation in England. "The people are frantic with rage," an American observer in London wrote to Seward, "and were the country polled, I fear 999 men out of a thousand would declare for war." As the English press fumed 11,000 British troops embarked for Canada to the strains of a volunteer band playing "Dixie."

To win European recognition, the Confederacy sent James M. Mason (above) to England and John Slidell (below) to France.

Seward Backs Down, but the South Fails to Find Allies

By 1861 haughty, 77-year-old Lord Palmerston (above) had been a British statesman for 54 years and had once served a Foreign Secretary to Earl Russell (below) who now shared power with him in a government that was Liberal in name only The Punch cartoon by John Tenniel at left is typical of that magazine's disparaging attitude toward the Union cause

AMERICA ANOTHER FEDERAL DEFEAT

VERY PROBABLE.

Lord Punch. "THAT WAS JEFF DAVIS, PAM! DON'T YOU RECOGNISE HIM?"
Lord Pam. "HM! WELL, NOT EXACTLY——MAY HAVE TO DO SO SOME OF THESE DAYS."

Lord Palmerston, the British Prime Minister, considered the *Trent* affair an affront to his country's honor and prestige, and his Foreign Secretary, Earl Russell, drafted a strong protest to the U.S. government. Before it was dispatched to America on November 30, 1861, however, Prince Albert, Victoria's consort, had the message toned down. Then Lord Lyons, the British Ambassador in Washington, obligingly delayed presenting Seward with the seven-day ultimatum which demanded the release of Mason and Slidell and an apology for their seizure. In London, Lord Russell confided to Palmerston: "I still incline to think Lincoln will submit, but not until the clock is 59 minutes past 11."

On December 27 Seward replied to Lyons. The mistake, he explained, had been in removing the Confederate envoys from the *Trent;* instead, the captain of the Union ship should have taken the vessel into port for adjudication by a prize court. "The comparative unimportance of the captured persons themselves," Seward concluded, no longer required their detention. They would be released.

Southern elation was short-lived, however, for British and French recognition proved as illusory as the South's belief that the need for cotton would force Britain to come to its aid. Most of the 1860 bumper crop had already been shipped at war's outset, and there was a surplus of raw cotton in England. New sources in India and Egypt were developing, and England suffered little from lack of American cotton. From now on, the South's search for allies would be plagued by the existence of slavery.

"UP A TREE."
Colonel Bull and the Yankee 'Coon.
'Coon. "AIR YOU IN ARNEST, COLONEL?"
Colonel Bull. "I AM."
'Coon. "DON'T FIRE—I'LL COME DOWN."

This brutal Punch *cartoon, also by John Tenniel, appeared at the height of the storm raised by the* Trent *affair. Lincoln, as a timorous raccoon, has been treed by a stalwart, bombastic John Bull.*

Lord Lyons (left), a shy, amicable bachelor, was scrupulously neutral, although he felt slavery made the Rebel cause "loathsome to the civilized world."

257

Emancipation: Changing War Aims

The quarrel, cover it with cotton as we may," the British *Spectator* editorialized in June, 1861, "is between freedom and slavery, right and wrong, the dominion of God and the dominion of the Devil, and the duty of England, we submit, is clear." By the summer of 1862 Lincoln, sensitive to the mounting pressure for abolition, was seriously considering action that would put the war on just such a footing.

On July 22 the President read a preliminary draft for an emancipation proclamation to his cabinet. Seward demurred. The step would be interpreted abroad, he argued, "as the last measure of an exhausted government, a cry for help . . . our last shriek on the retreat." Lincoln agreed; the proclamation was quietly returned to his desk; and not until September 22—five days after Union victory at Antietam—was it issued.

For years Great Britain had urged abolition of the slave trade, and the British working class was solemnly committed to emancipation. English textile workers, even though they were unemployed during periods of cotton shortage, nevertheless rallied to the cause. To Manchester workers expressing sympathy with the Proclamation, Lincoln wrote: "I cannot but regard your decisive utterances as an instance of sublime Christian heroism." By and large the British government and press viewed the Proclamation as "direct encouragement to servile insurrection" and were hostile at first. But "if they become once fully aroused to a sense of the importance of this struggle as a purely moral question," Adams wrote Seward on January 22, 1863, "I feel safe in saying there will be an end of all effective sympathy in Great Britain with the rebellion." And so it proved.

In the 1864 lithograph at left, Lincoln is surrounded by such allegorical symbols as the Bible, scales of justice, and the Presidential oath, which, the artist intimated, aided him in drafting the Emancipation Proclamation.

Confederate caricaturist Adalbert Volck, hinting darkly at slave uprisings, showed a satanical Lincoln composing the Proclamation with one foot on the Constitution. A. A. Lamb viewed emancipation more positively (below).

The Laird Rams Bring a New Crisis

On June 4, 1861, James D. Bulloch, a Georgian of Scotch ancestry, arrived in Liverpool with instructions from Confederate Secretary of the Navy Mallory to "get cruising ships of suitable type afloat with the quickest possible despatch." The Confederacy was determined to build a navy in England, and to circumvent British laws which forbade construction of warships for belligerents, contracts were secretly negotiated, and bogus purchasers were listed. The vessels were to leave British harbors as unarmed merchantmen, to be armed in friendly ports later.

When the first of Bulloch's ships, the *Florida*, left Liverpool on March 22, 1862, Charles Francis Adams became alarmed. With information supplied by Thomas Dudley, American Consul at Liverpool, Adams prepared a case against the second vessel, known only as No. 290, then being built there by the Laird brothers. The evidence was forwarded to the British government just at the time the Queen's Advocate went insane, and the documents remained untouched on his desk for a crucial five-day period. On July 29 No. 290 steamed out of Liverpool, ostensibly on a trial run. Visitors were soon sent to shore in a tug, however; the ship proceeded to the Azores, where it was armed; and the *Alabama* made its debut as a Confederate raider. Methodically, Adams bombarded the British government with reports of ships sunk by the *Alabama,* together with bills for reparations that were not to be settled until 1872.

As the *Alabama* was making its escape the obliging Lairds began construction of two ironclad rams, designed to break the blockade and, perhaps, shell defenseless Northern port cities. First the French Emperor was listed as owner, then the Pasha of Egypt, although it was an open secret that the rams would go to the Rebels.

The canny Confederate agents transferred legal ownership of the rams to a French company under an agreement to repurchase them once they were safely at sea, and there appeared to be nothing the British could do. Adams was coldly furious. On September 5, 1863, he presented a note to Earl Russell. Should the rams be permitted to leave England, Adams stated grimly, "It would be superfluous in me to point out to your Lordship that this is war . . ." But the British had already taken steps to detain the Laird rams, and in mid-October they were formally seized.

A crisis had been averted; the Rebels were thwarted in their efforts to build ironclads; and Charles Francis Adams was credited with a great diplomatic victory. "None of our generals, nor Grant himself," James Russell Lowell wrote later, "did us better or more trying service than he in his forlorn outpost of London."

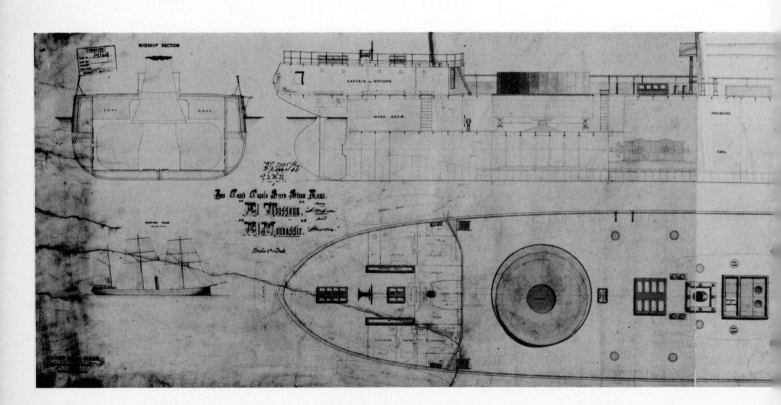

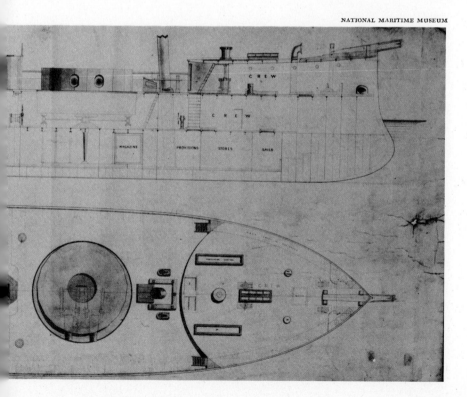

Several blockade-runners were outfitted in British ports. The American Consul at Bristol had this photograph of the Old Dominion *made to aid in its interception.*

The sophisticated design of the Laird rams is shown in the contemporary plans at left. Each of the twin-turreted vessels was 230 feet long, with a 40-foot beam, and armored with 4½-inch iron plate. The 7-foot submerged curve at the prow (top drawing, right), called the "piercer," gave the ironclads the character of rams. Here the vessels are listed under their Egyptian names, El Tousson *and* El Monasir; *later they were incorporated into the British fleet as the* Scorpion *and* Wivern.

Russian Visitors and a Mexican Emperor

The crew of the Russian ship Osliaba *posed for this picture at Alexandria. Not until 50 years later was it learned that the Russian fleet actually visited American ports in 1863 to protect itself should France and Britain declare war over the Czar's suppression of Poland.*

Implicit in the North's concern over the threat of British intervention was a certain knowledge that other European powers would follow England's lead. Indeed, Napoleon III's France was often openly sympathetic to the Confederate cause; but Russia, in September, 1863, made a move which was widely interpreted in the North as a gesture of support from the Czar. Ships of the Russian fleet put in at New York and San Francisco, to receive wildly enthusiastic welcomes. Later, when the ships stopped at Alexandria, Virginia, Lincoln held a reception in the White House in honor of the visitors.

By this time France was posing a threat to the hallowed Monroe Doctrine. In 1861 Mexico had defaulted on its foreign debts, and Great Britain, Spain, and France launched a military expedition to force payment. When the allies drifted apart, Napoleon moved to set up a puppet empire in Mexico. By June, 1863, French forces were in Mexico City, and Napoleon offered the nonexistent throne of Mexico to a fatuous young Hapsburg prince, Archduke Ferdinand Maximilian of Austria.

Seward knew he was powerless to act. "But why should we gasconade about Mexico when we are in a struggle for our own life?" he asked. Public opinion, however, viewed the matter more aggressively. "As for Mexico," screeched the New York *Herald*, "we will, at the close of the rebellion . . . send fifty thousand Northern and fifty thousand Southern troops . . . to drive the invaders into the Gulf."

Although 50,000 troops *were* rushed to the Mexican border at war's end, Seward, ever the diplomat, bided his time. At last, oppressed by enormous expenses, disillusioned by hostile opinion at home, and harassed by continuing guerrilla warfare under Juárez, Napoleon withdrew his soldiers from Mexico in the spring of 1867. Maximilian's chimerical empire toppled, and the hapless Archduke was executed by the outraged Mexicans.

Urged on by his lovely, ambitious wife, Carlota, Maximilian undertook the foolhardy Mexican venture. When the empire collapsed, she escaped to Europe, to linger on in tragic insanity until 1927.

263

STALEMATE, EAST AND WEST

AFTER the failure of the great Southern counteroffensive in the fall of 1862, the North tried to pick up the lost threads afresh. Its problem, then as always, was deceptively simple: to use its immense preponderance of physical strength in a sustained, increasing pressure that would collapse the Confederate defenses and destroy the Confederate armies and the government which they supported. In the spring it had seemed that success was very near; by autumn the vast difficulties that lay across the path were much more clearly visible. Momentum, so important to military success, had been lost, and in the East and in the West a new start would have to be made.

In this effort three armies would be chiefly involved —the Army of the Potomac in Virginia, the Army of the Cumberland in central Tennessee, and the Army of the Tennessee along the Mississippi River. The Army of the Potomac was led now by Major General Ambrose E. Burnside, a handsome, likable, unassuming West Pointer with a legendary growth of side whiskers, a man whose sincere desire to do the right thing was a good deal stronger than his ability to discern what that right thing might be. McClellan had at last been removed. He had let six weeks pass after Antietam before he crossed the Potomac and began a new offensive, and then he moved, as always, with much deliberation; Lincoln had lost patience, McClellan

was in retirement, and Burnside now had the army.

It lay in the neighborhood of Warrenton, Virginia, east of the Blue Ridge. Burnside did not like the advance down the Orange and Alexandria Railroad which McClellan seemed to have projected, and he devised a new plan: go east to Fredericksburg, cross the Rappahannock there and force Lee to give battle somewhere between Fredericksburg and Richmond, and then drive on toward the Confederate capital. By the middle of November, Burnside had the army on the move.

The Army of the Cumberland was just below Nashville, Tennessee. Like the Army of the Potomac, this army had a new commander: bluff, red-faced William S. Rosecrans, who had taken Buell's place when that officer proved unable to overtake Bragg on the retreat from Kentucky. Rosecrans was well-liked by his troops, and he was a stout fighter. He had commanded the portion of Grant's force which won the bloody battle at Corinth, and although Grant had been critical of the way he pursued Van Dorn's beaten army after the battle (it seemed to Grant that that army should have been destroyed outright), Rosecrans' general record of performance was good. He devoted some weeks now to refitting and reorganization, and late in December he began to move south from Nashville with 45,000 men. The Confederate army under Braxton Bragg lay in camp at Murfreesboro, behind Stones River, thirty

Andrew Humphreys leads his untried Pennsylvanians against a Rebel "sheet of flame" at Fredericksburg.

miles away. At the moment it numbered some 37,000 soldiers.

The third army, Grant's, held western Tennessee, and it had two principal functions: to occupy the western third of the state, holding Memphis and the important network of railroads that ran east and northeast from that city and north from the Mississippi border to the upper Mississippi River; and to move down the great river, capture the Confederate stronghold at Vicksburg, join hands with the Union forces which held New Orleans and Baton Rouge, and so open the river from headwaters to gulf. Grant had 80,000 men in his department, but half of them were needed for occupation duties. When he moved against Vicksburg he would be able to put fewer than 40,000 in his field army. He would follow the north-and-south railroad that ran to the Mississippi capital, Jackson, forty miles east of Vicksburg, and then he would swing west. Opposing him was an undetermined number of Confederates led by Lieutenant General John C. Pemberton, a Pennsylvania-born West Pointer who had cast his lot with the South.

These three Federal armies, then, would move more or less in concert, and if all went well, the Confederacy would be pressed beyond endurance. If all did not go well, the Lincoln administration might be in serious trouble. The Emancipation Proclamation was meeting with a mixed reception in the North, and the fall elections had gone badly. The Democrats had sharply reduced the Republican majority in Congress and had elected Horatio Seymour governor of New York; and to the Republican radicals, Seymour, lukewarm about the war at best, looked no better than an arrant Copperhead. In the Northwest war weariness was clearly visible, and Lincoln was being warned that if the Mississippi were not soon opened, there would be an increasing demand for a negotiated peace with the South. For political reasons he needed new military successes.

For the immediate present he did not get them. Instead he got one disaster and a series of checks which looked almost as bad.

First there was Burnside. He got his army to the Rappahannock, opposite Fredericksburg, and if he could have crossed the river at once, he might have made serious trouble for Lee, who did not have all of his men on hand just yet. But the pontoon trains which Burnside needed to bridge the river had gone astray somewhere, and Burnside could think of nothing better to do than wait quietly where he was until they arrived. They reached him, eventually, but a fortnight had been lost, and by the end of it Lee had both Jackson and Longstreet in position on the opposite shore—75,000 veteran fighters of high morale, ably led, ready for the kind of defensive battle in which they were all but unbeatable.

Burnside lacked the mental agility to change his plan, and he tried to go through with it even though the conditions essential for success had gone. He built his bridges, crossed the Rappahannock, and on December 13 assailed Lee's army in its prepared positions. As made, the attack had no chance to succeed. Solidly established on high ground with a clear field of fire, the Confederates beat off a succession of doomed assaults in which the Federals displayed great valor but an almost total lack of military acumen. At the end of the day the Army of the Potomac had lost more than 12,000 men, most of them in front of a stone wall and a sunken road that ran along the base of Marye's Heights. The Confederates had lost fewer than half that many men, and at no time had they been in any serious danger of being dislodged. Burnside called for new assaults the next day—he proposed to lead them in person, there being nothing wrong with his personal courage—but his subordinates managed to talk him out of it, and the Army of the Potomac sullenly withdrew to the north side of the river, its morale all but ruined. The two armies glowered at each other from opposite banks of the river for several weeks; then Burnside tried to move upstream, to cross beyond Lee's left flank and fight a new battle, but three days of steady, icy rain turned the unpaved roads into bottomless mud and left his army completely bogged down. In the end the soldiers managed to pull themselves, their wagons, and their artillery out of the mire and came slogging back to camp, utterly dispirited. This fiasco was too much for everybody, and Burnside was removed from command. To all intents and purposes the Army of the Potomac was out of action for the winter.

In central Tennessee things went better, although what was gained cost a good deal more than it was worth. Rosecrans moved down to Murfreesboro, and Bragg waited for him, and on December 31 their armies fought a desperate, inconclusive battle on a desolate frozen field. Tactically, the fight presented an interesting oddity; each general prepared to hold with his right and attack with his left, and if the two plans had been carried out simultaneously the armies would have swung around like a huge revolving door. As it happened, however, Bragg's men struck first, crushing the Federal right wing and compelling Rosecrans to abandon all thought of an advance with his left. For a time it appeared that the Union army would be completely routed, but Rosecrans' center was commanded by George Thomas, and that stolid Virginian was very hard to dislodge. His corps hung on while the shattered right was re-formed far to the rear, and the sound of musket fire rose to such a deafening pitch that Confederates charging across a weedy cotton field stopped and plucked raw cotton from the open bolls and stuffed it in their ears before going on with the advance.

When night came, Rosecrans' line, which had been more or less straight at dawn, was doubled back like a jackknife with a partly opened blade, but it had not been driven from the field. Bragg notified Richmond that he had won a signal victory—and then, unaccountably, failed to renew the attack the next day. Through all of January 1 the armies faced each other, inactive; late in the afternoon of January 2 Bragg finally assailed the Union left, but his columns were broken up by Federal artillery, and at nightfall the armies were right where they had been at dawn. On January 3, again, they remained in contact, with sporadic firing along the picket lines but no real activity. Then, after dark, the unpredictable Bragg drew off in retreat, marching thirty-six miles south to Tullahoma. Rosecrans moved on into Murfreesboro, but his army was too badly mangled to go any farther. Six months would pass before it could resume the offensive.

No one quite knew who had won this battle, or what its military significance was, if indeed it had any. The Federals did occupy the field, and the Confederates had retreated, so the North accepted it as a victory; but nothing of any consequence had been gained, Bragg's army was still in position squarely across the road to Chattanooga, the key city which the Federals wanted to possess, and the only concrete result seemed to be that both armies had been immobilized for some time to come. Since the North could not possibly win the war if armies were immobilized, this victory was not quite worth the price.

The casualties had been shocking. The Federals had lost 13,000 men and the Confederates 10,000 or more—in each case, more than a fourth of the army's total strength. Few Civil War battles ever cost more or meant less.

If the Federals were to get anything at all out of the winter's operations, they would have to get it from Grant, and for a long time it did not seem that his luck was going to be any better than anybody else's.

He started out brightly enough, beginning in November to advance down the line of the railroad. He established a base of supplies at the town of Holly Springs, two dozen miles south of the Tennessee-Mississippi border, and went on with a methodical advance toward the town of Grenada. His progress, however, was first delayed and then brought to a complete halt by two unexpected developments—a strange case of military-political maneuvering among the Federals, and a display of highly effective aggressiveness by

Confederate cavalry led by Van Dorn and Forrest.

Grant had hardly begun his advance before he began to realize that something odd was going on in the rear. He was moving so as to approach Vicksburg from the east—the only point from which that riverside stronghold could really be attacked with much hope of success. But as he moved he got persistent reports that there was also going to be an expedition straight down the river, some sort of combined army-navy operation apparently intended to break the river defenses by direct assault. He had planned no such operation, but it was going to take place in his department, and although he could get no clear information about it from Halleck, it seemed that the business would be more or less under his command if he played his cards carefully. It took him a long time to find out what was really in the wind, and when he did find out he was obliged to revise his plans.

What was in the wind was an ambitious attempt by one Major General John A. McClernand to find and to use a new route to victory. McClernand had been prominent in Democratic politics in Illinois before the war, and as a prominent "War Democrat" his standing with the administration was very high; he had been given a brigadier general's commission and then he had been made major general, and he had led troops under Grant at Fort Donelson and at Shiloh. He was not a West Pointer, and Grant considered him too erratic and opinionated for independent command, but he was a good fighter and leader of men, and on the whole his combat record was good. He had taken leave of absence late in September and had gone to Washington to see Lincoln and Stanton, and he had persuaded them that unless a conclusive victory were won soon in the Mississippi Valley, the whole Northwest might fall out of the war. Since this jibed with what they already had been told, the President and the Secretary of War listened attentively.

McClernand's proposal was unorthodox but direct. He had a solid following among the Democrats of the Northwest. He believed that he could organize enough fresh troops in that area to form a new army. With such an army, he believed, he could go straight down the Mississippi, and while Grant and the others were threshing about inland he could capture Vicksburg, opening the waterway to the sea and providing the victory which would inspire the Northwest and make possible a final Federal triumph. Lincoln and Stanton liked the idea and gave McClernand top-secret orders to go ahead. In these orders, however, they wrote an escape clause which McClernand seems not to have noticed; what McClernand did was to be done in Grant's department, and if Halleck and Grant saw fit, Grant could at any time assume over-all command over McClernand, McClernand's troops, and the entire venture.

McClernand went back to Illinois and began to raise troops, and rumors of the project trickled out. Halleck could not tell Grant just what was up, but he did his best to warn him by indirection: also, he saw to it that as McClernand's recruits were formed into regiments the regiments were sent downstream to Grant's department. In one way and another, Grant finally came to see what was going on. There was going to be an advance on Vicksburg by water, and Halleck wanted him to assume control of it; wanted him, apparently, to get it moving at once, before McClernand (for whose abilities Halleck had an abiding distrust) could himself reach the scene and take charge.

The upshot of all this was that in December Grant recast his plans. He sent his most trusted subordinate, William T. Sherman, back to Memphis, with orders to organize a striking force out of Sherman's own troops and the new levies that were coming downstream from Illinois, and to proceed down the river with it at the earliest possible date and put his men ashore a few miles north of Vicksburg. Grant, meanwhile, would bring his own army down the line of the railroad, and Pemberton could not possibly meet both threats; if he concentrated against one Federal force, the other would strike him in the rear, and since he would be outnumbered he could not possibly meet both threats at once. Sherman hurried to get things in motion, and Grant went on with his own advance.

At this point the Confederates took a hand. The General Van Dorn who had been beaten at Corinth took a cavalry force, swung in behind Grant, and captured the vast Federal supply base at Holly Springs; and at the same time Bedford Forrest rode up into western Tennessee, cutting railroads and telegraph lines, seizing enough Federal weapons, horses, and equipment to outfit the new recruits who joined him in that stoutly secessionist area, and creating vast confusion and disorganization deep in the Federal rear. In consequence, Grant was brought to a standstill, and he could not get word of this to Sherman, who by now was en route to Vicksburg with 30,000 men, many of whom belonged to the absent McClernand.

So Sherman ran into trouble, because Pemberton was able to ignore Grant and give Sherman all of his attention. The Federals attacked on December 29 and were decisively repulsed, losing more than 1,700 men. Sherman withdrew to the Mississippi River, and on January 2 he was joined there by the indignant McClernand, who was beginning to realize that things were not working out quite as he had hoped. McClernand assumed command, and—for want of anything better to do—he and Sherman, with the help of the navy's gunboats, went up the Arkansas River to capture Confederate Fort Hindman: a nice little triumph, but not precisely what had been contemplated earlier. From Fort Hindman they returned to make camp on the west shore of the Mississippi at Young's Point and Milliken's Bend, some dozen miles above Vicksburg.

There, at the end of the month, Grant showed up, bringing with him most of the men with whom he had attempted the advance down the railroad. His arrival reduced McClernand to the position of a corps commander—a demotion which McClernand protested bitterly but in vain—and gave Grant a field force which numbered between 40,000 and 50,000 men. It also gave Grant a position from which it was all but impossible even to get at the Confederate stronghold, let alone capture it.

Grant's move to the river had been inevitable. There was going to be a Federal column operating on the river, whether Grant liked it or not—Washington had settled that, and the decision was irreversible—and it was clearly unsound to try to co-ordinate that column's movements with the movements of a separate army operating in the interior of the state of Mississippi. The only sensible thing to do was concentrate everything along the river and make the best of it. But in this area geography was on the side of the Confederates.

Vicksburg occupied high ground on the east bank of the Mississippi, and it could be attacked with any chance of success only from the east or southeast. The Yazoo River entered the Mississippi a short distance north of Vicksburg, with steep bluffs along its left bank, and Pemberton had entrenched these bluffs and put troops in them; Sherman's December experience had shown the futility of trying an assault in that area. North of there, the fertile low country of the Yazoo delta ran for two hundred miles, cut by innumerable rivers, creeks, and bayous—fine land for farming, almost impossible land for an army of invasion to cross with all of its guns and supplies.

To the south things looked little better. The Louisiana shore of the Mississippi was low, swampy, intersected like the Yazoo delta by many streams, and if the army did go south it could not cross the river without many steamboats, and there did not seem to be any good way to get these past the Vicksburg batteries. Even if steamboats were available, Confederates had mounted batteries to cover most of the downstream places where a crossing might be made.

What all of this meant was that the army must somehow get east of Vicksburg in order to assault the place, and there did not seem to be any way to get east without going all the way back to Memphis and starting out again on the overland route which Grant had tried in December. This was out of the question because it would be an obvious, unmitigated confession of defeat, and an unhappy Northern public which was trying to digest the bad news from Fredericksburg and Murfreesboro probably could not swallow one more defeat.

Apparently, then, the Northern war machine was stalled, on dead center. It was perfectly possible that the Federals had broken the great Confederate counteroffensive in the fall only to let their hopes of victory die of sheer inanition during the winter. The Army of the Potomac had a new commander—Major General Joseph Hooker, handsome, cocky, a hard drinker and a hard fighter—and Hooker was doing his best to get the army back into shape. By reorganizing his supply and hospital services, shaking up the chain of command, overhauling his cavalry, and instituting a program of constant drills, Hooker was restoring morale, but it would be the middle of the spring before the army could be expected to do anything. (No one except Hooker himself was really prepared to bet that it would then fare any better against Lee than McClellan, Pope, and Burnside had fared.) At Murfreesboro lay the Army of the Cumberland, licking its wounds and recuperating. It had suffered no decline in morale, but it had been cruelly racked at Stones River, and Rosecrans was going to take his time about resuming the offensive.

It was up to Grant, even though he did seem to be stymied. He had hardly reached the Mississippi before he began to try every possible means to solve the problem which faced him. There seemed to be four possibilities. He would try them all.

Opposite Vicksburg the Mississippi made a hairpin turn. If a canal could be cut across the base of the narrow finger of land that pointed north on the Louisiana side, the Mississippi might pour through it, bypassing the city entirely. Then gunboats, transports, and everything else could float downstream unhindered, and Vicksburg would be a problem no longer. Dredges were brought down, and Sherman's corps was put to work with pick and shovel, and the canal was dug. (In the end it did not work; perversely, the Mississippi refused to enter it in any volume, and Sherman's men had their work for nothing.)

Fifty miles upstream from Vicksburg, on the Louisiana side, a backwater known as Lake Providence lay near the river. It might be possible to cut a channel from river to lake and to deepen the chain of streams that led south from Lake Providence. If that worked, steamers could go all the way down to the Red River, coming back to the Mississippi 150 miles below Vicksburg. Using this route, the army could get east of the river, roundabout but unhindered; it also could draw supplies and substantial reinforcements from New Orleans. So this too was tried; after two months it could be seen that this was not quite going to work, partly because the shallow-draft steamers needed could not be obtained in quantity.

A good 300 miles north of Vicksburg, streams tributary to the Yazoo flowed from a deep-water slough just over the levee from the Mississippi. Cut the levee, send transports and gunboats through, get into the Yazoo, and cruise down to a landing point just above the fortified chain of bluffs; put troops ashore there, take the fortifications in flank—and Vicksburg is taken. Engineer troops cut the levee, gunboats and transports steamed through: and where the Tallahatchie and Yalobusha rivers unite to form the Yazoo, they ran into Confederate Fort Pemberton, which was not particularly strong but was situated in a place that made it practically impregnable. It was surrounded by water, or by half-flooded bottom land, and could be attacked only from the river, and the river just here came up to the fort in a straight, narrow reach which was fully controlled by the fort's guns. The gunboats moved in to bombard, got the worst of it—and the whole expedition had to go ignominiously back to the Mississippi. The Yazoo venture was out.

A fourth possibility involved a fearfully complicated network of little streams and backwaters which could be entered from the Mississippi near the mouth of the Yazoo. Gunboats and transports might go up this chain for a hundred miles or more and, if their luck was in, safely below Fort Pemberton go on over to the Yazoo, coming down thereafter to the same place which the other expedition had tried to reach. This too was tried, with troops under Sherman and gunboats under the David Porter who had commanded Farragut's mortar boats below New Orleans. This move was a total fiasco. Porter's gunboats got hung up in streams no wider than the boats were, with an infernal tangle of willows growing up ahead to block further progress, and with busy Confederates felling trees in the rear to cut off escape. The whole fleet narrowly escaped destruction. It finally got back to the Mississippi, but it had demonstrated once and for all that this route to Vicksburg was no good. (The four routes are shown on the map on pages 310–11.)

Four chances, and four failures: and as spring came on Grant sat in the cabin of his headquarters steamer at Milliken's Bend, stared into the wreaths of cigar smoke which surrounded him, and worked out the means by which he would finally be enabled to attack Vicksburg. If he failed, his army would probably be lost, and with it the war; if he succeeded, the North would at last be on the road to victory. Either way, everything was up to him.

The spires and buildings of Fredericksburg loom through the early morning fog, appearing to

Burnside Draws up Before Fredericksburg

Fredericksburg, a charming colonial town on the southwest bank of the Rappahannock River, was in the fall of 1862 one more barrier to the Union march on Richmond. A week after self-effacing Ambrose E. Burnside reluctantly assumed command of the Army of the Potomac, he proposed a movement south

...ch the same as they did to Burnside's army, waiting to cross the Rappahannock in December, 1862.

through Fredericksburg. Lincoln approved his plan, noting, "it will succeed, if you move very rapidly; otherwise not."

Almost at once Burnside began moving his huge army, now reorganized into three Grand Divisions of two corps each, to the Rappahannock. When Edwin Sumner's Right Grand Division arrived opposite Fredericksburg on November 17, only a handful of Confederates held the town; but almost immediately a fierce storm lashed the area, the Rappahannock River began to rise, and the impatient Burnside had to wait a week for the arrival of pontoons.

The day after Sumner's arrival Robert E. Lee had shifted Longstreet's I Corps to Fredericksburg. Taking advantage of his foe's procrastination, Lee sent for Stonewall Jackson, who came up on November 30. While two armies—122,000 Union troops and 78,500 Confederates—faced one another, Burnside waited another ten days to strike.

271

Ambrose Burnside felt himself unfit for high command, a view borne out by the one major battle he directed—the Fredericksburg debacle.

Bridging the Rappahannock

In the fog-shrouded dawn of December 11 a Confederate fieldpiece boomed out on the heights behind Fredericksburg. A Louisiana lieutenant waited: "The deep roar of a second gun was heard, and we knew what we had to do." The Union army was forcing a crossing of the ice-choked Rappahannock. That day and the next Federal engineers bridged the river at three points, and by December 13 Burnside had sent two of his Grand Divisions onto the level bottoms below Fredericksburg and into the streets of the town.

Riding out to observe the deployment of the superior enemy force, Stonewall Jackson was asked what he intended to do. "We will give them the bayonet," he answered grimly.

right; the Sacking of Fredericksburg — & Bidney afunir

BANK OF VIRGINIA

Fredericksburg residents fled the artillery bombardment which covered the Union crossing. A Northern officer, horrified at the sack of the town (above), noted that his men "seemed to delight in destroying everything."

Union bridge builders, sketched at left by A. R. Waud, were targets for tenacious Mississippi sharpshooters in Fredericksburg. "Confederate hornets . . . stinging the Army of the Potomac into a frenzy," Longstreet proudly called them.

Part of Sumner's Right Grand Division crossed the Rappahannock over the middle bridge and marched up into Fredericksburg along Rock Lane, pictured at right. Sumner, mistrusted for his rashness, was kept behind in Falmouth.

The Attack Moves into the Open

Rebel sharpshooters fired from Fredericksburg houses like the one above, still pocked with bullet holes. From the Court House steeple (left) Union General Darius Couch watched the desperate attacks against Marye's Heights, where the stately mansion at bottom left stands. Confederate troops were entrenched behind the Sunken Road's Stone Wall (below, right).

Jackson's men, concealed in greater strength than Burnside realized, awaited the Union advance in this woods.

On the morning of December 13 the lifting fog revealed William B. Franklin's Left Grand Division preparing to advance. Jackson's corps, hidden in the woods at Hamilton's Crossing below Fredericksburg, was the objective. Dashing into the open with just two fieldpieces, impetuous John Pelham of Alabama held off the movement until Jeb Stuart sent him a frantic message—"Get back from destruction you infernal, gallant fool." Freed from this interference, Franklin sent Meade's division into the wooded swamp. The Union soldiers stumbled through a gap between two Southern brigades and gained the second line of Rebel forces before being driven back. But Franklin refused to renew the offensive as the battle intensified to his right.

The meandering canal above funneled the Union attack against Lee's strongest salient and protected the weaker Confederate left flank.

OVERLEAF: *Union Lieutenant Frederic Cavada painted this version of the futile assault on Marye's Heights. Untried Pennsylvanians were told by a commander that only the bayonet would do; firing was useless.*

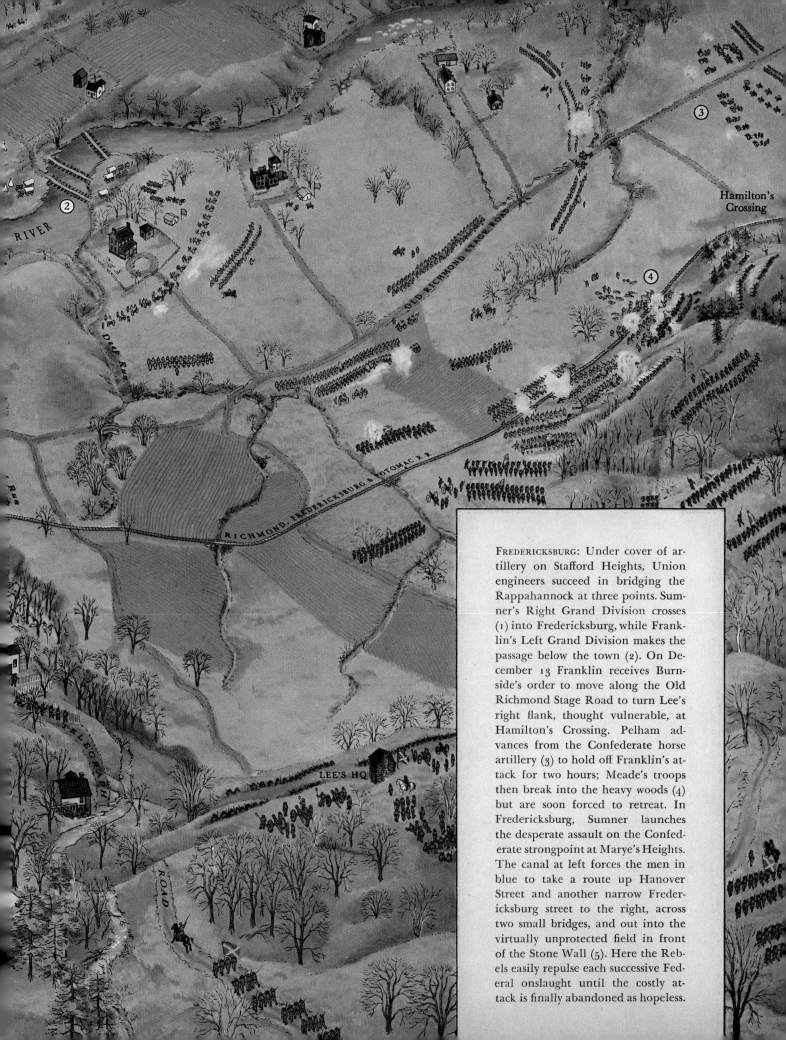

FREDERICKSBURG: Under cover of artillery on Stafford Heights, Union engineers succeed in bridging the Rappahannock at three points. Sumner's Right Grand Division crosses (1) into Fredericksburg, while Franklin's Left Grand Division makes the passage below the town (2). On December 13 Franklin receives Burnside's order to move along the Old Richmond Stage Road to turn Lee's right flank, thought vulnerable, at Hamilton's Crossing. Pelham advances from the Confederate horse artillery (3) to hold off Franklin's attack for two hours; Meade's troops then break into the heavy woods (4) but are soon forced to retreat. In Fredericksburg, Sumner launches the desperate assault on the Confederate strongpoint at Marye's Heights. The canal at left forces the men in blue to take a route up Hanover Street and another narrow Fredericksburg street to the right, across two small bridges, and out into the virtually unprotected field in front of the Stone Wall (5). Here the Rebels easily repulse each successive Federal onslaught until the costly attack is finally abandoned as hopeless.

John Richards' painting above is based on a Harper's engraving which appeared shortly after the battle of Fredericksburg and was, no doubt, inspired by the carnage there. Amputations were performed directly in front of nervous reserves waiting to join the attack.

Valor and Blunders
Produce Fredericksburg's Carnage

Robert E. Lee had been watching the battle to his right through field glasses. As a Federal drive into the woods near Deep Run was driven back, he saw the pursuing Carolinians weep with disappointment when commanded to retire in the face of withering Union artillery fire. Turning to an aide, Lee murmured, "It is well that war is so terrible—we should grow too fond of it."

Now Lee's attention was focused on the heavier fighting that had been raging on his left, in front of Marye's Heights. Sensing that the Federal assault against Jackson was failing, Burnside sent wave after wave of Sumner's Right Grand Division against the impregnable Confederate line behind the Stone Wall along the Sunken Road. Asked if he could hold this line against such massive Union attacks, Longstreet answered confidently, "If you put every man now on the other side of the Poto-

mac in that field to approach me over the same line, and give me plenty of ammunition, I will kill them all before they reach me." It was not an idle boast.

Out on the murderous plain, Union soldiers were forming breastworks with the bodies of their fallen comrades. That day some 9,000 Federals fell in front of Marye's Heights; Confederate losses there were slightly over 1,500.

Across the river in Falmouth an anguished Burnside was pacing the floor. "Oh those men! Those men over there! I am thinking of them all the time." On the night of December 14-15 he pulled the defeated Army of the Potomac back across the Rappahannock, and a disgusted Northern correspondent summed up the Battle of Fredericksburg: "It can hardly be in human nature for men to show more valor, or generals to manifest less judgment."

Rain checked Burnside's move up the Rappahannock after the battle. A. R. Waud's drawing of the famous "Mud March" indicates the cause for an officer's humorous request for "50 men, 25 feet high, to work in mud 18 feet deep."

The ubiquitous Rosecrans (third from left) was undaunted when a cannon ball decapitated his chief of staff, next to him in Henri Lovie's sketch. Below, another panel from the Travis panorama (see page 72) shows the Federals retreating before a Rebel charge at Murfreesboro, on December 31.

Rosecrans Takes Charge in the West

Early in November, 1862, William S. Rosecrans, who had replaced Don Carlos Buell as commander of the Union Army of the Cumberland, advanced to Nashville. He was brave, well-liked by the men who fought under him, and a brilliant strategist; but "Old Rosy" was badly handicapped by a firecracker temper and an almost hypnotic self-complacency. He spent nearly two months preparing his offensive, and on December 26 sent his army in three columns southeast toward the little town of Murfreesboro, Tennessee, where Braxton Bragg's Confederate Army of Tennessee had been encamped for a month.

Bragg, widely censured for his indecisive Kentucky campaign, had taken a defensive position above Murfreesboro, astride Stones River, a narrow stream that loops off northward to join the Cumberland River. To the east of Stones River, on the low hills which dominate the terrain, Bragg had posted a detached division under John C. Breckinridge, the former Vice-President of the United States. West of the river, where a heavy growth of scrub cedar badly obscured vision, he concentrated his main force.

On the evening of December 29 Rosecrans' army began arriving in the vicinity of Murfreesboro, and by nightfall two-thirds of his force was in position along the Nashville Turnpike, less than 700 yards in front of the Confederate line. By next day Rosecrans' army numbered nearly 44,000, against Bragg's 38,000, and the two commanders worked out their respective battle plans. By some weird coincidence they were identical: each general had decided to hold with his right and attack with his left. Bragg, who had previously reported his troops "all ready and confident," now telegraphed his superiors, "Enemy very cautious, and declining a general engagement. Both armies in line of battle within sight." The advantage would fall to the man who moved first.

Major General William S. Rosecrans

Bragg Anticipates a Victory

At dawn on December 31 Confederate General William J. Hardee moved with clocklike precision against the Union right flank, catching some of the Federals cooking breakfast at their camp sites. The Union troops put up a stiff resistance against the relentless tide of the Confederate onslaught, but brigade by brigade the Union right swung back like a door on a hinge; and by 10 A.M. the line stood at almost right angles to what it had been when the attack began. One hard-hit Northern brigade had suffered 500 casualties in the first few minutes.

Confederate cavalry, pursuing the fleeing Union troops, had intercepted Federal ammunition trains; and by 11 A.M. Union troops were forced to retire with empty cartridge belts.

Some Ohio boys were told to "Fix bayonets and hold your ground!" and an unfortunate Illinois regiment, not equipped with bayonets, was ordered to club their muskets when the ammunition was exhausted. Phil Sheridan's men stood fast until the last minute and then executed an orderly retreat to a point behind their own lines.

The tireless Rosecrans was everywhere. To a subordinate's plea for reinforcements on his crumbling right, he thundered, "Tell [him] to contest every inch of ground." Inspecting the ford by which he still hoped to cross Stones River and assault the lightly held Confederate right, the general asked if the position could be held. "I will try, sir," replied the officer in charge. Rosecrans

repeated the question. "I will die right here," came the answer. Not until he asked the same question for a third time and got the desired reply, "Yes, sir!" did Rosecrans ride off, satisfied. At 6 A.M. that morning he had sent a division under General Van Cleve across the river, and now, sensing that he was in serious trouble, Rosecrans recalled this force to the dwindling Union salient. By 4 P.M. he had completely re-formed his lines; further Confederate charges were repulsed; and the battle sputtered out.

Bragg was confident that his beleaguered opponent would pull the battered Union army back to Nashville the next day. Exulting in his victory, he telegraphed Richmond, "God has granted us a Happy New Year."

In the above scene from the Travis panorama, Union troops are cheered by the sight of General Rosecrans (right) and rally near the railroad (left).

At Murfreesboro the 21st Michigan formed a part of Sheridan's division, forced to retire from heavy fighting on the right when it ran out of ammunition.

Typical of the hardened Southerners who fought at Murfreesboro were these men of the 9th Mississippi Infantry, photographed in 1861 at Pensacola, Florida.

285

MURFREESBORO

December 31, 1862
January 2, 1863

FIELD OF JANUARY 2ND

STONES RIVER

BRAGG
JA...

6

7

4

3

5

2

ROSECRANS
HQ

NASHVILLE & CHATTANOOGA R.R.

NASHVILLE TURNPIKE

FIELD

David Greenspan

MURFREESBORO (or Stones River): At dawn on December 31 Bragg launches his sledge-hammer attack near the Widow Smith House, catching some of the Federals at breakfast (1). This assault completely turns the Union right, an entire corps being driven back some three miles before rallying on the Nashville Turnpike. As succeeding waves of Confederates crash through the scrub cedar, men under Phil Sheridan fight valiantly (2) but are forced to retire for lack of ammunition, which has been held up by Rebel cavalry forays at far left. Imperturbable George H. Thomas, whose very glance seemed to freeze would-be skulkers in their tracks, falls back and begins to form a new Union line (3), at right angles to the original one. Astride the railroad tracks, Colonel William B. Hazen's artillery stubbornly holds its original position—the only Union detachment to do so—at the center cf the line (4). The first day's battle draws to a close with the Federals formed in a salient around Rosecrans' Headquarters (5). On January 2 Breckinridge is ordered to make a charge across an open field (6), vulnerable to Union artillery at the river's edge. Only when Union reinforcements are hurried across the river (7) is this final Confederate assault halted.

Murfreesboro

G'S HQ
C. 31

WIDOW
SMITH
HOUSE

① 1

GRISCOM
HOUSE

Overall's Creek

At a critical moment in the battle of January 2, sketched here by Henri Lovie, Ohio and Illinois regiments splashed across Stones River to drive back the final Confederate charge on their left.

The Indecisive Fight at Stones River

New Year's Day, 1863, was cold and fair. The two watchful commanders seemed to be avoiding another major engagement; and Rosecrans' efforts to re-form were misinterpreted by Bragg as the prelude to a Union withdrawal. Van Cleve led his division of Federals across Stones River for a third time, taking up the position for the postponed attack on the Confederate right, while Rosecrans strengthened his forward line along the west bank and took measures to protect his supply trains and convoys from Rebel cavalry raids.

Bragg was surprised to discover on the morning of January 2 that the Union army still confronted him. After a quiet forenoon he suddenly ordered Breckinridge's division to dislodge the Union left from the east bank of Stones River. Although Breckinridge protested the order, the attack was set for 4 P.M. With spirit the Southerners charged across 500 yards of open ground, completely exposed to Union artillery. Seeing frightened rabbits scurrying before the shelling, one Rebel called out, "Go it, cotton-tail; I'd run too if I hadn't a reputation." Within twenty minutes the heroic Confederate charge was repulsed, and Breckinridge's men fell back—minus some 1,800 of their comrades.

That evening Bragg was informed that reinforcements for Rosecrans' army had arrived. Disheartened, he wrote, "Common prudence and the safety of my army . . . left no doubt on my mind as to the necessity of my withdrawal from so unequal a contest." In the two separated days of fighting he had lost nearly 12,000 men to the Union loss of 13,000. Bragg retired some 36 miles, for the winter; and Rosecrans, making no effort at pursuit, moved into Murfreesboro for a six months' encampment. Riding about camp the following day, he acknowledged the cheers of his men, "All right, boys, all right; Bragg's a good dog, but Hold Fast's a better."

289

Stones River as it appears today.

THE SOUTH'S LAST OPPORTUNITY

IN THE spring of 1863 the Northern grip on the Confederacy was slowly tightening; yet there was still a chance for the South to upset everything, and for a few unendurably tense weeks that chance looked very good. With Rosecrans inactive in Tennessee, and with Grant seemingly bogged down hopelessly in the steaming low country north of Vicksburg, attention shifted to the East, and it appeared that a Southern victory here might restore the bright prospects that had gone so dim in the preceding September. Robert E. Lee set out to provide that victory; winning it, he then made his supreme effort to win the one final, unattainable triumph that would bring the new nation to independence. He never came quite as close to success as men supposed at the time, but he did give the war its most memorable hour of drama.

Joe Hooker had done admirably in repairing the Army of the Potomac. He displayed genuine talents as an organizer and an executive, which was something of a surprise, for he was believed to be a dashing heads-down fighter and nothing more. He saw to it that the routine chores of military housekeeping were performed properly, so that the men got enough to eat and lived in decent camps; he turned his cavalry corps into an outfit that could fight Jeb Stuart's boys on something like even terms; and he restored the weary army's confidence in itself. He himself had abundant confidence—too much, Mr. Lincoln suspected, for Hooker's jaunty remark that the question was not whether he could take Richmond, but simply when he would take it, struck the President as a little too optimistic. But when April came, and the spring winds dried the unpaved roads so that the armies could use them, Hooker led his troops off on a new offensive with the highest hopes.

Hooker had a greater advantage in numbers than McClellan had ever had. The manpower shortage was beginning to handicap the Confederacy. Union troops were moving about the Virginia landscape on the south side of the lower James River, apparently with aggressive intent; to hold them in check, and to keep that part of the country open so that its bacon and forage could be used, Lee had had to detach James Longstreet and most of Longstreet's army corps early that spring, and when Hooker began to move, Lee's army in and around Fredericksburg numbered hardly more than 60,000 men of all arms. Hooker had more than twice that many, and he was handling them with strategic insight.

He would not repeat Burnside's mistake, butting head-on against the stout Confederate defenses at

Their capture at Gettysburg ended the fighting days of these three lean, tough Confederate soldiers.

Fredericksburg. Instead, he left a third of his army at Fredericksburg to hold Lee's attention, and took the rest on a long swing up the Rappahannock, planning to cross that river and the Rapidan twenty-five miles away, and then march in on Lee's unprotected left and rear. He made the move competently and swiftly, and he sent his cavalry on ahead to make a sweep across Lee's lines of communication near Richmond. He would compel Lee to retreat, his own army would lie on Lee's flank when the retreat began, Lee would have to attack this army on ground of Hooker's choice —and, all in all, this might be the recipe for a resounding Union victory.

It might have worked, except for two things. At the critical moment Hooker lost his nerve—and Lee refused to act by the script which Hooker had written. What followed was one more dismal Union defeat, and the end of another of those "on to Richmond" drives that never seemed to get anywhere.

The first part of Hooker's plan went very smoothly. Hooker got more than 70,000 men established around Chancellorsville, a crossroads a dozen miles back of Lee's left flank, and his cavalry went swooping down to cut the Richmond, Fredericksburg, and Potomac Railroad farther south. But Lee ignored the cavalry raid and used Stuart's cavalry to control all of the roads around Chancellorsville, so that Hooker could not find out where the Confederates were. Worried and somewhat bewildered, Hooker called a halt and put his troops in sketchy fieldworks near Chancellorsville, instead of pushing on to the more open country half a dozen miles to the east, which was where he had originally planned to take position. Then Lee, in the most daring move of his whole career, split his army into three pieces and gave Joe Hooker an expensive lesson in tactics.

Lee left part of his men at Fredericksburg to make sure that the massed Federals there did not do anything damaging. With 45,000 men he went to Chancellorsville to face Hooker; and after making a quick size-up of the situation he gave Stonewall Jackson 26,000 of these and sent him on a long swing around Hooker's exposed right. Two hours before dusk on May 2 Jackson hit that right flank with pile-driver force, shattering it to pieces, driving a whole Yankee army corps in wild rout, and knocking Hooker's army completely loose from its prepared position. Two or three days of confused and desperate fighting ensued —around Chancellorsville clearing and back at Fredericksburg, where the Federals forced a crossing and then found they could accomplish nothing in particular—and in the end Hooker beat an ignominious retreat, pulling all of his troops north of the Rappahannock. He had lost 17,000 men, he had let an army half the size of his own cut him to pieces, and he had handled his men so poorly that a very substantial part of his immense host had never been put into action at all. Chancellorsville was Lee's most brilliant victory. It had been bought at a heavy cost, however, for Stonewall Jackson was mortally wounded, shot down by his own troops in the confused fighting in the thickets on the night of May 2.

Once more, Lee had taken the initiative away from his Federal opponent. The next move would be his, and after conferences with President Davis and his cabinet in Richmond, that move was prepared: Lee would invade Pennsylvania, trying in the early summer of 1863 the move that had failed in the fall of 1862.

This decision may have been a mistake: a thing which is more easily seen now than at the time it was made. It would be a gamble, at best—a bet that the magnificent Army of Northern Virginia could somehow win, on Northern soil, an offensive victory decisive enough to bring the war to a close. The army was certain to be outnumbered. The thrust into the Northern heartland was certain to stir the Federals to a new effort. The business would have to be a quick, one-punch affair—a raid, rather than a regular invasion—for Confederate resources just were not adequate to a sustained campaign in Northern territory. If it failed, the Confederacy might lose its army and the war along with it. When he marched for Pennsylvania, Lee would be marching against long odds. He would have Longstreet and Longstreet's soldiers, which he had not had at Chancellorsville, but he would greatly miss Stonewall Jackson.

But the fact is that no really good move was available to him. If he stayed in Virginia, holding his ground, the North would inevitably refit the Army of the Potomac and in a month or so would come down with another ponderous offensive. That offensive might indeed be beaten back, but the process would be expensive, and the campaign would further consume the resources of war-racked Virginia. European recognition and intervention—that will-o'-the-wisp which still flickered across the Confederate horizon—could never be won by defensive warfare. A good Confederate victory in Pennsylvania might, just possibly, bring it about.

Furthermore, the Confederacy was beginning to feel

the pressure which Grant was applying in the Vicksburg area. An invasion of the North might very well compel the Federals to pull troops away from the Mississippi Valley; certainly, a Southern victory in Pennsylvania would offset anything that might be lost in the West . . . for it was beginning to be obvious that a great deal was likely to be lost in the West, and fairly soon at that.

For Grant, having tried all of the schemes that could not work, had finally hit upon one that would work, and he was following it with an energy and a daring fully equal to Lee's own.

To get east of the river, where he could force his enemy to give battle, Grant had followed the simplest but riskiest plan of all. He would march his troops downstream on the Louisiana side of the river; he would use gunboats and transports—which first must run the gantlet of the powerful Vicksburg batteries—to get the soldiers over to the eastern shore; and then he could march to the northeast, destroying any field army that might come to face him, cutting Pemberton's lines of communication with the rest of the Confederacy, herding Pemberton's troops back inside of the Vicksburg entrenchments, and then laying siege to the place and capturing army, fortress, and all. Like Lee's move at Chancellorsville, this would be a dazzling trick if it worked. If it did not work, the North would lose much more than it could afford to lose.

As the month of May wore along Grant was making it work.

The area which his army would have to traverse on the Louisiana side was swampy, with a tangle of bayous and lakes in the way. The western pioneers in Grant's army were handy with the axe and the spade, and they built roads and bridges with an untaught competence that left the engineer officers talking to themselves. Downstream the army went; and downstream, too, came Admiral Porter's gunboats and enough transports to serve as ferries, after a hair-raising midnight dash past the thundering guns along the Vicksburg waterfront. The navy proved unable to beat down the Confederate defenses at Grand Gulf, twenty-five miles below Vicksburg, but Grant got his troops across a few miles farther down, flanked the Grand Gulf defenses, beat an inadequate force which Pemberton had sent down to check him, and then started out for the Mississippi state capital, Jackson, fifty miles east of Vicksburg. Jackson was a supply base and railroad center; if the Richmond government sent help to Vicksburg, the help would come through Jack-

son, and Grant's first move was to take that piece off the board before it could be used.

Grant made his river crossing with some 33,000 men. (He had more soldiers in the general area, and would have many more than 33,000 before long, but that was what he had when he started moving across the state of Mississippi.) At this time the Confederates had more troops in the vicinity than Grant had, but they never could make proper use of them; Grant's swift move had bewildered Pemberton much as Lee's had bewildered Hooker. Just before he marched downstream, Grant had ordered a brigade of cavalry to come down from the Tennessee border, riding between the parallel north-south lines of the Mississippi Central and the Mobile and Ohio railroads. This brigade was led by Colonel Benjamin H. Grierson, and it was eminently successful; it went slicing the length of the state, cutting railroads, fighting detachments of Confederate cavalry, and reaching Union lines finally at Baton Rouge. For the few days that counted most, it drew Pemberton's attention away from Grant and kept him from figuring out what the Yankees were driving at.

From Port Gibson, a town in the rear of Grand Gulf, Grant moved on Jackson. Joe Johnston was at Jackson. He had recovered from his wounds, and Davis had sent him out to take general command in the West—an assignment which Johnston did not care for, because Pemberton's and Bragg's armies, for which he now had responsibility, were widely separated, and Johnston did not see how he could control both of them at once. He was trying now to assemble enough of a force to stave Grant off and then, with Pemberton, to defeat him outright, but Grant did not give him time enough. On May 14, having driven off a Confederate detachment at the town of Raymond, Grant occupied Jackson, and Johnston, moving north, sent word to Pemberton to come east and join him. (It was clear enough to Johnston that Pemberton would lose both his army and Vicksburg if he were ever driven into his entrenchments and compelled to stand siege.)

Pemberton was in a fix. From Richmond, Davis was ordering him to hold Vicksburg at any cost; Johnston, meanwhile, was telling him to leave the place and save his army; and Pemberton, trying to do a little of both, came quickly to grief. He marched east to find Grant, heeded Johnston's orders too late and tried to swing to the northeast, and on May 16 he was brought to battle on the rolling, wooded plateau known as Champion's Hill, halfway between Vicksburg and

Jackson. Grant beat him and drove him back to the west, followed hard and routed his rear guard the next day at the crossing of the Big Black River, and sent him headlong into his Vicksburg lines. Grant's army followed fast, occupying the high ground along the Yazoo River—the ground that had been the goal of all the winter's fruitless campaigning—and establishing there a secure base, where steamboats from the North could reach it with all the supplies and reinforcements it might need. On May 19 and again on May 22 Grant made an attempt to take Vicksburg by storm. He was repulsed both times, with heavy loss, so he resorted to siege warfare. He drew lines of trenches and redoubts to face the entire length of the Confederate lines—all in all, Grant's entrenched line was fifteen miles long by the time it was finished—he detached a sufficient force eastward to hold Joe Johnston at bay, and then he settled down grimly to starve the place into submission. Johnston was building up his relieving army, but he never could make it strong enough. He had perhaps 25,000 men, and Pemberton had 30,000, but Grant was reinforced until he had 75,000, and he could handle both Pemberton and Johnston without difficulty. By the first of June, Pemberton was locked up, Johnston was helpless, and it seemed likely that Vicksburg's fall would only be a question of time.

So when Lee prepared for his own campaign, the inexorable pressure of Grant's grip on Vicksburg was an important factor in his plans. It may be that his best move then would have been to stay on the defensive in Virginia and send troops west so that Johnston could beat Grant and raise the siege of Vicksburg, but to argue so is to indulge in the second-guessing that is so simple long after the event. The move would have been very chancy, at best, and there was no guarantee that the Federals in Virginia would permit it. The Army of the Potomac had been disgracefully beaten at Chancellorsville, but it had not been disorganized, and the battle somehow had not left the depression and low morale which had followed Second Bull Run and Fredericksburg. The army would be ready for action very soon, and if it began a new campaign of invasion, Lee would need every man he could get. To send west enough troops to turn the tables on Grant might be to invite a disastrous defeat in Virginia . . . and so, in the end, the idea was dropped, and Lee prepared to head north.

Lee began his move on June 3, shifting his troops northwest from Fredericksburg behind the line of the Rappahannock River, aiming to reach the Shenandoah Valley and cross the Potomac west of the Blue Ridge. His army was divided into three corps, now: one led by the redoubtable Longstreet (who took a very dim view, incidentally, of this invasion of Pennsylvania), and the others commanded by two new lieutenant generals, Richard S. Ewell and A. P. Hill. Longstreet's corps led off, pausing at Culpeper Court House while Ewell's corps leapfrogged it and went on to drive scattered Federal detachments out of the lower Valley. Hill stayed in Fredericksburg to watch the Yankees.

The movement was made with skill, and Hooker was given no real opening for an attack on the separated segments of Lee's army. Hooker did propose, once he saw what was going on, that he himself simply march toward Richmond, in the belief that that would force Lee to return quickly enough. But Washington did not approve. Hooker's mishandling of the army at Chancellorsville had aroused the gravest distrust of his abilities; and although the administration could not quite nerve itself to remove him (he enjoyed the powerful backing of Secretary of the Treasury Salmon P. Chase), it apparently was unwilling to let him try a new offensive. Hooker was told to act strictly on the defensive, and to follow Lee wherever Lee might go.

By June 14 Lee had pulled Hill out of Fredericksburg, and the whole army was on the move, with Longstreet holding the gaps in the Blue Ridge, and Ewell, behind him, moving toward the Potomac crossings. Hooker's army was sidling toward the northwest, determined, whatever happened, to keep between Lee and Washington. Between the two armies the rival cavalry sparred and skirmished, each commander trying to get news of the enemy's army and deny to the enemy news of his own. Out of all of this sparring came a moment of inspiration to Jeb Stuart. He acted on it, and thereby helped Lee lose the campaign.

As Lee's army crossed the Potomac and wheeled eastward, Stuart and his cavalry were to move on its right flank and front, keeping Lee informed about the Union army's movements. It occurred to Stuart that he could best get his horsemen across the Potomac by riding all the way around Hooker's army—a feat which would bring Stuart much acclaim—and so Stuart, with Lee's permission, undertook to do it that way. But the Federal army occupied more ground and was much more active than Stuart had supposed, and Stuart, driven far to the east, was completely out of touch with Lee for ten days. Lacking Stuart, Lee during those ten days was completely out of touch with Hooker. Invading the enemy's country, Lee was in effect moving blindfolded.

Lee got his army into Pennsylvania, its three corps widely separated—the advance of the army, as June neared its end, was at York, and the rear was at Chambersburg—and he believed that this dispersion was proper, since, as far as he knew, Hooker had not yet come north of the Potomac. (Stuart surely would have notified Lee if the Federals had moved.) But the Army of the Potomac had actually crossed the river on June 25 and 26, and on June 28 Lee learned that the whole Yankee army was concentrated around Frederick, Maryland, squarely on his flank. He also learned that it was Hooker's army no longer. Hooker had at last been relieved, and the command had gone to the short-tempered, grizzled, and competent Major General George Gordon Meade.

Lee hastened to concentrate, and the handiest place was the town of Gettysburg. Moving north to bring him to battle, Meade collided with him there, and on July 1, 2, and 3 there was fought the greatest single battle of the war—Gettysburg, a terrible and spectacular drama which, properly or not, is usually looked upon as the great moment of decision.

In the fighting on July 1 the Federals were badly outnumbered, only a fraction of their army being present, and they were soundly beaten. On the next two days Lee attacked, striking at both flanks and at the center in an all-out effort to crush the Army of the Potomac once and for all. Nothing quite worked. The climactic moment came in the afternoon of July 3, when 15,000 men led by a division under Major General George Pickett made a gallant but doomed assault on the central Federal position on Cemetery Ridge. The assault almost succeeded, but "almost" was not good enough. Broken apart and staggered by enormous losses, the assaulting column fell back to the Confederate lines, and the Battle of Gettysburg was over. The Federals had lost 23,000 men, and the Confederates very nearly as many—which meant that Lee had lost nearly a third of his whole army. He could do nothing now but retreat. Meade followed, but his own army was too mangled, and Meade was too cautious to try to force another battle on Lee north of the Potomac. Lee got his army back into Virginia, and the campaign was over.

Stuart's absence had been expensive. (He finally reached Lee on the evening of the second day of the battle.) Lee had been forced to fight before he was ready for it, and when the fighting began he had not felt free to maneuver because, with Stuart away, he could never be sure where the Yankees were. At the close of the first day's fighting Longstreet had urged Lee to move around the Federal left flank and assume a position somewhere in the Federal rear that would force Meade to do the attacking, but with the knowledge he then had Lee could not be sure that such a move would not take him straight to destruction. He had felt compelled to fight where he was, and when the fighting came he desperately missed Stonewall Jackson: Ewell, leading Jackson's old troops, proved irresolute and let opportunities slip, while Longstreet was sulky and moved with less than his usual speed. All in all, Lee was poorly served by his lieutenants in the greatest battle of his career.

But if Gettysburg was what took the eye, Vicksburg was probably more important; and the climax came at Vicksburg, by odd chance, at almost exactly the same time that it came at Gettysburg. Grant's lines had grown tighter and tighter, and Pemberton's army was strained to the breaking point; and on July 3, just about the time when Pickett's men were forming for their hopeless charge, Pemberton sent a white flag through the lines and asked for terms. Grant followed the old "unconditional surrender" line, but receded from it quickly enough when Pemberton refused to go for it; and on July 4 Pemberton surrendered the city and the army, on terms which permitted his men to give their paroles and go to their homes. Halleck, back in Washington, complained that Grant should have insisted on sending the whole army north as prisoners of war, but Grant believed that this was not really necessary. The 30,000 soldiers whom Pemberton had surrendered were effectively out of the war. Vicksburg itself was taken, within a week the Confederates would surrender the downstream fortress at Port Hudson—and, as Lincoln put it, the Father of Waters would roll unvexed to the sea.

Gettysburg ruined a Confederate offensive and demonstrated that the great triumph on Northern soil which the South had to win if it was to gain recognition abroad could not be won. But Vicksburg broke the Confederacy into halves, gave the Mississippi Valley to the Union, and inflicted a wound that would ultimately prove mortal. Losing at Gettysburg, the Confederates had lost more than they could well afford to lose; at Vicksburg, they lost what they could not afford at all.

Edwin Forbes' sketch above shows the Federal army approaching the Rappahannock River fords on its way to Chancellorsville. Hooker replaced supply wagons with pack mules (right) to speed the march.

Lincoln appointed Joe Hooker (below) to army command reluctantly; despite his good combat record and his popularity with the troops, Lincoln saw that Hooker was an intriguer and an egotist at heart.

The Road to Chancellorsville

The Army of the Potomac's new commanding officer, "Fighting Joe" Hooker, was a debonair general with a good combat record, an Apollo-like presence, and a vast amount of self-confidence. Upon presenting his plans to Washington for the 1863 spring campaign in the East, Hooker remarked, "May God have mercy on General Lee, for I will have none."

McClellan had tried to take the Rebel capital from the east; Burnside had tried it from the north; Hooker would now essay a wide sweep to his right and come in on Lee from the west. This called for a long hike up the Rappahannock, crossings of that river and its tributary, the Rapidan, then another march down the south bank of the two streams through a tangled maze of second-growth woodland known locally as the Wilderness. If Joe Hooker could achieve all this quickly, under cover of various diversions, he would be in the rear of the Rebel army, on good fighting ground, and with a solid numerical advantage. The one hitch was that Robert E. Lee refused to sit still and let Hooker outflank him.

Leaving one wing of his army at Fredericksburg to deceive Lee, Hooker crossed the Rapidan on the night of April 29, and the next day was at Chancellorsville, another of those nondescript crossroads in the middle of nowhere whose name war would stain immutably.

The Federals were just twelve miles from Lee's Fredericksburg lines and well behind them; however, they were still in the Wilderness, and Lee, alert to his danger, was marching hard for Chancellorsville.

The Army of the Potomac crossed the Rapidan at Germanna and Ely's fords; the latter appears in the photographs above (taken from a modern-day bridge) and below. Bonfires on each bank guided the long blue columns during the night crossing, and several Northern soldiers were swept away by the swift, roily waters in spite of the cavalry "lifeguards" stationed at the fords.

This is Scott's Run, near one of the narrow Wilderness roads on which Jackson moved around the Union flank.

Lee and Jackson Prepare a Surprise

On May 1 Hooker had his army on the march toward Fredericksburg, but the moment it ran into Rebel fire he unaccountably pulled back to Chancellorsville. Lee had struck sooner than he expected, and Hooker's nerve failed: "I just lost confidence in Joe Hooker," he later admitted.

The ugly duckling of this Union army was O. O. Howard's XI Corps, composed in part of Germans ostracized by the other boys for their alien ways. Hooker posted this corps on his extreme right, as far away from the enemy as possible, but when Stuart's cavalry found this wing invitingly unprepared, Lee made the most daring decision of his military career. Outnumbered 70,000 to 50,000, he nevertheless sent Jackson with 26,000 men on a long, concealed flank march directly across the front of Hooker's army. By late afternoon of May 2 Stonewall was set to throw a Sunday punch at the hapless XI Corps.

The tablet above marks the site of the final war council between Lee and Jackson, on the night of May 1. The following dawn they met briefly, for the last time, as painted at left by E. B. F. Julio; that evening Jackson was mortally wounded. At right, the scene of the Rebel flank attack, looking toward the Federal line.

Jackson's
Last Charge

Major General O. O. Howard

Above, Federal reserves at Chancellorsville, sketched by Alfred Waud during the fighting on May 1. The Chancellor House, Hooker's headquarters, is at right.

Jackson's target was particularly vulnerable because of the rashness of Daniel Sickles, who commanded the Union center. When Sickles saw what was the end of Jackson's column moving off through the woods, he deduced that the Confederates were retreating, and attacked. This came to little, and it left the Federal right completely isolated. When Jackson's men reappeared on the Union flank, bursting from the forest in a mile-wide assault wave, Howard's XI Corps crumbled and fled in headlong panic down the gloomy roads toward Chancellorsville. Fresh troops, artillery, and darkness finally slowed the Rebel tide, but Hooker's right wing was gone.

About 9 P.M. a North Carolina regiment fired at what it thought was Yankee cavalry. Instead, it was Jackson and his staff on a scouting mission, and Stonewall reeled in the saddle with three wounds.

Waud's sketch below shows the Union II Corps advancing to meet Jackson's flank attack of May 2, as the tangled remnants of the XI Corps stream to the rear.

Jackson's wounds necessitated the amputation of his left arm at a field hospital behind the lines. The stone below marks the spot where the limb is buried.

301

CHANCELLORSVILLE

Second Day: May 2, 1863

TO RAPPAHANNOCK RIVER

RIVER ROAD

TO SALEM CHURCH

TURNPIKE

Mott's Run

Chancellorsville

HOOKER'S HQ

ORANGE PLANK ROAD

FAIRVIEW CEMETERY

7

2

...WERT ...OUSE

HAZEL GROVE

6

FURNACE ROAD

CATHERINE FURNACE

1

JACKSON'S FLANK MARCH

CHANCELLORSVILLE: At first light on May 2 Jackson begins a flank march (lower right) across the Union front. Sickles glimpses the tail of this column, moves forward from Hazel Grove, and attacks (1). His minor success convinces Hooker that the Confederates are in full retreat, and that Lee's probing attacks (2) are merely rear-guard actions. Jackson, meanwhile, has gone into position athwart the Union right flank, which faces south along the Turnpike. At 6 P.M. he drives forward (3), routing the XI Corps, his wide battle line overlapping the desperate Union attempts to form (4). The victorious Confederates sweep up the Turnpike, past the Wilderness Church and Dowdall's Tavern. Here remnants of the XI Corps make a last stand (5) and, reinforced with a few guns, delay Jackson's men long enough for the rest of the troops to make good their escape. Sickles falls back to Hazel Grove, where Union guns knock back a Rebel attack (6) threatening this key position. The fire of Hooker's massed artillery at Fairview Cemetery (7) finally halts the Southern advance. At 9 P.M. Jackson and his staff, returning from a reconnoitering mission to locate the new Federal positions, are fired on by a nervous Confederate regiment, and Jackson is fatally wounded (8).

The Fight for Chancellorsville Clearing

Dan Sickles' recklessness had left the XI Corps unsupported; and when that outfit was demolished, Sickles was isolated. Regaining his lines at Hazel Grove, he started back toward the rest of the Union army. The result was a fiery, confused battle in the smoky, moonlit night.

A Northern general recalled the "infernal and yet sublime combination of sound and flame and smoke, and dreadful yells of rage, of pain, of triumph, or of defiance." Part of Sickles' men reached the main lines, and part stayed at Hazel Grove. Strong Federal batteries in Fairview Cemetery finally stopped the attackers, breaking up troop concentrations poised to renew the battle. Their fire nearly annihilated the party evacuating the wounded Jackson and hit A. P. Hill with a shell fragment.

Oddly enough, Joe Hooker was not in a particularly bad spot as May 3 dawned. Reinforcements from Fredericksburg gave him a two-to-one edge, and he was squarely between the two halves of Lee's army. But Hooker was a beaten man, thinking only of defense. He recalled the rest of Sickles' men, abandoning Hazel Grove. Jeb Stuart had taken over for Jackson, and he began shifting to his right to rejoin Lee.

With Lee and Stuart sending their men forward relentlessly, the fighting reached a savage pitch again. The Union salient became more and more constricted, and Lee's artillery had it in a cross fire. Chancellorsville clearing became a maelstrom of plunging shell. Hooker was stunned by a shot that smashed into his headquarters, and reinforcements and supply trains were scattered. The Rebel cannoneers even fired pieces of railroad rail.

At last the Federals fell back to a new position covering the Rappahannock fords. General Charles Griffin worked his guns into position, exclaiming, "I'll make 'em think hell isn't half a mile off!" and beat back the final Rebel charge.

304

At dawn on May 3 Hooker ordered the evacuation of Hazel Grove (above), an open, high plateau which was an ideal artillery position. Lee's gunners immediately moved in to pour a converging fire into the massed Federal troops.

Federal artillery emplacements are still visible at Fairview Cemetery.

A Union trench near the Orange Plank Road, held by Slocum's XII Corps.

This narrow lane, Mineral Spring Road, was part of Hooker's last line.

Fredericksburg and Salem Church

At the time Jackson made his flank attack, Hooker had decided that Major General John Sedgwick's VI Corps—nearly 25,000 troops threatening Jubal Early's 10,000 Confederates at Fredericksburg—had better come to his rescue. On May 3, while Lee was driving Hooker toward the Rappahannock, Sedgwick sent his men against the rugged Marye's Heights lines that had stopped Burnside the previous December.

Early's thin ranks repulsed two attacks. As a third formed, the lead regiment was told, "You will advance at double-quick. . . . you will not stop until you get the order to halt. You will never get that order." One end of the Rebel line gave way, the rest came under enfilading fire, and Marye's Heights was won.

Sedgwick put his men on the roads to Chancellorsville, but Lee, leaving Stuart and just four divisions to keep an eye on Hooker, turned and held him off at Salem Church, half a dozen miles short of his goal. On the night of May 5 Hooker ordered a general withdrawal across the Rappahannock.

In its simplest terms, Chancellorsville demonstrated the complete dominance of one general, Robert E. Lee, over another, Joseph Hooker. Hooker had frittered away an excellent start and several good chances, letting an army half the size of his defeat him, and losing 17,000 men in the bargain.

For the Confederacy, however, Chancellorsville was a barren victory. On May 10, murmuring, "Let us cross over the river, and rest under the shade of the trees," Stonewall Jackson died. Lee said, "I have lost my right arm," and the Army of Northern Virginia was never quite the same again.

Above, a rare action photograph of a Union battery during Sedgwick's attack on Marye's Heights. Below, the Sunken Road as it looked after the battle.

At right, sunset at Salem Church, site of the final blow to Hooker's hopes for victory at Chancellorsville.

The photograph above looks across the Confederate positions north of Vicksburg (Fort Hill is visible at left) toward the Mississippi's 1863 channel, now a backwater called the Yazoo Canal.

A fellow officer said that Grant (at left, photographed by Brady in 1863) "habitually wears an expression as if he had determined to drive his head through a brick wall, and was about to do it."

The Mississippi made a loop at Vicksburg, and Grant set his men to digging in an unavailing attempt to divert the river and bypass the city completely. The engraving at right is from Leslie's.

Vicksburg: Key to the Mississippi

Major General Earl Van Dorn

"The spinal column of America," William T. Sherman called the Mississippi River. Like most Federal strategists he was convinced that the Confederacy would die a quick death if the North could seize control of the river and cut off the Old South from its Western allies. When General U. S. Grant set out to do the job, he hardly suspected that it would take him eight months.

By November, 1862, approximately 250 miles of the river—from Vicksburg, Mississippi, to Port Hudson, Louisiana—remained in Southern hands. Vicksburg was the key: hilly, heavily fortified, perched atop bluffs on the east bank, it was impregnable to attack from the river.

Grant learned much about mili-tary strategy during his Vicksburg campaign, and the first lesson was the difficulty of co-ordinating two widely separated armies operating in enemy territory. His teachers were Earl Van Dorn and Bedford Forrest, who destroyed his supply depot and cut his communications as he tried to cut off Vicksburg by invading central Mississippi. With Grant stymied, the Rebel garrison in Vicksburg met Sherman, advancing down-river, and easily repulsed him at Chickasaw Bluffs north of the city.

Then Grant joined Sherman across the Mississippi, just above Vicksburg, and spent the winter digging canals, cutting levees, and widening bayous in an effort to bypass the citadel's formidable batteries.

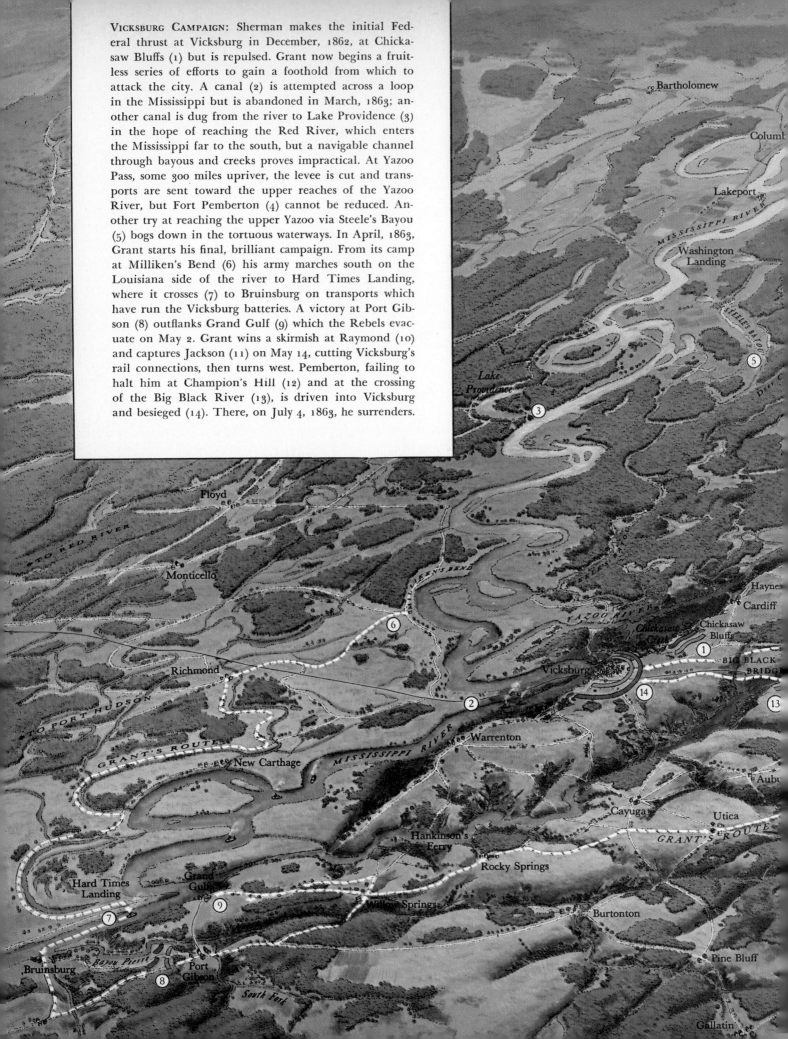

VICKSBURG CAMPAIGN: Sherman makes the initial Federal thrust at Vicksburg in December, 1862, at Chickasaw Bluffs (1) but is repulsed. Grant now begins a fruitless series of efforts to gain a foothold from which to attack the city. A canal (2) is attempted across a loop in the Mississippi but is abandoned in March, 1863; another canal is dug from the river to Lake Providence (3) in the hope of reaching the Red River, which enters the Mississippi far to the south, but a navigable channel through bayous and creeks proves impractical. At Yazoo Pass, some 300 miles upriver, the levee is cut and transports are sent toward the upper reaches of the Yazoo River, but Fort Pemberton (4) cannot be reduced. Another try at reaching the upper Yazoo via Steele's Bayou (5) bogs down in the tortuous waterways. In April, 1863, Grant starts his final, brilliant campaign. From its camp at Milliken's Bend (6) his army marches south on the Louisiana side of the river to Hard Times Landing, where it crosses (7) to Bruinsburg on transports which have run the Vicksburg batteries. A victory at Port Gibson (8) outflanks Grand Gulf (9) which the Rebels evacuate on May 2. Grant wins a skirmish at Raymond (10) and captures Jackson (11) on May 14, cutting Vicksburg's rail connections, then turns west. Pemberton, failing to halt him at Champion's Hill (12) and at the crossing of the Big Black River (13), is driven into Vicksburg and besieged (14). There, on July 4, 1863, he surrenders.

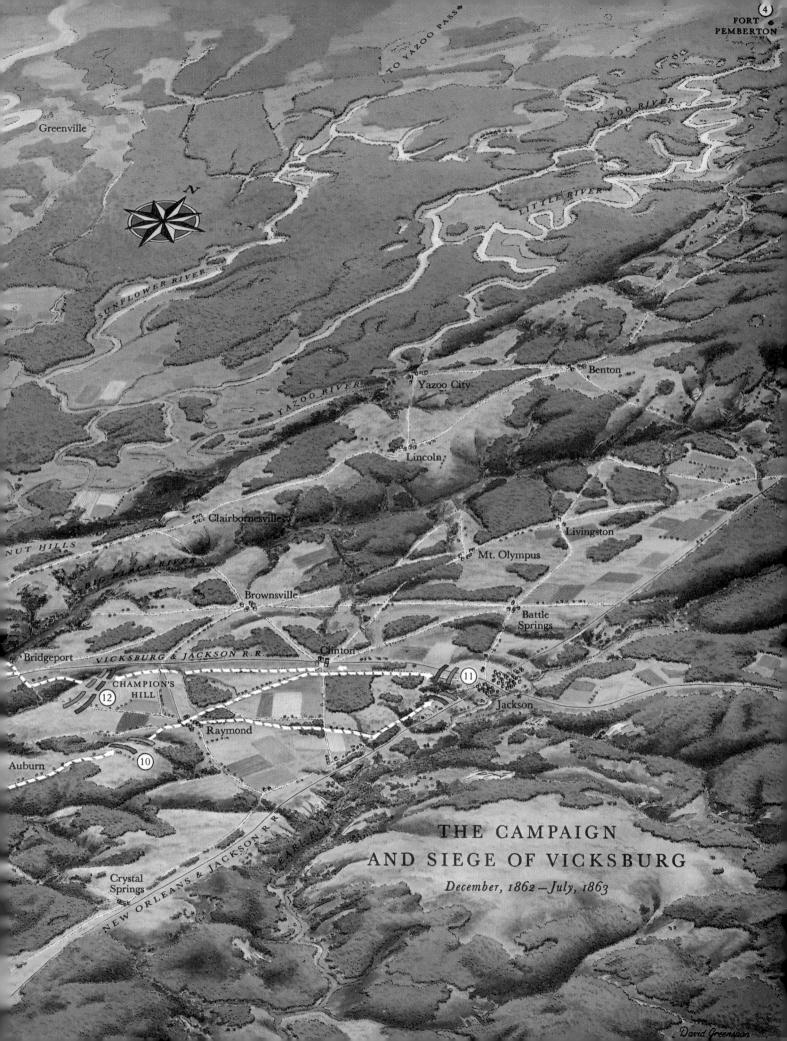

THE CAMPAIGN
AND SIEGE OF VICKSBURG
December, 1862 – July, 1863

David Greenspan

In the Currier and Ives print above, Porter's gunboats, with transports and barges lashed to their sides, run Vicksburg's guns. A month before, Farragut's New Orleans fleet had failed to knock out Port Hudson, 250 miles downstream. His flagship Hartford is the lead craft in Edward Arnold's 1864 painting below.

The Union Navy Assists in a Daring Plan

The Union navy was represented at Vicksburg by Rear Admiral David D. Porter, a tough, bluff, aggressive sailor. While the Confederate high command in the West was confused and divided, the Federals —Grant, his trusted lieutenant Sherman, and Porter—worked together in harmony. This was fortunate, for during the months of unavailing effort to find a way to get at Vicksburg, a great number of influential Northerners railed at their management of the campaign.

By April, 1863, Grant finally committed himself to a course of action. His army would make the difficult march south through the swampy lowland on the west shore and cross the river below Vicksburg on transports which Porter would have to run past the city's batteries. This would put him, as he said later, "on dry ground on the same side of the river with the enemy." It was a risky, unorthodox plan: his supply line would be tortuous; the navy, once past the batteries, would be irretrievably below Vicksburg, for the underpowered gunboats could not beat their way upstream past the guns again; and initially, at least, Grant would be outnumbered while operating in enemy territory.

Porter successfully ran the Vicksburg batteries the night of April 16, and two weeks later Grant was across the river. To Sherman he outlined a radical plan: they would carry "what rations of hard bread, coffee and salt we can and make the country furnish the balance."

Rear Admiral David Dixon Porter, "brave, resolute and indefatigable."

Grierson Provides a Smoke Screen

Grierson's cavalry on review near Baton Rouge after the raid through Mississippi, shown in a remarkable photograph by Confederate secret service agent Andrew D. Lytle. The troopers at right have already dismounted and unsaddled. Grierson reported that "the Confederacy was a hollow shell."

Colonel Benjamin H. Grierson

President Davis had sent Joseph E. Johnston, now recovered from his Fair Oaks wounds, to assume command in the West. At Jackson, about fifty miles east of Vicksburg, he pulled together what troops he could and worried about how John C. Pemberton's Rebel army at Vicksburg should be used. Davis had ordered Pemberton to hold Vicksburg at all costs; but Johnston was well aware that the city could be a fatal trap for its defenders.

Grant needed to screen his movements, and he began by sending a former Illinois music teacher named Benjamin Grierson off on a cavalry raid with 1,700 men. Heading south from the Tennessee border, Grierson drove through central Mississippi, tearing up railroads and upsetting Pemberton's troop deployments before reaching Union-held Baton Rouge.

As Grant prepared to cross the river below Vicksburg he ordered Sherman to make a diversionary attack on the northern approaches to the city. Pemberton was now confused to Grant's satisfaction. "All right," he wrote Sherman, "join me below Vicksburg." The next step was a push inland to Jackson, to cut Pemberton's railroad lifeline and hold Joe Johnston at bay.

315

This sturdy old live oak stands on the site of the Champion House, used as a Union hospital at the Battle of Champion's Hill. The house was burned when the Federals moved on to besiege Vicksburg.

The Vicksburg Citadel Is Isolated

As the Federal Army of the Tennessee moved swiftly on Jackson, Pemberton began to see the light. He wired Jefferson Davis that Grant "threatens Jackson and if successful cuts off Vicksburg and Port Hudson from the East." Pemberton sought to sever Grant's supply lines while he was busy at Jackson, but he soon discovered there was no supply line. The Yankees were living off the country.

Brushing aside light opposition, on May 14 Grant chased Joe Johnston out of Jackson, and his Westerners, acting on Sherman's orders "to destroy everything public not needed by us," took the town apart.

Grant now turned toward Vicksburg. On May 16 Pemberton tried to make a stand at Champion's Hill, twenty miles east of Vicksburg, but after a stiff fight which made the place a "hill of death" he was defeated. His rear guard was routed the next day at the Big Black River. Johnston warned: "If it is not too late, evacuate Vicksburg . . . and march to the northeast." It was too late; Pemberton was trapped.

The now-abandoned road and gravel pit at Champion's Hill (above) were the scenes of heavy fighting. Soldiers hurrying forward to the battle scooped drinking water from rutted roads like that at left.

This four-gun Confederate water battery was typical of the well-protected artillery defending Vicksburg.

Grant Closes the Ring

Skillful Confederate engineers had been at work on the Vicksburg land and river defenses ever since Farragut's fleet had threatened the city the previous year. An officer in Grant's army recorded his impression of their work: "A long line of high, rugged, irregular bluffs, clearly cut against the sky, crowned with cannon which peered ominously from embrasures to the right and left as far as the eye could see . . . The approaches to this position were frightful."

Pemberton's 30,000 troops threatened to swamp the city, and one woman resident, watching them march into the lines, wrote in her diary: "Wan, hollow-eyed, ragged, footsore, bloody, the men limped along unarmed . . . followed by siege-guns, ambulances, gun-carriages, and wagons in aimless confusion." Another diarist reported on May 17, "The day of our doom appears close at hand."

Grant's first move was to seize the high ground overlooking the Yazoo River north of the city, where Sherman had been repulsed five months before. Pemberton let it go without a fight, giving the Federals a base for supplies and reinforcements sent up the Yazoo from the Mississippi.

Joe Johnston, some 40 miles to the northwest, had less than 25,000 men, and eventually would manage to scrape up a few thousand more. But he knew the South could never hope to match the flow of Union reinforcements which would arrive now that Grant's supply line was re-established. Already the Union commander had 50,000 men, and within a month he would have half again as many more.

At right, dugouts behind the center of the Union lines encircling Vicksburg, from which sapping operations underneath a Rebel fort were begun.

318

Union Frontal Attacks Fail

Lt. Gen. John C. Pemberton

On May 19 Grant tried to take Vicksburg by storm. Believing Pemberton's men to be demoralized by their recent defeats, he wanted to capture the city before Johnston could gather a force to raise a siege. But the Rebels had regained their confidence, now that they were behind strong defensive works.

"God! what a charge it was! . . . My men came on so gallantly; not one to falter. . . . We did all mortal men could do—but such slaughter!" recalled a Union officer. Sherman wrote his wife: "The heads of columns have been swept away as chaff from the hand on a windy day."

By May 22 Grant was ready with another major attack, for his aggressive instincts recoiled at the thought of a lengthy siege. At 10 A.M., after a severe bombardment, his three corps, under Sherman, James McPherson, and John McClernand, surged forward. They struggled through the cunning defenses, captured a few outlying trenches, but were soon stymied. The Confederates sent artillery shells with lit fuzes rolling into their ranks and launched vicious counterattacks. When McClernand insisted that he was close to making a breakthrough on his front, Grant ordered a renewal of the assault, but the only result was to increase Union casualties to 3,200.

Convinced at last that a siege was necessary, Grant set his men to emplanting batteries and digging trenches around the city.

Vicksburg (below) was a bustling commercial center of 4,500 when the Civil War began, with strong economic ties to the North. Its besieged citizens remembered ironically that in 1860 a majority of them had opposed secession.

The water color above is an anonymous, primitive view of Grant's May 19 attack on Vicksburg. Below, Frank Schell's sketch for Leslie's shows slaves from Jefferson Davis' nearby plantation entering Union lines at Vicksburg.

City Under Siege

Even without the obstacles such as ditches and felled trees which the Confederates put in the Yankees' path, the approaches to Vicksburg were rugged, as these two photographs demonstrate. Above is Fort Hill on Pemberton's extreme left, which Sherman's XV Corps faced. At right is a view from the Southern lines of the broken terrain across which Grant's men had to make their attacks.

Vicksburg has the melancholy distinction of being the only sizable American city to endure total siege. It was ringed so tightly, a Rebel soldier admitted, that "a cat could not have crept out of Vicksburg without being discovered." Under the steady shelling of Porter's fleet and Grant's army, the populace went underground, "packed in, black and white, like sardines in a box." It was spring, and in her diary a woman mused, "In the midst of all this carnage and commotion . . . birds are singing . . . flowers are in perfection . . . and the garden bright and gay. . . . all save the spirit of man seems divine."

As Grant's lines crept closer the city's food supply dwindled; mule meat and peas formed a typical diet. At last, on July 3, Pemberton requested surrender terms.

On June 25 the Yankees exploded a mine under a Rebel fort and briefly occupied the crater it made (at left center in Frank Schell's drawing above), but to little advantage. The Vicksburg courthouse is visible beyond the crater. Below is a pen sketch by Theodore R. Davis of Grant (at left) and Pemberton discussing the surrender terms between the lines.

Victory Clears the Great River

As the generals discussed surrender the men in the ranks took advantage of the cease fire to visit with their opposite numbers. A private noted that "several brothers met, and any quantity of cousins. It was a strange scene."

Grant agreed to the paroling of Pemberton's army instead of the unconditional surrender terms he originally proposed. He did not want his transportation system tied up by the necessity of sending captured Confederates north to prison camps, and

he felt that the presence of 30,000 parolees, who considered themselves out of the war and were eager to get home, would put a strain on the Southern economy. On July 4 the final articles were signed. Not until 1945, near the end of a global war for survival, did Vicksburg officially celebrate Independence Day again.

Including battle casualties, the South had lost approximately 40,000 men during the Vicksburg Campaign, a manpower drain it could ill afford; Grant's casualties totaled

about one-fourth of that number.

Port Hudson, under siege by a Federal force commanded by Nathaniel Banks, was isolated now and surrendered on July 9. The entire length of the Mississippi was in Union hands, and the Confederacy was split in two. Two weeks later Sherman pushed Joe Johnston's army away from the vicinity of Vicksburg. Jackson, Mississippi's desolated capital, was dubbed Chimneyville by Sherman's men after they sacked it for the second time.

Soon after the surrender Yankee soldiers raised the Stars and Stripes over the Vicksburg courthouse, as sketched above. The Kilroy type below them waves the shot-torn regimental flag of the 45th Illinois.

Private Samuel A. Burhans of the 12th Wisconsin made the drawing at left, of Vicksburg's capture, for the folks back home. White flags fly from the Confederate works as Federal troops form to march into the city.

A great deal of precious Confederate ordnance was lost with the fall of Vicksburg, including 60,000 small arms and 172 cannon. The captured artillery park above includes caissons and several rifled guns.

The site of Grant's and Pemberton's conference is marked by a stone shaft (left). A nearby oak tree fell prey to 1863 souvenir hunters; the monument has suffered similarly at the hands of modern-day tourists.

325

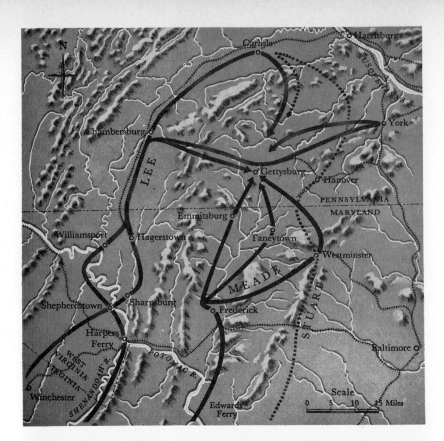

At one point in his invasion of Pennsylvania (right), Lee's army was spread out over 100 miles, and before concentrating at Gettysburg some of his advance elements were as far east as the Susquehanna River. As shown on the map, Stuart's ride around the Union army left Lee without a scouting force.

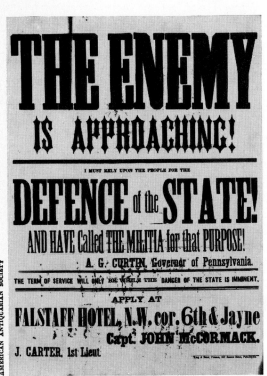

Storm warnings in the form of posters (above) appeared in Pennsylvania with the news of Lee's advance. The militia, Sunday soldiers at best, were understandably nervous at the thought of meeting the Rebel veterans.

Major General George Gordon Meade (right) was a hot-tempered professional to whom army command was wholly unexpected. He became the fifth man to command the Army of the Potomac in less than a year.

Lee Launches a Second Invasion

In mid-May, after the brilliant Chancellorsville victory, Robert E. Lee and Jefferson Davis agreed that an offensive thrust northward was the logical course for the triumphant Army of Northern Virginia. Invasion might loosen Grant's grip on Vicksburg; while a decisive victory on Northern soil could affect the Union's will to continue the war. Equally important, ravaged northern Virginia was unable to support Lee's troops much longer—"The question of food," he said, "gives me more trouble and uneasiness than everything else combined."

In early June Lee shifted his army around the western flank of Hooker's force guarding the Rappahannock and moved into the Shenandoah Valley. By the end of the month his forces were in Pennsylvania, concentrated in an east-west arc from Chambersburg to a point north of a locally important road center named Gettysburg. Lee had lost his "eyes," however, for Stuart's cavalry was off somewhere to the east, effectively out of the campaign.

The Army of the Potomac was moving northward fast, and tough, capable George G. Meade was now in command. As usual, Lee knew his opponent: "General Meade will make no blunder on my front," he remarked.

Before he was relieved of command, Hooker skillfully kept the Federal army within striking distance of Lee. In David G. Blythe's painting General Abner Doubleday's division splashes across the Potomac in pursuit on June 7.

The quiet market town of Gettysburg (above) accidentally became a battleground when Harry Heth's Rebels, seeking shoes there, ran into Union cavalry.

At left is Alfred Waud's sketch of the death of Union General John Reynolds, the victim of a sharpshooter as he rallied his troops west of Gettysburg.

The Civil War's greatest battle began near the McPherson Farm (right) on the Chambersburg Pike. A statue of General Reynolds is visible at left.

Cavalryman John Buford (below, with his staff) was a hard fighter whose troopers, with their new repeating carbines, held off the Rebels for two hours.

Gettysburg: The Great Battle Begins

On the morning of July 1, 1863, John Buford's Federal cavalry was patrolling the roads northwest of Gettysburg, on the lookout for Rebels. The night before, Buford had prophetically told an aide, "They will attack you in the morning and they will come booming.... You will have to fight like the devil until supports arrive." By 8 A.M. Harry Heth's division of A. P. Hill's corps was trading fire with the dismounted cavalry.

Buford's men were soon in trouble, and he called on John Reynolds' I Corps for infantry support. Shouting "Forward! for God's sake, forward!" Reynolds rushed his lead division into action, including the crack Iron Brigade, and briefly stabilized the situation west of the town. Then a sharpshooter's bullet killed him. Hill's men were pouring into line rapidly, and their numbers began to tell.

Howard's XI Corps, so badly mauled at Chancellorsville, came up just as Stonewall Jackson's veteran corps, now under Dick Ewell, bore down from the north. Robert Rodes' division piled directly into the XI Corps, and then Jubal Early overlapped its right flank. Lee had not wanted to fight here, but, opportunist that he was, he now ordered the entire Confederate line forward. The ill-fated XI Corps collapsed, and with it the Federal right wing, uncovering the left wing which was facing Hill west of town.

The Iron Brigade and some artillery tried to make a stand along Seminary Ridge, and a gunner recalled, "for seven or eight minutes ensued probably the most desperate fight ever waged between artillery and infantry at close range without a particle of cover on either side ... bullets hissing, humming and whistling everywhere; cannon roaring; all crash on crash and peal on peal, smoke, dust, splinters, blood, wreck and carnage indescribable." The Southern pressure was relentless, and soon the entire Union line was gone, with survivors fleeing through Gettysburg to high ground beyond.

COLLECTION OF ALEXANDER MC COOK CRAIGHEAD

The First Day:

A Climactic Struggle Opens

James Walker's painting records the massive charge of A. P. Hill's Rebel divisions as they swept in on Gettysburg from the west along the Chambersburg Pike, early in the first day's fighting. Hill's men have overrun the thin Union line on McPher-

son's Ridge and are trading volleys with John Reynolds' I Corps massed to meet them.

Eventually the Northern troops were outflanked and driven back to a last-stand position among some trees around the Lutheran theologi-

cal seminary building on Seminary Ridge in the middle distance. At left is the cut of an unfinished rail-road, scene of savage hand-to-hand fighting, which became a slaughter pen for the men of both armies.

Beyond Gettysburg, and in a di-

rect line with the turnpike, Culp's Hill and Cemetery Hill are visible. At right center are the twin eminences known as the Round Tops. On the second and third days of the battle these four areas of high ground anchored the Union line.

Ewell Fails to Exploit the Advantage

By the time the Federals managed to pull together their shattered forces on Cemetery Hill, south of Gettysburg, it was dusk. The two Union army corps involved thus far had been outnumbered and soundly whipped, and their losses were appalling. The XI Corps lost 4,000 men as prisoners alone, and the I Corps had suffered 7,500 casualties. The Iron Brigade was finished as an effective force. All told, only about 5,000 Yankees were present for action on Cemetery Hill.

If the Army of the Potomac was to make a stand at Gettysburg, it was imperative that these men hold on. The only good defensive ground available to Meade was Cemetery Ridge, running straight south to the Round Tops; Cemetery Hill anchored its northern end, where the ridge turned off at right angles, ending at Culp's Hill. It was a strong line, but if the Confederates got possession of any of these hills, it would be untenable.

Lee perceived this immediately and ordered Ewell to take Cemetery Hill "if possible." Jackson would have grasped at once the implications of Lee's courteous order, but Jackson was gone, and Dick Ewell was suffering a strange mental paralysis in his new role as corps commander. He did nothing. A few Southern patrols did threaten Culp's Hill, but Hancock, whom Meade had sent to take command, saw the danger and got a division there in time. For the moment the Union army was safe, and soon Meade arrived to take personal command. That night Lee told his officers, "we will attack . . . in the morning as early as practicable."

When Stonewall Jackson died, Lee said, "I know not how to replace him." In the command reorganization that followed, most of Jackson's men went to eccentric Lieutenant General Richard S. Ewell (above) who had lost a leg at Second Bull Run.

The four Union officers at left played key roles at Gettysburg, and all four were wounded there. Seated is the II Corps' commander, Winfield Scott Hancock; standing, left to right, are generals Francis Barlow, David Birney, and John Gibbon.

Arriving on the battlefield after the first day's fighting, Meade made his headquarters in a tiny farmhouse on the rear slope of Cemetery Ridge. Although badly damaged by Confederate shellfire, the building was repaired and survives today (above).

The Iron Brigade, one of the best units in the Army of the Potomac, was decimated at Gettysburg; at right, in Timothy O'Sullivan's photograph, are some of the dead from one of its regiments, the 24th Michigan, which lost 80 per cent of its men.

These four paintings by Edwin Forbes show stages in the second day's fighting at Gettysburg. At the top, Union artillery and infantry brace to meet Hood's attack across the Wheat Field and the Peach Orchard. After breaking this line, the Rebels advance on the Round Tops, in the second picture. By evening the action had shifted to the Union right, where, in the third painting, Edward Johnson's Rebels storm the breastworks atop Culp's Hill. At the bottom, Confederates under Jubal Early force a temporary break in the Union line at Cemetery Hill, near the Evergreen Cemetery gate, in the final action of the day.

334

Gettysburg: The Second Day's Action Begins

When his 9th Massachusetts battery was called from the artillery reserve to support the Union left, Charles W. Reed made this quick sketch of Sickles' headquarters. The general stands among his mounted couriers and staff.

As Meade prepared to meet Lee's expected offensive on July 2 he considered Culp's Hill, on his right, to be the likeliest point of attack. In this he was only half right; Lee planned to strike simultaneous blows at both Union flanks.

Since Longstreet's corps had not fought the previous day, Lee assigned him the major effort of turning the Union left at Little Round Top. But Longstreet took his time, and it was late afternoon before he was ready. As John B. Hood remembered it, Longstreet said, "The general is a little nervous this morning; he wishes me to attack; I do not wish to do so without Pickett. I never like to go into battle with one boot off." But George Pickett's division failed to arrive in time. His date with destiny

would not come until the next day.

The delay was actually to the Confederates' advantage, for Dan Sickles became nervous and repeated the mistake he had made at Chancellorsville. It very nearly cost the North the battle, and it did cost Sickles a leg.

His corps held the Union left, and Sickles decided to occupy the slightly higher ground a half mile in front of Cemetery Ridge. This move isolated him from Hancock's II Corps, holding the center, and it left him in an exposed salient too large to hold if he was to cover Little Round Top as well. Before Meade could correct this, Longstreet's guns opened, and Hood's magnificent shock troops came pounding in on Devil's Den at the foot of Little Round Top.

Hood was wounded, but his men broke through and began scrambling up the rocky slopes. At the crest Meade's acting chief of staff, Gouverneur Warren, found "not a man on the hill." If Little Round Top were lost, the Union line on Cemetery Hill would be exposed to a deadly enfilading fire.

Warren pushed two brigades forward, and they fought the Rebels toe to toe. A man in the 20th Maine remembered: "The lines at times were so near each other that the hostile gun barrels almost touched." When their ammunition ran out, the New Englanders fixed bayonets and charged. Their effort, and an equally gallant charge by the 140th New York, saved Little Round Top. But the respite was only momentary.

GETTYSBURG

Second Day: July 2, 1863

Gettysburg

CULP'S HILL ⑦

⑧

CEMETERY HILL

ZIEGLER'S GROVE

MEADE'S HQ

SEMINARY RIDGE

CODORI HOUSE

CEMETERY RIDGE

⑥

ROGERS HOUSE

⑤

TROSTLE FARM

PEACH ORCHARD

WHEAT FIELD

③

WARFIELD HOUSE

EMMITSBURG ROAD

ROSE HOUSE

David Greenspan

GETTYSBURG: The action on the second day opens with a Confederate artillery barrage at 4 P.M. An hour later Hood's Rebel division sweeps in around the Union left flank, overruns Devil's Den (1), and begins the ascent of the undefended Little Round Top, which dominates the entire Federal position. Warren hastens troops to the crest, and they repulse Hood's men after a bitter struggle (2). As the battle shifts steadily northward, Longstreet sends in McLaws, who shatters Sickles' salient (3), embracing the Peach Orchard and the Wheat Field, and advances toward a gap in Meade's line (4). Artillery is rushed forward to hold together the battered Union line until reinforcements arrive. At the Trostle Farm, Barksdale's Mississippians manage to take a Yankee battery (5), but Barksdale is mortally wounded and his brigade wrecked. The Rebels strike at the Union center (6), where they meet stiff resistance, including a doomed counterattack by the 1st Minnesota, and are stopped. At dark Ewell demonstrates against the Federal right, but fails to take the strong position on Culp's Hill (7). In the day's final action Jubal Early gets two Rebel brigades in among the Union batteries on Cemetery Hill (8), but they are not strong enough to resist counterattacks and are driven off.

Wheat Field and Peach Orchard

In Alexander Gardner's photograph, a dead Southern sharpshooter lies behind a stone breastwork he had built in Devil's Den, at the foot of Little Round Top.

Major General Lafayette McLaws

Sickles' salient enclosed the Wheat Field and the Peach Orchard (two more ordinary pieces of American landscape that have earned capitalization at a terrible price), and after the expulsion of the Confederates from Little Round Top these two spots again came into Union hands—temporarily.

Longstreet had another fresh division, under Lafayette McLaws, which now joined the assault, aiming for the gap between Sickles and Hancock. William Barksdale's Mississippi Brigade spearheaded this charge, and although Barksdale was shot down, the Confederates soon reclaimed the Peach Orchard and the Wheat Field. Sickles was down with a shattered leg, and his III Corps was virtually demolished.

Hancock, thundering and swearing at the top of his voice, prodded troops forward to seal the gap, but for agonizing minutes the sector was simply a vast chaos of intermingled battle lines and crashing musketry. A. P. Hill threw a division against the Union center, but soon the Federal artillery sorted itself out, and its fire tipped the balance.

The guns, jammed to the muzzles with canister, tore great gaps in the charging Rebel lines. The 1st Minnesota counterattacked, was trapped, and came back with only 47 of the 262 men who had started out.

By now it was nearly dark, and the thunder of battle on the Union left finally dwindled to a mutter, an occasional volley crackling in the smoky haze like summer lightning.

Union General Gouverneur Warren's statue stands guard on Little Round Top.

DAVID E. SCHERMAN

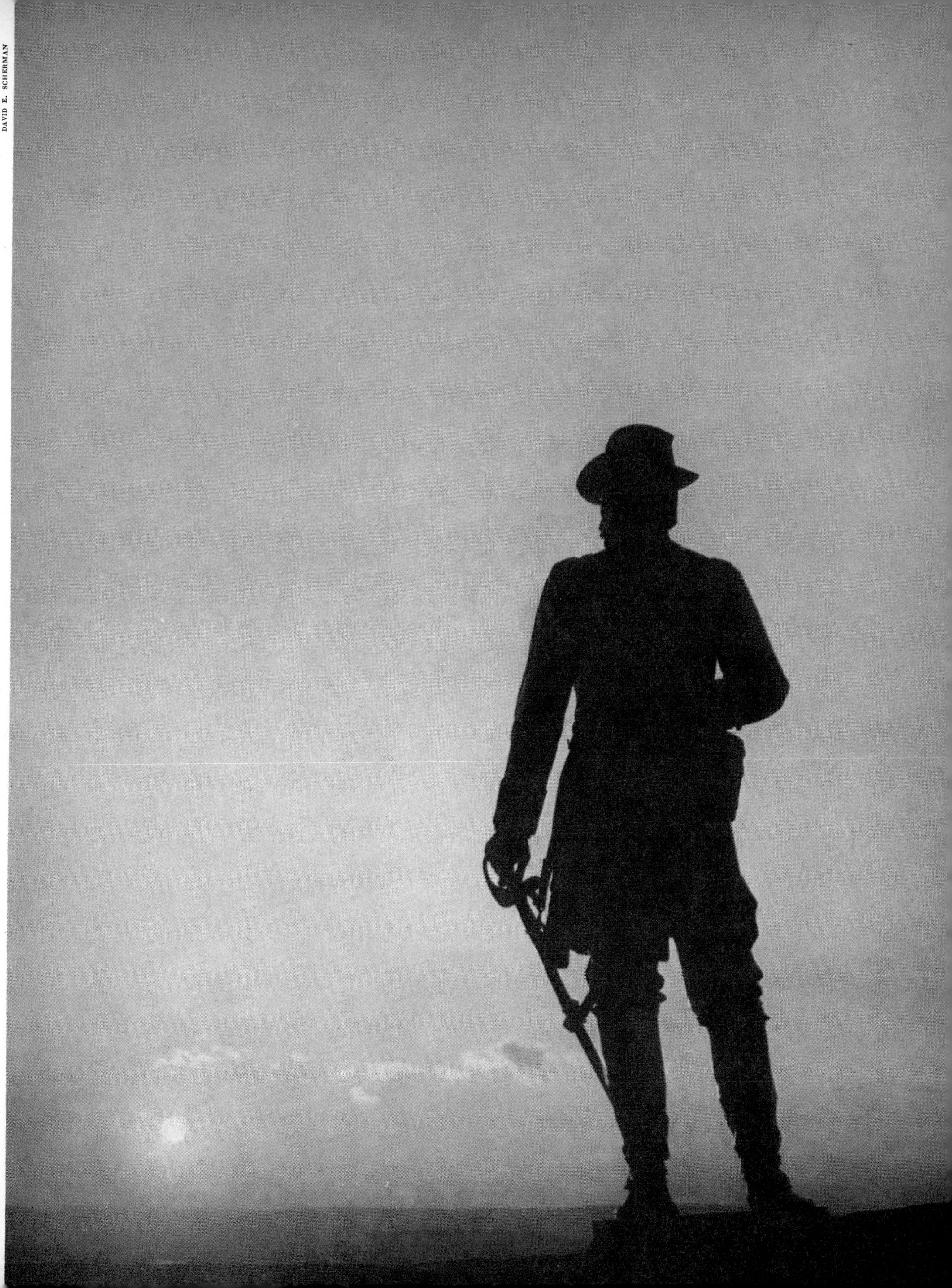

Crisis on the Union Right

BOTH: KOSTI RUOHOMAA, BLACK STAR

Spangler's Spring (above), near Culp's Hill, was the scene of a skirmish on the night of July 2, as men of both armies, filling their canteens, tangled in the smoky darkness. The view at right looks toward Culp's Hill from Cemetery Hill; the gun marks the site of a Federal battery seized briefly by the Rebels.

Lee had intended that Dick Ewell make a demonstration against the Union right—Cemetery and Culp's hills—as soon as he heard Longstreet's guns. This Ewell did, opening with artillery, but the heavier Union fire soon silenced his batteries. Then Ewell, who was very conscious of his missed opportunity of taking Cemetery Hill the previous day, ordered his infantry forward.

One division, under Edward Johnson, had the unenviable task of attacking Culp's Hill. There was only a single Federal brigade holding it, but these New Yorkers were protected by sturdy log barricades, and they beat off four separate attacks.

As Johnson's assault lost steam Jubal Early pushed two brigades up a ravine separating Culp's Hill from Cemetery Hill. It was a somewhat undermanned attack, but the two brigades were good ones, including the rough and ready Louisiana Tigers. The Northern line was thin here, as a result of demands from the

beleaguered left, and Early's men lunged out of the gathering darkness to capture several Federal batteries in bitter hand-to-hand fighting. Suddenly the Confederates were struck hard in a counterattack by some of Hancock's troops and remnants of the Iron Brigade, and the breach was finally mended.

So ended the second day at Gettysburg. Lee had failed to turn either Union flank, and the value of the ground he had gained was hardly worth the terrible cost. That night Meade called a council of war, where his generals agreed that they would neither retreat nor attack but would await Robert E. Lee's next move.

General John Gibbon commanded the Union division holding the center of Cemetery Ridge (his position included two now-famous features, a clump of trees and a stone wall) and as the council of war broke up Meade called Gibbon aside and warned him, "If Lee attacks tomorrow, it will be in your front."

The Great Confederate Frontal Assault

At daylight on July 3 the Rebel attack on Culp's Hill was renewed, but the position was simply too strong, and by 10:30 an unearthly quiet had settled over the scorching field. The Yankees watched as cannon after Confederate cannon was moved into position a mile west of Cemetery Ridge. Finally some 150 of them were zeroed in on the center of Meade's line.

At 1 P.M. the Rebel guns loosed a torrent of shot and shell on Cemetery Ridge, but by some quirk the Southerners were firing a shade too high, and noncombatants on the reverse slope got the worst of it. Federal artillery fired slowly in return, conserving ammunition.

Longstreet's attack waves—six battle-hardened brigades, plus George Pickett's fresh division, close to 15,000 in all—moved forward, and as the smoke of the cannonade lifted, a Union eyewitness saw "an overwhelming resistless tide of an ocean of armed men sweeping upon us! . . . on they move, as with one soul, in perfect order . . . over ridge and slope, through orchard and meadow and cornfield, magnificent, grim, irresistible."

At the base of the Virginia monument on Seminary Ridge (above), a bugler, shadowed by Lee's statue, signals the advance. The North Carolina monument (right) captures the tense moment of Pickett's Charge. In Charles Reed's sketch below, Pickett's Confederates form for the charge.

Pickett's Charge

As the Confederate infantrymen came on steadily and quietly, nearing the awful climax of the war's greatest battle, Union artillery fire shook their ranks with deadly accuracy, and then both sides exploded in a tremendous clash of musketry. The Rebel flanks were smashed in, but the spearhead, led by Lewis Armistead, drove on to the clump of trees and the stone wall at the Union center—soon known simply as the Angle. Yankee artillerist Alonzo Cushing, wounded three times, fired triple loads of canister from his remaining gun until he was killed and the position overrun. Hancock and Gibbon were down, and Armistead mortally wounded. The battle noise was "strange and terrible, a sound that came from thousands of human throats . . . like a vast mournful roar."

Suddenly it was over. Union reinforcements swarmed into the breach, and the Confederates withdrew sullenly. Watching the survivors return, Lee said, "All this has been my fault."

NEW HAMPSHIRE HISTORICAL SOCIETY

GETTYSBURG NATIONAL MILITARY PARK; COURTESY *Time* (GEORGE STROCK)

James Walker's painting above shows, from behind the Union center, nearly the entire Gettysburg battlefield. As the Rebel charge reaches the trees at left center, Yankee reinforcements rush forward. General Meade is visible just right of center, mounted, with field glasses; receiving aid in the left foreground is the dying Confederate General Lewis Armistead.

At left is the Confederate high tide at Gettysburg, from Paul Philippoteaux' cyclorama painting. Armistead's Virginians surge through the Union line at left while Federal gunners work desperately to remove the remnants of Cushing's wrecked battery. With their flank support demolished, the Southerners at length withdrew, leaving half their number dead.

OVERLEAF: *The Angle, focal point of Pickett's Charge, as it looks today, calm and peaceful in the July heat.*

KOSTI RUOHOMAA, BLACK STAR

345

Edwin Forbes' painting shows Federal troops marching in the rain in pursuit of Lee's army after Gettysburg.

Lee's Beaten Army Heads South

A downpour that "washed the blood from the grass" fell July 4, and after resting a day, Lee began his long retreat to Virginia. Meade pursued slowly, catching up at the Potomac, where high water prevented a crossing. But Lee dug in, and Meade refused to attack an entrenched, dangerous enemy. By July 14 Lee was across the river, his dream of victory in the North dead forever.

The two armies had been dreadfully mangled, the casualties totaling about 50,000 for the three-day battle. There was a certain terrible majesty and pageantry to Pickett's Charge, but the aftermath revealed the true face of war. A 17-mile train of springless wagons jolted southward, carrying Confederate wounded, uncared for, pelted with rain and hail, in unutterable agony. Gettysburg and nearby towns were swamped with wounded, and a Quaker nurse wrote, "There are no words in the English language to express the sufferings I witnessed today."

Meade's trains approaching the Potomac crossing, long after Lee's escape.

General Robert E. Lee, painted by W. B. Cox in Richmond in 1865. Lee refused to sit for portraits, so Cox apparently based his work on the Vannerson photograph shown on page 149.

349

The Gettysburg Address

Lincoln's "Second Draft" of the Gettysburg Address, from which he spoke.

Because of the epic proportions of the Battle of Gettysburg it seemed only fitting that the dead, North and South, should be interred with a proper ceremony. Seventeen acres were set aside on Cemetery Hill, the battlefield was cleaned up, and on November 19, 1863, the military cemetery was dedicated. The noted orator Edward Everett spoke for two long hours; then Abraham Lincoln delivered the "few appropriate remarks" requested of him, and in ten sentences did unforgettable justice to the thousands of young Americans who had struggled with incredible bravery in the Peach Orchard, on Little Round Top, and at the Angle.

At left, the procession en route to Cemetery Hill for the dedication ceremonies of the military cemetery.

Lincoln's Gettysburg Address was delivered at a point just beyond the fence of the civilian cemetery at right.

350

THE ARMIES

THE STATESMEN and the diplomats did their best to control and direct the war, but the real load was carried from first to last by the ordinary soldier. Poorly trained and cared for, often very poorly led, he was unmilitary but exceedingly warlike. A citizen in arms, incurably individualistic even under the rod of discipline, combining frontier irreverence with the devout piety of an unsophisticated society, he was an arrant sentimentalist with an inner core as tough as the heart of a hickory stump. He had to learn the business of war as he went along because there was hardly anyone on hand qualified to teach him, and he had to pay for the education of his generals, some of whom were all but totally ineducable. In many ways he was just like the G.I. Joe of modern days, but he lived in a simpler era, and when he went off to war he had more illusions to lose. He lost them with all proper speed, and when the fainthearts and weaklings had been winnowed out, he became one of the stoutest fighting men the world has ever seen. In his own person he finally embodied what the war was all about.

The first thing to remember about him is that, at least in the beginning, he went off to war because he wanted to go. In the spring of 1861 hardly any Americans in either section had any understanding of what war really was like. The Revolution was a legend, and the War of 1812 had been no more than an episode, and the war with Mexico had never gone to the heart.

Right after Fort Sumter war looked like a great adventure, and the waving flags and the brass bands and the chest-thumping orators put a gloss of romance over everything; thousands upon thousands of young Northerners and Southerners hastened to enlist, feeling that they were very lucky to have the chance. Neither government was able to use all of the men who crowded the recruiting stations in those first glittering weeks, and boys who were rejected went back home with bitter complaints. Men who went off to camp were consumed with a fear that the war might actually be over before they got into action—an emotion which, a year later, they recalled with wry grins.

In the early part of the war the camps which received these recruits were strikingly unlike the grimly efficient training camps of the twentieth century. There were militia regiments which hired civilian cooks and raised mess funds to buy better foods than the government provided. In the South a young aristocrat would as likely as not enlist as a private and enter the army with a body servant and a full trunk of spare clothing; and in the North there were volunteer regiments which were organized somewhat like private clubs—a recruit could be admitted only if the men who were already in voted to accept him. In both sections the early regiments were loaded down with baggage, as well as with many strange notions. These sons of a rawboned democracy considered it degrading to give immediate and unquestioning obedience

This Confederate camp in Virginia was typical of the log cabin villages which were constructed for winter quarters.

Forgotten faces from the North.

to orders, and they had a way of wanting to debate things, or at least to have them explained, before they acted. In the South a hot-blooded young private might challenge a company officer to a duel if he felt that such a course was called for, and if the Northern regiments saw no duels, they at least saw plenty of fist fights between officers and men. The whole concept of taut, impersonal discipline was foreign to the recruits of 1861, and many of them never did get the idea.

The free and easy ways of the first few months were substantially toned down, of course, as time went on, and in both armies it presently dawned on the effervescent young volunteer that his commanders quite literally possessed the power of life and death over him. Yet the Civil War armies never acquired the automatic habit of immediate, unquestioning obedience which is drilled into modern soldiers. There was always a quaint touch of informality to those regiments; the men did what they were told to do, they saluted and said "Sir" and adjusted themselves to the army's eternal routine, but they kept a loose-jointed quality right down to the end, and they never got or wanted to get the snap and precision which European soldiers considered essential. The Prussian General von Moltke remarked in the 1870's that he saw no point in studying the American Civil War, because it had been fought by armed mobs, and in a way—but only in a way—he was quite right. These American armies simply did not follow the European military tradition.

One reason why discipline was imperfect was the fact that company and regimental officers were mostly either elected by the soldiers or appointed by the state governor for reasons of politics: they either were, or wanted to be, personally liked by the men they commanded, and an officer with political ambitions could see a postwar constituent in everybody in the ranks. Such men were not likely to bear down very hard, and if they did the privates were not likely to take it very well. On top of this, neither North nor South had anything resembling the officer-candidate schools of the present day. Most officers had to learn their jobs while they were performing them, and there is something pathetic in the way in which these neophytes in shoulder straps bought military textbooks and sat up nights to study them. They might be unqualified for military command, but as a general thing they were painfully conscientious, and they did their best. A regiment which happened to have a West Pointer for a colonel, or was assigned to a brigade commanded by a West Pointer, was in luck; such an officer was likely to devote a good deal of time to the instruction of his subordinates.

There is one thing to remember about Civil War discipline. In camp it was imperfect, and on the march it was seldom tight enough to prevent a good deal of straggling, but in battle it was often very good. (The discipline that will take soldiers through an Antietam, for instance, has much to be said for it, even though it

Four unsung Confederate heroes.

is not recognizable to a Prussian martinet.) The one thing which both Northern and Southern privates demanded from their officers was the leadership and the physical courage that will stand up under fire, and the officers who proved lacking in either quality did not last very long.

The training which a Civil War soldier got included, of course, the age-old fundamentals—how to stand at attention, how to pick up and shoulder a musket, how to do a right face, and so on—but beyond this it was designed largely to teach him how to get from a formation in which he could march into a formation in which he could fight. A division moving along a country road would go, generally, in column of fours; moving thus, it would be a spraddled-out organism eight feet wide and a mile long. When it reached the battlefield, this organism had to change its shape completely, transforming length into width, becoming, on occasion, six feet long and a mile wide. It might form a series of lines, each line one or more regiments in width; it might temporarily throw its regiments into boxlike shapes, two companies marching abreast, while it moved from road to fighting field; if the ground was rough and badly wooded, the ten companies of a regiment might go forward in ten parallel columns, each column two men wide and forty or fifty men deep; and the fighting line into which any of these formations finally brought itself might lie at any conceivable angle to the original line of march, with underbrush

and gullies and fences and swamps to interfere with its formation. Once put into action, the fighting line might have to shift to the right or left, to swing on a pivot like an immense gate, to advance or to retreat, to toss a swarm of skirmishers out in its front or on either flank—to do, in short, any one or all of a dozen different things, doing them usually under fire, and with an infernal racket making it almost impossible to hear the words of command.

A regiment which could not do these things could not fight efficiently, as the First Battle of Bull Run had abundantly proved. To do them, the men had to master a whole series of movements as intricate as the movements of a ballet; had to master them so that doing them became second nature, because they might have to be done in the dark or in a wilderness and almost certainly would have to be done under great difficulties of one sort or another. As a result an immense amount of drill was called for, and few generals ever considered that their men had had enough.

Oddly enough, the average regiment did not get a great deal of target practice. The old theory was that the ordinary American was a backwoodsman to whom the use of a rifle was second nature, but that had never really been true, and by 1861 it was very full of holes. (Here the Confederacy tended to have an advantage. A higher proportion of its men had lived under frontier conditions and really did know something about firearms before they entered the army.) In some cases—

Winslow Homer's eyewitness drawing captures the motion of ramrods and muskets on the firing line.

notably at Shiloh—green troops were actually sent into action without ever having been shown how to load their muskets; and although this was an exceptional case, very few regiments ever spent much time on a rifle range. As late as the summer of 1863 General George Gordon Meade, commanding the Army of the Potomac, felt compelled to call regimental officers' attention to the fact that the army contained many soldiers who apparently had never fired their weapons in action. On the field at Gettysburg his ordnance officers had collected thousands of muskets loaded with two, three, or even ten charges; in the excitement of the fight many men had feverishly loaded and reloaded without discharging the pieces.

This musket was one great source of woe for the Civil War soldier. It looked like the old weapon of infantry tradition, but in actual fact it was a new piece, and it compelled a radical change in infantry tactics. The change was made late and slowly, and thousands of lives were lost as a result.

Infantry tactics at that time were based on the use of the smoothbore musket, a weapon of limited range and accuracy. Firing lines that were much more than a hundred yards apart could not inflict very much damage on each other, and so troops which were to make an attack would be massed together, elbow to elbow, and would make a run for it; if there were enough of them, and they ran fast enough, the defensive line could not hurt them seriously, and when they

got to close quarters the advantage of numbers and the use of the bayonet would settle things. But the Civil War musket was rifled, which made an enormous difference. It was still a muzzle-loader, but it had much more accuracy and a far longer range than the old smoothbore, and it completely changed the conditions under which soldiers fought. An advancing line could be brought under killing fire at a distance of half a mile, now, and the massed charge of Napoleonic tradition was miserably out of date. When a defensive line occupied field entrenchments—which the soldiers learned to dig fairly early in the game—a direct frontal assault became almost impossible. The hideous casualty lists of Civil War battles owed much of their size to the fact that soldiers were fighting with rifles but were using tactics suited to smoothbores. It took the generals a long time to learn that a new approach was needed.

Much the same development was taking place in the artillery, although the full effect was not yet evident. The Civil War cannon, almost without exception, was a muzzle-loader, but the rifled gun was coming into service. It could reach farther and hit harder than the smoothbore, and for counterbattery fire it was highly effective—a rifled battery could hit a battery of smoothbores without being hit in return, and the new three-inch iron rifles, firing a ten-pound conoidal shot, had a flat trajectory and immense penetrating power. But the old smoothbore—a brass gun of four-and-one-half-

Digging in under fire, by Charles W. Reed.

Edwin Forbes sketched Union artillery impeded by the Wilderness' glutinous mud.

inch caliber, firing a twelve-pound spherical shot—remained popular to the end of the war; in the wooded, hilly country where so many Civil War battles were fought, its range of slightly less than a mile was about all that was needed, and for close-range work against infantry the smoothbore was better than the rifle. For such work the artillerist fired canister—a tin can full of lead slugs, with a propellant at one end and a wooden disk at the other—and the can disintegrated when the gun was fired, letting the lead slugs be sprayed all over the landscape. In effect, the gun then was a huge sawed-off shotgun, and at ranges of 250 yards or less it was in the highest degree murderous.

The rifled cannon had a little more range than was ordinarily needed. No one yet had worked out any system for indirect fire; the gunner had to see his target with his own eyes, and a gun that would shoot two miles was of no especial advantage if the target was less than a mile away. Shell fuzes were often defective, and most gunners followed a simple rule: never fire over your own infantry, except in an extreme emergency. (The things were likely to go off too soon, killing friends instead of enemies.) Against fixed fortifications, or carefully prepared fieldworks, the gunners liked to use mortars, which gave them a high-angle fire they could not get from fieldpieces. They would also bring up siege guns—ponderous rifled pieces, too heavy to be used in ordinary battles, but powerful enough to flatten parapets or to knock down masonry walls. These large guns were somewhat dangerous to the user. They tended to be weak in the breech, and every now and then one of them would explode when fired.

The Federals had a big advantage in artillery, partly because of their superior industrial plant and partly because, having larger armies, they could afford to use more batteries. On most fields they had many more guns than the Confederates, with a much higher percentage of rifled pieces. (An important factor at Antietam was that Federal artillery could overpower the Confederate guns, and Southern gunners for the rest of the war referred to that fight as "artillery hell.") It appears too that Northern recruits by and large had a little more aptitude for artillery service, just as Southerners outclassed Northerners in the cavalry.

For at least the first half of the war Confederate cavalry was so much better than that of the Federals that there was no real comparison. Here the South was helped both by background and tradition. Most of its recruits came from rural areas and were used to horses; and the legends of chivalry were powerful, so that it seemed much more knightly and gallant to go off to war on horseback than in the infantry. Quite literally, the Confederate trooper rode to the wars on his own charger, cavalry horses not being government issue with the Richmond administration. In the beginning this was an advantage, for many Confederate squadrons were mounted on blooded stock that could run

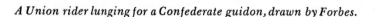

A Union rider lunging for a Confederate guidon, drawn by Forbes.

rings around the nags which sharpshooting traders were selling to the Yankee government. In the long run, though, the system was most harmful. A trooper who lost his horse had to provide another one all by himself, and he usually could get a furlough so that he might go home and obtain one. Toward the end of the war replacements were hard to come by.

In any case, both horses and riders in the Confederate cavalry were infinitely superior to anything the Yankees could show for at least two years. There were plenty of farm boys in the Federal armies, but they did not come from a horseback country; most horses on Northern farms were draft animals, and it never occurred to a Northern farm boy that he could acquire social prestige simply by getting on a horse's back. Being well aware that it takes a lot of work to care for a horse, the Northern country boy generally enlisted in the infantry. The Union cavalry got its recruits mostly from city boys or from nonagricultural groups; and before this cavalry could do anything at all, its members had first to be taught how to stay in the saddle. Since Jeb Stuart's troopers could have taught circus riders tricks, the Yankees were hopelessly outclassed. Not until 1863 was the Army of the Potomac's cavalry able to meet Stuart on anything like even terms.

In the West matters were a little different. Here the Confederacy had a very dashing cavalry raider in the person of John Hunt Morgan, who made a number of headlines without particularly affecting the course of the war, and it had the youthful Joe Wheeler, who performed competently; but most of all it had Nathan Bedford Forrest, an untaught genius who had had no military training and who never possessed an ounce of social status, but who was probably the best cavalry leader in the entire war. Forrest simply used his horsemen as a modern general would use motorized infantry. He liked horses because he liked fast movement, and his mounted men could get from here to there much faster than any infantry could; but when they reached the field they usually tied their horses to trees and fought on foot, and they were as good as the very best infantry. Not for nothing did Forrest say that the essence of strategy was "to git thar fust with the most men." (Do not, under any circumstances whatever, quote Forrest as saying "fustest" and "mostest." He did not say it that way, and nobody who knows anything about him imagines that he did.) The Yankees never came up with anybody to match Forrest, and tough William T. Sherman once paid him a grim compliment: there would never be peace in western Tennessee, said Sherman, until Forrest was dead.

Aside from what a man like Forrest could do, cavalry in the Civil War was actually of secondary importance as far as fighting was concerned. It was essential for scouting and for screening an army, but as a combat arm it was declining. Cavalry skirmished frequently with other cavalry, and the skirmishes at times rose to the level of pitched battles, but it fought in-

The casual glamour of the cavalryman is suggested by Homer's study of boots at left. Few jobs were more prosaic than that of his teamster (below).

Building Corduroy Roads from Belle Plain to Fredericksburg, H.C.

To make boggy roads passable by guns and wagons, men laid logs side by side across them, to corduroy them.

fantry only very rarely. It enjoyed vast prestige with the press and with back-home civilians, but neither infantry nor artillery admired it. The commonest infantry wisecrack of the war was the bitter question: "Who ever saw a dead cavalryman?"

Infantry, artillery, cavalry—these were the three major subdivisions of a Civil War army. Numerically very small, but of considerable value, were the engineer troops. They built bridges, opened roads, laid out fortifications, and performed other technical chores; pontoon trains were in their care, and they were supposed to do any mining or countermining that was done, although in actual practice this was frequently done by troops of the line. Indeed, it was the engineer officer rather than the engineer battalion that was really important. In the Northern armies the average regiment contained men of so many different skills that with proper direction they could do almost anything an engineer outfit could do; it was the special skill and ability of the trained officer that really counted. The Confederate regiments contained fewer jacks-of-all-trades, but this shortage never proved a serious handicap. At the top the South had the best engineer officer of the lot in the person of Robert E. Lee.

It is hard to get an accurate count on the numbers who served in the Civil War armies. The books show total enlistments in the Union armies of 2,900,000 and in the Confederate armies of 1,300,000, but these figures do not mean what they appear to mean. They are fuzzed up by a large number of short-term enlistments and by a good deal of duplication, and the one certainty is that neither side ever actually put that many individuals under arms. One of the best students of the matter has concluded that the Union had the equivalent of about 1,500,000 three-year enlistments, from first to last, and that the Confederates had the equivalent of about 1,000,000. Anyone who chooses may quarrel with these figures. Nobody will ever get an exact count, because the records are very confusing, and some figures are missing altogether. In any case, approximately 359,000 Federal soldiers and 258,000 Confederate soldiers lost their lives in the course of the war. These figures, to be sure, include deaths from disease as well as battle casualties, but a young man who died of dysentery is just as dead as the one who stopped a bullet, and when these figures are matched against the total possible enrollment, they are appalling.

For the unfortunate Civil War soldier, whether he came from the North or from the South, not only got into the army just when the killing power of weapons was being brought to a brand-new peak of efficiency; he enlisted in the closing years of an era when the science of medicine was woefully, incredibly imperfect, so that he got the worst of it in two ways. When he fought, he was likely to be hurt pretty badly; when he stayed in camp, he lived under conditions that were very likely to make him sick; and in either case he had almost no chance to get the kind of medical treat-

Kindness was often the only medicine available to the wounded man.

ment which a generation or so later would be routine.

Both the Federal and Confederate governments did their best to provide proper medical care for their soldiers, but even the best was not very good. This was nobody's fault. There simply was no such thing as good medical care in that age—not as the modern era understands the expression.

Few medical men then knew why wounds become infected or what causes disease; the treatment of wounds and disease, consequently, ranged from the inadequate through the useless to the downright harmful. When a man was wounded and the wound was dressed, doctors expected it to suppurate; they spoke of "laudable pus" and supposed that its appearance was a good sign. The idea that a surgical dressing ought to be sterilized never entered anyone's head; for that matter, no physician would have known what the word "sterilized" meant in such a connection. If a surgeon's instruments were so much as rinsed off between operations at a field hospital, the case was an exception.

In camp, diseases like typhoid, dysentery, and pneumonia were dreaded killers. No one knew what caused them, and no one could do much for them when they appeared. Doctors had discovered that there was some connection between the cleanliness of a camp and the number of men on sick call, but sanitation was still a rudimentary science, and if a water supply was not visibly befouled or odorous, it was thought to be per-

fectly safe. The intestinal maladies that took so heavy a toll were believed due to "miasmic odors" or to even more subtle emanations in the air.

So the soldier of the 1860's had everything working against him. In his favor there was a great deal of native toughness, and a sardonic humor that came to his rescue when things were darkest; these, and an intense devotion to the cause he was serving. Neither Yank nor Reb ever talked very much about the cause; to listen to eloquence on the issues of the war, one had to visit cities behind the lines, read newspapers, or drop in on Congress, either in Washington or in Richmond, because very little along that line was ever heard in camp. The soldier had ribald mockery for high-flown language, and he cared very little for the patriotic war songs which had piped him down to the recruiting office in the first place. In his off hours, at camp or in bivouac, he was a sentimentalist, and one of the most typical of all Civil War scenes is the campfire group of an evening, supper finished, chores done, darkness coming on, with dim lights flickering and homesick young men singing sad little songs like "Lorena" or "Tenting Tonight." No matter which army is looked at, the picture is the same. On each side the soldier realized that he personally was getting the worst of it, and when he had time he felt very sorry for himself. . . . But mostly he did not have the time, and his predominant mood was never one of self-pity. Mostly he was ready for whatever came to him.

A SPECIAL PICTURE PORTFOLIO

Stacked arms—Conrad W. Chapman's quiet tribute to the weapons of war.

It is monotonous, it is not monotonous, it is laborious, it is lazy, it is a bore, it is a lark, it is half war, half peace, and totally attractive, and not to be dispensed with from one's experience in the nineteenth century." So wrote Theodore Winthrop, a New York private, describing camp life shortly before he was killed at Big Bethel in June, 1861. To the common soldier, North and South, the Civil War was not important battles, famous generals, or grand military strategy. It was an intensely moving personal experience.

The story of that common soldier is presented in this special picture portfolio. It is the story of uniforms, of foraging for food, of hospitals, of the singing of songs by boys away from home and lonely. Had young Winthrop lived, he might have seen much of war that is terrible; but those who did experience the horror along with the exhilaration did not pity themselves. "Instead of growling and deserting," a Confederate said, "they laughed at their own bare feet, ragged clothes and pinched faces; and weak, hungry, cold, wet, worried with vermin and itch, dirty with no hope of reward or rest, marched cheerfully to meet the . . . enemy."

1

2

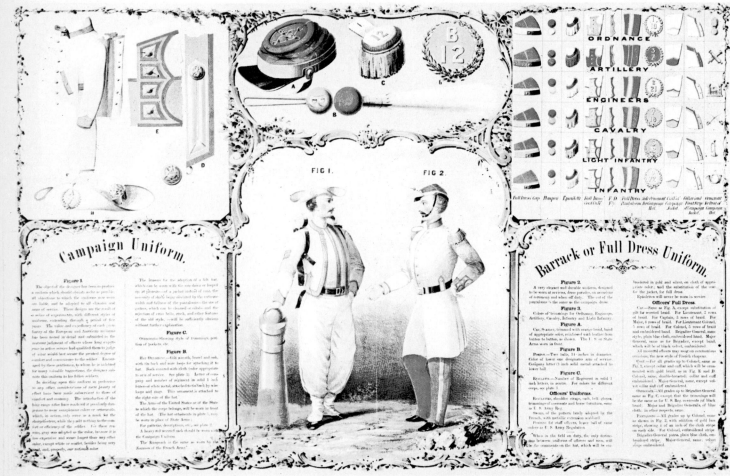

Campaign Uniform.

Barrack or Full Dress Uniform.

ELLSWORTH'S CAMPAIGN & BARRACK OR DRESS UNIFORMS.

PLATE I

The Regulation Soldier

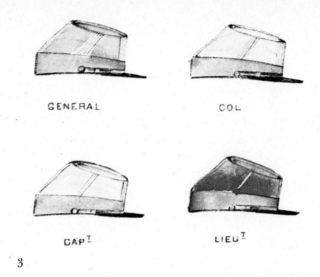

GENERAL   COL

CAP^T   LIEU^T

3

ALL: COLLECTION OF MRS. JOHN NICHOLAS BROWN

4

5

"Never mind the raggedness," Lee once counseled a British visitor, staring at the tattered breeches of a parading unit, "the enemy never sees the backs of my Texans." Almost from the beginning the Confederate uniform was a nondescript, improvised affair—deficiencies being supplied by packages from home or scavenging among the Federal dead.

Even in the North, better equipped to clothe its fighting men, the picture of the ideal soldier was enough to make a veteran smile. "And these poor infantry . . ." wrote a volunteer aide in 1864, "the more they serve, the less they look like soldiers and the more they resemble day-laborers who have bought second-hand military clothes."

(1) This handsome specimen, posing successively in the regulation full-dress uniform of a cavalry corporal (left), ordnance sergeant (center), and infantry private (right), was the beau ideal of the Union fighting man. (2) In the 1861 design for the campaign uniform (left) of Ellsworth's Zouaves, it was claimed, "Considerations of mere beauty and taste have been made subservient to those of economy and comfort." The full-dress uniform (right) of this Federal unit was frankly called "very elegant." (3) Confederate caps were patterned after the French kepi. Shown here, from left to right, are the caps of a general, cavalry colonel, infantry captain, and lieutenant of artillery. (4) Rank was denoted by gold braid on the sleeve and collar insignia— two stars for this lieutenant colonel. Branch of service, artillery, was indicated by the red trim on the jacket. (5) Light blue trousers were officially prescribed for, but seldom worn by, the Southern infantryman. The jacket was to be cadet gray, but due to an improvised dye, it usually came out a yellow-brown, or butternut color.

1

2

Cavalry and Artillery

3

4

5

Advising on the enlistment prospects of a younger brother, a Rebel foot soldier wrote home in January, 1863: "The Infantry is the worse place he can possibly be put into in this war—so if he wants to have a good time Join the Cavalry." Such candid admiration was rare among infantrymen; yet the universal faith of the cavalry, both Blue and Gray, in its own superiority was never in doubt. "I would rather be corporal in company F of the Texas Rangers," a Southerner boasted, "than to be first Lieu in a flat foot company."

The dashing cavalier lent a vanishing touch of glory to this interminable war, but the artillery provided a forecast of the future. Although constant innovations were made, the 12-pound, smoothbore, muzzle-loading Napoleon was the basic artillery piece on both sides—a coincidence partly explained by Confederate General E. P. Alexander's postwar claim: "Gradually we captured Federal guns to supply most of our needs . . ."

(1) Horses and ammunition chests are safely to the rear, and guns are at ready in the foreground in this photograph of the Keystone Battery at drill. (2) Winslow Homer drew the lancers of the 6th Pennsylvania Cavalry during the Peninsular Campaign. (3) Jeb Stuart's Horse Artillery, here sketched by Frank Vizetelly, effectively combined speed and surprise. (4) A Rebel cavalryman posed for this sketch by Conrad Wise Chapman. (5) Another Chapman drawing shows one of the heavy Confederate guns used in the 1863 defense of Charleston. The pulley device raised shells to the mouth of the muzzle-loader.

OVERLEAF: Even the horses are in step in this painting of the 4th Pennsylvania Cavalry by an unknown artist.

GARBISCH COLLECTION, NATIONAL GALLERY OF ART

1

2

3

4

Northern Camp Life

5

6

"The first thing in the morning is drill, then drill, then drill again," commented a Pennsylvania boy after six months of service. "Between drills, we drill and sometimes we stop to eat a little and have a roll call." Almost from the beginning the novelty of camp life was replaced by the inevitable boredom of a soldier's existence. Soon actual combat replaced drilling, but still there were the long stretches between campaigns when the armies went into winter quarters. "After breakfast there is little for the well men to do," a Northerner wrote in 1864. "The forenoon is spent in poke, poke, poking around till the appetite says it is dinner time."

(1) Drummer boys like the one Julian Scott painted sounded daily camp calls and took such chores as barbering and burying the dead. At night they stood alone at the head of a camp street and tapped out the beat which gave "Taps" its name. (2) Artist Edwin Forbes pictured a mess call at the Army of the Potomac's 1862–63 winter encampment at Falmouth, Virginia. The third man in the soup line is Walt Whitman, who was searching for a wounded brother. (3) Charles W. Reed, a soldier-artist with the 9th Massachusetts Artillery, sketched the dreaded moment in every soldier's life—the morning call. (4) Servants relieved most officers of such tiresome chores as cooking and washing clothes. This group arrested what may have been lightning movements long enough to pose for a photographer at Yorktown in May, 1863. (5) Another subject for Forbes was a camp barber at work on a supremely relaxed soldier in August, 1863. (6) In building winter quarters, the men displayed infinite ingenuity and a wide range of taste, as revealed by Pvt. David James' view of a Federal camp at Culpeper, Virginia, in 1864.

1

2

3

The Sick and the Wounded

As staggering as casualty figures for Civil War battles are, even more appalling are the statistics of deaths from disease. It has been estimated that two and one-half Union deaths resulted from disease for every single combat loss, while the ratio on the Confederate side was three to one. The North Carolina soldier who wrote that "these Big Battles is not as Bad as the fever" knew of what he told.

Clara Barton, who would later found the American Red Cross, left her Patent Office desk to find means of channeling medicine to the sick and wounded; and Sally Tompkins of Richmond was commissioned a Confederate captain for her hospital work. Volunteers of the U.S. Sanitary Commission set themselves the task of raising hygienic standards in camps and hospitals. Yet, despite these efforts, hospitals remained fearful places, and doctors were generally distrusted. "I insisted on takeing the field . . ." wrote an Ohioan ordered to the hospital, "thinking that I had better die by rebel bullets than Union Quackery."

(1) Philadelphia's busy refreshment saloon fed the boys en route to war. (2) The sutler's cart, where tobacco, sweets, and other delicacies could be purchased, was the camp's social center, especially if attended by an attractive lady as in Alfred Waud's sketch. (3) Jarring rides from the battlefield in one of these two-wheeled ambulances (sketch by Charles Reed) often proved fatal to the badly wounded. (4) An impromptu, al fresco tooth extraction caught Charles Reed's eye. (5) This converted passenger coach served as a Federal hospital car, holding 33 wounded. Alternate seats were removed and replaced with wooden slats. The least seriously wounded rode in stretchers hung from above. (6) An unknown Rebel painted Howard's Grove Hospital, near Richmond.

LIBRARY OF CONGRESS

4

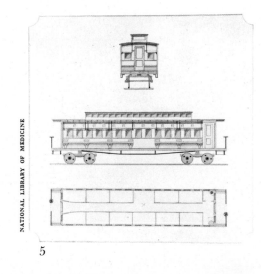

NATIONAL LIBRARY OF MEDICINE

5

CHICAGO HISTORICAL SOCIETY

6

371

1

2

3

"O Maw yon goes
de last hive"

Living off the Land

4

5

In classic understatement, William Tecumseh Sherman recalled the march from Atlanta to the sea: "The skill and success of the men in collecting forage," he wrote in his *Memoirs,* "was one of the features of this march." A Union lieutenant with a lively memory described one of Sherman's "bummers" loaded with "first, a bundle of fodder for his mule; second, three hams, a sack of meal, a peck of potatoes; third, a fresh bed quilt, the old mother's coffee pot, a jug of vinegar . . ."

Too often the distinction between necessary foraging and senseless looting and pillaging became blurred. Soldiers of both armies, however, learned how to relieve the monotony of hardtack, salt pork, and coffee; "fowls and pigs and eatables don't stand much chance," one Rebel recorded during Lee's invasion of Pennsylvania in 1863. "If God Almighty had yet in store another plague worse than all the others," Zebulon Vance, the querulous governor of North Carolina, wrote later that year to the Confederate Secretary of War, "I am sure it must have been a regiment or so of half-armed, half-disciplined Confederate Cavalry."

(1) The happy end of a foraging expedition appears in an A. R. Waud drawing. "Every hog seen," a Wisconsin lad noted, "is a 'wild hog' of course." (2) This frank, unabashed acknowledgment of foraging is from Federal cavalryman Nathan B. Webb's diary. (3) An Ohio soldier justified the stealing of Southern chickens by claiming that "they are always sure to cackle at the Stars and Stripes . . ." This pair's sheer delight in their prize catch is registered in an unsigned sketch. (4) With split-rail fences at hand soldiers could not be bothered with chopping down trees for firewood. (5) This attempt on a beehive, drawn by Charles Reed, ended in bitter rout.

373

1

2

No. 3. Soldiers
Amusement
"Louse Race

3

4

Southern Camp Life

The hardships and privations endured by the Union soldiers were, in many cases, intensified in the toilsome life of the Confederate soldier. During campaigns they often went without food, adequate shelter, or warm clothing. And, like their Northern counterparts, they found winter camp overpoweringly boring: "Oh how tiresome this camp life to me," complained a Mississippi boy in 1864, "one everlasting monotone, yesterday, today, and tomorrow." Yet the Southern spirit proved indomitable. As late as May, 1864, one of Lee's men stated: "As for myself, I am getting pretty tired of it, but am not ready yet for a while to say Enought. I think I can stand thru three more years yet and I think before that time [the enemy] will get middling tired of it."

(1) Conrad Chapman's sketch portrays a relaxed Southern camp group.
(2) A Confederate picket on duty.
(3) Private Harry St. John Dixon of the 28th Mississippi Cavalry turned artist to sketch a "louse race" for an entry in his diary on June 20, 1864.
(4) The first war sketch received by *Harper's* was this, of Rebels at Camp Las Moras, Texas, in March, 1861.
(5) A sense of drama and excitement animates Chapman's delicate painting of Rebel troops leaving a camp.
(6) William Cooper enlivened his diary with a crude sketch of a Rebel cavalry ball, held on Christmas, 1862.
(7) Many Rebel officers were accompanied by Negro slaves. Chapman made this thoughtful study in 1863.

OVERLEAF: Conditions at the Confederate camp at Corinth, Mississippi, in May, 1862, were not quite so idyllic as portrayed in this chromolithograph after a Chapman painting. As many Rebels died from disease here in the seven weeks following Shiloh as perished in the battle itself.

5

6

7

Inscribed to the 8th Wisconsin Regt.

"OLD ABE" THE BATTLE EAGLE

SONG & CHORUS
Poetry by
L. J. BATES ESQ.

MUSIC BY
T. MARTIN TOWNE
Author of "Our boys are coming home"

OLD ABE the Battle Eagle when history is well known throughout the North West was carried by the Eighth Wisconsin Regiment in all their battles, and was equally exposed with them during their three years service. He now belongs to and is supported by the State in quarters fitted up for him in the State House Park at Madison.

MILWAUKEE
Published by H. N. HEMPSTED 410 Main St.

378

COLLECTION OF MRS. JOHN NICHOLAS BROWN

At a high point in the Battle of the Wilderness in May, 1864, the Union IX Corps was thrown back by a savage Rebel flank attack. Suddenly one of the men raised his voice in the stirring words of the song which begins "We'll rally round the flag; Boys, we'll rally once again"; and the boys in blue returned to the fight.

Generally speaking, the type of patriotic fervor symbolized by such songs (in this instance, George F. Root's "The Battle Cry of Freedom") more often moved the home folks than it did the men in the front lines. The Civil War fighting man, Blue or Gray, was frankly sentimental and often preferred such lachrymose ballads as "Just Before the Battle, Mother," or "Somebody's Darling." Quite naturally, the men sang of their sweethearts—"Aura Lea," "Lorena," and "The Yellow Rose of Texas." A great Rebel favorite was "All Quiet Along the Potomac," which spoke of the picket's endless loneliness. Gathered about their campfires, Northern boys would sing "Tenting Tonight on the Old Camp Ground" and "Weeping Sad and Lonely" ("When this cruel war is over")—songs which expressed simple homesickness.

Paradoxically, the two songs that, in memory at least, best represent the Union and Confederacy were each borrowed from the other side. "Dixie" was a Northern minstrel tune, composed by Dan Emmett, the son of an Ohio abolitionist. "The Battle Hymn of the Republic" marked Julia Ward Howe's attempt to dignify an already popular marching song—"John Brown's Body"—which was sung to the melody of a Southern camp-meeting hymn first heard in Charleston in the 1850's. The song sheet covers reproduced here are a representative selection.

1

2

3

4

Recreation and Punishment

5

"Sometimes we are granted a pass to visit the Citty," a Southerner stationed near Richmond in 1864 wrote. "If not we run the Blockade, visit the Theaters maybe get on a big Whope & Paint the thing red." Drunkenness, gambling, and even assaulting officers could be dismissed as minor vices, the result of pent-up emotions in those troubled times; but desertion could not. During the war 141 Union men were executed for desertion, although a sympathetic President Lincoln granted an untold number of pardons, preferring, he said, to "take the risk on the side of mercy."

(1) Jeff Davis hanged in effigy (left, background) added a unique touch to Christmas decorations at this Northern camp near Washington in 1861. Visiting ladies and officers watch the men chase a greased pig (left), play football (center), and attempt to climb a pole (right) for an elusive prize. (2) These Union officers seem to anticipate the Keystone Cops in this horseplay, staged for the cameraman. (3) In Winslow Homer's painting titled "Playing Old Soldier" a suspiciously healthy-looking Northern lad feigns illness to avoid active service. (4) Wrists tied to tree limbs and bayonets gagged in their mouths, these men are suffering the consequences of drunkenness and unruly conduct. (5) Two Federal pranksters tip over the improvised chimney of a snug winter shelter in Charles Reed's sketch. (6) Flanked by soldiers carrying reversed arms, this Massachusetts soldier is drummed out of camp. The placard identifies his crime as theft of money from a wounded friend.

OVERLEAF: Federal prisoners play baseball at Salisbury, North Carolina. Abner Doubleday, who later became a Union general, is often credited with inventing the game as a Cooperstown, New York, lad in 1835.

6

1

Camp Scene Evening Amusements (Annapolis)

2

3

A Connecticut Corporal

All that is positively known of Corporal J. E. Shadek is his name and his record of service with Company A of the 8th Connecticut Volunteers. Yet this man from the ranks is memorialized in an aging, dog-eared sketchbook—measuring no more than seven by three inches and containing only 100 pages—which he prepared for Captain Henry M. Hoyt of his unit.

The primitive, yet finely drawn sketches in pen, pencil, and water colors form an unofficial log of the 8th Connecticut—from its first duty station at Annapolis, through the Cape Hatteras and Roanoke Island expeditions early in 1862, to Antietam the following September. The regiment went on to fight at Fredericksburg, Cold Harbor, and Petersburg, and was in the trenches before Richmond when the Confederacy collapsed in April, 1865.

On the last numbered page of the picture diary appears a hushed, autumnal view of Burnside's Bridge after the Battle of Antietam. The remaining 30 pages of the book are blank except for a few preliminary sketches and a calendar that abruptly ends on October 24, 1862. Records indicate that Shadek was discharged for disability the following December 13; his regiment, in its four years of service, lost 464 men.

(1) Shadek's powers of humorous observation more than make up for his lack of proportion in a milking scene. (2) A quiet evening camp scene at Annapolis, Maryland, early in the war. (3) An eerie sense of apocalyptic vision illuminates this untitled sketch. (4) Shadek's 8th Connecticut, fresh from its triumphs on the North Carolina coast, marches past the unfinished Capitol en route to Antietam. (5) The Company A cook, it would appear, was an orderly, efficient man. (6) The sketchbook's dedicatory page.

Mortar firing in N° 36   Capt Simonds
13 inch Shells

1

Fire in one of Co A's tents.
Soldiers who would not stand fire

2

3

A Cincinnati Artist

4

5

"A person gets almost tired of seeing soldiers . . ." James W. McLaughlin wrote from Washington on July 2, 1861, "in fact the distinction is to be a civilian for the gentlemen in plain clothes bear just about the proportion of 1 in 10." The promising young Cincinnati architect had come to the capital, possibly to win an officer's appointment; by the following winter he was in Missouri, serving with the Benton Cadets. His unit, he complained, was becoming "famous for brilliant expeditions that don't amount to much." April, 1862, found McLaughlin at New Madrid on the Mississippi, where the action suited him better. "I feel remarkably well," he wrote home, "with the exception of the aching produced by the 20 mile ride on horseback . . . but will soon get used to it and enjoy myself."

That month James McLaughlin received encouragement from *Leslie's* for sketches he had been submitting. Henceforth, he directed his family, letters should be sent to "Frank Leslie's artist, care of St. Chas. Hotel, Cairo." Some of McLaughlin's original sketches, handed down in the family, are here reproduced for the first time. At war's end McLaughlin followed a distinguished architectural career in Cincinnati. He lived until 1923.

(1) James McLaughlin sketched this 13-inch mortar, firing from the deck of a Union gunboat during Flag Officer Foote's siege of Fort Pillow on the Mississippi River in April, 1862.
(2) An overheated stove caused one type of fire, artist McLaughlin wryly noted, that soldiers could not stand.
(3) This raffish hospital steward apparently had one remedy for all ills.
(4) Colonel Lew Marshall of the Benton Cadets, McLaughlin's first unit.
(5) The distribution of clothing in December, 1861, was a riotous affair.

1

2

An Artistic French Visitor

3

4

Europe, in the 1860's, was at the midpoint of a century of almost uninterrupted peace. As a proving ground for sizing up time-honored military tactics and modern weaponry, the Civil War attracted wide-scale interest abroad, and high-ranking visitors crossed the Atlantic to observe the hostilities. Among these distinguished visitors were the Comte de Paris and the Duc de Chartres, accompanied by their uncle, Admiral Prince de Joinville, the third son of King Louis Philippe of France. The two younger men donned Federal blue as volunteer aides and, with their uncle, followed the Peninsular Campaign of McClellan—once a foreign observer himself during the Crimean War.

During his years of exile from France, following the Revolution of 1848, the Prince de Joinville had studied painting. He further developed his very considerable talents as a water-colorist in America, leaving an arresting record of his two years as a military observer. Four of the Prince's water colors, owned by the present Comte de Paris, pretender to the French throne, are reproduced here for the first time in color.

(1) An unending blue column crosses the Potomac River at Harpers Ferry.
(2) A treetop sentinel guards a picnic.
(3) The Comte de Paris and the Duc de Chartres (right) posed in uniform for their uncle at a Northern camp.
(4) This reconnaissance scene was painted along the Warwick River, near Yorktown, scene of the Revolutionary French-American triumph.

OVERLEAF: Featured in this 1865 lithograph, typical of many issued in the postwar period to commemorate individual units, are the 1861 departure of New York's 14th Regiment, its moment of glory at Gettysburg, and its delirious 1864 homecoming.

"THE PRICE OF LIBERTY,"

MEMO

14th Reg

DEPARTURE FROM FORT GREENE, MAY 18th 1861.

BULL RUN	July 21st 1861
BINNS HILL	Nov 10th
FALMOUTH	Apr 17th 1862
RAPPAHANNOCK STATION	Aug 21st
BEVERLY FORD	22d
SULPHUR SPRINGS	26th
GAINESVILLE	28th
GROVETON	29th
BULL RUN 2d	30th
SOUTH MOUNTAIN	Sept 14th

CAPTURE OF A REG

LITH & PUBLISHED

Y. S. M.

"IS ETERNAL VIGILANCE"

RECEPTION AT FULTON FERRY, MAY 25TH 1864.

EXCELSIOR

ANTIETAM	Sept 17th 1862.
FREDERICKSBURGH	Dec 13th
PORT ROYAL	April 23d 1863
FITZHUGH CROSSING	29th
CHANCELLORSVILLE	May 3d & 4th
SEMINARY HILL	July 1st
GETTYSBURGH	2d & 3d
MINE RUN	Nov 30th
WILDERNESS	May 6th 7th 1864
LAUREL HILL	8th 10th & 12th
SPOTTSYLVANIA	12th to 21st

MEADE, JULY 1ST 1863.

TWO
ECONOMIES
AT WAR

THE INNER meaning of Gettysburg was not immediately visible. It had been a fearful and clamorous act of violence, a physical convulsion that cost the two armies close to 50,000 casualties, the most enormous battle that had ever been fought on the North American continent, and all men knew that; but the deep mystic overtones of it, the qualities that made this, more than any other battle, stand for the final significance of the war and the war's dreadful cost—these were realized slowly, fully recognized only after Abraham Lincoln made them explicit in the moving sentences of the Gettysburg Address.

In that speech Lincoln went to the core of the business. The war was not merely a test of the Union's cohesive strength, nor was it just a fight to end slavery and to extend the boundaries of human freedom. It was the final acid test of the idea of democracy itself; in a way that went far beyond anything which either government had stated as its war aims, the conflict was somehow a definitive assaying of the values on which American society had been built. The inexplicable devotion which stirred the hearts of men, displayed in its last full measure on the sun-scorched fields and slopes around Gettysburg, was both the nation's principal reliance and something which must thereafter be lived up to. Gettysburg and the war itself would be forever memorable, not merely because so

many men had died, but because their deaths finally did mean something that would be a light in the dark skies as long as America should exist.

. . . Thus Lincoln, considering the tragedy with the eyes of a prophet. Yet while the mystical interpretation may explain the meaning of the ultimate victory, it does not explain the victory itself. The Confederate soldier had fully as much selfless devotion as the Unionist, and he risked death with fully as much heroism; if the outcome had depended on a comparison of the moral qualities of the men who did the fighting, it would be going on yet, for the consecration that rests on the parked avenues at Gettysburg derives as much from the Southerner as from the Northerner. The war did not come out as it did because one side had better men than the other. To understand the process of victory it is necessary to examine a series of wholly material factors.

Underneath everything there was the fact that the Civil War was a modern war: an all-out war, as that generation understood the concept, in which everything that a nation has and does must be listed with its assets or its debits. Military striking power in such a war is finally supported, conditioned, and limited by the physical scope and vitality of the basic economy. Simple valor and devotion can never be enough to win, if the war once develops past its opening stages. And for such a war the North was prepared

Some 3,000 cannon for Union armies were manufactured at the West Point foundry, painted here by J. F. Weir.

393

and the South was not prepared: prepared, not in the sense that it was ready for the war—neither side was in the least ready—but in the resources which were at its disposal. The North could win a modern war and the South could not. Clinging to a society based on the completely archaic institution of slavery, the South for a whole generation had been making a valiant attempt to reject the industrial revolution, and this attempt had involved it at last in a war in which the industrial revolution would be the decisive factor.

To a Southland fighting for its existence, slavery was an asset in the farm belt. The needed crops could be produced even though the army took away so many farmers, simply because slaves could keep plantations going with very little help. But in all other respects the peculiar institution was a terrible handicap. Its existence had kept the South from developing a class of skilled workers; it had kept the South rural, and although some slaves were on occasion used as factory workers, slavery had prevented the rise of industrialism. Now, in a war whose base was industrial strength, the South was fatally limited. It could put a high percentage of its adult white manpower on the firing line, but it lacked the economic muscle on which the firing line ultimately was based. Producing ample supplies of food and fibers, it had to go hungry and inadequately clad; needing an adequate distributive mechanism, it was saddled with railroads and highways which had never been quite good enough and which now could not possibly be improved or even maintained.

The North bore a heavy load in the war. The proliferating casualty lists reached into every community, touching nearly every home. War expenditures reached what then seemed to be the incomprehensible total of more than two million dollars a day. Inflation sent living costs rising faster than the average man's income could rise. War profiteers were numerous and blatant, and at times the whole struggle seemed to be waged for their benefit; to the very end of the war there was always a chance that the South might gain its independence, not because of victories in the field but because the people in the North simply found the burden too heavy to carry any longer.

Yet with all of this the war brought to the North a period of tremendous growth and development. A commercial and industrial boom like nothing the country had imagined before took place. During the first year, to be sure, times were hard: the country had not entirely recovered from the Panic of 1857, and when the Southern states seceded the three hundred million dollars which Southerners owed to Northern businessmen went up in smoke, briefly intensifying the depression in the North. But recovery was rapid; the Federal government was spending so much money that no depression could endure, and by the summer of 1862 the Northern states were waist-deep in prosperity.

In the twentieth century boom times often leave the farmer out in the cold, but it was not so during the Civil War. The demand for every kind of foodstuff seemed insatiable. Middle-western farmers, who used to export corn and hogs to Southern plantation owners, quickly found that government requirements more than offset the loss of that market—which, as a matter of fact, never entirely vanished; a certain amount of intersectional trade went on throughout the war, despite efforts by both governments to check it.

Not only were grain and meat in demand, but the government was buying more leather than ever before —marching armies, after all, need shoes, and the hundreds of thousands of horses and mules used by the armies needed harness—and the market for hides was never better. A textile industry which could not get a fraction of all the cotton it wanted turned increasingly to the production of woolen fabrics (here likewise government requirements had skyrocketed), and the market for raw wool was never livelier. Taking everything into consideration, there had never before been such a prodigious rise in the demand for all kinds of Northern farm produce.

This increased demand Northern farms met with effortless ease. There might have been a crippling manpower shortage, because patriotic fervor nowhere ran stronger than in the farm belt and a high percentage of the able-bodied men had gone into the army. But the war came precisely when the industrial revolution was making itself felt on the farm. Labor-saving machinery had been perfected and was being put into use—a vastly improved plow, a corn planter, the two-horse cultivator, mowers and reapers and steam-driven threshing machines—all were available now, and under the pressure of the war the farmer had to use them. Until 1861 farm labor had been abundant and cheap, and these machines made their way slowly; now farm labor was scarce and high-priced, and the farmer who turned to machinery could actually expand his acreage and his production with fewer hands.

The expansion of acreage was almost automatic. All along the frontier, and even in the older settled areas of the East, there was much good land that had not yet been brought into agricultural use. Now it was put into service, and as this happened the government confidently looked toward the future. It passed, in 1862, the long-sought Homestead Act, which virtually gave away enormous quantities of land, in family-sized chunks, to any people who were willing to cultivate it. (The real effect of this was felt after the war rather than during it, but the act's adoption in wartime was symptomatic.) Along with this came the Morrill Land Grant Act, which offered substantial Federal support to state agricultural colleges, and which also was passed in 1862. In the middle of the war the government was declaring that all idle land was to be made available for farming, and that the American farmer was going to get the best technical education he could be given.

As acreage increased, with the aid of laborsaving machinery, the danger of a really crippling manpower shortage vanished; indeed, it probably would have vanished even without the machinery, because of the heavy stream of immigration from Europe. During 1861 and 1862 the number of immigrants fell below the level of 1860, but thereafter the European who wanted to come to America apparently stopped worrying about the war and concluded that America was still the land of promise. During the five years 1861–65 inclusive, more than 800,000 Europeans came to America; most of them from England, Ireland, and Germany. In spite of heavy casualty lists, the North's population increased during the war.

With all of this, the Northern farm belt not only met wartime needs for food and fibers, but it also helped to feed Great Britain. More than 40 per cent of the wheat and flour imported into Great Britain came from the United States. The country's wheat exports tripled during the war, as if it was Northern wheat rather than Southern cotton that was king.

But if the farms enjoyed a war boom, Northern industry had a growth that was almost explosive. Like the farmer, the manufacturer had all sorts of new machinery available—new machinery, and the mass-production techniques that go with machinery—and the war took all limits off his markets. The armies needed all manner of goods: uniforms, underwear, boots and shoes, hats, blankets, tents, muskets, swords, revolvers, cannon, a bewildering variety of ammunition, wagons, canned foods, dressed lumber, shovels, steamboats, surgical instruments, and so on. During the first year industry was not geared to turn out all of these things in the quantities required, and heavy purchases were made abroad while new factories were built, old factories remodeled, and machinery acquired and installed. By 1862 the government practically stopped buying munitions abroad, because its own manufacturers could give it everything it wanted.

The heavy-goods industries needed to support all of this production were available. One of the lucky accidents that worked in favor of American industry in this war was the fact that the canal at Sault Sainte Marie, Michigan, had been built and put into service

a few years before the war, and the unlimited supply of iron ore from the Lake Superior ranges could be brought down to the furnaces inexpensively. Pittsburgh was beginning to be Pittsburgh, with foundries that could turn out cannon and mortars, railroad rails, iron plating for warships or for locomotives—iron, in short, for every purpose, iron enough to meet the most fantastic demands of wartime.

There was a railroad network to go with all of this. During the 1850's the Northern railroad network had been somewhat overbuilt, and many carriers had been having a hard time of it in 1860, but the war brought a heavy traffic that forced the construction of much new mileage. New locomotives and cars were needed, and the facilities to build them were at hand. The Civil War was the first of the "railroad wars," in a military sense, and the Northern railway nexus enabled the Federal government to switch troops back and forth between the Eastern and Western theaters of action with a facility the South could never match.

Altogether, it is probable that the Civil War pushed the North into the industrial age a full generation sooner than would otherwise have been the case. It was just ready to embrace the factory system in 1861, but without the war its development would have gone more slowly. The war provided a forced draft that accelerated the process enormously. By 1865 the northeastern portion of America had become an industrialized nation, with half a century of development compressed into four feverish years.

One concrete symbol of this was the speedy revision of tariff rates. Southern members had no sooner left the Congress than the low tariff rates established in 1857 came in for revision. A protective tariff was adopted, partly to raise money for war purposes but chiefly to give manufacturers what they wanted, and the policy then adopted has not since been abandoned.

The North had little trouble in financing the war. As in more modern times, it relied heavily on war loans, to float which Secretary Chase got the aid—at a price—of the Philadelphia banker Jay Cooke. Cooke sold the bonds on commission, with a flourish very much like the techniques of the 1940's, and during the war more than two billion dollars' worth were marketed. Congress also authorized the issuance of some four hundred and fifty million dollars in "greenbacks"—paper money, made legal tender by act of Congress but secured by no gold reserve. The value of these notes fluctuated, dropping at times to no more than forty cents in gold, but the issue did provide a circulating medium of exchange. More important was the passage in 1863 of a National Bank Act, which gave the country for the first time a national currency.

Wartime taxes were moderate by present-day stand-

395

ards, but the Federal government had never before levied many taxes, and at the time they seemed heavy. There was a long string of excise taxes on liquor, tobacco, and other goods; there were taxes on manufacturers, on professional men, on railroads and banks and insurance companies, bringing in a total of three hundred million dollars. There was also an income tax, although it never netted the Federal treasury any large sums. One point worth noting is that the supply of precious metals in the country was always adequate, thanks to the California mines and to lodes developed in other parts of the West, notably in Colorado and Nevada.

It remains to be said that the North's war-born prosperity was not evenly distributed. Prices, as usual, rose much faster than ordinary incomes: in the first two years of the war wages rose by 10 per cent and prices by 50 per cent, and people who lived on fixed incomes were squeezed by wartime inflation. In such places as the Pennsylvania coal fields there was a good deal of unrest, leading to labor troubles which, in the eyes of the government, looked like outbreaks of secessionist sympathy, but which actually were simply protests against intolerable working conditions. There were many war profiteers, some of them men apparently devoid of all conscience, who sold the government large quantities of shoddy uniforms, cardboard shoes, spavined horses, condemned weapons imperfectly reconditioned, and steamboats worth perhaps a tenth of their price, and these men did not wear their new wealth gracefully. The casualty lists produced by such battles as Stones River and Gettysburg were not made any more acceptable by the ostentatious extravagance with which the war contractors spent their profits. Yet it was not all ugly. Some of the war money went to endow new colleges and universities, and such war relief organizations as the U.S. Sanitary Commission and the Christian Commission got millions to spend on their work for the soldiers.

Thus in the North, where an economy capable of supporting a modern war was enormously expanded by war's stimulus. In the South the conditions were tragically reversed. Instead of expanding under wartime pressures, the Southern economy all but collapsed. When the war began, the Confederacy had almost nothing but men. The men were as good as the very best, but their country simply could not support them, although the effort it made to do so was heroic and ingenious. The South was not organized for war or for independent existence in any of the essential fields—not in manufacturing, in transportation, or in finance—and it never was able during the course of the war to remedy its deficiencies.

Until 1861 the South had been almost strictly an agricultural region, and its agricultural strength rested largely on cotton. The vain hope that England and France would intervene in order to assure their own supplies of raw cotton—the hoary "cotton is king" motif—kept the Confederacy from sending enough cotton overseas during the first year of the war to establish adequate credit, and the munitions and other manufactured goods that might have been imported then appeared only in a trickle. When the government finally saw that its rosy expectations were delusions and changed its policy, the blockade had become effective enough to thwart its aims. As a result the South was compelled to remake its entire economy. It had to achieve self-sufficiency, or something very close to it, and the job was humanly impossible.

A valiant effort was made, and in retrospect the wonder is not that it failed but that it accomplished so much. To a great extent the South's farmers shifted from the production of cotton to the growth of foodstuffs. Salt works were established (in the days before artificial refrigeration salt was a military necessity of the first importance, since meat could not be preserved without it), and textile mills and processing plants were built. Powder mills, armories, and arsenals were constructed, shipyards were established, facilities to make boiler plate and cannon were expanded, and the great Tredegar Iron Works at Richmond became one of the busiest factories in America. Moonshiners' stills were collected for the copper they contained, sash weights were melted down to make bullets, all sorts of expedients were resorted to for saltpeter; and out of all these activities, together with the things that came in through the blockade and war material which not infrequently was captured from the Yankee soldiers and supply trains, the South managed to keep its armies in the field for four years.

But it was attempting a job beyond its means. It was trying to build an industrial plant almost from scratch, without enough capital, without enough machinery or raw materials, and with a desperate shortage of skilled labor. From first to last it was hampered by a badly inadequate railway transportation network, and the situation here got progressively worse because the facilities to repair, to rebuild, or even properly to maintain the railroads did not exist. From the beginning of the war to the end, not one mile of railroad rail was produced in the Confederacy; when a new line had to be built, or when war-ruined track had to be rebuilt, the rails had to come from some branch line or side track. The situation in regard to rolling stock was very little better. When 20,000 troops from the Army of Northern Virginia were sent to northern Georgia by rail in the fall of 1863, a Confederate general quipped that never before had such good soldiers been moved so far on such terrible railroads. Much of the food shortage which plagued Confederate armies and civilians alike as the war grew old came not from any lack of production but from simple inability to move the products from farm to ultimate consumer.

To make matters worse, there was constant and increasing Federal interference with the resources the South did have. The Union armies' advance up the Tennessee and Cumberland rivers in the winter of 1862 meant more than a simple loss of territory for the Confederacy. It put out of action a modest industrial network; there were ironworks, foundries, and small manufacturing plants in western Tennessee which the South could not afford to lose. The early loss of such cities as New Orleans, Nashville, and Memphis further reduced manufacturing capacity. Any Union army which got into Confederate territory destroyed railway lines as a matter of course. If the soldiers simply bent the rails out of shape, and then went away, the rails could quickly be straightened and re-used; as the war progressed, however, the Federals developed a system of giving such rails a spiral twist, which meant that they were of no use unless they could be sent to a rolling mill . . . of which the Confederacy had very few.

Increasingly, the war for the Confederates became a process of doing without. Until the end the soldiers had the guns and ammunition they needed, but they did not always have much of anything else. Confederate soldiers made a practice of removing the shoes, and often the clothing, of dead or captured Federals out of sheer necessity, and it was frequently remarked that the great *élan* which the Southern soldier displayed in his attacks on Federal positions came at least partly from his knowledge that if he seized a Yankee camp he would find plenty of good things to eat.

As in the North, there were war profiteers in the South, although there were not nearly so many of them, and they put on pretty much the same sort of display. The blockade-runners brought in luxury goods as well as necessities, and the Southerner who had plenty of money could fare very well. Few people qualified in this respect, but the ones who did qualify and who chose to spend their money on themselves found all kinds of things to buy.

Perhaps the shortage that hit the Confederacy hardest of all was the shortage—or, rather, the absolute lack —of a sound currency. This compounded and intensified all of the other shortages; to a nation which could neither produce all it needed nor get the goods which it did produce to the places where they were wanted, there came this additional, crushing disaster of leaping inflation. As a base for Confederate currency the new government possessed hardly more than one million dollars in specie. Credit resources were strictly limited, and an adequate system of taxation was never devised. From the beginning the nation put its chief reliance on printing-press money. This deteriorated rapidly, and kept on deteriorating, so that by 1864 a Confederate dollar had a gold value of just five cents. (By the end of 1864 the value had dropped very nearly to zero.) Prices went up, and wages and incomes were hopelessly outdistanced. It was in the South during the Civil War that men made the wisecrack that was re-used during Germany's inflation in the 1920's—that a citizen went to market carrying his money in a basket and came home with the goods he had bought in his wallet.

Under such conditions government finances got into a hopeless mess. One desperate expedient was a 10 per cent "tax in kind" on farm produce. This did bring needed corn and pork in to the armies, but it was one of the most unpopular taxes ever levied, and it contributed largely to the progressive loss of public confidence in the Davis administration. To supply its armies, the government at times had to wink at violations of its own laws. It strictly prohibited the export of raw cotton to Yankee consumers, for instance, but now and then it carefully looked the other way when such deals were made: the Yankees might get the cotton, but in return the Southern armies could sometimes get munitions and medicines which were otherwise unobtainable.

By the spring of 1865, when the military effort of the Southland was at last brought to a halt, the Confederate economy had suffered an all but total collapse. The nation was able to keep an army in the field at all only because of the matchless endurance and determination of its surviving soldiers. Its ability to produce, transport, and pay for the necessities of national life was almost entirely exhausted; the nation remained on its feet only by a supreme and despairing effort of will, and it moved as in a trance. Opposing it was a nation which the war had strengthened instead of weakened—a nation which had had much the greater strength to begin with and which had now become one of the strongest powers on the globe. The war could end only as it did end. The Confederacy died because the war had finally worn it out.

Northern machine shops, such as the chisel and steel-square works at Shaftsbury, Vermont (pictured above and below), gave the Union the industrial superiority which proved decisive.

Denied cotton, the North perfected its infant woolen goods industry with new textile machinery (left) in order to meet the demand for uniforms.

As the Union's most reliable source of supply, the Du Pont powder mills (right) were guarded day and night. Horse-drawn cars were used to eliminate the danger of flying sparks.

The North's Industrial Muscle

The North can make a steam engine, locomotive or railway car; hardly a yard of cloth or a pair of shoes can you make. You are rushing into war with one of the most powerful, ingeniously mechanical and determined people on earth—right at your doors. You are bound to fail." It was Christmas Eve, 1860, and William Tecumseh Sherman was lecturing a Southern friend on the futility of the looming contest.

As early as 1851 such symbols of American inventiveness and technology as the McCormick reaper, the Colt revolver, and Goodyear rubber products had won grudging praise at London's Crystal Palace Exhibition. Three years later British manufacturers were complaining of the threat of U.S. imports.

By 1860 the North possessed all the requirements of a potentially great manufacturing nation: natural resources, a cheap labor supply, and mechanical genius. Yet even in the more important industries production was fragmented among scores of petty establishments, and corporate organization had advanced little beyond the stage of family ownership. It would take the Civil War to shock the country into industrial maturity —bringing greater centralization, giant strides in manufacturing techniques, and fundamental changes in a newly urbanized society's way of life.

On November 24, 1861, the New York *Herald,* in an editorial entitled "The Great Rebellion a Great Revolution," concluded that "everything the finger of war touches is revolutionized." It was a prophecy as well as a judgment.

E. I. DU PONT DE NEMOURS AND COMPANY

King Corn
Replaces King Cotton

A major source of sectional hostility in the ante-bellum period was the South's long-standing opposition to high protective tariffs on manufactured goods. The South, which sold most of its agricultural products abroad, wanted cheap imports to fill the gap in its own economy and cared not a whit for the infant industries in the North. When Southern legislators withdrew from Congress, that body passed, on March 2, 1861, a high-tariff act sponsored by Vermont's Senator Justin S. Morrill. Added to the war's incessant demands, this protection from foreign competition insured the continued expansion of Northern industry. American factories were soon able to fill nearly all the needs of the Union armies, and imports of munitions virtually ceased after the first year of the war.

The Federal blockade soon proved that Europe could survive without Southern cotton; but apparently it could not get along without Northern wheat. Ideal weather conditions, year after year, plus improved farming methods, proved such a stimulus to agriculture that the North was raising more corn and wheat than it could consume. And so the excess was shipped overseas. Between 1861 and 1863 the North supplied Great Britain with 40 per cent of its wheat and flour.

"Wave the stars and stripes high o'er us, Let every freeman sing," penned a Northern versifier, "Old King Cotton's dead . . . brave young Corn is King."

In this period photograph a forest of masts, symbolic of the Union's commerce, chokes New York's waterfront.

401

Hard-working, efficient Montgomery Meigs (left) was the organizing genius who kept the river of supplies flowing to Union armies. Above, a Negro soldier guards an unbroken line of parked 12-pounders, brought to City Point, Virginia, in 1864 for the siege of Petersburg. Mountains of army staples such as pork, hardtack, sugar, and coffee rose at various commissary depots. The one in the 1864 photograph below was at Cedar Level, Virginia.

Supplying the Federal Armies

In May, 1861, a captain of army engineers, Montgomery C. Meigs, was taken off the job of supervising the Capitol's remodeling, promoted to brigadier general, and given the post of Quartermaster General of the U.S. Army. The zealous Meigs was to serve in that capacity throughout the war, though it would keep him from the field command which, for a man of such talent, might have been a surer path to fame and glory.

To feed, clothe, and supply the largest armies ever gathered on the North American continent would have daunted a lesser man. And even when Northern industry could furnish Meigs with almost everything he needed, there were critical problems. "The mania for stealing seems to have run through all the relations of Government," lamented a New York congressman. "Nearly every man who deals with the Government seems to feel or desire that it would not long survive, and each had a common right to plunder while it lived." In Louisville, 485 horses sold to the army for $58,200 were found to be "blind, spavined . . . and with every disease that horseflesh is heir to." A stand of outdated carbines, which the government disposed of at two dollars apiece, was purchased by a contractor and sold back to the army at $22 each. Young Jim Fisk, down from Vermont to launch a financial career that would reach spectacular heights by the 1870's, glibly remarked: "You can sell anything to the government at almost any price you've got the guts to ask."

Revelations of scandals, graft, and corruption in the filling of war contracts soon toppled Simon P. Cameron from his position as Secretary of War; but Montgomery Meigs stayed on the job. At war's end Secretary of State Seward reviewed the Quartermaster General's handling of supply problems: "without the services of this eminent soldier," he wrote, "the national cause must have been lost or deeply imperilled."

The South
Learns a Hard Lesson
About Cotton

In the cartoon above a smug Northerner offers captured cotton for sale to England's John Bull. Confederates often destroyed cotton to keep it from the Yankees. Frank Vizetelly sketched Rebel cotton burners below, being surprised by Federal scouts.

Cotton production, in the peak year of 1860, reached the fantastic total of 5,198,077 bales. But Southern armies were going to need food, not cotton, and early in the war the Confederacy was forced to reconsider its heavy reliance on this cash crop. Several Southern states passed laws limiting its production, and the Confederate Congress approved a resolution asking planters to forsake cotton and tobacco for food crops. "If all citizens were intelligent and patriotic," declared the Richmond *Examiner,* "not another leaf of tobacco or pod of cotton would be seen in the fields of the South until peace is declared."

Loyal Southerners responded to this demand, and the presence of invading armies limited cotton planting still further. Production dropped to 1,500,000 bales in 1862; 500,000 in 1863; and to an abysmal yet encouraging low of 300,000 bales by 1864. A woman passing through the cotton belt of Mississippi and Alabama in 1862 noted corn growing everywhere, with scarcely an acre of cotton to be seen. In January, 1863, Jefferson Davis triumphantly reported to Congress that Southern fields were "no longer whitened by cotton . . . [but were] devoted to the production of cereals and the growth of stock formerly purchased with the proceeds of cotton." Salty William Tecumseh Sherman viewed the feat from another angle: "Convey to Jeff. Davis my personal and official thanks for abolishing cotton and substituting corn and sweet potatoes in the South," he wrote as he began his invasion of Georgia. "These facilitate our military plans much, for food and forage are abundant."

Cut off from sea lanes by the blockade, Charleston's Union Wharf (right) presented a forlorn scene of stranded ships and cotton lying useless on the docks for want of transportation.

The Confederacy Builds a War Machine

A symbol of Richmond's industrial importance was the imposing Virginia Armory above. Its capacity of 5,000 small arms per month was the largest in the South. Another Richmond establishment, the Confederate States Laboratory, turned out percussion caps and cartridges.

Joseph Reid Anderson (above) had a brief career as a brigadier general but performed his most valuable service for the Confederacy as civilian director of the Tredegar Iron Works (below, photographed in 1865 after the fall of Richmond).

When war began, secessionists had seized military supplies in Federal arsenals throughout the South. From this source the Confederacy obtained 135,000 infantry weapons, but a great many were antiquated muskets. Emissaries were hastily dispatched to purchase more arms abroad, while the Confederacy sought to create, overnight, an industry capable of sustaining a nation at war.

When they evacuated Harpers Ferry, Federal authorities had burned the armory there (containing the only machinery in the South for making rifles), but some machinery was salvaged and brought to Richmond, the most important industrial center in the South. The removal of the Confederate capital from Montgomery, Alabama, to Richmond in June, 1861, was motivated in part by the necessity of securing the large Tredegar Iron Works on the banks of the James River; and subsequent Southern military strategy was often designed to protect this leading iron manufactory as well as to safeguard the Rebel seat of government.

Joseph Reid Anderson, the prewar owner of the Tredegar Iron Works, performed yeoman service as director of the South's largest manufacturing establishment. Under his imperturbable management Tredegar turned out projectiles, gun carriages, plates for ironclads, wheels and axles for railway rolling stock, and furnaces for a chain of smaller factories which the Confederacy was establishing from Richmond south to Selma, Alabama.

Although Anderson more than once offered to turn the entire plant over to the Confederate authorities, the government was well satisfied with his efficient performance. Until April, 1865, Anderson operated Tredegar as a semiautonomous domain. A Negro laborer employed there was once asked if he was working for the government. "No, suh," he answered indignantly. "I'm with the other concern."

The Long War Demands Southern Sacrifices

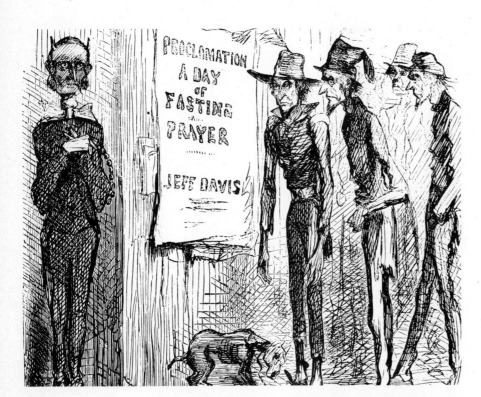

A Harper's artist enjoyed showing gaunt Southern citizens staring with sunken eyes at a proclamation of fasting posted by the horned Jefferson Davis at left.

In 1863, looking back at prewar conditions, a Mississippi editor wrote that "We were so poor, and so helpless, the Yankees had to take care of us like so many children. . . . Let us resolve never more to be dependent on that people . . ."

By this time the Southerners had already shown their determination to follow this advice, with a demonstration of courage, ingenuity, and improvisation that was truly remarkable. Enthusiasm for making everything soon caused the Confederate Congress to set up a patent office, and applications poured in at a rate of about 70 a month.

But enthusiasm was not enough. Some shortages could not be overcome, and the South was forced to do without or to pay exorbitant prices for articles which had once been considered necessities but were now unattainable luxuries. By mid-1864 a lady's bonnet cost $250, and women began wearing hats made

Life on the Rebel homefront required sacrifice and devotion, as Adalbert Volck's drawings above indicate. At left, medicine is smuggled across the lines; in the center, ladies make clothes for the boys at the front; and at right, a sanctimonious group meets an appeal for church bells to be melted down for cannon.

from cornhusks and palmetto leaves. A reporter, forced to pay $5 for a cup of coffee in Richmond in 1864, wrote angrily: "The *acme* of extortion is reached . . ." It was a common joke that innkeepers did not allow guests to pay for a night's lodging until the following morning, lest the price rise during the night.

By March, 1865, loaves of bread were being made in three sizes, for sale at one, two, and three dollars. "The first is only visible by microscopick aid; the second can be discerned with the naked eye, and the third can be seen with outline and shape distinct," a Richmond newspaper reported. The tenacity and determination of the South in the face of such grim prospects were noted by *The Illustrated London News:* "The South with no advantage except that of 'immortal hate,'" it concluded, "has maintained the contest with a heroism that has carried men's hearts captive with admiration."

Breech-loading guns like this Rebel 12-pounder, photographed after its capture by Union troops, had to run the blockade, since the South made only muzzle-loaders.

Sherman's men could tear apart railroads as well as build them. The tracks in Georgia were easily pried loose (above, left) and then heated in special ovens (above, right) to be twisted into "Sherman hairpins," which decorated tree trunks all the way to the sea.

Herman Haupt served as chief of U.S. military rail transportation. A prewar authority on railroad construction, Haupt scorned military red tape to get his job done. In the photograph below, Haupt (standing at right) directs work on a Virginia line in 1863.

Transportation and Communication

In fighting a defensive war, the Confederacy lacked one essential component which would have facilitated the repulse of the invading Union armies—adequate railroad transportation. Symptomatic of this shortcoming was the 40-mile gap in the railroad between Danville, Virginia, and Greensboro, North Carolina. Jefferson Davis proposed the building of this section of the road in November, 1861; Congress appropriated funds the following February; but not until May, 1864, was the line completed—and then only by tearing up the tracks on another line to supply the shortage of rails.

Meanwhile, Union generals were using railroads to great advantage. "The quicker you build the railroad, the quicker you'll get something to eat," Sherman told his men in 1863. To block his drive toward Atlanta, the Confederates tore up miles of track and even blasted a tunnel near Dalton, Georgia, but Sherman's ability to rebuild and repair lines was the despair of his opponents. "Oh, hell," a Rebel soldier supposedly remarked, "don't you know Sherman carries along a duplicate tunnel?"

Another nineteenth-century invention which played an important part in this war was the object of daily attention by a tall, angular figure who emerged from the White House, walked across the lawn to the War Department building, and went into the telegraph office where news from the front was received. "I come here to escape my persecutors," Lincoln told the operators, yet it could hardly have been a comforting refuge, for here the President received news of some of the war's greatest disasters and sadly wrote out in longhand his anguished replies to queries and complaints from a long string of disappointing generals.

During the heated Battle of Fredericksburg, army Signal Corps teams, drawn above by A. R. Waud, scurried about laying telegraph wires to relay news to Washington.

William Waud's drawing below shows the U.S. military railroad which Grant built south from the existing City Point line to aid his protracted siege of Petersburg.

The Problem of Financing the War

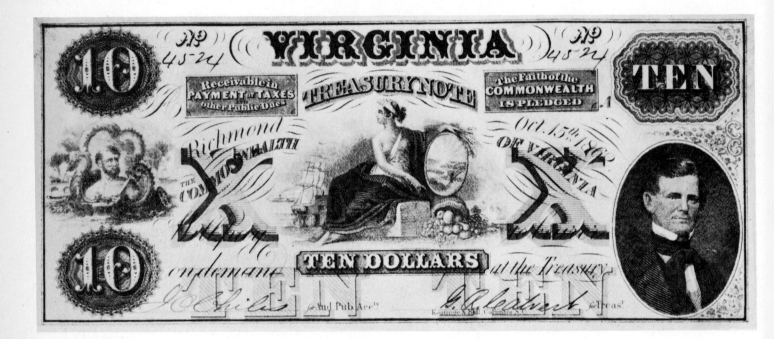

The one billion dollars' worth of Confederate currency is-sued was never declared legal tender—patriotism alone was supposed to lend it value. Above is a $10 Virginia note; Stonewall Jackson's portrait adorns the $500 bill below.

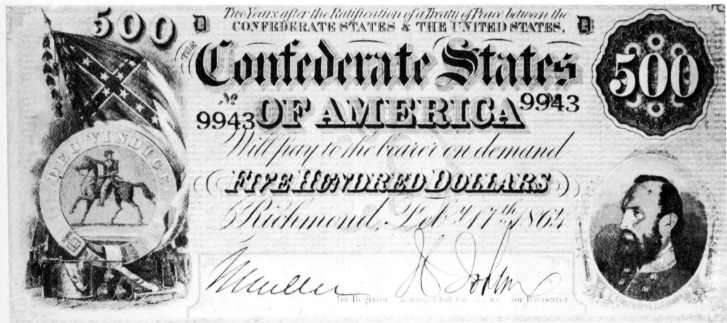

In January, 1862, a discouraged Lincoln slouched into the office of Quartermaster General Montgomery Meigs, seated himself before the fire, and asked wearily: "What shall I do? The people are impatient; Chase has no money and he tells me he can raise no more . . . The bottom is out of the tub." Secretary of the Treasury Chase had been forced, in the first year of the war, to borrow money at the ruinous rate of 7.3 per cent; and in December, 1861, the government had suspended specie payments. Into this financial morass stepped shrewd Jay Cooke, a self-made Philadelphia banker.

Cooke opened a Washington office early in 1862, and the following October Chase named him a special treasury agent. Cooke's first big assignment was the sale of $500,000,000 worth of 6 per cent government bonds. With a dazzling commission of $1,750,000 in the offing Cooke enthusiastically launched a subscription campaign. By January 21, 1864, his agents had persuaded some 600,-000 citizens to share in the war's expenses; and the loan had actually been oversubscribed by about $13,-000,000. The people, a Cooke report noted somewhat pompously, had placed "their treasure on the altar of their country with patriotic confidence and generous hands."

In Richmond, meanwhile, the Confederacy was struggling with absolutely insoluble financial problems. The South had gone to war largely financed by a $500,000 loan from Alabama and $389,267 in bullion seized from the Federal mint at New Orleans. A domestic loan brought in some $100,000,000; and after April, 1863, an extremely unpopular 10 per cent tax in kind was leveled on all produce. But the South relied most heavily on the printing press. "An oak leaf," predicted a Georgian in 1863, "will be worth just as much as the promise of the Confederate treasury to pay one dollar." And by war's end he was right.

Jay Cooke (above) was the North's financial wonder. Below is the prospectus for a Confederate loan, backed by cotton, which Paris bankers offered for sale in Europe.

SEVEN PER CENT. COTTON LOAN

OF THE

CONFEDERATE STATES OF AMERICA.

FOR

£3,000,000 STERLING, AT 90 PER CENT.

The BONDS to bear INTEREST at the rate of 7 per cent. per annum in Sterling, from 1st March, 1863, payable Half-yearly in London, Paris, Amsterdam, or Frankfort.

The BONDS exchangeable for COTTON on application, at the option of the Holder, or redeemable at par in Sterling in Twenty Years, by Half-yearly drawings, commencing 1st March, 1864.

Agents for the Contractors in Liverpool :—Messrs. FRASER TRENHOLM & Co., 10, RUMFORD PLACE.

This Loan has been contracted with Messrs. EMILE ERLANGER & Co., Bankers of Paris, by the Government of the Confederate States of America, and is specially secured by an undertaking of the Government to deliver Cotton to the holders of the Bonds, on application after sixty days' notice, on the footing aftermentioned.

The nature of the arrangement is fully set forth in Article IV. of the Contract made with Messrs. E. ERLANGER & Co., which is as follows :—

The Union Continues to Grow

There is a great, grand, and glorious future to our country when the slaveholders' hellish revolt is crushed out," Joseph Medill, editor of the Chicago *Tribune,* was writing in the summer of 1863. "Emigration from Europe is already pouring into New York at the rate of 1,000 a day, which will fill the gap made by the war in our labor population." He might also have noted how easily the North could find the manpower with which to quell Indian uprisings in Minnesota and continue populating the vast Western territories.

In the ante-bellum period Northerners had often felt their natural exuberance restrained by a South resistant to change. For ten years Southern legislators had opposed the distribution of free land, fearful that antislavery settlers would rush into the Western territories. With Southern seats empty, Congress passed the Homestead Act on May 20, 1862. Henceforth any person over 21 or the head of a family could obtain 160 acres of surveyed land out of the public domain after a five-year continuous residence and payment of a nominal registration fee.

Similarly, the South had long blocked a transcontinental railroad, desirous of its own route to the Pacific. On July 1, 1862, the Pacific Railway Act became law. The Union Pacific Railroad was authorized to build west from Nebraska to meet the Central Pacific out of California. The railroad would not be completed until 1869, and thereafter would become the great route to the West, but already a resilient America had staked out its path to the future.

In the whimsical lithograph above an Irishman is contemplating emigration to America. The woodcut below shows John Bull vainly attempting to retain British labor. During the war immigration slowed but never halted, as hundreds of thousands sought a new life.

There were few people on Salt Lake City's main street on October 22, 1861, to celebrate the joining of the eastern and western sections of the transcontinental telegraph (above); yet it was a historic moment of Union solidarity. The unassuming folks below, photographed in 1864, might well have been waiting at this way station on the Oregon Trail for the coming hordes of settlers.

THE DESTRUCTION OF SLAVERY

A SINGULAR fact about modern war is that it takes charge. Once begun it has to be carried to its conclusion, and carrying it there sets in motion events that may be beyond men's control. Doing what has to be done to win, men perform acts that alter the very soil in which society's roots are nourished. They bring about infinite change, not because anyone especially wants it, but because all-out warfare destroys so much that things can never again be as they used to be.

In the 1860's the overwhelming mass of the people, in the North and in the South, were conservatives who hated the very notion of change. Life in America had been good and it had been fairly simple, and most people wanted to keep it that way. The Northerner wanted to preserve the old Union, and the Southerner wanted to preserve the semifeudal society in which he lived; and the unspoken aim in each section was to win a victory which would let people go back to what they had had in a less turbulent day. But after a war which cuts as deeply and goes on as long as the Civil War, no one "goes back" to anything at all. Everybody goes on to something new, and the process is guided and accelerated by the mere act of fighting.

One trouble was that once this war was well begun there was no way, humanly speaking, to work out a compromise peace. The thing had to end in total victory for one side or the other: in a completely independent Confederacy, or in a completely restored Union and the final evaporation of the theory of the right of secession. The longer the war went on and the more it cost, the less willing were patriots on either side to recede from this position. The heroic dead, who were so tragically numerous and who had died for such diametrically opposite causes, must not have died in vain, and only total victory would justify what had been done. And because total victory was the only thinkable outcome, men came to feel that it was right to do anything at all that might bring victory nearer. It was right to destroy railroads, to burn factories and confiscate supplies of food or other raw materials, to seize or ruin any kind of property which was helpful to the enemy.

This feeling rested with especial weight on the North because the North was of necessity the aggressor. The Confederacy existed and it had to be destroyed—not merely brought to the point where its leaders were willing to talk about peace, but destroyed outright. It had to be made incapable of carrying on the fight; both its armies and the industrial and economic muscle which supported them must be made helpless. And so the North at last undertook to wipe out the institution of human slavery.

Lincoln had made this official with the Emancipation Proclamation, but that strange document had to

417

The precipitous summit of Lookout Mountain, overlooking Chattanooga, photographed after its capture by Federal troops.

be ratified by the tacit consent of the people at home and by the active endorsement of the soldiers in the field. And most of the soldiers had not, in the beginning, felt very strongly about slavery. There were, to be sure, many regiments of solid antislavery sentiment: New Englanders, many of the German levies, and certain regiments from abolitionist areas in the Middle West. But these were in a minority. The average Federal soldier began his term of service either quite willing to tolerate slavery in the South or definitely in sympathy with it. He was fighting for the Union and for nothing more. Lincoln's proclamation was not enthusiastically accepted by all of the troops. A few regiments, from border states or from places like southern Illinois and Indiana where there were close ties of sentiment and understanding with the South, came close to mutiny when the document was published, and a good many more grew morose with discontent.

Yet in the end all of the army went along with the new program; became, indeed, the sharp cutting edge that cut slavery down. This happened, quite simply, because the Federal armies that were being taught to lay their hands on any property which might be of service to the Confederate nation realized that the most accessible and most useful property of all was the Negro slave. They had little sympathy with the slave as a person, and they had no particular objection to the fact that he was property; indeed, it was his very status as property which led them to take him away from his owners and to refer to him as "contraband." As property, he supported the Southern war effort. As property, therefore, he was to be taken away from his owners, and when he was taken away, the only logical thing to do with him was to set him free.

The war, in other words, was taking charge. To save the Union the North had to destroy the Confederacy, and to destroy the Confederacy it had to destroy slavery. The Federal armies got the point and behaved accordingly. Slavery was doomed, not so much by any proclamation from Washington as by the necessities of war. The soldiers killed it because it got in their way. Perhaps the most profound miscalculation the Southern leaders ever made was that slavery could be defended by force of arms. By the middle of the nineteenth century slavery was too fragile for that. It could exist only by the tolerance of people who did not like it, and war destroyed that tolerance.

So where the Northern armies went, slavery went out of existence. In Virginia this meant little, partly because in Virginia the Federal armies did not go very far, and partly because in the fought-over country most Southerners got their slaves off to safety as fast as they could. But in the West, in Tennessee and northern Mississippi and Alabama, Federal armies ranged far, destroying the substance of the land as they ranged. They burned barns, consuming or wasting the contents. They burned unoccupied homes, and sometimes rowdy stragglers on the fringes of the armies burned occupied homes as well; they seized any cotton that they found, they broke bridges and tore up railway tracks and ruined mills and ironworks and similar installations . . . and they killed slavery. Grim General Sherman, the author of so much of this destruction, remarked not long after the victory at Vicksburg that all the powers of the earth could no more restore slaves to the bereaved Southerners than they could restore their dead grandfathers. Wherever Union armies moved, they were followed by long lines of fugitive slaves—unlettered folk who did not know what the war was about and could not imagine what the future held, but who dimly sensed that the road trodden by the men in blue was the road to freedom.

Neither the soldiers nor the generals were entirely happy about this increasing flood of refugees. In a clumsy, makeshift manner camps were set up for them; thousands of the refugees died, of hunger or disease or simple neglect, but most of them survived —survived in such numbers that the Federals had to do something about them. Negro labor could be used to build roads or fortifications, to harvest cotton in plantations that lay inside the Union lines, to perform all manner of useful military chores about the camps.

The refugee camps needed guards, to keep intruders out and to police the activities of the refugees themselves, and the Federal soldiers almost unanimously objected to performing such service. (They had enlisted to save the Union, not to guard a milling herd of bewildered Negroes.) It seemed logical, after a time, to raise guard detachments from among the Negroes themselves, outfitting them with castoff army uniforms. Then it appeared that the immense reserve of manpower represented by the newly freed slaves might be put to more direct use, and at last the government authorized, and even encouraged, the organization of Negro regiments, to be officered by whites but to be regarded as troops of the line, available for combat duty if needed.

To this move the soldiers made a good deal of objection—at first. Then they began to change their minds. They did not like Negroes, for race prejudice of a malignity rarely seen today was very prevalent in the North at that time, and they did not want to associate with them on anything remotely like terms of equality, but they came to see that much might be said for Negro regiments. For one thing, a great many enlisted men in the Northern armies could win officers' commissions in these regiments, and a high private who saw a chance to become a lieutenant or a captain was likely to lose a great deal of his antagonism to the notion of Negro soldiers. More important than this was the dawning realization that the colored soldier could stop a Rebel bullet just as well as a white soldier could, and when he did so, some white soldier who would otherwise have died would go on living. . . . And so by the middle of 1863 the North was raising numbers of Negro regiments, and the white soldiers who had been so bitter about the idea adjusted themselves rapidly.

All told, the Federals put more than 150,000 Negroes into uniform. Many of these regiments were used only for garrison duty, and in many other cases the army saw to it that the colored regiments became little more than permanent fatigue details to relieve white soldiers of hard work, but some units saw actual combat service and in a number of instances acquitted themselves well. And there was an importance to this that went far beyond any concrete achievements on the field of battle, for this was the seed of further change. The war had freed the slave, the war had put freed slaves into army uniforms—and a permanent alteration in the colored man's status would have to come out of that fact. A man who had worn the country's uniform and faced death in its service could not, ultimately, be anything less than a full-fledged citizen, and it was going to be very hard to make citizens out of some Negroes without making citizens out of all.

The armies moved across the sun-baked American landscape in the summer of 1863, trying to preserve the cherished past and actually breaking a way into the unpredictable future; and after Gettysburg and Vicksburg the center of attention became central Tennessee and northern Georgia, where the chance of war gave the South one more opportunity to restore the balance.

Nothing of much consequence would happen just now in Virginia. Both armies had been badly mangled at Gettysburg, and the rival commanders were being very circumspect. Lee had not the strength to make a real offensive campaign, and Meade was little better off; the two maneuvered up and down around the Orange and Alexandria Railroad, sparring for position, neither one willing to bring on a stand-up fight unless he could do so to real advantage, each one careful to give the other no opening. There were skirmishes, cavalry engagements, and now and then sharp actions between parts of the armies, but nothing really important took place, and as the summer gave way to fall it became apparent that there would not be a really big campaign in Virginia before 1864.

In Mississippi there was a similar lull. After the capture of Vicksburg, Grant wanted to go driving on.

There was nothing in the South that could stop his army, and he believed that he could sweep through southern Mississippi and Alabama, taking Mobile and compelling Bragg to hurry back from in front of Chattanooga. The authorities in Washington, however, clung to the notion that the important thing in this war was to occupy Southern territory, and Grant was compelled to scatter his troops. Some of them he had to send to Louisiana, where Major General Nathaniel P. Banks was preparing to invade Texas. Others went to Missouri and to Arkansas, and those that were left were engaged in garrison duty in western Tennessee and Mississippi, occupying cities and guarding railroad lines, effectively immobilized.

Virginia and Mississippi were, so to speak, the wings of the war front. The center was in middle Tennessee, where Rosecrans with the Army of the Cumberland faced Bragg with the Army of Tennessee; and at the end of June Rosecrans at last began to move, hoping to seize Chattanooga and thus to make possible Federal occupation of Knoxville and eastern Tennessee—a point in which President Lincoln was greatly interested, because eastern Tennessee was a stronghold of Unionist sentiment.

Rosecrans made his move late, but when he did so he moved with much skill. Bragg, covering Chattanooga, had weakened his force sending troops to Joe Johnston, and in his position around the town of Tullahoma he had perhaps 47,000 men, of which a disproportionate number were cavalry. (Forrest's cavalry though, mostly, and hence of value against infantry.) The Confederates held good defensive ground, and considering everything Rosecrans' field force of 60,000 was none too large for the job at hand.

Old Rosy, as his troops called him, feinted smartly and moved with speed. He made as if to swing around Bragg's left flank, then sliced off in the opposite direction, and despite seventeen consecutive days of rain his troops got into the rear of Bragg's right before Bragg realized what was going on. Rosecrans bluffed an attack and then slipped off on another flanking movement, and Bragg found himself compelled to retreat. By July 4 the Confederate army was back in Chattanooga, and Rosecrans, calling in vain for reinforcements (the government was sending pieces of Grant's army off in all directions, but somehow it could not spare any for Rosecrans), was trying to find a line of advance that would force Bragg to retreat still farther. He presently found it, and in August he made an unexpected crossing of the Tennessee River thirty miles west of Chattanooga. Establishing a base of supplies at Bridgeport, Alabama, on the Tennessee, Rosecrans moved over into a mountain valley with nothing between him and Chattanooga but the long rampart of Lookout Mountain. Refusing to make a frontal assault on Bragg's defensive position, he then went southeast, going through a series of gaps in Lookout Mountain and heading for the Western and Atlantic Railroad, which ran from Chattanooga to Atlanta and was Bragg's supply line. Bragg had to evacuate Chattanooga, Union troops entered the place, and Old Rosy had completed a brilliant and virtually bloodless campaign.

The only trouble was that Rosecrans did not know that he had completed it. He might have concentrated in Chattanooga, paused to renew his supplies and let his hard-marching army catch its breath, and then he could have advanced down the railroad line to good effect. Instead, he tried to keep on going, and as he moved through the mountain passes his three army corps became widely separated. Furthermore, Bragg had stopped retreating and was making a stand at La Fayette, Georgia, about twenty-five miles from Chattanooga, awaiting reinforcements. These he was getting; troops from Knoxville, from Mississippi, and two divisions from the Army of Northern Virginia itself, led by James Longstreet. (The move the Richmond government had refused to make in June was being made now, with troops from Lee going to fight in the West.) Thus reinforced, Bragg moved in for a counterattack, and Rosecrans, waking up in the nick of time, hastily pulled his troops together to meet him. On the banks of Chickamauga Creek, about twelve miles below Chattanooga, Bragg made his attack, and on September 19 and 20 he fought and won the great Battle of Chickamauga. Part of Rosecrans' army was driven from the field in wild rout, and only a last-ditch stand by George Thomas saved the whole army from destruction. The Union troops retreated to Chattanooga, Bragg advanced and entrenched his men on high ground in a vast crescent, and the Army of the Cumberland found itself besieged.

The name Chickamauga was an old Cherokee word, men said, meaning "river of death," and there was an awful literalness to its meaning now. Each army had lost nearly a third of its numbers, Bragg's casualty list running to 18,000 or more, and Rosecrans' to nearly 16,000. Rosecrans' campaign was wrecked, and his own career as a field commander was ended; he was relieved and assigned to duty in St. Louis, and Rock-of-Chickamauga Thomas took his place. Bragg, the victor, had not added greatly to his reputation. He had made the Federals retreat, but if he had handled his army with more energy he might have destroyed the whole Army of the Cumberland, and his subordinates complained bitterly about his inability to make use of the triumph the troops had won. Their complaints echoed in Richmond, and President Davis

came to Tennessee to see whether Bragg ought to be replaced; concluded, finally, that he should remain, and went back to Richmond without ordering any change.

Chickamauga was a Union disaster, but at least it jarred the Federal campaign in the West back onto the rails. It forced the government to drop the ruinous policy of dispersion and concentrate its forces, and in the end this was all to the good. Additionally, it gave new powers and a new opportunity to U. S. Grant, who knew what to do with both. Thus it may have been worth what it cost, although the soldiers of the Army of the Cumberland probably would have had trouble seeing it that way.

As September ended these soldiers were in serious trouble. They held Chattanooga, but they seemed very likely to be starved into surrender there. The Confederate line, unassailable by any force George Thomas could muster, ran in a vast semicircle, touching the Tennessee River upstream from Chattanooga, following the high parapet of Missionary Ridge to the east and south, anchoring itself in the west on the precipitous sides of Lookout Mountain, and touching the Tennessee again just west of Lookout. The Confederates had no troops north of the river, nor did they need any there; that country was wild, mountainous, and all but uninhabited, and no military supply train could cross it. Supplies could reach Thomas only by the river itself, by the railroad which ran along the river's southern bank, or by the roads which similarly lay south of the river, and all of these were firmly controlled by Bragg. The Union army could not even retreat. (No army under Thomas was likely to retreat, but physical inability to get out of a trap is a handicap any way you look at it.) As far as Bragg could see, he need only keep his army in position for a month or two longer, and the Unionists would have to give up.

Neither by a military nor a political calculation could the Federal cause afford a catastrophe like the outright loss of the Army of the Cumberland, and the crisis at Chattanooga had a galvanic effect on the Federal nerve center in Washington. Two army corps were detached from Meade, placed under the command of Joe Hooker, and sent west by rail. This was the most effective military use of railroads yet made anywhere, and the soldiers were moved with surprising speed; leaving the banks of the Rappahannock on September 24, they reached Bridgeport, Alabama, just eight days later. Sherman was ordered to move east from Memphis with part of the Army of the Tennessee, and Grant was put in command of all military operations west of the Alleghenies (except for Banks' venture in the New Orleans-Texas area) and was ordered over to Chattanooga to set things straight.

This Grant proceeded to do, his contribution being chiefly the unflagging energy with which he tackled the job. Plans for loosening the Confederate strangle hold had already been made, and what Grant did was to make certain that they were put into effect speedily. He brought Hooker east from Bridgeport, used a brigade of Thomas' men in a sudden thrust at the Confederate outpost on the Tennessee River west of Lookout Mountain, and presently opened a route through which supplies could be brought to Chattanooga. The route combined the use of steamboats, scows, a pontoon bridge, and army wagons, and it could not begin to supply the army with everything it needed, but at least it warded off starvation. Thomas' men dubbed it "the cracker line" and began to feel that life might be worth living after all.

Sherman, leaving Memphis, had about three hundred miles to march, and for some reason Halleck had given him orders to repair the line of the Memphis and Charleston Railroad as he moved, so his progress was glacial. Grant told him to forget about the track-gang job and to come as fast as he could; and by early November the Federal force in Chattanooga, no longer half-starved, had powerful reinforcements at hand and was ready to try to break the ring that was around it. Bragg, meanwhile, acted with incredible obtuseness. A Federal force under General Burnside had come down through the Kentucky-Tennessee mountain country to occupy Knoxville, and although it had got into the place it was not, for the moment, doing any particular harm there; but Bragg sent Longstreet and 12,000 men away to try to dislodge this force, and he detached his cavalry and still more infantry to help—so that when it came time for the big fight Bragg would be badly outnumbered, facing the best generals the Federals could muster, Grant, Sherman, and Thomas.

The big fight came on November 24 and 25. Hooker with his men from the Army of the Potomac drove the Confederate left from Lookout Mountain—less of an achievement than it looked, since Bragg had only a skeleton force there, which was dug in along the slopes rather than on the crest, but it was one of the war's spectacular scenes for all that. There had been low-lying clouds all day, and when these finally lifted and the sun broke through, the Northern flag was on the top of Lookout, and war correspondents wrote enthusiastically about the "battle above the clouds." Sherman took his Army of the Tennessee units upstream and attacked the Confederate right. He made some progress but not enough, and was getting not much more than a bloody nose for his pains; and on the afternoon of November 25 Grant told Thomas to push his Army of the Cumberland forward and take the Rebel rifle pits at the base of Missionary Ridge. This pressure might force Bragg to recall troops from Sherman's front.

At this point Thomas' soldiers took things into their own hands. They had been suffering a slow burn for a month; both Hooker's and Sherman's men had jeered at them for the Chickamauga defeat and had reminded them that other armies had to come to their rescue, and the Cumberlands had had all they cared to take. Now they moved forward, took the Confederate rifle pits as ordered—and then, after a brief pause for breath, went straight on up the steep mountain slope without orders from either Grant or Thomas, broke Bragg's line right where it was strongest, drove the Confederate army off in complete retreat, and won the Battle of Chattanooga in one spontaneous explosion of pent-up energy and fury.

Chattanooga was decisive. The beaten Confederates withdrew into Georgia. Burnside's position in Knoxville was secure. Grant, with new laurels on his unassuming head, was very clearly going to become general in chief of the Union armies, the South had definitely lost the war in the West—and, when spring came, the Federals would have a chance to apply more pressure than the Confederacy could hope to resist.

William Travis titled the scene above, from his Civil War panorama, "Emancipation"; the slaves are fleeing a Tennessee manor house in order to follow a column of the Army of the Cumberland visible in the distance.

The photograph below of a guard detail of the 107th U.S. Colored Infantry was taken at Fort Corcoran, near Washington. The regiment saw action late in the war in the capture of Fort Fisher and in the Carolinas.

Emancipated Negroes Pose a Problem

Returning to Vicksburg after a raid into central Mississippi early in 1864, General Sherman reported, "We bring in some 500 prisoners, a good many refugees and about ten miles of Negroes." His booty was symptomatic of the collapse of slavery as the Federal armies, particularly in the Western theater, pressed relentlessly on toward the deep South.

Wherever they went, the Yankees were followed by swarms of ex-slaves, carrying their possessions on their backs, pathetically eager to sample their new freedom. The government tried to meet this influx by setting up refugee camps, forming labor battalions, and, early in 1863, enlisting the black man in the Union army.

The average Yankee soldier objected at first to any contact with the Negro. An Ohioan wrote early in the war, "I don't think enough of the Niggar to go and fight for them," and a Michigan man considered "a system of servitude & serfdom better for both whites & blacks than immediate emancipation." Yet by 1863 emancipation was a fact, and the men soon adjusted to it. For one thing, noncoms had a chance at rank, for most Negro regiments had white officers; "The prospect of . . . $120. or $130 per month is no small temtation," admitted one.

Although the majority of colored soldiers served as noncombatants— teamsters, guards, cooks, laborers—a number of all-Negro regiments saw combat action. With proper training and discipline they proved to be good fighters. General Ben Butler, a staunch abolitionist, explained his extensive use of Negro troops: "I knew that they would fight more desperately than any white troops, in order to prevent capture, because they knew . . . if captured they would be returned to slavery."

Above, a gun crew of the 2nd U.S. Colored Light Artillery, which took part in the Battle of Nashville. Their two white officers stand at right. Major Martin R. Delany (below), a graduate of Harvard Medical School, was the first Negro officer to hold a field command.

Rosecrans and Bragg Jockey for Position

Three Confederate stalwarts from Braxton Bragg's Army of Tennessee.

On the heels of their wearing fight at Murfreesboro, Bragg's Army of Tennessee and Rosecrans' Army of the Cumberland lay inactive for six months, less than 40 miles apart. Then, while Grant closed in on Vicksburg, Rosecrans at last headed toward the rail center of Chattanooga.

In a brilliant maneuver Rosecrans slipped around Bragg's right flank, forcing the Confederate out of Tennessee without a fight. He swung in on Chattanooga from the southwest, aiming for Bragg's supply line; Bragg evacuated the city and withdrew to northwestern Georgia to await reinforcements from Virginia. Finally, after fumbling for each other in the mountainous terrain, the two armies collided on September 19, 1863, near Chickamauga Creek, a dozen miles south of Chattanooga.

At left is Lee and Gordon's Mill on Chickamauga Creek, the site of an abortive Confederate attempt to turn the Federal flank on September 18.

Closing on Chattanooga, the Federals crossed the Tennessee River (above) near Stevenson, Alabama. In Travis' painting Rosecrans is at left, waving his sword.

Alfred Waud's drawing below shows Hood's division, rushed west from Lee's army, driving Yankee cavalry away from a Chickamauga Creek bridge before the battle.

CHICKAMAUGA

Second Day: September 20, 1863

BROTHER
HOUSE

POE
HOUSE

KELLY
HOUSE

THOMAS'
HQ

SNODGRASS HILL

SNODGRASS
HOUSE

TO ROSSVILLE AND CHATTANOOGA

David Greenspan

BRAGG'S HQ

OSBURN HOUSE

LAFAYETTE ROAD

VINIARD HOUSE

JACKSON HOUSE

ROSECRANS HQ

DYER HOUSE

WITHERS HOUSE

DRY VALLEY ROAD

VILLETOE HOUSE

West Chica

③

CHICKAMAUGA: At dawn on September 20 Rosecrans' Federal line roughly parallels the Lafayette Road, with Thomas holding a salient on the left at the Kelly House. The second day's battle starts at 9 A.M., when Bragg sends Polk's wing against Thomas' breastworks (1); Thomas repulses the heavy assaults. Wood's division pulls out of line to go to Thomas' aid, leaving a hole in the Union center. At this moment, shortly before noon, Longstreet charges with the Confederate left wing, breaking through the gap between the Brotherton and Viniard houses (2). The Federal right is crushed and flees in disorder (3); swept along with it are Rosecrans and two of his three corps commanders, Crittenden and McCook. Longstreet now turns north and hits Thomas' lightly defended flank (4) on Snodgrass Hill. Thomas patches up a line, standing firm and earning his sobriquet, "The Rock of Chickamauga." Longstreet is sliding toward Thomas' rear when Granger, on his own initiative, orders Steedman's division from the Union reserve to the front. Steedman's arrival (5) checks Longstreet's turning movement about 2:30 P.M. Thomas continues to repel stiff Rebel attacks the rest of the afternoon, then joins the retreat to Rossville and Chattanooga at sundown. Bragg permits the Federal army to escape to safety.

Federal Rout at Chickamauga

Above, a Yankee firing line and cavalry reserve at Chick-amauga, painted by James Walker. General Thomas made his headquarters near the Snodgrass House at left center.

William Travis' version of the battle (below) pictures in gory detail blue and gray battle lines locked in hand-to-hand combat as Union reinforcements rush up at left.

B ragg intended to turn the Federal left flank at Chickamauga and push Rosecrans into a mountain cul-de-sac. But that flank, under George Thomas, was not where it was thought to be, and Bragg's assault bogged down. Soon most of the units in both armies were involved in the fierce fight on the Federal left. At nightfall Thomas' line was battered but unbroken.

Longstreet arrived from Virginia that night, and Bragg gave him the left wing and Bishop Polk the right. Polk was to engage Thomas again the next morning, and as Rosecrans met this threat Longstreet would advance.

At 9 A.M. on September 20 Polk attacked, and soon Thomas had to call for help. In the confusion of reinforcing him, Rosecrans left a gap in his center at precisely the spot where Longstreet's heavy assault wave struck. The Rebels poured through unchecked, splitting Rosecrans' army in half, and the routed Yankees streamed toward Chattanooga, carrying Rosecrans with them. "No order could be heard above the tempest of battle. . . . Fugitives, wounded, caissons, escort, ambulances, thronged the narrow pathways," a Northern officer wrote, adding that Rosecrans believed "the day was lost."

Longstreet surveyed his handiwork and then turned to make the rout complete by disposing of Thomas.

At upper right is the woodland where Longstreet mustered his attack; at right, Waud's drawing of a Rebel charge against Thomas; above, Hood, his arm still in a sling from Gettysburg, gets a wound that cost him a leg.

Major General George H. Thomas

Bragg Allows
a Beaten Enemy
to Escape

George Thomas was a West Pointer, a Virginian who chose the Union in 1861. Now he prepared coolly to make the fight of his life. He put together a defensive line to cover his exposed flank, and his men repulsed repeated Rebel assaults. A Confederate remembered how "the dead were piled upon each other in ricks, like cord wood, to make passage for advancing columns. The sluggish . . . Chickamauga ran red with human blood."

General Gordon Granger was in command of the Federal reserve, and without orders he dispatched a division to Thomas' aid, plus a fresh supply of ammunition. By sunset, however, the pressure exerted by Polk and Longstreet proved too

430

General Braxton Bragg

great, and Thomas' command joined the grim retreat to Chattanooga. His stand had bought an afternoon's time for the rest of the army.

Bragg was stunned by his 17,800 casualties (Rosecrans' were only 1,200 less) and would not believe he had won a decisive victory. Polk, Longstreet, and Forrest pleaded with him to crowd his routed enemy and recapture Chattanooga, but Bragg shook his head and went to bed.

The outraged Polk reported to President Davis that Bragg had "allowed the fruits of the great but sanguinary victory to pass from him by the most criminal negligence." A week later Forrest's frayed temper snapped, and he thundered at Bragg, "You have played the part of a damned scoundrel, and are a coward, and if you were any part of a man I would slap your jaws."

Bragg finally took position on Missionary Ridge and Lookout Mountain, overlooking Chattanooga, and prepared to besiege Rosecrans. The discontented Polk and D. H. Hill were relieved, and Forrest was given an independent command.

Grant Takes Command at Chattanooga

In late September, 1863, Braxton Bragg seemed to have the Army of the Cumberland in the palm of his hand. Less than two months later he was in serious trouble.

Washington finally awoke to the fact that an entire Union army was trapped at Chattanooga, down to quarter-rations and in danger of starvation or capture. Grant was given command in the West, and things began to hum: Thomas replaced Rosecrans; Sherman brought two army corps east from Memphis to help; two more moved west from the Army of the Potomac.

Late in October the Yankees seized Brown's Ferry, downstream from Chattanooga, opening a supply route into the beleaguered city. Now that the Federals could again "board at home," Lincoln said, they should try to break Bragg's siege. On November 23 Thomas took Orchard Knob, a good spot from which to assault Missionary Ridge. The next day Joe Hooker's Easterners seized Lookout Mountain.

Above is Lookout Mountain, viewed from Chattanooga across the Tennessee River and Moccasin Point; its rugged heights are shown at right.

On the night of October 26 William Hazen's brigade from Thomas' army drifted down the Tennessee on pontoon rafts (painted below by Travis) to take Brown's Ferry, key to the Chattanooga supply line.

Hooker's capture of Lookout Mountain (Hooker is on the white horse at left center) was more dramatic than decisive, and Grant regarded it simply as a first step in his general assault on Bragg's main Missionary Ridge line. The Rebels,

outnumbered six to one, were driven from successive positions on the rocky
slopes. Late in the day a heavy mist shrouded the action until only the gun
flashes, "like swarms of fire-flies," could be seen. This painting is by James Walker.

The Federal Army of the Cumberland was besieged within the fortifications of Chattanooga (1) when Grant arrived on October 23, 1863, over an inadequate, almost impassable road across the mountains to the north of the river. Braxton Bragg's Confederate Army of Tennessee, on Missionary Ridge (foreground) and Lookout Mountain (left), completely dominated the Federal lines. On the twenty-seventh the Federals pried open a route, dubbed "the cracker line," to their supply depots at Bridgeport via Brown's Ferry (2). Less than a month later Grant took the offensive. On November 23, George Thomas' Army of the Cumberland seized Orchard Knob (3), high ground in the plain before Missionary Ridge. The next day General Joseph Hooker stormed up Lookout Mountain (4) to threaten Bragg's left flank. At the same time, Sherman crossed the Tennessee (5), but his misdirected attack struck too far north (6). On November 25, Sherman having made no progress against Pat Cleburne's division in the area of the tunnel (7) on the Confederate right, Grant ordered Thomas to apply pressure on Bragg's center. The Army of the Cumberland overran the Confederate positions at the base of Missionary Ridge (8); after a pause for breath, the Yankees drove on up the slope and over the crest of the ridge (9), forcing the Confederates to flee in confusion.

MAP: DAVID GREENSPAN

RAISING THE SIEGE OF
CHATTANOOGA

Orchard Knob: November 23, 1863
Lookout Mountain: November 24, 1863
Missionary Ridge: November 25, 1863

TO KNOXVILLE

Chickamauga Creek

TENNESSEE RIVER

FORT
GROSE

WESTERN & ATLANTIC R.R.

CHATTANOOGA & CLEVELAND R.R.

THE
TUNNEL

GRANT'S
HQ

ORCHARD
KNOB

BRAGG'S
HQ

MISSIONARY RIDGE

RETREAT TO GEORGIA

David Greenspan

Above, cannon on Missionary Ridge, ghostly in the morning mist. Below, a sketch of Grant and Sherman; this was the last battle the two men fought together.

Yankee Victory at Missionary Ridge

As Grant planned it, Sherman's role would be decisive in the attack of November 25; he was to roll up the Confederate right flank while Thomas in the center and Hooker on the left kept Bragg from reinforcing his right. There were, however, two miscalculations in this scheme: first, Pat Cleburne, the best division commander in Bragg's army, blocked Sherman's path; and second, Thomas' Army of the Cumberland, scorned by Hooker's Easterners and Sherman's veterans, was tired of playing the poor relation in this campaign.

Sherman drove his men forward at daylight on the twenty-fifth, and for more than eight hours they struggled with Cleburne's Confederates defending the north end of Missionary Ridge. When the Rebels found their cannon would not depress enough to hit the charging Yankees, they lit the shells and threw them down the slopes. They even launched a surprise counterattack from a railroad tunnel. By 3 P.M. Sherman was stalled, and one of his gunners admitted, "We have gained nothing in the shape of ground all day."

With Hooker delayed in bridging a stream on his front, the Army of the Cumberland was ordered to make a diversion against Missionary Ridge itself. Thomas' men were so eager that even "servants, cooks, clerks, found guns in some way," and at 3:30 they ran forward, heading for the rifle pits at the base of the ridge.

The first Rebel line soon fell, but the Yankees were still exposed to killing fire from above. Without orders, they leaped from the captured rifle pits and began charging up the steep face of Missionary Ridge.

A Northern lieutenant noted that "little regard to formation was observed. Each battalion assumed a triangular shape, the colors at the apex. . . . [a] color-bearer dashes ahead of the line and falls. A comrade grasps the flag. . . . He, too, falls. Then another picks it up . . . waves it defiantly, and, as if bearing a charmed life, he advances steadily towards the top . . ." Another soldier remembered: "Amid the din of battle the cry 'Chickamauga! Chickamauga!' could be heard."

Grant and Thomas, watching from Orchard Knob, were incredulous; General Granger confirmed to Grant that the men charged without orders, and added, "When those fellows get started all hell can't stop them." Bragg's men fired desperately, the cannoneers pouring hatfuls of musket balls into their pieces, shooting them like giant shotguns. Bragg, "cursing like a sailor," tried to rally his force, but it fled in hopeless rout as the Army of the Cumberland poured over the crest.

Chattanooga was delivered, and the effects were momentous: Grant became commander of all the Union armies and Sherman took over in the West; Bragg was relieved as general of the Army of Tennessee; and in the spring Chattanooga became the springboard for an invasion of the South's heartland.

This unsigned drawing shows a Federal unit storming Missionary Ridge. As the Rebel defenders fled an amazed Yankee cried, "My God, come and see 'em run!"

THE
NORTHERN VISE
TIGHTENS

O<small>N THE</small> ninth of March, 1864, U. S. Grant was made lieutenant general and given command of all the Union armies, and the hitherto insoluble military problem of the Federal government was at last on its way to solution. President Lincoln had learned that it took a soldier to do a soldier's job, and he had at last found the soldier who was capable of it: a direct, straightforward man who would leave high policy to the civilian government and devote himself with unflagging energy to the task of putting Confederate armies out of action. There would be no more side shows: from now on the whole weight of Northern power would be applied remorselessly, with concentrated force.

There had been a number of side shows during the last year, and the net result of all of them had been to detract from the general effectiveness of the Union war effort. An army and navy expedition had tried throughout the preceding summer to hammer its way into Charleston, South Carolina. It had reduced Fort Sumter to a shapeless heap of rubble, but it had cost the North a number of ships and soldiers and had accomplished nothing except to prove that Charleston could not be taken by direct assault. In Louisiana, General Banks was trying to move into Texas, partly

for the sake of the cotton that could be picked up along the way and partly because the government believed that Napoleon III would give up his Mexican adventure if a Northern army occupied Texas and went to the Rio Grande. The belief may have been justified, but Banks never came close, and his campaign was coming to grief this spring. Early in April he was beaten at Mansfield and Pleasant Hill, Louisiana, far up the Red River, and he retreated with such panicky haste that Admiral Porter's accompanying fleet of gunboats narrowly escaped complete destruction. (The water level in the Red River was falling, and for a time it seemed that the gunboats could never get out; they were saved at the last when a backwoods colonel in the Union army took a regiment of lumbermen and built dams that temporarily made the water deep enough for escape.) In Florida a Union expedition in which white and Negro troops were brigaded together attempted a conquest that would have had no important results even if it had succeeded; it had failed dismally, meeting defeat at Olustee late in February. Union cavalry under William Sooy Smith had tried to sweep across Mississippi during the winter and had been ignominiously routed by Bedford Forrest.

All of these ventures had dissipated energy and

Lieutenant General Ulysses S. Grant, photographed at
City Point, Virginia, during the siege of Petersburg.

manpower that might have been used elsewhere. (Banks' Texas expedition had been the chief reason why Grant had not been allowed to exploit the great opportunity opened by the capture of Vicksburg.) They had won nothing, and they would not have won the war even if all of them had succeeeded. Now, it was hoped, there would be no more of them. Grant had intense singleness of purpose, and the government was giving him a free hand. He would either win the war or be the man on the spot when the Union confessed that victory was unattainable.

Grant considered the military problem to be basically quite simple. The principal Confederate armies had to be destroyed. The capture of cities and "strategic points" and the occupation of Southern territory meant very little; as long as the main Confederate armies were in the field the Confederacy lived, and as soon as they vanished the Confederacy ceased to be. His objectives, therefore, would be the opposing armies, and his goal would be to put them out of action as quickly as possible.

There were two armies that concerned him: the incomparable Army of Northern Virginia, led by Robert E. Lee, and the Army of Tennessee, commanded now by Joseph E. Johnston. Bragg's inability to win had at last become manifest even to Jefferson Davis, who had an inexplicable confidence in the man. Bragg had made a hash of his Kentucky invasion in the late summer of 1862, he had let victory slip through his grasp at Murfreesboro, and he had utterly failed to make proper use of his great victory at Chickamauga. After Chattanooga, Davis removed him —bringing him to Richmond and installing him as chief military adviser to the President—and Johnston was put in his place.

Davis had scant confidence in Johnston and had grown to dislike the man personally, and Johnston felt precisely the same way about Davis. But the much-abused Army of Tennessee, which had fought as well as any army could fight but which had never had adequate leadership, revered and trusted Johnston profoundly, and his appointment had been inevitable. His army had recovered its morale, and it was strongly entrenched on the low mountain ridges northwest of Dalton, Georgia, a few miles from the bloodstained field of Chickamauga. It contained about 60,000 men, and Lee's army, which lay just below the Rapidan River in central Virginia, was about the same size.

These armies were all that mattered. The Confederacy had sizable forces west of the Mississippi, under the over-all command of Edmund Kirby Smith, but the trans-Mississippi region was effectively cut off now that the Federals controlled the great river, and what happened there was of minor importance. The Southern nation would live or die depending on the fate of Lee's and Johnston's armies. Grant saw it so, and his entire plan for 1864 centered on the attempt to destroy those two armies.

In the West everything would be up to Sherman. Grant had put him in control of the whole Western theater of the war, with the exception of the Banks expedition, which was flickering out in expensive futility. Sherman was what would now be called an army group commander. In and around Chattanooga he had his own Army of the Tennessee, under Major General James B. McPherson; the redoubtable Army of the Cumberland, under Thomas; and a small force called the Army of the Ohio—hardly more than an army corps in actual size—commanded by a capable regular with pink cheeks and a flowing beard, Major General John M. Schofield. All in all, Sherman had upwards of 100,000 combat men with him. When he moved, he would go down the Western and Atlantic Railroad toward Atlanta; but Atlanta, important as it was to the Confederacy, was not his real objective. His objective was the Confederate army in his front. As he himself described his mission after the war, "I was to go for Joe Johnston."

Grant, meanwhile, would go for Lee.

Although he was general in chief, Grant would not operate from headquarters in Washington. The demoted Halleck was retained as chief of staff, and he would stay in Washington to handle the paper work; but Grant's operating headquarters would be in the field, moving with the Army of the Potomac. General Meade was kept in command of that army. With a fine spirit of abnegation, Meade had offered to resign, suggesting that Grant might want some Westerner in whom he had full confidence to command the army; but Grant had told him to stay where he was, and he endorsed an army-reorganization plan which Meade was just then putting into effect. Grant made no change in the army's interior chain of command, except that he brought a tough infantry officer, Phil Sheridan, from the Army of the Cumberland and put him in charge of the Army of the Potomac's cavalry corps. But if Grant considered Meade a capable officer who deserved to retain his command, he himself would nevertheless move with Meade's army, and he would exercise so much control over it that before long people would be speaking of it as Grant's army.

Grant's reasons were simple enough. The Army of the Potomac had much the sort of record the Confederate Army of Tennessee had—magnificent combat performance, brought to nothing by repeated failures in leadership. It had been unlucky, and its officer corps was badly clique-ridden, obsessed by the memory of the departed McClellan, so deeply impressed by Lee's superior abilities that its talk at times almost had a defeatist quality. The War Department had been second-guessing this army's commanders so long that it probably would go on doing it unless the general in chief himself were present. All in all, the Army of the Potomac needed a powerful hand on the controls. Grant would supply that hand, although his presence with the army would create an extremely difficult command situation.

This army was in camp in the general vicinity of Culpeper Court House, on the northern side of the upper Rapidan. (A measure of its lack of success thus far is the fact that after three years of warfare it was camped only a few miles farther south than it had been camped when the war began.) Facing it, beyond the river, was the Army of Northern Virginia. Longstreet and his corps were returning from an unhappy winter in eastern Tennessee. When the spring campaign opened, Lee would have rather more than 60,000 fighting men. The Unionists, who had called up Burnside and his old IX Corps to work with the Army of the Potomac, would be moving with nearly twice that number.

The mission of the Army of the Potomac was as simple as Sherman's: it was to head for the Confederate army and fight until something broke. It would move toward Richmond, just as Sherman was moving toward Atlanta, but its real assignment would be less to capture the Confederate capital than to destroy the army that was bound to defend that capital.

Grant was missing no bets. The irrepressible Ben Butler commanded a force of some 33,000 men around Fort Monroe, denominated the Army of the James, and when the Army of the Potomac advanced, Butler was to move up the south bank of the James River toward Richmond. At the very least his advance would occupy the attention of Confederate troops who would otherwise reinforce Lee; and if everything went well (which, considering Butler's defects as a strategist, was not really very likely), Lee would be compelled to retreat. On top of this there was a Union army in the Shenandoah, commanded by the German-born Franz Sigel, and this army was to move down to the town of Staun-

ton, whence it might go east through the Blue Ridge in the direction of Richmond. All in all, three Federal armies would be converging on the Confederate capital, each one with a powerful numerical advantage over any force that could be brought against it.

Everybody would move together. Sherman would march when Grant and Meade marched, and Butler and Sigel would advance at the same time. For the first time in the war the Union would put on a really co-ordinated campaign under central control, with all of its armies acting as a team.

On May 4, 1864, the machine began to roll.

Public attention on both sides was always centered on the fighting in Virginia. The opposing capitals were no more than a hundred miles apart, and they were the supremely sensitive nerve centers. What happened in Virginia took the eye first, and this spring it almost seemed as if all of the fury and desperation of the war were concentrated there.

The Army of the Potomac crossed the Rapidan and started to march down through a junglelike stretch of second-growth timber and isolated farms known as the Wilderness, with the hope that it could bring Lee to battle in the open country farther south. But one of Lee's distinguishing characteristics was a deep unwillingness to fight where his opponent wanted to fight. He liked to choose his own field, and he did so now. Undismayed by the great disparity in numbers, he marched straight into the Wilderness and jumped the Federal columns before they could get across. Grant immediately concluded that if Lee wanted to fight here, he might as well get what he wanted, and on May 5 an enormous two-day battle got under way.

The Wilderness was a bad place for a fight. The roads were few, narrow, and bad, and the farm clearings were scarce; most of the country was densely wooded, with underbrush so thick that nobody could see fifty yards in any direction, cut up by ravines and little watercourses, with brambles and creepers that made movement almost impossible. The Federal advantage in numbers meant little here, and its advantage in artillery meant nothing at all, since few guns could be used. Because a much higher percentage of its men came from the country and were used to the woods, the Confederate army was probably less handicapped by all of this than the Army of the Potomac.

The Battle of the Wilderness was blind and vicious. The woods caught fire, and many wounded men were burned to death, and the smoke of this fire together with the battle smoke made a choking fog that intensified the almost impenetrable gloom of the woods. At the end of two days the Federals had lost more than 17,000 men and had gained not one foot. Both flanks had been broken in, and outright disaster had been staved off by a narrow margin. By any indicator one could use, the Army of the Potomac had been beaten just as badly as Hooker had been beaten at Chancellorsville a year earlier. On May 7 the rival armies glowered at each other in the smoldering forest, and the Federal soldiers assumed that the old game would be repeated: they would retreat north of the Rapidan, reorganize and refit and get reinforcements, and then they would make a new campaign somewhere else.

That night, at dusk, the Army of the Potomac was pulled back from its firing lines and put in motion. But when it moved, it moved south, not north. Grant was not Hooker. Beaten here, he would sideslip to the left and fight again; his immediate objective was a crossroads at Spotsylvania Court House, eleven miles southwest of Fredericksburg. It was on Lee's road to Richmond, and if Grant got there first, Lee would have to do the attacking. So the army moved all night, and as the exhausted soldiers realized that they were not retreating but were actually advancing they set up a cheer.

Grant had made one of the crucial decisions of the war, and in retrospect the Battle of the Wilderness became almost a Federal victory. This army was not going to retreat, it was not even going to pause to lick its wounds; it was simply going to force the fighting, and in the end Lee's outnumbered army was going to be compelled to play the sort of game which it could not win.

It was not going to be automatic, however. Lee saw what Grant was up to and made a night march of his own. His men got to Spotsylvania Court House just ahead of the Federals, and the first hot skirmish for the crossroads swelled into a rolling battle that went on for twelve days, from May 8 to May 19. No bitterer fighting than the fighting that took place here was ever seen on the American continent. The Federals broke the Southern line once, on May 12, at a spot known ever after as "Bloody Angle," and there was a solid day of hand-to-hand combat while the Federals tried unsuccessfully to enlarge the break and split Lee's army into halves. There was fighting every day, and Grant kept shifting his troops to the left in an attempt to crumple Lee's flank, so that Federal

soldiers who were facing east when the battle began were facing due west when it closed. Phil Sheridan took the cavalry off on a driving raid toward Richmond, and Jeb Stuart galloped to meet him. The Unionists were driven off in a hard fight at Yellow Tavern, in the Richmond suburbs, but Stuart himself was killed.

Elsewhere in Virginia things went badly for the Federals. Sigel moved up the Shenandoah Valley, was met by a scratch Confederate force at New Market, and was routed in a battle in which the corps of cadets from Virginia Military Institute greatly distinguished itself. Ben Butler made his advance up the James River most ineptly and was beaten at Bermuda Hundred. He made camp on the Bermuda Hundred peninsula, the Confederates drew a fortified line across the base of the peninsula, and in Grant's expressive phrase Butler was as much out of action as if he had been put in a tightly corked bottle. He would cause Lee no worries for some time, and from the army which had beaten him Lee got reinforcements that practically made up for his heavy battle losses thus far.

There were brief lulls in the campaign but no real pauses. From Spotsylvania the Army of the Potomac again moved by its left, skirmishing every day, looking for an opening and not quite finding one. It fought minor battles along the North Anna and on Totopotomoy Creek, and it got at last to a crossroads known as Cold Harbor, near the Chickahominy River and mortally close to Richmond; and here, because there was scant room for maneuver, Grant on June 3 put on a tremendous frontal assault in the hope of breaking the Confederate line once and for all. The assault failed, with fearful losses, and the Union and Confederate armies remained in contact, each one protected by impregnable trenches, for ten days more. Then Grant made his final move—a skillful sideslip to the left, once more, and this time he went clear across the James River and advanced on the town of Petersburg. Most of the railroads that tied Richmond to the South came through Petersburg, and if the Federals could occupy the place before Lee got there, Richmond would have to be abandoned. But General William F. Smith, leading the Union advance, fumbled the attack, and when the rest of the army came up, Lee had had time to man the city's defenses. The Union attacks failed, and Grant settled down to a siege.

The campaign thus far had been made at a stunning cost. In the first month the Union army had lost 60,000 men. The armies were never entirely out of contact after the first shots were fired in the Wilderness; they remained in close touch, as a matter of fact, until the spring of 1865, and once they got to Petersburg they waged trench warfare strongly resembling that of World War I. Across the North people grew disheartened. Lee's army had not been broken, Richmond had not been taken, and no American had ever seen anything like the endless casualty lists that were coming out. At close range the achievement of the Army of the Potomac was hard to see. Yet it had forced Lee to fight continuously on the defensive, giving him no chance for one of those dazzling strokes by which he had disrupted every previous Federal offensive, never letting him regain the initiative. He tried it once, sending Jubal Early and 14,000 men up on a dash through the Shenandoah Valley into Maryland. Early brushed aside a small Federal force that tried to stop him on the Monocacy River and got clear to the Washington suburb of Silver Spring, less than a dozen miles from the Capitol building; but at the last minute Grant sent an army corps north from the Army of the Potomac, and after a skirmish at Silver Spring (witnessed by a worried Abraham Lincoln, in person) Early had to go back to Virginia. No longer could a threat to Washington induce the administration to recall an army of invasion. Early's march had given the government a severe case of nerves, but it had been barren of accomplishment.

Sherman's campaign in Georgia followed a different pattern from Grant's. Sherman had both the room and the inclination to make it a war of maneuver, but Johnston was an able strategist who could match paces with him all the way. Maneuvered out of his lines at Dalton, Johnston faded back, Sherman following. Often the Confederates would make a stand; when they did, Sherman would confront them with Thomas' Army of the Cumberland, using McPherson's and Schofield's troops for a wide flanking maneuver, and while these tactics usually made Johnston give ground, they never compelled him to fight at a disadvantage, and Sherman's progress looked better on the map than it really was. He had been ordered to go for Joe Johnston, and he could not quite crowd the man into a corner and bring his superior weight to bear. There were several pitched battles and there were innumerable skirmishes, and both armies had losses, but there was nothing like the all-consuming fighting that was going on in Virginia. Johnston made a stand once, on the slopes of Kennesaw Mountain, and Sherman tired of his flanking operations and tried to crack the center of the Confederate line. It refused to yield, and Sherman's men were repulsed with substantial losses; then, after a time, the war of movement was resumed, like a formalized military dance performed to the rhythmic music of the guns.

By the middle of July Sherman had crossed the Chattahoochee River and reached the outskirts of Atlanta, but he had by no means done what he set out to do. Johnston's army, picking up reinforcements as it retreated, was probably stronger now than when the campaign began, and Sherman for the moment was at a standstill. Grant and Meade were stalled in front of Petersburg, and Sherman was stalled in front of Atlanta. The Confederate strongholds were unconquered, and Northerners began to find the prospect discouraging.

They became even more discouraged late in July, when Grant's army failed in a stroke that should have taken Petersburg. Frontal attacks on properly held entrenchments were doomed to failure, and even Grant, not easily convinced, had had to admit this. But at Petersburg a new chance offered itself. A regiment of Pennsylvania coal miners dug a five-hundred-foot tunnel under the Confederate lines, several tons of powder were planted there, and at dawn on July 30 the mine was exploded. It blew an enormous gap in the defensive entrenchments, and for an hour or more the way was open for the Federal army to march almost unopposed into Petersburg.

Burnside's corps made the attempt and bungled it fearfully; the assault failed, and Grant's one great chance to end the war in one day vanished.

The people of the North were getting very war-weary as the month of July ended. Grant did not seem to be any nearer the capture of Richmond than he had been when the campaign began; Sherman was deep in Georgia, but he had neither whipped the Confederate army which faced him nor taken Atlanta. The pressure which the Confederacy could not long endure was being applied relentlessly, but it was hard for the folks back home to see that anything was really being accomplished. They only knew that the war was costing more than it had ever cost before, and that there seemed to be nothing of any consequence to show for it; and that summer President Lincoln privately wrote down his belief that he could not be re-elected that fall. If the electorate should repudiate him, the North would almost certainly fall out of the war, and the South would have its independence.

A New Campaign Begins

In the spring of 1864, as the Federal high command mustered its forces for a new campaign against Robert E. Lee, it had to face a thorny problem: the three-year enlistments of the veteran regiments which comprised the hard core of the Army of the Potomac were about to expire.

One soldier remarked that he had "no desire to monopolize all the patriotism there is, but am willing to give others a chance." His attitude was hardly surprising, for few other armies had been so ineptly led, and at such terrible cost in human life. Even so, more than half the men who had enlisted in the bright, far-off days of 1861 finally decided to sign up again, quietly determined to finish the job.

U. S. Grant traveled with this army now, and he too was quietly determined. In the Rebel camps across the Rapidan, where morale was high, one of Lee's aides believed that "if we whip the Yankees good again this year they will quit in disgust," and he added that Lee was eager to test "the present idol of the North." To Longstreet, however, whose corps had returned from Tennessee, Grant was a general "who will fight us every day and every hour till the end of the war."

Grant's strategy, like Joe Hooker's the previous spring, was to force Lee out of his entrenchments. But unlike 1863, when Lee was at Fredericksburg, east of the Rapidan fords, 1864 found him west of these crossings. Grant meant to move quickly through the Wilderness, turn Lee's right flank, and bring him out of his lines to protect Richmond.

On May 4 Grant began crossing the Rapidan. Soon his long supply trains fell behind, and late in the day he called a halt to let them catch up. Like Hooker, Grant was unable to move out of the gloomy, tangled Wilderness before Lee could hit him. He deployed his troops to cover the roads by which Lee must come—the Orange-Fredericksburg Turnpike and the Orange Plank Road, and the veterans bedded down with "a sense of ominous dread."

On the morning of May 5 Ewell's Confederate corps, advancing along the turnpike, collided with Gouverneur Warren's V Corps. As the firing grew heavier Grant called up John Sedgwick's corps and ordered Hancock's troops, in the Federal van, to retrace their steps.

Although he was outnumbered, Lee had no intention of letting the Yankees get clear of the Wilderness without a stiff fight.

In Timothy O'Sullivan's photograph at left, Federal artillery crosses the Rapidan at Germanna Ford on May 4, 1864, at the opening of Grant's campaign. Above, Grant, drawn by Charles Reed, sits calmly whittling during the first day's fight in the Wilderness.

General Hancock's description of the Wilderness as "almost impenetrable by troops in line of battle" is evident in Alfred Waud's sketch (below) of James Wadsworth's Union division in action on May 6.

The Fight in the Wilderness

Essentially, the Rebel attack consisted of two army corps on parallel roads—Ewell on the turnpike, A. P. Hill on the Orange Plank Road—advancing at right angles to Grant's line of march. Lee planned to wait until the remaining third of his army, under Longstreet, reached him before taking the offensive, but the brisk Federal action taken against Ewell brought the battle to a boil.

Brigadier General Charles Griffin of Warren's corps pushed Ewell's men back down the turnpike, but his reinforcements got tangled in the underbrush, their flanks became uncovered, and Ewell counterattacked. He regained the ground he had lost and, since he was under orders to avoid a general engagement until Longstreet arrived, entrenched.

On the Orange Plank Road, A. P. Hill was also waiting for Longstreet. Hancock, meanwhile, prepared to attack him, and late in the afternoon sent his men forward. Until dark the lines swayed back and forth in vicious charge and countercharge. The woods caught fire, and the blinding smoke from timber and underbrush was increased by that from the guns. A Northern private wrote that "it was a blind and bloody hunt to the death, in bewildering thickets, rather than a battle."

At 5 A.M. on May 6 Grant resumed the offensive. On the turnpike Ewell repulsed the Federal advance with heavy loss, but on the plank road Hill's battered troops were unable to contain Hancock's aggressive, mile-wide assault. "Tell General Meade we are driving them most beautifully!" Hancock shouted to an aide. For a time Lee's army was close to disastrous defeat.

Then came one of those moments of pure drama that seemed to be a specialty of the Army of Northern Virginia. Longstreet's corps surged to the front at last, Lee himself rallied them, and a Rebel officer announced "I would charge hell itself for that old man."

Longstreet's men crashed head-on into the charging Yankees. Soon Longstreet discovered a weakness on Hancock's left flank and exploited it at once. General James Wadsworth was mortally wounded as he tried to realign his men to meet this new threat, but at the crucial moment Longstreet was shot accidentally by his own men, and the impetus was lost. Lee called a halt to reorganize his attacking columns.

Above, the Wilderness photographed at dusk looks little different than it did when one of Grant's men complained that "no one could see a hundred paces in any direction."

Heavy gunfire set the tinderlike Wilderness undergrowth ablaze, and burned to death countless soldiers too badly hurt to crawl to safety. Alfred Waud's drawing (left) shows wounded escaping the flames.

The Federals lost a first-rate division commander when Brigadier General James S. Wadsworth (right) was shot on May 6. He fell into Rebel hands and died two days later.

449

Impressions
of the
Wilderness

Grant Elects
to Head South

Winslow Homer's "A Skirmish in the Wilderness, 1864" (above) dramatically captures the battle which a soldier called "simply bushwhacking on a grand scale." The men in the foreground find shelter behind a tree as the battle line beyond them looses a volley at the unseen enemy and reinforcements advance at right. The photograph at left shows underbrush afire in the Wilderness today.

The lull on Hancock's front was broken by the assault of Burnside's IX Corps, brought in to plug the gap between Warren and Hancock. Burnside was soon halted, and Lee got Longstreet's battle lines aligned at last. At 4 P.M. he sent them charging out of the woods against the log breastworks thrown up by Federals along the Brock Road.

The Southerners had an ally here in the forest fire, which swept ahead of them, touching off parts of the breastworks and driving the Yankee defenders back. But Union reinforcements finally came up and pushed the Confederates back for good.

At dusk John B. Gordon led a victorious charge against the other end of the Union position. This seriously threatened Grant's supply line, but, as Gordon wrote, his men were "reveling in the chase, when the unwelcome darkness put an end to it."

The next day the two armies rested, licking their wounds. Grant had lost over 17,500, Lee less than 8,000; it was, seemingly, another Chancellorsville. That night, however, as the Federal army moved out, the men realized they were heading not for the Rapidan fords, but southward. When Grant rode by, they cheered.

453

When Grant decided to continue southward despite his defeat in the Wilderness, his army's "cheers echoed through the forest, and glad shouts of triumph rent the air." The scene above was sketched by Edwin Forbes.

Brigadier General Fitzhugh Lee (left) and Emory Upton, shown after becoming a major general late in 1864.

The Armies Move to Spotsylvania

During the night of May 7–8 the two armies stumbled down the dark roads in the exhausting, numbing race for a tiny settlement called Spotsylvania Court House. Southeast of the Wilderness, this was where the region's main roads crossed. If the Northerners got there first, they would be between the Rebels and their capital, and Lee would have to do the attacking.

But Fitzhugh Lee, the commanding general's nephew, delayed the Federal advance with his cavalry until Rebel infantry arrived, and once more the Confederates staved off disaster by the narrowest of margins. For two days Grant probed their lines west of Spotsylvania, and in the process lost able "Uncle John" Sedgwick, the popular commander of the VI Corps, who was killed by a Confederate sharpshooter just after reassuring his men that snipers "couldn't hit an elephant at this distance."

On May 10 Union Colonel Emory Upton split open the center of Lee's lines with a brilliant bayonet charge by twelve picked regiments. But Southern artillery wrecked Upton's support troops and he was driven back. Upton's technique of mass attack on a narrow front was appreciated by the resourceful Grant, who was heard to remark, "a brigade today—we'll try a corps tomorrow."

The death of Major General John Sedgwick, shot by a Rebel sniper at Spotsylvania, painted by Julian Scott.

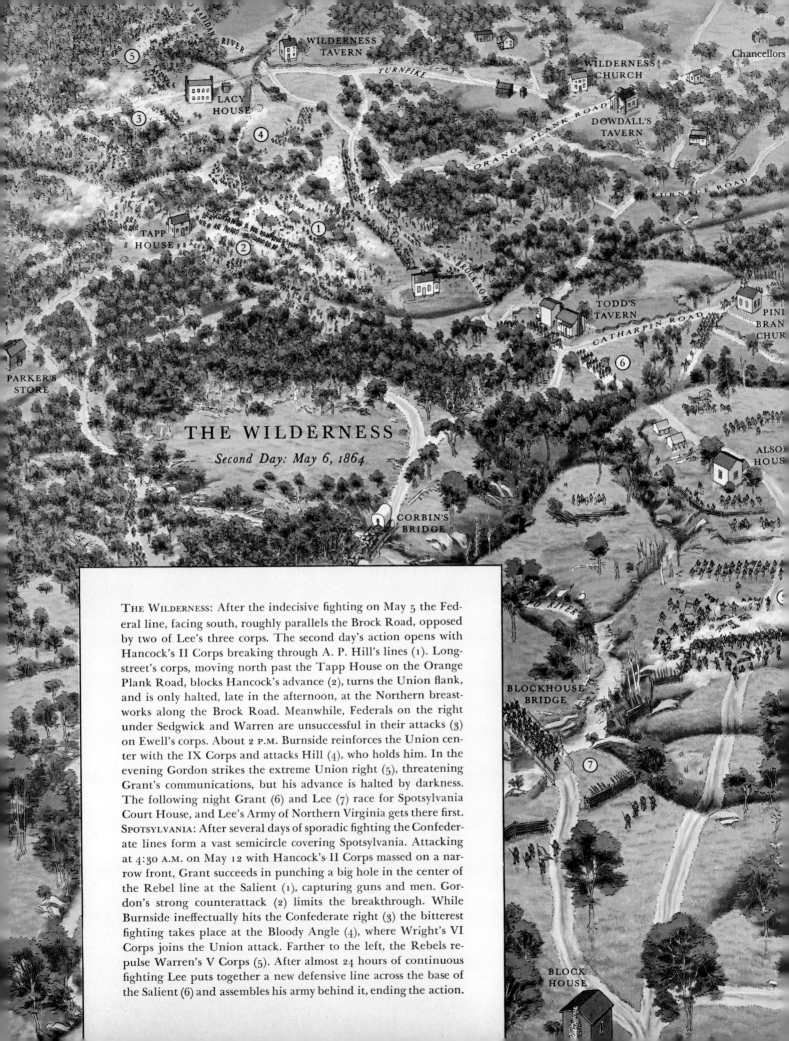

THE WILDERNESS

Second Day: May 6, 1864

THE WILDERNESS: After the indecisive fighting on May 5 the Federal line, facing south, roughly parallels the Brock Road, opposed by two of Lee's three corps. The second day's action opens with Hancock's II Corps breaking through A. P. Hill's lines (1). Longstreet's corps, moving north past the Tapp House on the Orange Plank Road, blocks Hancock's advance (2), turns the Union flank, and is only halted, late in the afternoon, at the Northern breastworks along the Brock Road. Meanwhile, Federals on the right under Sedgwick and Warren are unsuccessful in their attacks (3) on Ewell's corps. About 2 P.M. Burnside reinforces the Union center with the IX Corps and attacks Hill (4), who holds him. In the evening Gordon strikes the extreme Union right (5), threatening Grant's communications, but his advance is halted by darkness. The following night Grant (6) and Lee (7) race for Spotsylvania Court House, and Lee's Army of Northern Virginia gets there first.
SPOTSYLVANIA: After several days of sporadic fighting the Confederate lines form a vast semicircle covering Spotsylvania. Attacking at 4:30 A.M. on May 12 with Hancock's II Corps massed on a narrow front, Grant succeeds in punching a big hole in the center of the Rebel line at the Salient (1), capturing guns and men. Gordon's strong counterattack (2) limits the breakthrough. While Burnside ineffectually hits the Confederate right (3) the bitterest fighting takes place at the Bloody Angle (4), where Wright's VI Corps joins the Union attack. Farther to the left, the Rebels repulse Warren's V Corps (5). After almost 24 hours of continuous fighting Lee puts together a new defensive line across the base of the Salient (6) and assembles his army behind it, ending the action.

The Savage "Bloody Angle"

Brigadier General John B. Gordon

At dawn on May 12 Grant sent Hancock's men storming out of the fog and misty rain in a massive surprise attack on the so-called Mule Shoe Salient at the center of Lee's lines. They overran the defenders, as a Southerner recalled, "like a swollen torrent through a broken mill-dam."

The Yankees swept up twenty guns and thousands of prisoners, including two general officers and most of the famed Stonewall Brigade, but success so disorganized the Federals that a slashing counterattack by John B. Gordon's division knocked them back to the first line of captured trenches. They held there, and what followed was the most vicious struggle of the Civil War.

The front was so narrow that the Northerners were piled up thirty ranks deep, those in the rear passing loaded muskets forward. In many places, particularly at a bend in the lines called the Bloody Angle, there was hand-to-hand fighting of unbelievable savagery. Cannon fired canister at point-blank range, and soldiers were "stabbed to death with . . . bayonets thrust between the logs in the parapet which separated the combatants."

This "bloodshed surpassing all former experiences" continued in the rain and smoke and indescribable din until well past midnight, ending only when Lee completed a new line across the Salient.

The photograph above shows the scene of the Union attack of May 12 from a point behind a grassy, mounded Rebel trench at the Bloody Angle.

In Alfred Waud's drawing below, Yankee troops crouch in a captured trench and exchange fire with Southerners in trenches barely yards away.

Lee Loses Another Lieutenant

A Rebel killed in Ewell's attack on the Union right on May 19, 1864.

Spotsylvania was actually one sprawling, twelve-day battle, with continuous fighting somewhere along the opposing lines. The attack of May 12 was the bloodiest single day: at least 12,000 men fell in the struggle for one square mile of ground.

The next day Grant resumed his inexorable movement to the left, skirmishing, probing for a weak spot. Lee parried every thrust, but by May 19 he had to act or be cut off from Richmond. Ewell's corps, now down to 6,000, was sent to scout the strength of the Union right. It ran into a division of green troops fresh from the Washington fortifications, which, to everyone's surprise, fought the Rebels to a standstill. The next night found the determined Grant sliding southward again.

The two armies had been in contact since the Rapidan crossing less than three weeks before, and Grant's losses averaged 2,000 men a day. Lee's casualties had been considerably less, although his loss in prisoners was unusually heavy. A seemingly unending train of wagons with their ghastly cargo of wounded men trailed north toward Fredericksburg and south toward Richmond.

Lee bore more and more of the weight of command—Jackson was dead, Longstreet severely wounded, A. P. Hill always sick, Ewell still acting indecisively—and on May 12 a fresh blow came.

Phil Sheridan had moved on Richmond with a strong cavalry force, and Jeb Stuart met and held him at Yellow Tavern on the eleventh. It was Stuart's last battle; a Yankee trooper put a bullet in his stomach, and he died the next day. Lee commented sadly, "I can scarcely think of him without weeping."

This stark, simple cross in the Wilderness, near Chancellorsville, marks the grave of an unknown Union soldier.

461

The Battle of Cold Harbor

A pontoon bridge over the North Anna at Jericho Mills, where part of Grant's army crossed.

Throughout May the armies kept up their deadly, shuffling dance southeastward, Grant never quite able to catch his opponent at a disadvantage. There were constant skirmishes and probing attacks, with the crossings of the North Anna, Pamunkey, and Totopotomoy rivers marking the advance. By June 1 weary Rebels and Yankees began another race, this time for the barren, dusty crossroads of Cold Harbor; nearby, at Mechanicsville, Robert E. Lee had first fought the Army of the Potomac.

Grant ordered an attack for dawn on June 2, but high-command blundering forced its postponement for a day. By then Lee was ready. With no chance whatsoever against the expertly sited Southern entrenchments, 7,000 of Grant's men fell in just half an hour. A Rebel colonel noted that "the dead covered more than five acres of ground about as thickly as they could be laid."

Francis Barlow's brigades gained a foothold in Lee's lines at Cold Harbor, as sketched above by Alfred Waud, taking prisoners (right foreground) and turning captured guns on the Rebels. Their reinforcements shattered, Barlow's men were finally driven out. Portions of the Rebel Cold Harbor lines remain today (right). After the armies had moved on, a correspondent described them: "intricate, zig-zagged lines within lines, lines protecting flanks of lines, lines built to enfilade an opposing line . . . a labyrinth."

At left is the Federal high command, seated on pews from a nearby church, planning the Cold Harbor assault; at the far left Grant leans over the back of a pew to examine a map. Photographer Timothy O'Sullivan took his picture from the church steeple.

463

The Federal II Corps boarded transports to cross the James on June 14, drawn above by William Waud. Grant sits his horse (center); Hancock is in the chair.

Grant quickly found Petersburg's defenses impregnable to frontal assault. Below, the 22nd Colored Infantry, with bayonets fixed, makes a desperate charge June 16.

Opportunity at Petersburg

After ten days at Cold Harbor, Grant tried a new stratagem. He broke contact with Lee's army and, behind a cavalry screen, marched across the Peninsula east of Richmond and crossed the James River. Lee moved cautiously, unsure of Grant's exact goal.

The goal was Petersburg, twenty miles south of Richmond, through which passed all but one of the rail lines to the Confederate capital. If it fell into Union hands, and if that one remaining railroad were cut, both Richmond and Lee's army would be without food; at which point the Confederacy's days would be numbered.

It was a good plan, expertly carried out, but the wrong man had the job of taking Petersburg. As a result a dazzling chance to end the war in one stroke was missed.

William F. Smith's XVIII Corps reached Petersburg on June 15, where Beauregard had but 2,200 men to hold the fortifications. Smith finally attacked at dusk and soon held a large part of the works. While Petersburg lay undefended he halted, awaited Hancock's delayed troops, then took no action when they arrived. Hancock's veterans scented victory, and when no attack orders came, a soldier remembered that "the rage of the enlisted men was devilish." Beauregard was incredulous.

Beauregard reinforced and shortened his lines and repulsed badly mounted Federal attacks. Then Lee's army arrived, and all that remained to Grant was a siege.

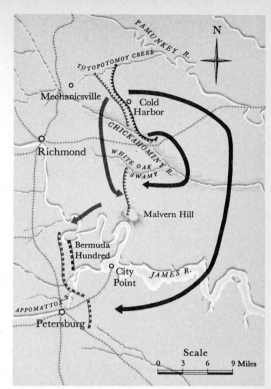

Grant's flanking march from Cold Harbor to Petersburg is shown in black, Lee's defensive moves in gray.

William Waud's panoramic drawing looks south from a signal station at Bermuda Hundred, where Butler's Army of the James had been bottled up by a small Rebel force, toward Petersburg, under siege and visible at the right. The Appomattox River is in the foreground.

OVERLEAF: *The armies' raw entrenchments soon scarred the land around Petersburg. These rugged outer works were abandoned by the Confederates early in the siege. In the left background are chevaux-de-frise, made of sharpened stakes and used as infantry obstacles.*

Battery of Mortars and light twelves. at. Jackson 1st C.

Above, a Union mortar and artillery battery at Petersburg, drawn by Alfred Waud. The comfort-loving gunners undoubtedly "borrowed" the couch visible at left from a local home.

At left, Alfred Waud's sketch of snipers. Men of both armies agreed with the Yankee who "hated sharpshooters, both Confederate and Union . . . I was always glad to see them killed."

At right, fouled water stands in the desolate trenches of Fort Sedgwick in Grant's Petersburg lines. After a heavy rain the men often had to stand in waist-deep water all day.

Below, a wash drawing by William Waud, Alfred's brother, shows the after-dark system of signaling by torch across the James River, used by Ben Butler's Federal Army of the James.

The Siege of Petersburg

A Pennsylvanian, writing about the siege of Petersburg, called it "hell itself. . . . simply awful. One-half of the line would fire while the other worked on the pits or tried to sleep."

Grant kept extending his lines westward around Petersburg, and by the end of June he had cut one of the railroads into the city. A great deal of digging by the enlisted men of both sides was required. "The men work after the manner of bees," wrote a Northern observer. "The mass throw up the earth; the engineer soldiers do the . . . interior facing of logs. . . . the engineer officers look as wise as possible."

The Army of Northern Virginia and the Army of the Potomac were of vastly different composition now. More than a third of Lee's general officers had been lost to him since the beginning of the campaign, many of them permanently, and several of his most valued units were decimated. In Grant's force a staggering 60 per cent of the men who had crossed the Rapidan were casualties. He had virtually a new army.

The soldiers settled into the routine of the siege: trenches were deepened and strengthened; covered ways dug leading to the rear; bombproofs built as protection against mortar fire and made as comfortable as possible; ditches and obstacles placed between the lines as insurance against surprise attack. Artillery duels were sometimes regular, sometimes begun on the spur of the moment, day or night. Sharpshooting was incessant. For six weeks there was blazing heat and no rain, then there was too much rain.

Most of the time the men performed their duties in a kind of stupor. A steady stream of casualties sapped each army—men who were killed and maimed to no particular purpose or advantage. Sickness, desertion, and battle fatigue took their toll. When someone observed to Grant that the campaign resembled the Kilkenny cats that devoured each other, he replied bluntly, "Our cat has the longer tail."

Alternatives to Siege Warfare

Civil War offensive strategy lagged far behind developments in defensive killing power, and the education of generals to this fact cost thousands of lives. By the summer of 1864, however, it was crystal clear that no frontal assault could succeed against Petersburg. Early in the siege a New Yorker, veteran of Spotsylvania and Cold Harbor, gave this version of a frontal attack: "We are going to run toward the Confederate earthworks and then we are going to run back. We have had enough of assaulting earthworks."

Other methods were needed to break Lee's defenses, or outflank him, or cut his supply line. Grant had the last alternative in mind when he dispatched James H. Wilson's cavalry to strike the railroads west of Petersburg and Richmond.

Wilson narrowly escaped destruction by Rebel cavalry under Wade Hampton and Fitz Lee, but not before he had destroyed 60 miles of vital trackage, severing rail connections for weeks and presenting Lee with a severe supply problem.

Ben Butler, meanwhile, was planning a grandiose scheme to clear the way for Yankee gunboats to reduce Richmond's James River defenses. Butler, the most incompetent of the Northern political generals, surpassed himself with this Dutch Gap canal project. The canal was not completed until the war was nearly over, and its only result was to straighten a bad bottleneck in the James, much to the benefit of Richmond's postwar commerce.

Long before Butler's folly was apparent, the long-suffering Army of the Potomac had been deprived by its inept officer corps of another golden chance to win the war.

Alfred Waud's drawing below shows Wilson's cavalrymen busily engaged in destroying Lee's railroad lifeline. Stacks of ties were crowned with rails and set afire; when red-hot, the rails were twisted around trees.

Ben Butler's troops work on the Dutch Gap canal under enemy fire, drawn above by William Waud. Butler's diggers removed over 65,000 cubic yards of dirt in cutting a channel to bypass a loop in the James River.

Late in July Grant launched a diversion north of the James, toward Richmond. In William Waud's sketch of the capture of a Rebel battery (below), the gunners flee with their sponge staffs, crippling the pieces.

A Confederate colonel at Petersburg, sketched by one of his men.

471

Federal Disaster at the Crater

Major General William Mahone

The 48th Pennsylvania held a section of the Petersburg lines only 130 yards from the Rebel trenches. The 48th contained many coal miners, and its colonel, Henry Pleasants, a mining engineer, persuaded high command to let him try to place a mine under the Confederate lines.

Within a month Pleasants had dug a tunnel and laid four tons of powder. A fresh colored division was especially trained to spearhead the assault. Grant feinted at Richmond, drawing Rebels from the mined sector; but at the last minute, for political reasons, the Negroes were replaced by war-weary white troops. The mine exploded at 4:45 A.M. on July 30 "with a muffled roar . . . as from the eruption of a volcano," and a 500-yard gap opened in the center of Lee's lines. By an incredible slip-up no provision had been made to get the attack columns over the steep parapets and through the obstacles between the lines. While two division commanders lay drunk in a dugout, the leaderless men trickled into the huge crater to gawk at the mine's carnage.

Hard-fighting William Mahone quickly rallied the stunned Confederates for a counterattack, and Lee's artillery zeroed in on the crater, turning it into "a cauldron of hell." By 1 P.M. the break was mended.

The moment the mine exploded, demolishing the Confederate entrenchments in "an enormous whirlwind," Federal artillery opened a heavy bombardment. Alfred Waud made this sketch.

Mahone's Confederates counterattack at the crater, painted above by John Elder. Writing of the
assault, Grant called it "a stupendous failure."

After the Battle of the Crater the routine of
trench warfare resumed. Below is Homer's painting of a bored, defiant soldier inviting a shot.

While Confederates Scrimp,
Union Supply Lines Are Choked
With Abundance

As autumn came to Virginia the armies prepared for the ordeal of winter in the trenches—the Confederates with increasing concern, the Federals with confidence born of their obvious strength. A visible symbol of Northern might was Grant's immense supply depot at City Point, painted here by E. L. Henry. A mile of wharves lined the shore, and food and war matériel of every sort poured ashore like a flood tide from transports and barges. The army ran 18 trains a day to the front lines over a 21-mile railroad it had built. A Southern churchman who saw City Point remarked, "Not merely profusion, but extravagance."

In Lee's trenches an officer wrote home, "It is hard to maintain one's patriotism on ashcake and water."

Sherman Takes the Offensive in the West

In Chattanooga, William Tecumseh Sherman, with some 100,000 veteran soldiers, had orders "to move against Johnston's army, to break it up, and to get into the interior of the enemy's country . . . inflicting all the damage you can." On May 6, 1864, as Grant and Lee fought in the Wilderness, Sherman went for Joe Johnston.

After a diet of martinet Braxton Bragg the average Rebel private was glad to have Johnston in command. "The joyous dawn of day seemed to have risen from the night," one of them wrote. The Army of Tennessee was fit and its morale was high.

Johnston was a counterpuncher, a defensive specialist quick to strike an overextended flank or a careless defense; Sherman had superior numbers and seldom made mistakes. Northern Georgia soon became a huge chessboard for their maneuvers.

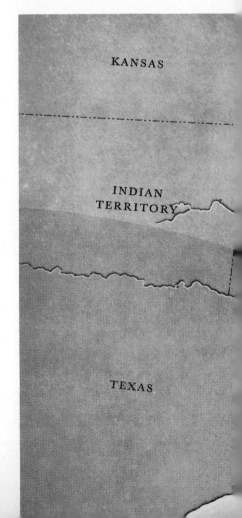

KANSAS

INDIAN TERRITORY

TEXAS

Advocating total war, Sherman wrote before his Atlanta Campaign that "war, like the thunderbolt, follows its laws and turns not aside even if the beautiful, the virtuous and the charitable stand in its path." This photograph of him was taken in 1864. The map (right) shows the 1864 Federal thrusts into the shrinking Confederacy; the dotted lines are the ultimate courses of Sherman and Grant.

Photographer George Barnard accompanied Sherman's invasion of Georgia and left an extensive pictorial record of the campaign. Above is his view of the Confederate fortifications guarding a railroad bridge over the Etowah River.

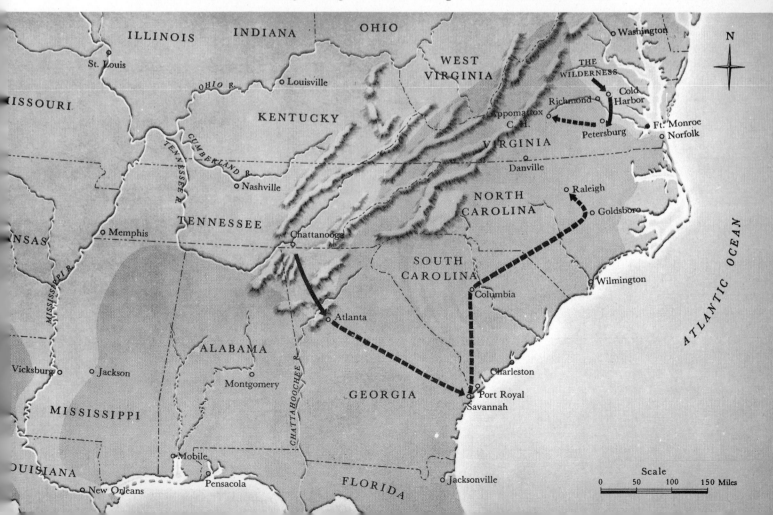

Maneuvers in Georgia

Rebel generals Hardee and Johnston witness the death of Bishop Polk.

Skillfully using his three armies, Sherman flanked Johnston out of successive defensive lines at Dalton, Resaca, Cassville, and Allatoona Pass. His rugged Westerners, prodigious marchers who saw little point in making frontal assaults on entrenchments, were ideal for this campaign of maneuver. John Schofield, commanding the Army of the Ohio, said his men fought "like they worked farms or sawmills, demanding a fair prospect that it would pay."

For four days the armies clashed indecisively at New Hope Church. The sharpest fighting occurred on May 25, when Hooker's attack on Alexander Stewart's Rebel division was stalled at the "Hell Hole" during a spectacular thunderstorm. By the end of the month Sherman forced Johnston into a new line, a few miles northwest of Marietta. A Rebel prisoner complained to his captors that "you-uns swings around your ends like a gate."

Here Johnston lost a corps commander and a guiding spirit of his army, Bishop Polk, who was killed by a Union artillery salvo as he reconnoitered from Pine Mountain. Johnston now withdrew to Kennesaw Mountain, where Sherman determined to attack him on June 27.

At left is Barnard's photograph of Confederate entrenchments in a thicket at New Hope Church, where the first major fighting of Sherman's campaign took place. Beyond the earthwork is an abatis of fallen, tangled trees to slow up attacking troops.

General Joseph E. Johnston (right) was admired by his troops, respected by his Federal opponents, and mistrusted by President Davis. Prideful and touchy, Johnston failed to explain candidly to Davis the reasons for his defensive strategy before Atlanta.

The photograph below looks west from the Confederate position atop Kennesaw Mountain. Sherman approached from Lost Mountain, visible in the distance, which, with Pine and Brush mountains, anchored Johnston's previous defensive lines.

The photograph above looks eastward toward Blackjack Mountain from the crest of Kennesaw Mountain. Outflanked after the battle here, Johnston retreated through Marietta (out of the picture at right) toward Atlanta. At left is a Confederate gun at the Kennesaw battlefield park, and below, the rocky, steep slope which faced Sherman's attackers. The unsigned wash drawing at right shows a Federal column charging that slope.

480

Hood Replaces Joe Johnston

Sherman learned at Kennesaw Mountain what Grant, three weeks earlier, had discovered at Cold Harbor: well-dug-in Confederates were impervious to frontal attack. Under a broiling Georgia sun Thomas' men bravely assaulted the divisions of Pat Cleburne and Benjamin Cheatham, and a defender wrote that "They seemed to walk up and take death as coolly as if they were automatic or wooden men." But the attack failed utterly. Among the mortally wounded was Colonel Daniel McCook, one of fifteen of Ohio's "Fighting McCooks" who fought for the North, and the fourth member of the family to be killed in action.

Sherman resumed his flanking strategy, forcing Johnston to the Chattahoochee River, less than ten miles from Atlanta—a city whose rolling mill, munitions factories, and railroad connections made it vitally important to the Confederacy.

Outnumbered two to one and sensing the political implications of war weariness in the North, Johnston had chosen to impede Sherman's juggernaut instead of attacking it. Lincoln's re-election in November seemed dubious, and Johnston thought the South's best hope was continued stalemate. Then he made his first serious tactical mistake: failing to anticipate Sherman's flanking move that sent McPherson far to the east to cross the Chattahoochee unopposed, Johnston had to fall back to the edge of Atlanta.

On July 17 Davis replaced Johnston with John Bell Hood. "This act," a Rebel soldier recalled, "threw a damper over this army from which it never recovered." Immediately Sherman braced his men for a battle, for Hood was an impetuous, gambling fighter. One of Sherman's officers recalled how, in a prewar army poker game, Hood "bet $2,500 with nary a pair in his hand."

THE
POLITICS
OF WAR

O<small>N EACH</small> side there was one man who stood at storm center, trying to lead a people who would follow no leader for long unless they felt in him some final embodiment of the deep passions and misty insights that moved them. This man was the President, given power and responsibility beyond all other men, hemmed in by insistent crowds yet always profoundly alone—Abraham Lincoln, in Washington, and Jefferson Davis, in Richmond.

They were very different, these two, alike only in their origins and in the crushing weight of the burdens they carried. On each rested an impossible imperative —to adjust himself to fate and yet at the same time somehow to control it. Miracles were expected of them by an age which had lost its belief in the miraculous.

Davis was all iron will and determination, a rigid man who might conceivably be broken but who could never be bent, proud almost to arrogance and yet humbly devoted to a cause greater than himself. Of the rightness of that cause he had never a doubt, and it was hard for him to understand that other men might not see that rightness as easily as he did. Essentially a legalist, he had been put in charge of the strangest of revolutions—an uprising of conservatives who would overturn things in order to preserve a cher-

ished *status quo*—and he would do his unwavering best to make the revolution follow the proper forms. He had had much experience with politics, yet it had been the experience of the aristocrat-in-politics. He had never known the daily immersion in the rough-and-tumble of ward and courthouse politics, where the candidate is hammered into shape by repeated contact with the electorate.

There were other handicaps, the greatest being the fact that the kind of government Southerners wanted was not the kind that could fight and win an extended war. The administration had to have broad wartime powers, but when Davis tried to get and use them he was bitterly criticized; fighting against strong central-ized government, he had to create such a government in order to win. States' rights made an impossible base for modern war. The doctrinaire was forever tripping up the realist.

Nor was that all. Davis' cabinet gave him little help. It contained some good men, the ablest perhaps being Judah P. Benjamin, a lawyer and former senator from Louisiana. He served, successively, as Attorney General, Secretary of War, and Secretary of State. He was a brilliant man and a hard worker, wholly devoted to the cause, and Davis trusted him and relied on him as much as a man of Davis' bristling independence could

Ben Butler is a subservient Sancho Panza to Lincoln's idealistic Don Quixote in this caricature by Volck.

483

be said to rely on anyone. Other men, in the cabinet and out of it, seemed to feel that Benjamin was just a little too clever, and he was never able to bring a broad national following to the President's support. Another good man, underestimated at the time, was Stephen Mallory of Florida, the Secretary of the Navy. Mallory had very little to work with, and the Confederacy's total inability to break the strangling blockade brought him much unjust criticism, but he did a good deal better with the materials at hand than there was any reason to expect. He and John H. Reagan of Texas, the Postmaster General, were the only two who held their cabinet posts from the Confederacy's birth to its death. There were six secretaries of war, and the one who held the job longest was James A. Seddon of Virginia; like those who preceded and followed him, Seddon found his path made difficult by the fact that Davis to all intents and purposes was his own Secretary of War.

Broadly speaking, the cabinet was undistinguished, and it never contained the South's strongest men. Alexander Stephens was Vice-President, as isolated in that office as an American Vice-President invariably is; Howell Cobb was never a member, Robert Toombs was in the cabinet only briefly, and as a general thing the cabinet did not contain the men who had been most influential in bringing about secession in the first place—the men who, just before the separation took place, would have been regarded as the South's strongest leaders. More and more as the war went on the Confederate government was a one-man show.

In the sense that the President was always dominant, the Northern government too was a one-man show, but in reality it was a team of powerful men—a team which was unruly, stubborn, and hard to manage, but which provided a great deal of service. Lincoln put in his cabinet men of force and ability, and although some of them fought against him at times and tried to wrest leadership from him, they added strength to his administration. Lincoln had a suppleness which Davis lacked, his political experience had taught him how to win a political fight without making personal enemies out of the men he defeated, and he had as well the ability to use the talents of self-assured men who considered themselves his betters.

William H. Seward, his Secretary of State, had opposed him for the Republican Presidential nomination, entered the cabinet reluctantly, and believed that he rather than Lincoln would actually run the show. Lincoln quickly disillusioned him on this point and then made a loyal supporter of him. Edwin M. Stanton, who became Secretary of War after Simon Cameron had demonstrated his own abysmal unfitness for the post, was harsh, domineering, ruthless, forever conniving with the radical Republicans to upset Lincoln's control of high policy; yet he, like Seward, finally came to see that the President was boss, and he was an uncommonly energetic and able administrator. Salmon P. Chase, Secretary of the Treasury, was another man who had sought the Republican Presidential nomination in 1860 and who, failing to get it, believed firmly that the better man had lost. He had no conception of the loyalty which a cabinet member might be supposed to owe to the president who had appointed him, and in 1864 he tried hard, while still in Lincoln's cabinet, to take the nomination away from him. But if he was a difficult man to get along with, he ran the Treasury Department ably; after removing him for unendurable political insubordination in 1864, Lincoln a few months later showed how highly he regarded Chase's services by making him Chief Justice of the United States.

Thus both Lincoln and Davis had to face intense political opposition as the war progressed. To sum up the quality of their respective cabinets, it can only be said that in the face of this opposition Lincoln's cabinet was in the long run a help to him, and that Davis' cabinet was not.

One queer aspect of the political phase of the war was the fact that it was the government at Richmond which was first and boldest in its assertion of centralized control over the armies. Despite the states' rights theory, the Confederate government became a truly national government, as far as matters like conscription were concerned, much earlier and much more unequivocally than the government at Washington.

When the war began, Confederate soldiers were enlisted for a term of twelve months, which meant that in the spring of 1862 the Confederate armies were in danger of dissolving. The administration and the Congress met this problem head-on, putting through a conscription act which placed exclusive control over all male citizens between eighteen and thirty-five in the hands of the Confederate President. With certain specified exceptions and exemptions, all men within those age limits were conscripted for the duration of the war. Some of the state governors, most notably the egregious Joseph E. Brown of Georgia, complained bitterly that this was a body blow at constitutional liberties, but the President and Congress were unmoved. There might be widespread complaint about the exemptions under the law—the owner or overseer of twenty slaves, for instance, could not be called into military service—and in the latter part of the war there was trouble enforcing the conscription act properly, but the act itself was courageous and straightforward, and it went unmodified.

It was the Northern government that found itself unable to assert adequate central control over the lives of its citizens, and although it was driven to conscription in 1863, it never was as bold or direct about it as the government at Richmond had been, and it never adopted as good a law.

Northern armies were composed of regiments raised by the several states, and the volunteer signed up, usually, for a three-year term. When new men were needed the Federal government set a total and assigned a quota to each state, and each state quota in turn was broken down into quotas for the separate Congressional districts. If any district or state could fill its quota with volunteers, there would be no draft, and since the draft was extremely unpopular, every state, town, and county did its best to promote volunteering. This led to the indefensible bounty system, which was enormously expensive and did the Union armies more harm than good. A state would offer a cash bounty for enlistments, cities and townships and counties would add their own contribution, the Federal government would make a further offer—and by 1864 there were many areas in which a man could receive more than a thousand dollars simply for joining the army.

The results were almost uniformly vicious. Men who had no intention of rendering any service at the front would enlist, collect their bounty, desert at the first opportunity, re-enlist under another name in some other locality, collect another bounty, desert again, and go on with the process indefinitely—the "bounty jumpers," who were detested by the veteran soldiers and who brought the very dregs of society into the army. Even when the high-bounty man did not desert, he did the cause little good; he was in the army because he was offered a great deal of money, not because of any patriotic impulse, and late in the war General Grant estimated that not one in eight of the high-bounty recruits ever did any useful service at the front.

On top of this, the draft act contained a couple of grotesque monstrosities. A drafted man could obtain exemption by paying a commutation fee of three hundred dollars; or, if he preferred—as well he might, since the exemption thus gained would last only until a new draft was called—he could hire a substitute to go to war in his place, thus obtaining permanent release from military service. The government could hardly have devised a worse law. It put the load on the poor man and gave special favors to the well-to-do, and it brought some very poor material into the army. The substitute broker—the dealer who, for a price, would find substitutes for well-heeled draft dodgers—would take any men he could get, and some of them were mentally or physically defective. Through bribery, the broker could often get these men accepted, but they were not of much use to the army.

All in all, the conscription law was an atrocity. Comparatively few men were actually drafted; the one virtue of the law was that it stimulated recruiting, and although the volunteers it brought in were by no means the equals of the men who had enlisted in 1861 and 1862, the army could make do with them. The high-bounty laws did have one good effect. Veteran soldiers whose three-year terms were expiring often re-enlisted because the proffered bounty and the furlough that went with re-enlistment looked attractive. In the final year of the war the heaviest part of the military load was carried by the old regiments which were entitled to denominate themselves "veteran volunteers."

That he accepted things like the bounty system and the conscription law simply indicates that Lincoln was always prepared to make political compromises to keep the war machine moving. He managed to keep his cabinet under moderately good control, and all things considered he got along with the Congress and with the state governors a good deal better than Davis was able to do. But the road was never smooth, and his problems multiplied as the war progressed. There were recurring cabinet crises. Lincoln had to hold the support of the radicals who followed Chase and Stanton and of the moderates who followed Seward, and there were times when it seemed all but impossible to head off an open break between the leaders of these factions. The innumerable political generals raised similar problems. Such men as Ben Butler, Nathaniel P. Banks, Franz Sigel, and John Charles Frémont were very poor generals indeed, but they held the confidence of large groups of citizens, and in the intricate game of war-plus-politics which Lincoln had to play it seemed, rightly or wrongly, that these generals must be retained in the government's service. The fearsome Congressional Joint Committee on the Conduct of the War was forever trying to interfere in the setting of administration policy and in the control of the armies; it was necessary for Lincoln to retain control without driving the energetic spellbinders who composed this committee into open opposition.

Lincoln was an adroit politician of extraordinary suppleness and agility. He had to be one, in 1864 especially, because there was about to be a Presidential election, and in the history of the world there had never been a canvass quite like this one. Never before had a democratic nation prepared to hold free elections while it was in the midst of a bloody attempt to win a violent civil war, and the results were unpredictable. As spring gave way to summer and autumn drew near it became increasingly apparent that when it voted on the Presidency, the nation might in effect be voting whether to drop out of the war or carry on to victory at any cost.

The Republicans would of course support Lincoln, even though the party's radicals wanted someone who would wage war with more vigor and with more bitterness. Secretary Chase's bid for the nomination had failed, and although a third party tried to advance General Frémont, it got nowhere, and Frémont presently withdrew. Lincoln was renominated, by a party which called itself the Union party in deference to the support it was getting from the War Democrats, and Andrew Johnson of Tennessee was named as his running mate. Lincoln would make no election campaign. What had been done in the war would, of necessity, be the principal issue. Fighting to defeat him for re-election, the Democrats would have great difficulty to keep from fighting for a different sort of war effort; and since the people who wanted a harder war were bound to support Lincoln, the Democrats were apt to speak, or at least to appear to speak, for a softer war— which, under the circumstances, would be likely to mean no war at all.

A great many people in the North were completely disillusioned about the war. Federal troops had to be used, in Ohio and Illinois and elsewhere, to put down uprisings provoked by the draft act; and New York City went through a few bloody days just after the Battle of Gettysburg when mobs stormed draft offices, killed or beat up any Negroes they could find, battled police and soldiers, and in general acted like revolutionists. The riots were at last suppressed, after combat troops had been sent in from the Army of the Potomac, but a thousand civilians had been killed or wounded and an immense amount of property had been destroyed, and the riots were a fearful symptom of deep underlying unrest and discontent. The 1864 Presidential election offered this discontent a chance to show its full strength.

In August the Democrats held their convention in Chicago, and the Copperhead wing was, if not in full control, very active and exceedingly vocal. (Copperhead: one of the anti-war Democrats, who wore in their lapels Indian heads cut from copper pennies.) They dictated a platform which declared the war a failure and called for re-establishment of the Union on the old basis, which amounted to an open confession of lack of will to go on fighting. They accepted the nomination of General McClellan as Presidential candidate, while George H. Pendleton of Ohio, friend of the Copperhead leader, Clement Vallandigham, was named for the Vice-Presidency. Then they sat back and waited for nation-wide war weariness and disillusionment to do the job.

It appeared that they might have things figured correctly. With the summer coming to a close, the campaigns that had been begun in the spring did look like failures. Neither Lee nor Johnston had been beaten, neither Richmond nor Atlanta had been taken, a Confederate army had recently menaced Washington itself, casualty lists were higher than they had ever been before, the administration had recently called for a new draft of 500,000 men, and Lincoln himself privately believed that he could not be re-elected. He believed, additionally, that if he were defeated, the man who beat him would win the election on terms which would make it humanly impossible to win the war; and although McClellan disavowed the peace plank in the Democratic platform and refused to say that the war was a failure, the Lincoln-McClellan contest was generally accepted as a test of the North's willingness to go on with the fight.

One factor in the public's war weariness was the presence of many thousands of Northern soldiers in Southern prison camps, where living conditions were atrocious and the death rate was alarmingly high. In the first years of the war the opposing governments had operated on a system of prisoner exchanges, by which prisoners were periodically repatriated on a man-for-man basis. This system had broken down by the time 1864 began, and when Grant took control of the Union armies he refused to put it in repair. The North now held more prisoners than the South held, and the manpower shortage was hurting the Confederacy much more than it hurt the Union. With lucid but pitiless logic Grant argued that to resume exchanges would simply reinforce the Confederate armies. (It would also reinforce Federal armies, but these would be reinforced anyway, and the Confederate armies would not.) Unionists in Southern prison camps, therefore, would have to stay there, and if they died like flies—from dysentery, typhoid, malnutrition, and homesick despair complicated by infected quarters—that was regrettable but unavoidable.

In actual fact the Union prisoners of war were very little worse off than the Southerners who were held in Northern prisons, but most people in the North did not realize this and would not have been consoled if they had realized it. All prison camps were death traps in that war. They were overcrowded, reeking from lack of sanitation, badly policed; housing was bad, food was worse, and medical care was sometimes worst of all. This was due less to any active ill-will on either side than to the general, unintended brutality and heartlessness of war. Army life in those days was rough, even under the best conditions, and disease killed many more men than bullets killed; in a prison camp this roughness was inevitably intensified (26,436 Southerners and 22,576 Northerners died in prison camps) even though nobody really meant it so.

No one in the North tried to analyze any of this in the summer of 1864. Heartsick parents could see only that their boys were dying in prisons because the administration, for some inscrutable reason, was refusing to bring them home. Grant was fighting the war on the theory that the North could stand heavier losses than the South could stand, and Lincoln was supporting him, but the immediate fruits of this policy did not make good election-campaign material.

Davis had no campaign problems that summer. The Confederate Constitution set the President's term at six years and ruled out a second term, and Davis did not need to ask for anybody's vote. He was devoting a good part of his attention, with a good deal of skill, to the task of making war-weary Northerners feel the burden of the war, and he was using for this purpose a device which a later generation would know as a fifth column.

This fifth column was directed from bases in neutral Canada, where certain Confederate emissaries, their operations amply financed by the sale of cotton, kept in touch with agents in the Northern states. They were in touch also with a good many of the Copperhead leaders, and they worked closely with a strange, amorphous, and slightly unreal secret society known variously as the Order of American Knights or the Sons of Liberty; a pro-Confederate peace organization which had proliferated all across the Middle West, claiming hundreds of thousands of members and supposedly preparing to take up arms against the Federal government. The plots that were laid for armed uprisings never came to anything—there was one scheme for a wholesale prison delivery in the Northern states, but it died a-borning—but their existence was an open secret, and the whole business tended to spread defeatist talk and defeatist feelings across the North as nothing else could have done. The fifth column attempted other things—to burn New York City, to capture a warship on the Great Lakes, to destroy railroad bridges, and to enrich the Confederacy with money taken from Yankee banks—and although the actual results were small, the program itself was as desperate as anything a modern fifth columnist would be likely to attempt.

Although Jefferson Davis lacked Lincoln's political address, he was adapting himself to the war situation with real skill. He was, to repeat, a legalist, insisting that the revolution which he led was in fact no revolution at all but something fully sanctioned by constitution and law; but he was laying his hands on a revolutionary weapon with genuine earnestness and ruthless energy, and it was no fault of his that the great fifth-column movement of 1864 came to so little. If the Northern Copperhead leaders had been able to deliver on a fifth of their promises, the Confederacy might that summer have given the Northern home front a good deal more than it could conveniently handle.

The Presidential campaign of 1864 was, all in all, about the most crucial political contest in American history, but it was a campaign in which what men said made very little difference. Speeches were of small account. It was what the men in uniform did that mattered. The war effort was alleged to be a failure; if most people felt, by election day, that it really was a failure, then it would in fact become one through the defeat of the candidate and the party which had had direction of the war effort. On the other hand, if by election day the war was clearly being won, the Democratic campaign would inevitably come to nothing. Everything depended on the fighting men. If they should start to win, Lincoln would win. He would not win otherwise.

The Radicals Harass Lincoln

Edwin M. Stanton, who first sneered at Lincoln as the "original gorilla," ingratiated himself with Radical leaders; then proved himself an energetic Secretary of War who learned to admire and trust the President.

As a Republican President, Abraham Lincoln was as often plagued by troubles from within his own party as by those raised by men who were more logically his political opponents. At the outset of the administration Ohio's "Bluff Ben" Wade heard that the new President would attempt a conciliatory policy. "If we follow such leadership," Wade howled, "we will be in the wilderness longer than the children of Israel under Moses." The war, Wade and his disciples decided, should be nothing less than a total assault on slavery. Acidulous Thaddeus Stevens, representative from Pennsylvania, viewed the conflict as a "radical revolution . . . [involving] the desolation of the South as well as emancipation . . ." To wage this type of war, the Radicals created the Joint Committee on the Conduct of the War. With Wade as chairman and resolute Zachariah Chandler of Michigan sitting at his elbow, the Committee, in time, became powerful enough to challenge Lincoln's role as Commander in Chief.

Republican governors multiplied the President's woes. Pudgy John A. Andrew of Massachusetts tirelessly raised troops for the Union cause, yet insisted on maintaining a degree of control over them. Oliver P. Morton, Indiana's alarmist war governor, whom Lincoln called "a good fellow, but . . . the skeeredest man I know of," refused to summon a Democratic-controlled legislature and for two years ruled as virtual dictator of Indiana.

Asked how he liked being President, Lincoln replied: "You have heard about the man tarred and feathered and ridden out of town on a rail? A man in the crowd asked him how he liked it, and his reply was that if it wasn't for the honor of the thing, he would much rather walk."

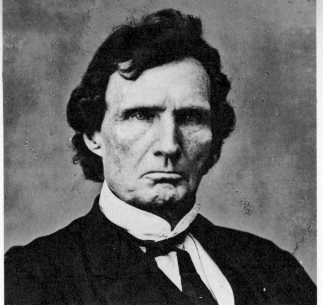

Thaddeus Stevens

John A. Andrew

Benjamin Wade

Oliver P. Morton

489

Zachariah Chandler

The Confederate Congress held its sessions in Virginia's stately capitol, designed on a classical scale by Jefferson.

Jefferson Davis Has Problems, Too

In Richmond, Jefferson Davis was beset by critics who were, if anything, more hostile and bitter than those opposing Lincoln. The Confederate Congress, frequently the scene of stormy sessions, often seemed intent on making war on Davis rather than against the Northern armies. Its fondness for secret sessions led one exasperated editor to complain that "nothing but motions to adjourn, tinker the currency, or appoint days of fasting and prayer, is done in open sessions." In the Senate, arrogant, venomous Louis T. Wigfall, who was "half drunk all the time" according to one observer, bullied and blustered against the Confederate President.

Within a frail, 100-pound frame, Vice-President Alexander H. Stephens harbored enough "hostility and wrath . . . to burst ten thousand bottles." The usual object of his spleen was Davis and his conduct of the war. Stephens absented himself from the capital for long periods of time and, when he did assume his duties as presiding officer of the Senate, used the office as a platform from which to hurl thunderbolts at Davis. Another obstacle to efficient management of the Confederacy was Georgia's pettifogging governor, Joe Brown, the "prince of Southern dem-

agogues." Brown, Davis claimed, persistently thwarted him at every turn.

The tactless Davis brought much of this criticism down upon his own head. The vituperative Richmond editor who found Davis "a literary dyspeptic who had more ink than blood in his veins, an intriguer, busy with private enemies," was expressing sentiments which many another Southerner held. Davis, who would have greatly preferred to be a general, told Robert E. Lee that "there has been nothing which I have found to require a greater effort of patience than to bear the criticisms of the ignorant."

Louis T. Wigfall

Alexander H. Stephens

Joseph E. Brown

The only official to win Jefferson Davis' full confidence was oleaginous Judah P. Benjamin, shown at left wearing the sly smile of inner amusement which infuriated his enemies and calmed the nervous President. Davis shifted him from post to post within the cabinet, retaining him as Secretary of State though the appointment was called "an ungracious and reckless defiance of popular sentiment."

Reporting the Civil War

Oliver Wendell Holmes, Boston's distinguished man of letters, followed the war news with interest. "We must have something to eat," Holmes wrote in the *Atlantic*, "and the papers to read. Everything else we can do without. . . . Only bread and newspapers we must have."

To satisfy the public appetite for news, a small army of Northern correspondents was organized—500, at one estimate. So thorough was their coverage that opposing generals sometimes learned more from enemy newspapers than from intelligence reports. Sherman, carrying on his own private war with the newspapers, grew apoplectic on the subject: "Reporters print their limited and tainted observations as the history of events they neither see nor comprehend," he wrote in fury.

The war also saw the dawn of pictorial journalism. Vivid eyewitness sketches by Alfred and William Waud, Henri Lovie, Winslow Homer, and Edwin Forbes turned up as engravings in *Harper's* and *Leslie's*, bringing the experiences of war vicariously to thousands who would never see a battlefield. At the same time Mathew Brady and other photographers were recording the tragic scenes of the great conflict.

That incomparable eccentric, Horace Greeley, was a leading public figure in his own right. Across the nation Greeley's *Tribune* was the family news Bible; men everywhere were convinced that Greeley wrote every word in the paper; and Horace himself was not above advising the President if necessary. Lincoln often invited reporters to the White House, in fact. "I am always seeking information," he explained, "and you newspapermen are so often behind the scenes at the front I am frequently able to get ideas from you which no one else will give."

Horace Greeley, photographed above while on an impromptu front-line tour, seemed to bear the entire burden of war, and once served as a semiofficial peace emissary. Below is a Forbes sketch of the arrival of newspapers in camp.

Debonair Frank Vizetelly (left), artist-correspondent for
The Illustrated London News, *was frankly pro-Southern.
Above is a Brady photograph of Alfred Waud, sketching
at Gettysburg. In the photograph below, left, Brady
appears, second from right, under fire with the Federal
artillery before Petersburg in June, 1864. The rakish
hero below delivered newspapers to the troops in camp*

Cloak and Dagger Activities by Femmes Fatales

Intrepid Belle Boyd once dashed through open fields, waving her bonnet, to give Stonewall Jackson information. She survived two imprisonments to marry a Union officer.

Darkly handsome Mrs. Rose Greenhow, shown below with her daughter in Old Capitol Prison, supplied the Rebels with information about Union troops before First Bull Run.

Early in the war Washington, a predominantly Southern town adjacent to Confederate territory, became both target and rendezvous for a network of secret agents, spies, and counterspies. The confidence of the mighty was sought and often won; bizarre costumes were donned (female spies favored uniforms to hide their curves); men rowed *agents provocateurs* across the Potomac after dark.

Ladies played spectacular roles as Rebel spies—Belle Boyd, Mrs. Rose O'Neal Greenhow, and the unsung heroine who was caught wearing a 50-pound petticoat of silk destined for a Confederate balloon—but it took men to catch them. Allan Pinkerton, chief of a celebrated detective agency, unveiled Mrs. Greenhow's activities by the simple expedient of peeping in her window. At the head of the North's Secret Service was Lafayette C. Baker. So notorious for tossing suspects in Old Capitol Prison was Baker that Lincoln once remarked to a citizen complaining about an organ-grinder: "Baker will steal the organ and throw its owner into the Old Capitol, and you'll never be troubled with the noise again."

When the photograph above was taken at McClellan's headquarters near Antietam, the man seated at right was known only as "Major Allen." In reality he was the famous detective Allan Pinkerton, who supplied the already cautious general with detailed and often grossly exaggerated reports of enemy strength.

Seductive Pauline Cushman, a theatrical ingénue, won Southern confidence by toasting the Rebels from a Kentucky stage. When she went South as a Federal agent she was captured, sentenced to death, left behind by the retreating Confederates, and then returned North to lecture on her exciting exploits.

495

A Fifth Column Menaces the Union Rear

Northern Copperheads were pictured in the 1863 cartoon above as snakes who would strike without warning. A supercilious Clement Vallandigham (center) sits with friends in the photograph below.

In this symbolic 1862 painting by D. G. Blythe, Lincoln, armed only
with a gun swab and fettered to strict constitutionality by Tam-
many Hall Democrats, tries to crush the dragon of rebellion.

Mayor Fernando Wood

Once during the grim winter of 1862–63 Lincoln was heard to remark that "The enemy behind us is more dangerous to the country than the enemy before us." He referred to subversive elements in the North such as Mayor Fernando Wood, New York's antiwar demagogue; the Knights of the Golden Circle, a spectral fifth column plotting rear-guard warfare; and Democrats advocating peace at any price (called Copperheads both for their serpentine qualities and for their lapel pins cut from copper pennies.)

The self-anointed leader of the Peace Democrats was a cold, calculating Ohio congressman, Clement L. Vallandigham. On January 14, 1863, Vallandigham rose in Congress to denounce the war. "Defeat, debt, taxation, sepulchres, these are your trophies," he told war supporters. "The war for the Union is . . . a most bloody and costly failure." Later that year he was deported to the Confederacy for declaring his sympathy with the enemy but soon returned, a pesky, tenacious foe to Lincoln through the 1864 elections.

The Propagandists at Work

Typical of Northern chauvinism is this 1861 eagle guarding its nest of states.

In the August 17, 1861, issue of *Harper's Weekly* appeared a fictitious picture of Rebel soldiers bayoneting Union wounded at Bull Run. Horrified readers were led to believe that "the savages who fought under the Confederate Flag systematically butchered the wounded, and this not only in obedience to their own fiendish instincts, but by order of their officers." It was the war's first major atrocity story.

People of the two sections had gone to war with the shibboleths of an exaggerated patriotism ringing in their ears; and soon artists, writers, and ministers were taking up the politician's war cries. In the North, Thomas Nast and others stirred millions with their vengeful cartoons. Among Southern propagandists the most skillful and vindictive was Adalbert Volck, a German immigrant, who took time out from his Baltimore dental practice to draw savage caricatures against the Union. Signing his work V. Blada (an anagram for Adalb. V.), he issued in 1863 a series of *Confederate War Etchings*. Two original drawings for the set appear on the opposite page.

As the bitter, bloody conflict lengthened into months, then years, mutual antagonism ripened into a hatred that was, too often, deliberately fostered. "The voice of reason is silenced," reported a North Carolinian. "Furious passion and thirst for blood consume the air."

498

In Volck's "Worship of the North" (above) Henry Ward Beecher sacrifices a white man to the deified Negro. Horace Greeley crouches at left as Ben Butler (foreground) kneels reverently before an altar which is topped by a bust of Lincoln in fool's cap. The drawing below is titled "Tracks of the Federal Armies."

The Failure of Prisoner Exchange

At the very outset of the war captured Rebel prisoners were released on parole, since there was no place to confine them. The Confederacy housed its first captives, for lack of a better place, in converted tobacco warehouses in Richmond. In this improvised war, prison sites were hastily selected and ill equipped. In the North, state penitentiaries, volunteer training camps like Camp Douglas near Chicago, a confiscated medical college, and a deserted slave pen in St. Louis were all pressed into service as prisons.

It took the two sides over a year to work out a system of exchange, and not until July, 1862, was a cartel signed. Under this arrangement all prisoners were to be discharged on parole and exchanged at a strict ratio—general for general, private for private, or 60 privates for one general. The cartel eventually collapsed over the knotty problem of exchanging former slaves, captured while serving in the Union armies. The South regarded the Negroes as runaways, to be returned to their masters; the North demanded that they be treated as any other prisoners of war. Another obstacle to any agreement was the fear that paroled soldiers would be returned to the front. In 1864 Grant wrote: "Every man we hold, when released on parole or otherwise, becomes an active soldier against us at once either directly or indirectly. If we commence a system of exchanges which liberates all prisoners taken, we will have to fight on until the whole South is exterminated." This meant, of course, that Northern boys would continue to languish in Rebel prisons. It was one more harsh reality which a North inured to horrors would have to accept.

In February, 1864, the Confederate government in Richmond, hard-pressed for an adequate food supply and threatened by a concerted Union drive against the city, cast about for prison sites farther South. One of the places chosen was Andersonville —"a name to be stamped so deeply by cruelty into the pages of American history"—a backwoods Georgia hamlet in the midst of dreary sand plains, deep, impenetrable pine forests, and swampy marshes.

In Richmond's notorious Libby Prison over 1,000 Union officers, confined in eight rooms like the one in David G. Blythe's painting at left, "endured . . . all the horrors of the middle-passage," a visitor wrote of conditions in the former tobacco warehouse.

Albert Moyer, a Pennsylvania private stationed at Camp Douglas, Illinois, painted the neat, precise view at right of that Northern prison camp. During the 1864 harvest season nearly 1,000 of its 7,500 Rebel prisoners were said to be suffering from scurvy.

At the Andersonville stockade in Georgia the death rate rose from 300 to 3,000 per month between March and August, 1864. The 26-acre plot, bisected by the dismal, sluggish stream shown in the photograph below, held nearly 32,000 Union prisoners.

A Confederate prisoner at Ohio's Camp Chase painted the water color above, showing
the arrival of the daily bread ration. In the crude painting below, John Omenhausser,
a Rebel confined at Point Lookout Prison, Maryland, depicted the sport of ratcatching.

Prison Camps: More Lethal Than Battles

CAMP-DOUGLAS SKETCHES

Visiting a Union Army mess in the summer of 1864, Abraham Lincoln pushed his plate away with a distressed sigh. Was the President ill? his host asked. "I am well enough," Lincoln replied, "but would to God this dinner or provisions like it were with our poor prisoners at Andersonville."

Stories filtering out of Andersonville and other Southern prisons had wrenched from Secretary of War Stanton the outraged charge that "the enormity of the crime committed by the rebels toward our prisoners . . . cannot but fill with horror the civilized world when the facts are fully revealed. There appears to have been a deliberate system of savage and barbarous treatment."

Horrors there were in Southern prisons; yet, too often, a self-righteous war psychosis blinded critics in the North to its own inhuman treatment of prisoners. The president of the U.S. Sanitary Commission visited Camp Douglas near Chicago and found there an "amount of standing water, of unpoliced grounds, of foul sinks, of general disorder, of soil reeking with miasmatic accretions, of rotten bones and emptying of camp kettles . . . [that was] enough to drive a sanitarian mad."

When the exchange cartel failed, a Confederacy unable to feed and clothe adequately its own soldiers was suddenly confronted with huge prisoner surpluses. The fact that the South's own men were being asked to fight on much the same fare as that handed out to Union prisoners failed to mitigate Northern criticism.

Prison life was not without its light moments, as is revealed in these sketches made in 1864 by Samuel Palmer, a Confederate prisoner at Camp Douglas, Illinois. The former soldiers staged the riotous free-for-all above in order to secure hay for bedding. The forlorn fellow at left is scanning an "Expriss List," possibly for news from home or a word on exchange. As a punishment men were sentenced to sit astride a sawhorse, called "Morgan's Mule" after Confederate raider John Hunt Morgan, who terrorized the Midwest in 1863.

CAMP-DOUGLAS SKETCHES "Morgan's MULE"

ALL: COLLECTION OF LT. COL. H. W. WILLIAMS, JR.

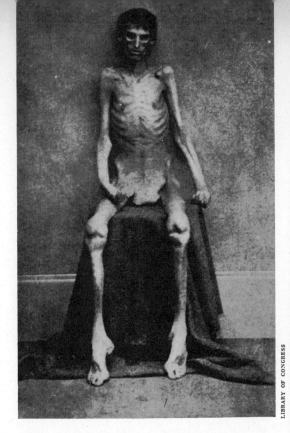

Pictures of Andersonville captives, like that above, horrified the North. General Lew Wallace based his sketch (left) of a prisoner shot trying to get a drink beyond the "dead line" on testimony at the Wirz trial. Below is Volck's drawing of Rebels at Camp Douglas.

Hatred Seeks a Scapegoat

A postwar report issued by the War Department listed 26,436 fatalities among the 220,000 Confederate prisoners held in the North, and 22,576 deaths among the 126,950 Union captives in the South. These figures, showing a higher ratio of deaths in Rebel prisons, did much to confirm, in the public mind, stories of Confederate atrocities.

Henry Wirz, the hapless Swiss immigrant who served as stockade commander at Andersonville, became the victim of postwar hysteria. Tried and convicted on a charge of conspiracy to impair the health and destroy the lives of prisoners, Wirz went to the scaffold on November 10, 1865, protesting his innocence. Forty years later a group of Confederate sympathizers erected a monument to his memory—overlooking the 12,884 Union graves at Andersonville.

William Waud's 1865 sketch above shows repatriated Union captives throwing their filthy prison rags off the transport bearing them North. In the 1864 photograph below, released Iowa prisoners pose disconsolately in a New Orleans yard after a ten-month imprisonment.

Volunteers Were the Nucleus of
Union and Confederate Armies

Whatever Northern lithographers may have lacked, it was not imagination. In 1862 some creative soul conjured up this nattily attired host of confident Yankee Doodles marching down the road to Dixie, as his contribution to the Union's recruiting drive.

So impatient did I become for starting," an Arkansas volunteer wrote in 1861, "that I felt like ten thousand pins were pricking me in every part of the body, and started off a week in advance of my brothers." His enthusiasm was typical of that felt by young men on both sides.

Although the North was fighting, for one thing, to assert national supremacy over states' rights, the recruiting and outfitting of volunteer regiments was, paradoxically, left entirely to local authorities. The result was an amateur army possessed of a dash and *élan* which would fade only as the war dragged on agonizingly.

For its part, the Confederacy authorized Jefferson Davis, in the first year of war, to accept only troops offered by state governors. This seemed to satisfy Davis, who declared in April of 1861 that "the gravity of age and the zeal of youth rival each other in the desire to be foremost for the public defense." By the end of the year, however, enlistments were falling off; and in January, 1862, the Confederate Congress issued a call for troops. Then, three months later, a more serious step was taken with the passage of the first conscription act in American history.

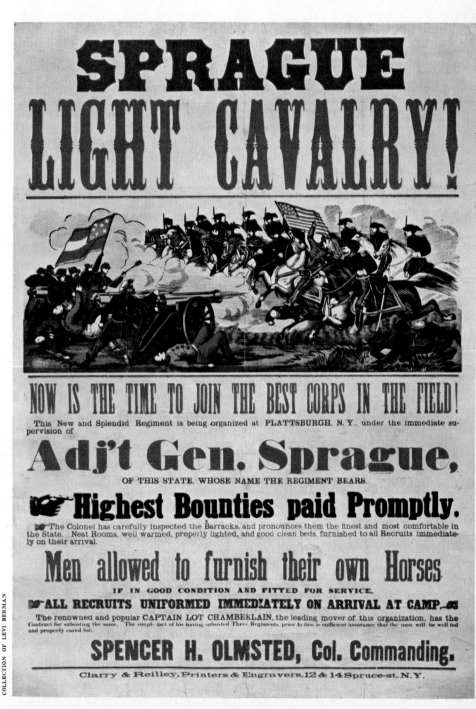

The man responding to this appeal could take his own horse along, and welcome.

MULLIGAN'S BRIGADE!

LAST CHANCE TO AVOID THE DRAFT!

$402 BOUNTY!

TO VETERANS!

$302 to all other VOLUNTEERS!

All Able-bodied Men, between the ages of 18 and 45 Years, who have heretofore served not less than nine months, who shall re-enlist for Regiments in the field, will be deemed Veterans, and will receive one month's pay in advance, and a bounty and premium of $402. To all other recruits, one month's pay in advance, and a bounty and premium of $302 will be paid.

All who wish to join Mulligan's Irish Brigade, now in the field, and to receive the munificent bounties offered by the Government, can have the opportunity by calling at the headquarters of

CAPT. J. J. FITZGERALD

Of the Irish Brigade, 23d Regiment Illinois Volunteers. Recruiting Officer. Chicago. Illinois.

Each Recruit, Veteran or otherwise, will receive

Seventy-five Dollars Before Leaving General Rendezvous,

and the remainder of the bounty in regular instalments till all is paid. The pay, bounty and premium for three years will average $24 per month, for Veterans; and $21.30 per month for all others.

If the Government shall not require these troops for the full period of Three Years, and they shall be mustered hono[r] out of the service before the expiration of their term of enlistment, they shall receive. UPON BEING MUSTERED O[UT] the whole amount of BOUNTY remaining unpaid, the same as if the full term [had] been served.

J. J. FITZGERALD.

Chicago, December, 1863.

Recruiting Officer, corner North Clark & Kenzie Stre[et]

A Lengthening War Requires
New Recruiting Measures

In the 1862 Congressional elections the people of the North, disgusted with the protracted war, gave the Republicans a severe political setback. The days of spontaneous, uncritical response to war demands had passed. The following March 3 a lame-duck Congress passed a conscription act making all men aged twenty to forty-five liable to military service, but exempting those who paid $300 or provided a substitute. "The blood of a poor man is as precious as that of the wealthy," one resentful Northerner complained.

A year earlier, on April 16, 1862, the Southern Congress had passed its conscription act, applicable to all men between eighteen and thirty-five. Exemptions claimed for physical disability were legion. "Rheumatism which was once dreaded as a torturing fiend," wrote a Southern satirist, "has become as popular as a beautiful coquet, tormenting and yet enchanting her spellbound victims." Gradually the scale of exemptions was pared down; age limits were extended; and, in March, 1865 —when it was too late—Negro slaves were authorized for active military service in Confederate ranks.

Through 1862 a steady clamor was growing in the North for the use of Negro troops; from the outset the South had employed Negroes as laborers and servants in its armies. For some time Lincoln ignored abolitionist pleas and vetoed the use of Negro soldiers by his field commanders. Not until he issued his Emancipation Proclamation in January, 1863, did the President call for the enlistment of Negro regiments.

SUBSTITUTE NOTICES.

Abuses forced the Confederacy to outlaw the hiring of substitutes in December, 1863. Prior to that, notices such as the one above from the Richmond Dispatch *appeared frequently. Negroes in the Union army served under volunteer white officers, as shown in the lithographed recruiting poster at left.*

The poster at left offered tangible inducements to volunteers.

509

THE VOLUNTARY MANNER IN WHICH SOME OF THE SOUTHERN VOLUNTEERS ENLIST.

The cartoon above mocks the Southern volunteer system, with an added dig (at bottom right) at the Rebel navy. Below is Volck's comment on the Northern substitute broker, offering the timid man at right his pick of derelicts.

Violent Reaction
to the Draft

These two Leslie's *engravings reveal the fury of the New York draft riots. The mob soon turned to looting and pillaging (above), and troops at last had to fire on them (below).*

Names drawn in New York's first draft were published in the Sunday papers on July 12, 1863. That afternoon protesting groups began forming in the city, and by Monday morning the mob had grown to 50,000. The poor were infuriated by the rich man's exemption and bitter over social injustices, aggravated by wartime hardships. In their anger they turned against all symbols of authority and even attacked helpless Negroes, whom they held responsible for the war. For four days violence ruled the city, until troops returning from Gettysburg were brought in to quell the riot.

In the four national draft calls of 1863–64, 776,829 names were drawn. Of these, amazingly few draftees— 46,347—were held for military service. It was still a volunteer's fight.

The President
Begins to Question His Chances
of Re-election

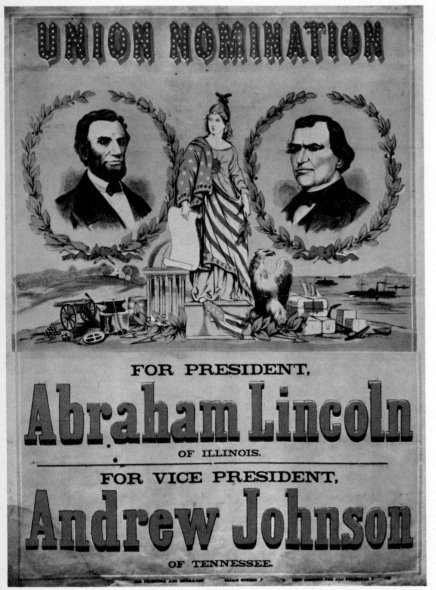

In the cartoon above, McClellan appears as Hamlet, holding the skull of Lincoln. "I knew him, Horatio; a fellow of infinite jest . . . where be your gibes now?" The President's earthy humor was often mistaken for shallowness.

The pro-Lincoln lithograph at right contrasts a dignified President on his platform, supported by the military, with an insecure McClellan toppling from a precarious perch on a cake of cheese.

The Lincoln-Johnson campaign poster at left offers the candidates with the simple declaration of a "Union Nomination." The lapel pin below was designed to be worn by Lincoln supporters.

Senator Samuel C. Pomeroy of Kansas issued, in February, 1864, a confidential letter designed to prevent Lincoln's renomination and promote the candidacy of Salmon P. Chase, the Secretary of the Treasury. "Even were the re-election of Mr. Lincoln desirable," the Pomeroy circular read, "it is practically impossible against the union of influences which will oppose him." Publication of the document, however, jolted the vain, ambitious Chase right out of the driver's seat of his own bandwagon, and that summer he was eased out of the cabinet. Quietly, Lincoln went about the business of securing the nomination.

On June 8, 1864, a coalition of Republicans and War Democrats unanimously renominated Lincoln on the first ballot, and Andrew Johnson, Tennessee's fiercely loyal Democratic governor, was selected as his running mate.

The following August the Democrats countered by nominating General George B. McClellan for President. Clement Vallandigham, now returned from exile, and his fellow Copperheads forced the adoption of a platform which stated that "justice, humanity, liberty, and the public welfare demand that immediate efforts be made for a cessation of hostilities . . ." The still popular McClellan accepted the nomination but maintained a discreet silence on the platform; and Lincoln began to fear for his chances of re-election.

Lincoln penned the gloomy forecast above and asked his cabinet to endorse it without seeing the contents.

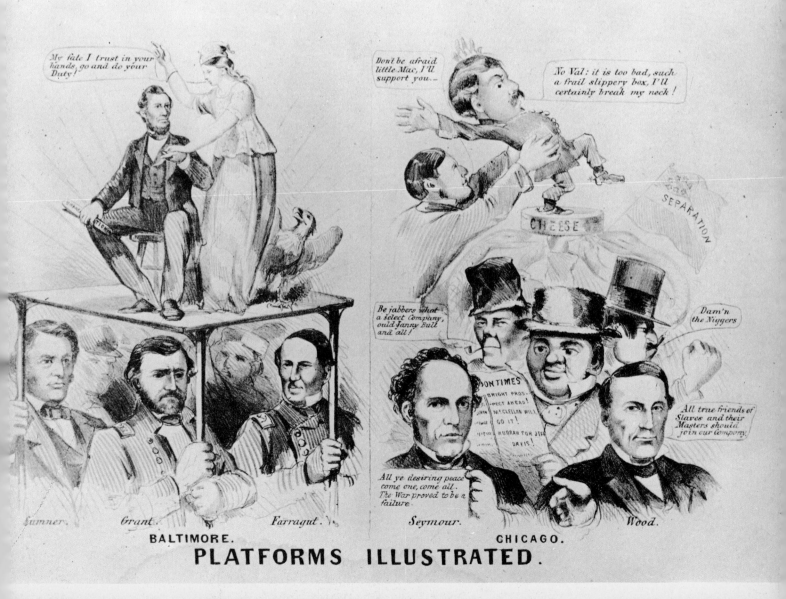

BALTIMORE.   CHICAGO.

PLATFORMS ILLUSTRATED.

TOTAL WARFARE

IN THE early summer of 1864 General Joseph E. Johnston understood the military situation very clearly. Sherman had driven him from the Tennessee border to the edge of Atlanta, and in Richmond this looked like the equivalent of a Confederate disaster; but to Johnston it looked very different. Sherman had done a great deal, but he had neither routed Johnston's army nor taken Atlanta, and until he did at least one of these things the Northern public would consider his campaign a failure. Feeling so, it might very well beat Lincoln at the polls—and this, as things stood in the fourth year of the war, represented the Confederacy's last and best hope for victory. As Johnston appraised things, his cue was to play a waiting game; stall for time, avert a showdown at all costs, let Sherman dangle ineffectually at the end of that long, tenuous supply line, and count on Northern depression and weariness to turn the tide.

But Davis saw it otherwise, and Davis had the final responsibility. He was a man beset by rising shadows, and as he struggled gallantly to keep life in a dying cause, refusing to recognize the omens of doom, he looked about him with the eyes of a soldier rather than with the eyes of a politician. What might happen in the November elections was a politician's con-

cern; to Davis the victories that would save the Confederacy must be won in the field, and they would never be won unless the Confederate armies turned and fought the invader until the invader had had enough. So Davis relieved Johnston of his command and put General John Bell Hood in his place. Doing so, he made one of the fateful decisions of the war.

Hood was a combat soldier of proved effectiveness. He had commanded a brigade and then a division in Lee's army, fighting with great dash and valor; had been badly wounded in the arm at Gettysburg, had recovered in time to fight at Chickamauga, and there had lost a leg. Patched up, and riding strapped to his saddle, he had been given corps command under Johnston, and he had been bitterly critical of Johnston's series of feints and retreats. He understood stand-up fighting, and now Davis wanted a stand-up fighter and gave Hood Johnston's job. Unfortunately, Hood was suited for subordinate command but not for the top job. The transfer worked to Sherman's immense advantage.

Hood was aware that he had been put in charge of the army to fight, and he lost no time in getting at it. Sherman had crossed the Chattahoochee River and was moving so as to come down on Atlanta from the north and east. Atlanta was ringed with earthworks, and Sherman had no intention of attacking these. He hoped to cut the four railroad lines that converged on the city and thus compel the Confederates either to retreat or to come out and make a stand-up fight in the open. Moving out to attack, Hood was doing just what Sherman wanted.

Hood was not being stupid, for Sherman had in fact incautiously left an opening. McPherson, with Schofield and rather less than half of the Federal troops, had moved to a point on the Georgia Railroad, east of the city, and was marching in, tearing up the railroad as he advanced. Thomas, with the rest of the army, was crossing Peachtree Creek, and there was a gap of several miles between his forces and the men of McPherson and Schofield; and on July 20 Hood attacked Thomas savagely, hoping to destroy him before Sherman could reunite his forces.

Hood's troops attacked with spirit, but there never was a better defensive fighter than George Thomas, and his troops were as good as their general. Hood's attack was beaten off, the Confederates had substantial losses, and Thomas' army was able to re-establish contact with McPherson and Schofield.

Two days later Hood struck again. This time he swung east, seeking to hit McPherson in the flank the way Jackson had hit Hooker at Chancellorsville. The fight that resulted, known as the Battle of Atlanta, was desperate, and it came fairly close to success. McPherson himself was killed, and for a time part of his army was being assailed from front and rear simultaneously. But the Unionists rallied at last, the Confederate assaults failed, and Hood pulled his men back inside the fortified lines. The two battles together had cost him upward of 13,000 men, and Sherman now was pinning him in his earthworks. The railroads that came to Atlanta from the north and east had been cut, and Sherman began to swing ponderously around by his right, hoping to reach the Macon and Western that ran southwest from Atlanta. Once more Hood came out to attack him, and there was a hard fight at Ezra Church west of the city; once again the Confederates were repulsed, with losses heavier than they could afford, and Sherman was a long step nearer the capture of Atlanta.

It was Atlanta that he wanted, now. He had started out to destroy the Confederate army in his front, and this he had never been able to do; since Hood replaced Johnston that army had been badly mangled, but it still existed as an effective fighting force, and Sherman had been changing his objective. If he could get the

city, the campaign would be a success, even though it would not be the final, conclusive success he had hoped to win. Hood alone could not keep him out of Atlanta indefinitely; Sherman had more than a two-to-one advantage in numbers now, and he could reach farther and farther around the city, snipping the railroad connections and compelling the defenders at last to evacuate. Sherman's chief worry now was his own rear—the railroad that went back to Chattanooga, down the Tennessee Valley to Bridgeport, and up through Nashville to Kentucky. There was in the Confederacy one man who might operate on that line so effectively that Sherman would have to retreat— Bedford Forrest—and as the siege of Atlanta began, Sherman's great concern was to put Forrest out of action.

Unfortunately for Sherman, all attempts to do this ended in ignominious defeat; the Federal army, apparently, contained no subordinate general capable of handling this self-taught soldier. Early in June, Sherman sent a strong cavalry column under Major General Samuel D. Sturgis down into Mississippi from Memphis, in the hope that Forrest could be forced into a losing battle. It did not work out as he hoped. Forrest met Sturgis, who had twice his strength, at Brice's Crossroads, Mississippi, on June 10, and gave him one of the classic beatings of the Civil War. Sturgis drew off in disgrace, and Sherman had to make another effort.

He made it in July. With his own army nearing Atlanta, Sherman ordered a powerful expedition under Major General A. J. Smith to move down from Memphis into Mississippi to keep Forrest busy. Top Confederate commander in that area was General Stephen D. Lee, and he and Forrest with a mixed force ran into Smith's expedition near the town of Tupelo. There was a brisk fight in which Forrest was wounded and the Confederates were driven off, a clear tactical victory for the Unionists; but Smith did not like the looks of things, and he beat a hasty retreat to Memphis, his withdrawal badly harassed by Forrest's cavalry. In August he was sent out to try again; and this time Forrest slipped past him and rode into Memphis itself—he was traveling in a buggy just now, his wounded foot propped up on a special rack, but he could still move faster and more elusively than any other cavalry commander. He could not stay in Memphis more than a moment, and he did no especial harm there, but he did force the authorities to recall Smith's expedition. The moral apparently was that no one could invade the interior of Mississippi as long as Forrest was around.

Brilliant as Forrest's tactics had been, however, the Federal moves had done what Sherman wanted done; that is, they had kept Forrest so busy in the deep South that he had not been able to get into Tennessee and strike the sort of blow against Sherman's long supply line that would have pulled Sherman back from Atlanta. With Forrest otherwise engaged, Hood could not hold the place forever. On August 25 Sherman broke off his intermittent bombardment of the Confederate lines and began another circling movement to the southwest and south of the city. Hood's efforts to drive the advancing columns back failed, and it was clear now that Atlanta was going to fall. Hood got his army out smartly, and on September 2 the Federals occupied the city.

Here was a victory which the administration could toss into the teeth of the Democrats who were basing their Presidential campaign on the assertion that the war was a failure. (The fact that this was not the kind of victory Sherman and Grant had hoped for in the spring was irrelevant; the fragmentation of the Confederacy was visibly progressing, and the capture of Atlanta was something to crow about.) The victory came on the heels of another one, at Mobile Bay, where tough old Admiral Farragut on August 5 had hammered his way past the defending forts and, after a hard fight, had taken the ironclad ram *Tennessee*. This victory effectively closed the port of Mobile, and although that city itself would hold out for months to come, it would receive and dispatch no more blockade-runners. One more Confederate gate to the outer world had been nailed shut, and there had been a spectacular quality to Farragut's victory that took men's imaginations. He had steamed in through a Confederate mine field (they called mines "torpedoes" in those days) and one of his monitors had run on one of the mines and had been lost, whereat the rest of the battle line hesitated and fell into confusion; but Farragut bulled his way in, and his "Damn the torpedoes—full speed ahead!" was a battle cry that stuck in the public's mind as if robust confidence in ultimate victory had been reborn.

Not long after this a third Federal triumph was recorded, and Northern spirits rose still higher.

Jubal Early had led his diminutive Confederate army to the very suburbs of Washington, but he had not been able to force his way in or to stay where he was, and he had retreated to the upper end of the Shenandoah Valley. The War Department had assembled troops to drive him away, but although Early was very badly outnumbered—he had about 15,000 men with him, and the Federals mustered three army corps and a good body of cavalry, 45,000 men or more—everybody was being very cautious, and Grant in front of Petersburg found it impossible to get aggressive action by remote control. He finally put Phil Sheridan in charge of the operation, went to the scene himself long enough to make sure that Sheridan understood what he was supposed to do, and returned to Petersburg to await results.

Sheridan was supposed to do two things—beat Early and take the Shenandoah Valley out of the war. This valley, running southwest from the Potomac behind the shield of the Blue Ridge, had been of great strategic value to the Confederacy ever since Stonewall Jackson had demonstrated its possibilities. A Confederate army moving down the Valley was heading straight for the Northern heartland, threatening both the capital and such cities as Philadelphia and Baltimore, to say nothing of the North's east-west railway connections; but a Northern army moving up the Valley was heading nowhere in particular, since the Valley went off into mountain country and led the invader far away from Richmond. The Valley was immensely fertile, producing meat and grain that were of great importance to Lee's army defending Richmond, and a Confederate army operating in the lower Valley could supply itself with food and forage from the Valley itself. All in all, a Federal army trying to take Richmond could never be entirely secure until the Confederates were deprived of all use of the Shenandoah Valley, and it was up to Sheridan to deprive them of it.

Grant's instructions were grimly specific. He wanted the rich farmlands of the Valley despoiled so thoroughly that the place could no longer support a Confederate army; he told Sheridan to devastate the whole area so thoroughly that a crow flying across over the Valley would have to carry its own rations. This work Sheridan set out to do.

And now, in September of 1864, total war began to be waged in full earnest. Grant and Sheridan were striking directly at the Southern economy, and what happened to Early's army was more or less incidental; barns and corncribs and gristmills and herds of cattle were military objectives now, and if thousands of civilians whose property this was had to suffer heartbreaking loss as a result, that also was incidental. A garden spot was to be turned into a desert in order that the Southern nation might be destroyed.

Sheridan began cautiously. Early was a hard hitter, and although his army was small, it was lean and sinewy, composed of veterans—altogether, an outfit to be treated with much respect. Sheridan did not really make his move until September, and on the nineteenth of that month he fought Early near the town of Winchester, Virginia. The battle began before half of Sheridan's army had reached the scene, and the morning hours saw a Union repulse, but by midafternoon Sheridan had all of his men in hand, and Early was badly beaten and compelled to retreat. Sheridan pursued, winning another battle at Fisher's Hill three days later, and Early continued on up the Valley while Sheridan's men got on with the job of devastation Grant had ordered.

Few campaigns in the war aroused more bitterness than this one. The Union troopers carried out their orders with a heavy hand, and as they did so they were plagued by the attacks of bands of Confederate guerrillas—irregular fighters who were of small account in a pitched battle, but who raided outposts, burned Yankee wagon trains, shot sentries and couriers, and compelled Sheridan to use a sizable percentage of his force for simple guard duty. The Federal soldiers considered the guerrillas no better than highwaymen, and when they captured any of them they usually hanged them. The guerrillas hanged Yankees in return, naturally enough; and from all of this there was a deep scar, burned into the American memory, as the romanticized "war between brothers" took on an ugly phase.

Guerrilla warfare tended to get out of hand. Most bands were semi-independent, and in some areas they did the Confederacy harm by draining able-bodied men away from the regular fighting forces and by stimulating the Federals to vicious reprisals. Best of the guerrilla leaders was Colonel John S. Mosby, who harassed Sheridan's supply lines so effectively that substantial numbers of Sheridan's troops had to be kept on duty patrolling roads back of the front, but most partisan leaders were far below Mosby's stature. In Missouri guerrilla warfare was especially rough; neighborhood feuds got all mixed in with the business of fighting the Yankees, and the notorious W. C. Quantrill, whose desperadoes sacked Lawrence, Kansas, in 1863, killing about 150 citizens, often looked more like an outlaw than a soldier.

The middle of October found Sheridan's army encamped near Cedar Creek, twenty miles south of Winchester. Early was not far away, but he had been beaten twice and it seemed unlikely that he retained any aggressive intentions, and Sheridan left the army briefly to visit Washington. At dawn on the morning of October 19, just as Sheridan was preparing to leave Winchester and return to camp, Early launched a sudden attack that took the Union army completely by surprise, broke it, and drove various fragments down the road in a highly disordered retreat. Sheridan met these fragments as he was riding back to camp, hauled them back into formation, got them to the battle front, put them in line with the soldiers who had not run away, and late in the afternoon made a furious counterattack which was overwhelmingly successful. Early was driven off, his army too badly manhandled to be a substantial menace any longer, and it was plain to all men that the Confederacy would never again threaten the North by way of the Shenandoah Valley.

This victory aroused much enthusiasm. Like Farragut's fight, it was intensely dramatic; men made a legend out of Sheridan's ride from Winchester and about the way his rallied troops broke the Confederate line, and a catchy little ballad describing the business went all across the North. Coming on the heels of Mobile Bay and Atlanta, Sheridan's conquest was a tonic that checked war weariness and created a new spirit of optimism. No longer could the Democrats make an effective campaign on the argument that the war was a failure. The war was visibly being won, and although the price remained high it was obvious that the last crisis had been passed. Sherman, Farragut, and Sheridan were winning Lincoln's election for him.

Which is to say that they were winning it in part. The victory which Lincoln was to gain when the nation cast its ballots in November was fundamentally of his own making. In his conduct of the war he had made many mistakes, especially in his handling of military matters in the first two years. He had seemed, at times, to be more politician than statesman, he had been bitterly criticized both for moving too fast on the slavery question and for not moving fast enough, and there had always been sincere patriots to complain that he had lacked drive and firmness in his leadership. But he had gained and kept, somehow, the confidence of the average citizen of the North. If his leadership had at times been tentative, almost fumbling, it had firmly taken the mass of the people in the direction they themselves deeply wanted. The determination and the flexible but unbreakable will that kept on waging war in the face of all manner of reverses had been his. The military victories won in the late summer and early fall of 1864 did reverse an unfavorable political current, but in the last analysis it was a majority belief in Lincoln himself that carried the day.

While these triumphs were being won, Grant's army was still dug in at Petersburg. It had had a fearful campaign. Coming to grips with Lee's army in the first week of May, it had remained in daily contact with its foes (except for the two-day interlude provided by the shift from Cold Harbor to Petersburg) for more than five months. It had fought the hardest, longest, costliest battles ever seen on the American continent, and its casualties had been so heavy that it was not really the same army it had been in the spring; most of the veterans were gone now, and some of the most famous fighting units had ceased to exist, and in all of this wearing fighting there had been nothing that could be pointed to as a clear-cut victory. The Army of the Potomac had won no glory, and it had been chewed up almost beyond recognition. It had done just one thing, but that one thing was essential to the final Union triumph: it had compelled Lee to stay in the immediate vicinity of Richmond and fight a consuming defensive fight which he could not win.

For the Army of Northern Virginia, doggedly barring the way to Richmond, had paid a price in this campaign too. It had been worn down hard, and if its losses were not nearly as heavy as the losses which it had inflicted, its numbers had never been as great, and the capacity to recuperate quickly from a hard bloodletting was gone. In all previous campaigns in Virginia this army, under Lee's direction, had been able to make a hard counterblow that robbed the Federals of the initiative and restored the offensive to the Confederacy. That had not happened in the 1864 campaign, partly because Grant had crowded Lee too hard, but even more because the Army of Northern Virginia was not quite the instrument it had been. The razor-sharp edge was gone. The army was still unconquerable on the defensive, and it was still knocking back offensive thrusts made by its rival, but it was no longer up to the kind of thing that had made Second Bull Run and Chancellorsville such triumphs.

In plain words, these two armies had worn each other out. The significance of this was the fact that the really decisive campaigns—the campaigns which would determine the outcome of the war—would therefore be made far to the south and west, where the Confederacy operated at a ruinous disadvantage. A stalemate in Virginia meant victory for the North. Only when the Army of Northern Virginia had the room and the strength to maneuver as of old could the nation which it carried on its shoulders hope to survive. Crippled and driven into a corner, it could do no more than protect the capital while the overwhelming weight of other Federal armies crushed the life out of the Confederacy.

Lincoln's re-election was the clincher. It meant that the pressure would never be relaxed; that Grant would be sustained in his application of a strategy that was as expensive as it was remorseless, and that no loss of spirit back home would cancel out what the armies in the field were winning. It should be pointed out that the Federal government used every political trick at its command to win the election; many soldiers were permitted to cast their ballots in camp, and where this was not possible, whole regiments were furloughed so that the men could go home and vote. However, Lincoln would have won even without the soldier vote. He got 2,203,831 votes to McClellan's 1,797,019, winning 212 electoral votes to 21 for his rival. In some states, notably New York, the winning margin was painfully narrow, and the fact that McClellan could get as much as 45 per cent of the total vote indicates that a surprisingly large number in the North were not happy about the course of events since March 4, 1861. However, 45 per cent remains a losing minority. By a substantial majority the people of the North had told Lincoln to carry the war on to a victorious conclusion. After November, triumph for the Union could only be a question of time.

That Devil Forrest

Major General Nathan Bedford Forrest

"Forrest is the very devil," Sherman wrote in June, 1864, and resolved to hound him "to the death, if it cost 10,000 lives and break the Treasury. There will never be peace in Tennessee till Forrest is dead."

Nathan Bedford Forrest, a rough, unlettered slave trader from Memphis, enlisted as a Confederate private in 1861; by December, 1863, he had risen to the rank of major general. Forrest brought a totally new concept to cavalry warfare. After Shiloh he began employing cavalry as mounted foot soldiers—using horses to give his men maximum mobility, to close in on the enemy for surprise attacks. His dogged pursuit wore out opponents, and when the foe was cornered, Forrest would demand surrender under the threat of total annihilation. When the Union commander at Fort Pillow on the Mississippi refused to capitulate in April, 1864, Forrest unleashed his men and later reported with glee that "The river was dyed with the blood of the slaughtered for two hundred yards." This brought charges in the North of a Rebel massacre, particularly of the Negro troops involved.

Forrest's supreme moment of glory came on June 10, 1864, at a heavily wooded intersection of two roads in northwestern Mississippi. Sherman, moving toward Atlanta and plainly worried about his tenuous supply lines, had sent Major General S. D. Sturgis south from Memphis to block a threatened Forrest raid into Tennessee. The two columns clashed at Brice's Crossroads, where Forrest's 3,300 dismounted troopers threw back Sturgis' 8,000-man force. The day-long fight was later described by a Tennessee participant as being "So close that guns once fired were not reloaded, but used as clubs . . . while the two lines struggled with the ferocity of wild beasts." Sturgis was badly beaten, and as Grant wrote years later, this "left Forrest free to go almost where he pleased . . ."

The Union advance—and retreat—at Brice's Crossroads
was over Tishomingo Creek, photographed above on
just such a breathless June day as that on which the battle was fought. The Federal retreat became a rout when
a traffic jam developed on a bridge across the creek.
At right is weedy, overgrown Bethany Cemetery, a
no man's land between the lines during the fighting.

In the map below, the Union advance from Memphis is
shown as a black arrow. Beyond Bethany Church, Federal cavalry met the Rebel advance guard and fell back to
form a defensive line around the crossroads. As Northern infantry reached this perimeter Forrest divided his
smaller force to execute a spectacular double envelopment that sent the enemy scrambling back to Ripley.

BOTH: BERN KEATING, BLACK STAR

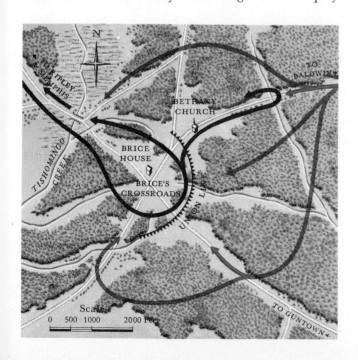

Hood
Takes the Offensive
at Atlanta

These pictures of the Rebel lines defending Atlanta are by George Barnard. Two frame houses below have been stripped to provide lumber for the fortifications.

Hood's appointment to command at Atlanta was in effect an order to take the offensive, and on July 20, after a careful look at Sherman's troop deployments, he concluded that it was time to strike.

The Georgia Railroad ran northeast from the city through Decatur. To prevent the Confederate government from reinforcing Hood with troops from Lee's army via this line, Grant told Sherman to put it out of commission. As Schofield and McPherson wheeled eastward toward Decatur to attend to this task, Thomas crossed Peachtree Creek, north of Atlanta. Incautiously, Sherman had left a gap between the two parts of his army; Hood spotted it, and immediately moved to attack Thomas.

Although Hood was not quite fast enough to catch Thomas crossing the creek, he nevertheless hit him hard, and the Yankee line sagged. Then the redoubtable Thomas brought up his guns and bloodily repulsed the Rebels.

Hood withdrew into the imposing Atlanta fieldworks. His cavalry brought word that McPherson's Army of the Tennessee—Sherman's old command—was exposed invitingly on the Federal left, and Hood decided to seize this second opportunity. About midnight on July 21 he pulled William Hardee's corps out of line and sent it on a long flanking march to come in behind McPherson. When Hardee's attack was well underway, Cheatham's corps would move out of the Atlanta lines, and between them they would roll up the Union left.

On the morning of July 22 Sherman supposed that Hood had evacuated the city, but soon the crash of musketry and the boom of artillery from his left wing warned him that the real battle for Atlanta had begun.

A grim Sherman was photographed (above) at Atlanta. The map shows Hood's July 20 thrust at Peachtree Creek and his flank attack two days later, known as the Battle of Atlanta.

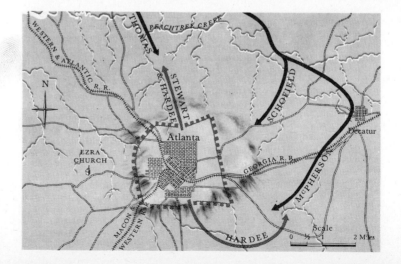

The Battle of Atlanta

These sections of the Atlanta Cyclorama show Cheatham's breakthrough in the Federal center. Above, Rebels defend captured Union trenches in the woods. The Georgia Railroad (right) leads into Atlanta. Below, Confederates overrun a battery by the brick house (at right of the railroad above) and, behind cotton bales, meet a counterattack. Union battery horses (center) are killed so the Rebels cannot remove the captured guns.

Hood's flank attack might well have repeated Jackson's success at Chancellorsville (on which it was modeled) had it not been for the unexpected presence of the XVI Corps under Grenville Dodge. Dodge's men were standing under arms in McPherson's left rear, awaiting orders, when Hardee's Confederates charged.

The surprise was mutual. The Yankees were pushed back slowly—"So persistent were [the Rebel] onslaughts," a Northern officer recalled, "that numbers were made prisoners by rushing directly into our lines" —but the stiff Union resistance took the steam out of Hardee's attack.

Cheatham's thrust from the Atlanta lines got off to a late start, but it met with temporary success. A hole was punched in the Union center, and the Federals of Dodge, Frank Blair, and "Black Jack" Logan had to fight on two fronts.

The Fall of Atlanta

The Battle of Atlanta put Sherman's faith in his pet Army of the Tennessee to a stern test, for he refused to reinforce it. He wanted the Army of the Cumberland free to move on Atlanta, but Thomas was too cautious and missed his chance.

McPherson, the most promising of Sherman's generals, was killed early in the fighting, and Sherman wept unashamedly when the body was brought to him. Yet the Yankees held on, sometimes rolling from one side of their earthworks to the other to halt consecutive charges from front and rear. At dark, Hood broke off the action, his flank attack a failure.

Sherman now gripped the city from north and east, and he pulled out the Army of the Tennessee, marched it behind his lines, and had it sweep in on Atlanta from the west. On July 28 Hood attacked at Ezra Church, and again was repulsed. The hardfisted XV Corps had beaten off twelve Rebel assault waves in a week.

Atlanta was now invested on three sides and its fall was inevitable. On September 2 Hood's army retreated southward, and Sherman wired Lincoln, "Atlanta is ours, and fairly won." The Richmond *Examiner* clearly foresaw the impact of the capture, which came, the paper said, "in the very nick of time when a victory alone could save the party of Lincoln."

Sherman was now less interested in Hood's army than in destroying Georgia's will and capacity for war. His first step was to order the citizens of Atlanta to evacuate their homes. "In the name of God and humanity, I protest," Hood wrote him, but Sherman was adamant. "You might as well appeal against the thunderstorm," he told Atlantans, "as against these terrible hardships of war."

The last train from Atlanta, piled high with refugees and their belongings, was photographed (above) by Barnard. At right is Atlanta after Sherman's departure; his men gutted a bank but left intact a bar and billiard parlor.

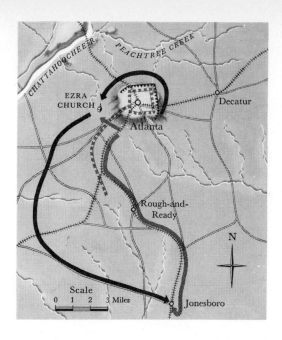

Sherman's investment of Atlanta is shown above in black. The map indicates the Battle of Ezra Church and Hood's evacuation of the city. At left is Major General James B. McPherson, killed in the Battle of Atlanta.

Sherman's march to the sea, as painted by primitive artist A. B. Carlin; Sherman is riding the dark horse at left center.

The March to the Sea Begins

Bedford Forrest was loose in Tennessee, and with Atlanta secured, Sherman dispatched Thomas to Nashville to restore order. Then Hood, too, threatened his vulnerable supply line, and for over a month he sparred with him north of Atlanta.

Then Sherman changed his tactics. "Damn him," he said of Hood, "if he will go to the Ohio River, I'll give him rations . . . my business is down South." Schofield and two corps would reinforce Thomas; and Sherman, with 62,000 men, would march eastward, "smashing things to the sea."

When Washington approved his plans, Sherman cut his communications, burned a good part of Atlanta, and, on November 15, 1864, began his march to the sea. "I can make . . . Georgia howl!" he promised.

Guerrilla Warfare

As the great armies advanced and retreated, blighting the landscape and leaving hate and bitterness behind, guerrilla bands sprang up in their wake to ravage further those areas on the fringe of the war.

In a few instances these bands served a legitimate function, harassing enemy communications and supply lines. But in the majority of cases there was little justification for their depredations, their indiscriminate robbery and murder, which were little short of organized outlawry. As often as not victims of the guerrilla bands were noncombatants, singled out because of their views on slavery or the Union, or simply because it was rumored that savings were hidden in their mattresses.

In western Virginia and in the Shenandoah Valley, guerrilla outfits roamed almost at will. John Singleton Mosby, the most effective Southern partisan, had a tight hold on the area north of the Rappahannock, and he was one reason that Grant, to protect his supply line, tied his 1864 campaign to the tidewater area.

The Confederate high command, however, generally discouraged partisan warfare, for the bands gave refuge to deserters and were as apt to attack Confederate sympathizers as Union supporters. Rebel cavalryman Thomas Rosser complained, "they roam broadcast over the country, a band of thieves, stealing, pillaging, plundering . . . an injury to the cause," and Lee stated flatly, "I regard the whole system as an unmixed evil."

Albert Bierstadt titled his 1862 canvas of Yankee troops firing from ambush at a band of Southern irregulars, "Guerrilla Warfare, Civil War."

531

The War West of the Mississippi

Sterling Price's Confederate raiders march through Kansas, herding captured militiamen. Artist Samuel J. Reader was one of the prisoners, but soon escaped. He also painted the picture at the right.

Senator James H. Lane of Kansas.

The most virulent brand of partisan warfare raged beyond the Mississippi, in Kansas, Missouri, and Arkansas. With a head start in civil strife dating from the 1850's, this area lived under a rule of terror during most of the Civil War.

Kansas Senator James H. Lane, a "lean, haggard, and sinewy figure," led Unionist troops in sacking and burning pro-Confederate settlements. In the Ozarks, Southern sympathizers hanged men "with no charge against them except that they had been feeding Union men."

The most murderous villain of all, however, was William C. Quantrill, whose followers included Bill Anderson, who tied the scalps of his victims to his horse's bridle, and a pair of infamous outlaws who learned their trade under Quantrill, Jesse James and Cole Younger.

On August 21, 1863, Quantrill and 450 of his bushwhackers raided Lawrence, Kansas, butchering some 150 unarmed citizens. "The whole business part of the town, except two stores, was in ashes," wrote a survivor. "The bodies of dead men . . . were laying in all directions." In October Quantrill committed another massacre at Baxter Springs, Kansas. Not until May, 1865, in Kentucky, was he caught and killed.

In the fall of 1864 the Confederacy made its last offensive thrust west of the Mississippi. Sterling Price and 12,000 troopers rode into Missouri, threatening St. Louis, Jefferson City, and Kansas City. On October 23 Samuel Curtis—the victor at Pea Ridge back in 1862—met Price near Westport, Missouri. With help from Alfred Pleasonton's cavalry, Curtis whipped the Rebels, drove them into Arkansas, and virtually ended the war in the trans-Mississippi West.

Above, the Federals fight a delaying action near the Big Blue River the day before defeating Price at Westport. Below, Union cavalryman Sherman Enderton's drawing of Quantrill's raid on Lawrence.

Another Southern Offensive in the Valley

As part of his grand strategy for 1864, Grant planned to lay waste the Shenandoah Valley, that rich granary upon which Lee was so dependent for food for his army. The Valley's summer harvest was vital to the South, for rations were running short; in April Lee wrote Davis, "I cannot see how we can operate with our present supplies."

At first Grant's plans were frustrated by the inept Union generals assigned to that region. Franz Sigel and David Hunter were carrying on the tradition of bungling set in the past by Patterson, Frémont, Banks, and Milroy.

Sigel had advanced up the Valley as far as New Market, where, on May 15, he met a scratch force assembled by John C. Breckinridge, which included the cadet corps of the Virginia Military Institute. Breckinridge attacked and, with the V.M.I. cadets distinguishing themselves, chased Sigel back down the Valley. This little victory assured Lee of the Valley's wheat harvest.

Hunter replaced Sigel and managed to get as far south as Staunton. In June he skirmished with Jubal Early, then beat an ignominious retreat into West Virginia, whereupon Early took the initiative in the Shenandoah. It was the Confederacy's last major offensive in the East.

Above, a golden harvest of wheat in the Shenandoah Valley. Decreeing total war, Grant wanted to "make all the Valley south of the Baltimore and Ohio Railroad a desert . . . all provisions and stock should be removed, and the people notified to get out."

At the Virginia Military Institute, Union Major General David Hunter claimed to have found a proclamation from the governor of Virginia "inciting . . . guerrilla warfare on my troops." On the strength of this he left V.M.I. the gutted ruin shown at left.

535

Partisan Warfare Stirs New Bitterness

Colonel John S. Mosby

Mosby's rangers, officially the 43rd Virginia Cavalry, are shown below returning from an obviously successful raid on a Yankee supply train in the Valley in the fall of 1864. Mosby is on the white horse at right.

The warfare waged in the Shenandoah Valley was poisoned by the activities of guerrillas. In theory, a Union army planted at the southern end of the Valley could effectively prevent the Confederacy from using it as a granary or a highway of invasion; but in practice, Rebel guerrillas, living off the land, could operate in such an army's rear so effectively as to make its position untenable.

John Singleton Mosby's partisans were so successful that a sizable portion of Virginia was known simply as Mosby's Confederacy. Although his rangers had been mustered into the Confederate army, their methods, and the methods used by the Federals to combat them, eventually led to the hanging of prisoners by both sides as reprisals. Thus one outrage bred another, until, in the end, the once-lovely Valley lay in blackened ruin.

By early July, Jubal Early's little army of invasion had raced down the Valley and across the Potomac. After levying tribute on Hagerstown and Frederick, Maryland, Early aimed a quick blow at Washington.

The city's defenses were rugged enough, mounting some 900 cannon, but to man them there was only "a mild-mannered set" of clerks and convalescent soldiers, and official Washington fell into a panic. "The Rebels are upon us," cried Secretary of the Navy Welles, but Grant dispatched the veteran VI Corps to the rescue. On July 12 Early probed the capital's defenses—affording President Lincoln a view of battle while sharpshooters' bullets whined around him —and then pulled back to the Valley.

On July 30 Rebel cavalryman John McCausland laid waste Chambersburg, Pennsylvania, in retaliation for Hunter's depredations in the Valley. Stirred to action, the government put Phil Sheridan in command in the Valley, and on August 7, 1864, Sheridan took over the newly christened Army of the Shenandoah, with orders to destroy both Early and the Shenandoah Valley.

COOK COLLECTION, VALENTINE MUSEUM

Lieutenant General Jubal A. Early

LIBRARY OF CONGRESS

In Charles Reed's sketch above, Early demands a $200,000 levy from the leading citizens of Frederick, Maryland. When Chambersburg, Pennsylvania, could not raise $500,000, two-thirds of the town was leveled (below).

KEAN ARCHIVES

537

Phil Sheridan Devastates the Valley

Above, Sheridan rides through his cheering troops as barns and corncribs blaze in the background. Below, Yankee cavalry seizes a fortified Confederate battery at the Battle of Winchester. Both of these drawings are by Leslie's artist James E. Taylor.

As he shook down his new command, the harsh, unyielding Sheridan methodically devastated the lower Valley. An army chaplain' wrote, "The time had fully come to peel this land." If, in the process, many staunch Unionists were burned out, and even the burners "could not but sympathize with the sufferers," it was now that kind of war.

On September 19 Sheridan attacked Early near Winchester. The assault was bungled and soon stalemated, but Sheridan was a far different soldier from his predecessors. He galloped to the front, waving his hat and shouting to his officers, "Give 'em hell . . . Press them, General, they'll run!" until he had the whole army surging forward irresistibly. The thin gray ranks broke and fled.

Early tried to make a stand at Fisher's Hill three days later, but was routed decisively. The Valley now belonged to Sheridan.

Major General Philip H. Sheridan

Sheridan's Ride

Sheridan pursued Early to the southern end of the Valley before withdrawing, preparatory to joining Grant at Petersburg. As they left, the Federals put the torch to the upper Valley, and a bitter Rebel saw "great columns of smoke which almost shut out the sun by day, and . . . the red glare of bonfires which . . . crackled mockingly in the night air." Sheridan left his army at Cedar Creek, south of Winchester, to attend a strategy conference in Washington.

Refusing to admit defeat, Early had followed the Yankees. When their scorched-earth policy forced him to choose between retreat and attack, he ignored the two-to-one odds and chose the latter.

The Federal left flank at Cedar Creek was protected by a river gorge thought to be impassable. The in-domitable Early, however, sent three divisions on a single-file night march through it. At dawn on October 19 the Confederates demolished the Union left, and with it an entire army corps. By afternoon the Yankees had been shoved back four miles.

Phil Sheridan was on his leisurely way back to Cedar Creek when the news reached him. He spurred through the backwash of defeat, a dramatic figure shouting at stragglers to "Turn back! Turn back! Face the other way!" Soon he had his men back into line and formed for a counterattack, swearing to give Early "the worst licking he ever had!" A blue tide of Yankees simply overwhelmed Early, with cavalry playing havoc among the retreating Rebels. The Confederacy's hold on the Shenandoah Valley was broken for good.

Above, Sheridan, on his fast black, "Rienzi," rallies his soldiers at Cedar Creek. Their response, wrote an officer, was "a wild cheer of recognition."

At left, Rebel Major General Stephen Ramseur is fatally wounded by Sheridan's charging Yankees. Ramseur had just learned of the birth of his first child.

After the Cedar Creek victory Sheridan sent Wesley Merritt's cavalry raiding into Mosby's Confederacy east of the Valley, with the results sketched at right.

E. TAYLOR

541

Lincoln Is Re-elected

William Waud sketched these soldiers voting near the Petersburg lines. The military vote went heavily for Lincoln.

Sherman's capture of Atlanta and Sheridan's triumphs in the Valley vastly brightened the Republicans' prospects, relieving them of the onus of a stalemated war and decreasing the appeal of the Democrats' peace platform. Yet all the cruel old epithets—ape, gorilla, ~~buffoon~~—were hurled at Lincoln by the supporters of General McClellan; and a Democratic whispering campaign had the President singing ribald songs while visiting a battlefield and demanding his salary in gold (soldiers were paid in greenbacks). "It is a little singular," the President noted sadly "that I, who am not a vindictive man, should have always been before the people in canvasses marked for their bitterness . . ."

But the Republicans could also play rough. To fill the party treasury, a 5 per cent levy was placed on the salaries of government employees; the moderate Postmaster General Montgomery Blair was unceremoniously dumped from the cabinet to placate the Radicals and assure the withdrawal of John C. Frémont as a third-party candidate; and the soldier vote was assiduously courted. Republican-controlled state legislatures passed laws allowing soldiers to vote in the field; and efforts were made to furlough others so that they could vote at home. Lincoln himself wrote to Sherman, asking that Indiana boys be released for the crucial election there. When Ohio politicians demanded the suspension of the unpopular draft, Lincoln finally put his foot down: "What is the Presidency worth to me," he asked them, "if I have no country?"

Election day, November 8, 1864, was cold and wet in Washington. A White House visitor found Lincoln alone. Only two cabinet members had appeared for a scheduled meeting; it seemed as if everyone was avoiding the President that day. At 7 P.M. he splashed through the rain to the War Department telegraph office to receive election returns, and learned to his surprise that Philadelphia had given him a 10,000-vote majority; Baltimore, 15,000; New York state, 40,000. As the Republican votes began to pile up Lincoln relaxed and started telling funny stories. At 2 A.M., when he left the telegraph office, his re-election appeared certain. "I earnestly believe that the consequences of this day's work," he told a group of boisterous serenaders, ". . . will be to the lasting advantage, if not to the very salvation, of the country."

Complete election returns gave Lincoln 2,203,831 votes to McClellan's 1,797,019, with an electoral count of 212 to 21. In Frank Bellew's cartoon at left, a giant "Majority" bears the well-satisfied President through troubled waters, as Little Mac falters to the rear. The election, Harper's said with its cartoon at right, made "Long Abraham Lincoln a Little Longer."

THE
FORLORN
HOPE

THE FEDERAL occupation of Atlanta led to a brief lull—a final intermission, so to speak, before the curtain should rise for the last act in the war. Sherman undertook to make a fortress out of Atlanta, and he ordered all noncombatants to leave— one of the harsh acts for which Georgians never forgave him. There was a brief truce, and Union army teamsters helped the exiles get their pathetic bundles of personal property south of the city and inside the Confederate lines. Not all civilians left Atlanta, but a great many did. The town was more than half depopulated, and many abandoned homes were looted or destroyed outright. Meanwhile, the rival commanders tried to devise new strategic plans.

Sherman welcomed the breathing spell. His army needed rest and a refit, and he himself needed time to decide on his next step. Under the program Grant had laid down in the spring, Sherman had not yet attained his true objective, the destruction of Hood's army; but as he studied the situation now he began to realize that the whole nature of the war had changed, and that a radical reconsideration of possible objectives might be necessary. He was in the very heart of the South, and he had subject to his

orders many more soldiers than his foe could bring against him. He could go anywhere he chose to go, and when he selected his goal he might not be bound by the tenets of military orthodoxy. He had broken the shell of the Confederacy, and—as he was to remark—he was finding hollowness within. His problem was to find the best way to exploit that hollowness.

Hood's problem was to get Sherman out of the South. The Confederate could hardly hope to do this by a direct attack. The inequality of the opposing forces ruled this out, and the battles around Atlanta had hurt Hood far more than they had hurt Sherman. If Sherman was to be dislodged, it must be by maneuver, and Hood concluded that his best hope was to go west of Atlanta, swing north, and attack Sherman's communications. This would force Sherman to follow him, and in the tangled country of northern Georgia an opportunity for a winning battle might somehow be developed.

So Hood put his army on the march, and as he did so Forrest went up into Tennessee and broke an important section of the railroad between Nashville and the Tennessee River. If this move had been made before the capture of Atlanta, it would have given Sherman serious trouble; even as it was, the Federals as-

Tennessee's imposing marble capitol appeared as a grim fortress during the 1864 Union defense of Nashville.

sembled 30,000 men to get Forrest out of Tennessee, and Sherman sent his ablest subordinate, Thomas, back to Nashville to make Tennessee secure. Forrest escaped the Federal net and withdrew to northern Mississippi. He got there early in October, just as Hood began his operations against Sherman's railroad line in Georgia.

Sherman left an army corps to hold Atlanta and set out after Hood, and for a fortnight or more the two armies sparred at long range and maneuvered for position. At Allatoona Pass on October 5 Hood saw an opportunity to capture large Federal stores of supplies, which were lightly guarded by a detachment under Brigadier General John M. Corse. The Confederates sent Corse a demand for immediate surrender "to avoid a needless effusion of blood," but the Unionist stoutly replied that he was ready for just such an effusion "whenever it is agreeable to you." From nearby Kennesaw Mountain, Sherman signaled Corse—an interchange of messages which inspired a popular patriotic ballad entitled "Hold the Fort"—and in the fight that followed Corse stubbornly held on, and the Rebels were eventually forced to retire.

Hood could never quite make a real break in Sherman's railroad, and Sherman could never pin the elusive Confederate down for a finish fight; and late in October the two armies turned their backs on one another and set off in opposite directions, each general having at last evolved a new program. Taken together, the decisions of Hood and Sherman put the war into its concluding phase.

Hood had settled on a bold and desperate gamble. He would go over into northern Alabama, and from that area he would march his entire army into Tennessee, in the belief that this would force Sherman to evacuate Atlanta and come after him. Joe Wheeler, with Hood's cavalry, would remain in Georgia to keep an eye on Sherman and hurt him as much as possible. When Hood crossed the Tennessee River and started north, Forrest would go with him in Wheeler's stead. Even if this move did not persuade the Federal authorities to call off Sherman's gigantic raid, Hood might possibly overwhelm Thomas and regain Tennessee for the Confederacy, and after refitting at Nashville, he could drive north into Kentucky. From that state, Hood reasoned, he could threaten Cincinnati, and he might even cross the Cumberland Mountains to fall upon Grant's rear and thus come to the aid of Lee before Richmond. It was a plan born of desperation, and, as it turned out, it was a strategic error of the

first magnitude, but the plain fact of the matter was that Hood had no good choice to make.

Sherman, meanwhile, was looking southeast to the sea, meditating a bold gamble of his own—a gamble all the more remarkable in that it involved a complete reversal of the strategic plan laid down by Grant six months earlier. Grant had insisted that Confederate armies were the chief objectives for Union strategy. What Sherman was saying now was that he would completely ignore the Confederate army which was supposed to be his target, and that he would go instead for a military intangible—the spirit that sustained the Confederate nation itself. He would march for Savannah and the seacoast, abandoning his own line of supply, living off the lush Georgia country—the harvest was in, there was corn in the bins and forage in the barns, plantation smokehouses were crammed with bacon and ham, and there were hogs and cattle in the fields. If 60,000 Union soldiers (Sherman argued) could go anywhere in the South they wanted to go, making the South support them as they moved and paying no attention to anything the South's army might try to do, they would prove once and for all that the Confederate nation was too weak to live. Lee and Hood might make war along the Southland's frontier; Sherman would make the Southern heartland his own, proving that the Confederacy could not protect the homes, the property, or the families of its own defenders. Grant was skeptical at first, but he finally approved Sherman's plan, and Sherman set off to implement it.

By November 16 the strangest movements of the war were under way: Hood was going north, striking for Nashville, and Sherman was marching southeast for Savannah. Atlanta Sherman left in flames: he had ordered that only buildings of some military potentiality should be destroyed, but his soldiers were careless with matches, and the place was full of empty dwellings, and as the Union army left most of Atlanta went up in smoke. With some 60,000 men Sherman set out for the sea.

Nowhere in Georgia was there any force that could give him serious opposition, and the march seemed to the soldiers more like a prolonged picnic than like regular war. The march was leisurely, and as it moved the army fanned out widely, covering a front sixty miles from wing to wing; and, by orders and by the inclination of its imperfectly disciplined soldiers, the army laid waste the land as it moved, doing much the same thing Sheridan had done in the Shenandoah Valley but doing it jocosely, like Halloween rowdies on a spree, rather than with the cold grimness of Sheridan's troopers. Regular foraging parties were sent out by each brigade, every morning, to bring in supplies, and these brought in far more than the army needed. Soldiers used to a diet of salt pork and hardtack ate chicken and sweet potatoes, fresh beef and southern ham, anything and everything that a rich agricultural region could provide. The supply wagons were always full, and when the army moved on, it destroyed or gave away to the runaway slaves who clustered about it more food than it had eaten.

In addition, the army was preceded, surrounded, and followed by a destructive horde of lawless stragglers. These included outright deserters, who had abandoned their regiments and had no intention of returning to them, and who were going along now on the fringe of the army just for the fun of it; they included, also, men temporarily absent without leave, who would return to duty later but who were freewheeling it for the time being; and they included, oddly enough, certain numbers of deserters from the Confederate army, who found kindred spirits among these lawless marauders and went with them for the sake of the loot. All of these characters, out from under anyone's control, went under the generic name of "bummers," and they made Georgia's lot far more grievous than Sherman's orders intended. They robbed and pillaged and burned all the way from Atlanta to the sea, not because they had anything against the people they were afflicting, but simply because they had gone outside of all normal controls—including their own.

Sherman probably could have suppressed them if he had tried hard. He did not try. He argued, with some justification, that his responsibility was to get his army safely to the sea, and that he could spare neither the manpower nor the energy to protect the people of Georgia while he got it there. But in point of plain fact the bummers were doing pretty largely what Sherman wanted done. They were undoubtedly being a great deal more brutal and wanton than he would have wanted them to be, but they were effectively laying waste the Confederate homeland, and that was all that mattered—to Sherman. He had said that he would make Georgia howl; Georgia was howling to the high heavens, and much of the impetus was coming from the work of the bummers. It is hard to imagine Sherman making a really serious effort to put all of these characters under proper restraint.

For this, again, was total war. Sherman's march to the sea was the demonstration that the Confederacy could not protect its own; it was also the nineteenth-century equivalent of the modern bombing raid, a blow at the civilian underpinning of the military machine. Bridges, railroads, machine shops, warehouses —anything of this nature that lay in Sherman's path was burned or dismantled. Barns were burned, with their contents; food to feed the army and its animals was taken, and three or four times as much as the army needed was simply spoiled . . . and partly because of all of this, Lee's soldiers would be on starvation rations, and the whole Confederate war effort would become progressively weaker. Wholesale destruction was one of the points of this movement. The process through which that destruction was brought about was not pretty to watch, nor is it pleasant to read about today.

Sherman went on toward the sea, taking his time about it, and the Confederacy could do nothing to stop him. Hood, who might have engaged his attention, was going on into central Tennessee, his gamble a failure before it was made. Thomas was assembling an army of more than 50,000 men at Nashville, and Hood was a great deal weaker. The odds were great, and the fact that they were so great was a conclusive demonstration of the North's overwhelming power; the Federal government could take Sherman's army clear off the board and still outnumber the best force Hood could bring to the field.

It took Thomas a certain amount of time, however, to get all of his forces together, and Hood was an aggressive fighter who would use his hitting power to the utmost. He was moving up from the Muscle Shoals crossing of the Tennessee, heading for Nashville by way of Franklin, and Federal General Schofield, commanding two army corps, was falling back from in front of him. Hood outmaneuvered Schofield and at Spring Hill had a chance to cut in behind him and put his whole force out of action—a blow which would have compelled the Federal high command to take Hood's movement very seriously indeed. Hood had particular admiration for the fighting qualities and generalship of the late Stonewall Jackson, and his move was now patterned after Jackson's spectacularly successful flanking march and attack at Chancellorsville. At Spring Hill he came very close to duplicating it, but at the last minute his command arrangements got completely snarled, in one way or another he failed to take advantage of his opportunity, and Schofield's army marched unmolested across the Confederate front, wagon trains and all, to escape the trap. On November 30 Hood overtook him at Franklin; furious because of the chance he had missed, Hood ordered a frontal assault on the Federal line, sending 18,000 men forward through the haze of an Indian-summer afternoon in an attack as spectacular, and as hopeless, as Pickett's famous charge at Gettysburg.

Never was a charge driven home more heroically, or at greater cost—to a more dismal defeat. In a few hours' time Hood's army lost 6,252 men, including five generals killed. The Union lines held firmly, and Hood gained nothing whatever by the assault. After dark Schofield drew away and continued his retreat to Nashville, and Hood was left in possession of the field, which he would have gained without fighting at all because Schofield had no intention of remaining there. Weaker than Thomas to begin with, Hood had further weakened his army; worse yet, his men had lost confidence in him, realizing that the whole battle had been useless.

No army in the war was unluckier than Hood's army, the gallant Army of Tennessee. It had fought as well as any army ever fought, but mistakes in leadership always intervened to cancel out gains that were won on battlefields. Bragg had taken it far up into Kentucky and then had been able to do nothing better than lead it back south again, its mission unaccomplished. The army had nearly destroyed Rosecrans at Murfreesboro only to see its near-victory turned into defeat. It had completely routed Rosecrans at Chickamauga, but Bragg's inept handling of it thereafter had made the victory barren. It had lost more men than it could afford to lose in the heroic assaults on Sherman's troops around Atlanta, and now, at Franklin, it had almost wrecked itself in an attack that should never have been ordered. It was at a dead end. It could continue to advance, but it was on the road to nowhere.

Hood followed hard, once the Battle of Franklin was over. The Federals in Nashville were solidly entrenched; they had been occupying the city for three years, and by now it was one of the best-fortified places in the country, and Thomas had put together a force at least twice the size of Hood's. Hood put his men in camp on high ground a few miles south of Nashville and waited—for what, it is hard to determine, since he had nothing to gain by hanging on in front of Nashville. He could not conceivably take the place by storm, his force was altogether too small

for him to lay siege to it, he could not side-step and march north without inviting Thomas to attack his flank and rear, and he believed that if he tamely retreated his army would disintegrate. In simple fact he had run out of strategic ideas, even of strategic possibilities, and as he waited he was no better than a sitting duck for the ablest Federal commander in the West.

Thomas was still holding back, preferring not to strike until everything was ready. Just when he completed his preparations a hard sleet storm came down, sheathing the roads and hills with glare ice and making movement impossible, so Thomas waited a few days longer for a thaw. Far off in Virginia, Grant, ordinarily a man without nerves, grew worried. He could not, at that distance, see how completely Thomas was in control of the situation; he feared that Hood would get away from him and march all the way north to the Ohio; and after fruitlessly bombarding Thomas with orders to attack at once, Grant prepared orders relieving the general from command and set out himself to go west and take control.

For the only time in his career Grant was suffering from a case of the jitters. The war was on the edge of being won, but if Hood eluded Thomas and kept on to the north the balance might be upset disastrously, and Grant was fretting about it, not realizing that Hood could do nothing whatever but await Thomas' assault. It appears that under everything there was some coolness between Grant and Thomas. Ordinarily a first-rate judge of soldiers, Grant apparently never quite rated Thomas at his true worth, and now he was unable to contain himself. It quickly became evident that Grant was indulging in a lot of quite needless worry.

Before the order relieving Thomas could be transmitted, and before Grant had got any farther on his way than Washington, Thomas struck, the ice at last having melted. On December 15 and 16 the Unionists attacked Hood's army, crushed it, and drove it south in headlong retreat. A rear guard of 5,000 men under Forrest fought a series of delaying actions, and the remnants of Hood's command at last got to safety south of the Tennessee River, but the Confederacy's great Army of Tennessee was no longer an effective fighting force. Hood was relieved from a command which had ceased to mean much, and the bits and pieces of the broken army were assigned to other areas of combat. For the one and only time in all the war, a Confederate army had been totally routed on the field of battle. It goes without saying that Grant never finished his trip west, and his order relieving Thomas was immediately canceled.

Meanwhile, Sherman had kept on moving. As far as the people of the North were concerned, he had disappeared from sight when he left Atlanta. He sent back no progress reports—could not, since all lines of communication with the North were cut—and if he and his whole army had gone underground they could not have been more completely out of touch with the home folks. Lincoln was somewhat worried, at times, but he comforted himself with the grim thought that even if Sherman's army were entirely lost, the North would still have enough soldiers to handle the Confederacy's declining armies; besides which, the President by this time had full confidence in Grant and Sherman, and he was willing to assume that they knew what they were about.

On December 10 Sherman reached the coast just below Savannah, capturing Confederate Fort McAllister, at the mouth of the Ogeechee River, and getting in touch with the U.S. fleet. News of his safe arrival went north promptly, and Sherman drew his lines to capture Savannah and the force of 10,000 which had been scraped together to defend it.

He succeeded in taking the city—it was bound to fall, once Sherman's army had attained full contact with the navy—but Confederate General William S. Hardee managed to get the garrison out safely. The Confederate troops moved up into South Carolina, and Sherman's men marched proudly into Savannah. On December 24 Sherman sent Lincoln a whimsical telegram, offering him the city of Savannah as a Christmas present.

So 1864 came to an end, and as it did the approaching end of the war was visible for all to see. The Confederacy still had an army west of the Mississippi, where it could have no effect on the outcome of the struggle, and it had isolated forces at Mobile and elsewhere in the deep South, but it had nothing to oppose Thomas' victorious troops in Tennessee, it had no chance to bring together enough men to keep Sherman from coming north from Savannah whenever he elected to try it, and Lee was still pinned in the lines at Petersburg, unable to do more than hold on. To all intents and purposes, the Confederacy at the beginning of 1865 consisted of the Carolinas and of the southern strip of Virginia.

One success the South had had, in December. An amphibious expedition under Benjamin Butler had tried to capture Wilmington, North Carolina, the one remaining seaport through which the South could communicate with the outer world. A Union fleet had bombarded Fort Fisher, which commanded the entrance to the Cape Fear River on which Wilmington was situated, Butler had put troops ashore—and then, growing panicky, had concluded that the place was too strong to be taken, had re-embarked his men, and had sailed north in disgraceful panic. But even the savor of this defensive victory did not last long. Butler was removed, and early in January Grant sent down a new expedition, with Admiral Porter commanding for the navy and General A. H. Terry commanding for the army. This time there was no hesitation. The navy pounded the fort hard, then Terry got his troops on the beach and sent them swarming over the defenses. Fort Fisher surrendered, and the Confederacy's last door to the outer world was closed.

Sherman was preparing to march north. In Tennessee a powerful Federal mounted force of 12,000 men armed with repeating carbines was getting ready to cut down into Alabama. Another Federal army was besieging Mobile. Grant was ordering 21,000 Western troops brought east, to move inland from captured Wilmington and join Sherman as he came north. The war was all but finished.

Hood Heads North

After the fall of Atlanta, John Bell Hood telegraphed Richmond for reinforcements and received the reply, "No other resource remains." Whether or not he realized Hood's plight, Sherman expected trouble. "It will be a physical impossibility to protect the roads," he complained, "now that . . . the whole batch of devils are turned loose without home or habitation." Then, like two boxers turning their backs on one another in the ring, Sherman and Hood moved apart—Sherman to slash across Georgia; Hood to invade Tennessee. Realizing the impossibility of stopping the Federal advance, Hood had determined "to resume active operations, move upon Sherman's communications, and avert, if possible, impending disaster from the Confederacy."

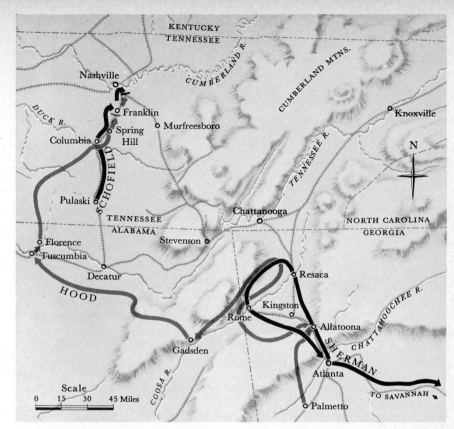

Hood's long, looping route from Atlanta toward Nashville is indicated on the map above. Below is a battery of colored troops, part of the force which Sherman sent to oppose Hood at Nashville.

551

Lieutenant General John Bell Hood

Hood Pursues Schofield to Franklin

"With twenty days' rations in the haversacks and wagons," Hood wrote later, "we marched, on the 22d of October, upon all the roads leading . . . in the direction of . . . the Tennessee River." Not until November 18, however, did Hood effect a delayed rendezvous with Nathan Bedford Forrest's 5,000-man cavalry force at Tuscumbia, Alabama; and the next day he began advancing northward with his Army of Tennessee, 30,000 strong.

Meanwhile, Union General John Schofield was falling back along a parallel line toward Columbia, Tennessee, with a 23,000-man army. For his invasion to prove successful, Hood would have to prevent Schofield from joining George H.

Thomas' additional 40,000 Federals at Nashville. Undismayed when Schofield beat him to Columbia by two days, Hood planned an elaborate flanking movement, designed to cut off Schofield at Spring Hill, eleven miles to the north.

The situation, he exulted, "presented an occasion for one of those interesting and beautiful moves upon the chess-board of war . . ." A few hours before dusk on November 29, Hood himself reached Spring Hill. A single Rebel division under Patrick Cleburne was repulsed by Schofield's advance guard, and—although the Union escape route to Nashville remained open—the Confederate army inexplicably went into bivouac for the night. Less than 600 yards away, with

only an occasional desultory challenge from a Rebel picket, Schofield's entire command streamed quietly past in the darkness.

The following morning, when he learned what had happened, Hood exploded. "The best move in my career as a soldier," he complained, "I was thus destined to behold come to naught." Mercilessly he drove his men after the enemy, and early in the afternoon found them entrenched just south of Franklin. Keeping Stephen D. Lee in reserve, Hood hastily dispatched the two corps of Alexander Stewart and Benjamin F. Cheatham against the Federal line. "I do not like the looks of this fight," Cheatham remarked before leading his men into battle.

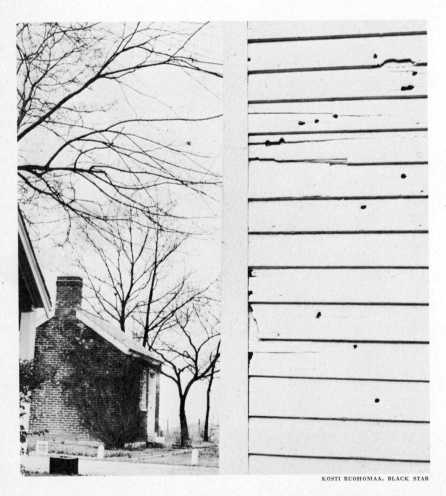

Union General John M. Schofield (above) formed his battle line at Franklin just south of the Carter House. This dwelling (left) is still marked by bullet holes. The Rebel approach to Franklin on the afternoon of November 30 marked a homecoming, after three years, for young Captain Tod Carter. The next morning his family found him on the battlefield and brought him home to die.

FRANKLIN: Having escaped the Rebels at Spring Hill, Schofield's army reaches Franklin by noon of November 30. The supply wagons are moved across the Harpeth River (1), as the troops form behind breastworks south of town. Hood approaches two hours later and at 3 P.M. orders the attack (2). This onslaught sweeps the Federal advance back along the Columbia Pike, and the Rebels pour through the Union line near the Gin House (3). At the Carter House (4) General Emerson Opdycke rallies enough Northerners to plug the gap. Further attacks along the Federal line (5) prove fruitless, and the battle sputters out at 9 P.M. That night Schofield pulled his army out of Franklin and joined Thomas' force at Nashville on December 1.

FRANKLIN

November 30, 1864

FORT GRANGER

TO NASHVILLE

Franklin

CARTER HOUSE

GIN HOUSE

COLUMBIA PIKE

LEWISBURG PIKE

HARPETH RIVER

NASHVILLE & DECATUR R.R.

These five Confederate generals died at Franklin. From left to right they are: H. B. Granbury, O. F. Strahl, States Rights Gist, John Adams, and Patrick Cleburne. A sixth general, John C. Carter, was mortally wounded; five others received lesser wounds; a twelfth was captured. After the battle, the owner of the Carnton House near Franklin had 1,500 Rebel dead removed to his family cemetery and buried in the plot photographed below.

Death in the Afternoon

The Carnton House porch held the bodies of five Confederate generals after the battle.

Through a long night and well into the warm, hazy morning of an Indian-summer day, the weary marchers of Schofield's army straggled, division by division, into Franklin on November 30. By noon the entire force had arrived and was entrenched in a vast semicircle. To ascertain Rebel intentions Schofield posted two brigades under George D. Wagner about half a mile to the front; Schofield himself crossed the Harpeth River behind Franklin to watch the action.

The Confederates appeared on the rim of hills south of Franklin about 2 P.M. and within an hour were in line of battle. "It was a grand sight such as would make a life-long impression . . ." a Federal officer recalled. "For the moment we were spell-bound with admiration, although they were our hated foes; and we knew that in a few brief moments . . . all that orderly grandeur would be changed to bleeding, writhing confusion . . ."

Behind that magnificent line, Confederate General O. F. Strahl was saying to his men: "Boys, this will be short but desperate." A signal volley was fired, the Rebel yell filled the air, and the Southerners swept forward "as steady and resistless as a tidal wave." Wagner's brigades were quickly overwhelmed, and the Union defenders to the rear were unable to fire upon the charging Rebels, so mixed were they with the fleeing men in blue. Again and again, the Confederates charged—some defenders counted thirteen separate assaults. "It is impossible to exaggerate the fierce energy with which the Confederate soldiers, that short November afternoon, threw themselves against the works, fighting with what seemed the very madness of despair," a Federal colonel wrote long afterwards. At some of the earthworks the press of men was so great that the dead, having no place to fall, remained in an upright position.

About 9 P.M. Hood halted the slaughter. Two hours later, under cover of darkness, Schofield pulled his army across the Harpeth, and the following day was safe in Nashville. Of the nearly equal forces involved, the North suffered 2,326 casualties, while the South's loss was 6,252.

Thomas Plans a Careful Attack

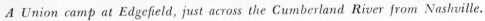

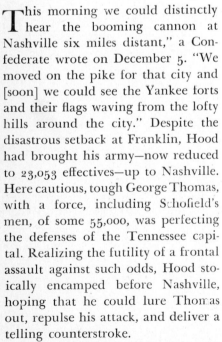

A Union camp at Edgefield, just across the Cumberland River from Nashville.

This morning we could distinctly hear the booming cannon at Nashville six miles distant," a Confederate wrote on December 5. "We moved on the pike for that city and [soon] we could see the Yankee forts and their flags waving from the lofty hills around the city." Despite the disastrous setback at Franklin, Hood had brought his army—now reduced to 23,053 effectives—up to Nashville. Here cautious, tough George Thomas, with a force, including Schofield's men, of some 55,000, was perfecting the defenses of the Tennessee capital. Realizing the futility of a frontal assault against such odds, Hood stoically encamped before Nashville, hoping that he could lure Thomas out, repulse his attack, and deliver a telling counterstroke.

Hood occupied a defensive position along a crooked, thinly held, five-mile line running from the Nashville and Chattanooga Railroad on the right to a series of incomplete redoubts along the Hillsboro Pike on the left. Early on the morning of December 15, Thomas checked out of his Nashville hotel room, paid the bill, and entrusted his packed valise to an orderly. The Rock of Chickamauga was about to oblige his enemy by attacking him.

In a dense fog at 6 A.M. Thomas sent the Negro troops of James B. Steedman on a secondary attack against Cheatham on the Rebel right, while he launched the principal Federal drive against Hood's weak left. One Union infantry corps was to press against the Rebel center and serve as a pivot on which James Wilson's cavalry and A. J. Smith's infantry would swing to envelop Stewart's Confederate left along the Hillsboro Pike. Miraculously, a detached Rebel artillery unit of 148 men held off a 4,000-man Union infantry division for two hours; then, according to Thomas' plan, the Confederate left began to crumble. Disregarding the continued pressure from Steedman, Hood recalled Cheatham to reinforce the hard-pressed left. Schofield, held in reserve until then, was brought up behind A. J. Smith; and the odds against Hood became too great.

Mary Bradford, a plucky Southern girl, rushed out among Hood's fleeing soldiers and, with tears streaming down her face, unavailingly begged them to halt. At nightfall Thomas, convinced he had won, called off the battle, but Schofield was skeptical. "You don't know Hood," he said. "He'll be right there, ready to fight, in the morning."

556

Thomas turned Nashville into an armed camp. The steps of the state capitol (above) served as gun emplacements, and supplies and reinforcements continued to pour through the busy railroad yards at left, photographed in 1864. Although Washington fumed at the delay, Thomas put off attacking Hood for two weeks after the latter's arrival before the Tennessee capital. Carefully, he was strengthening his defensive lines, while devising a brilliant offensive plan.

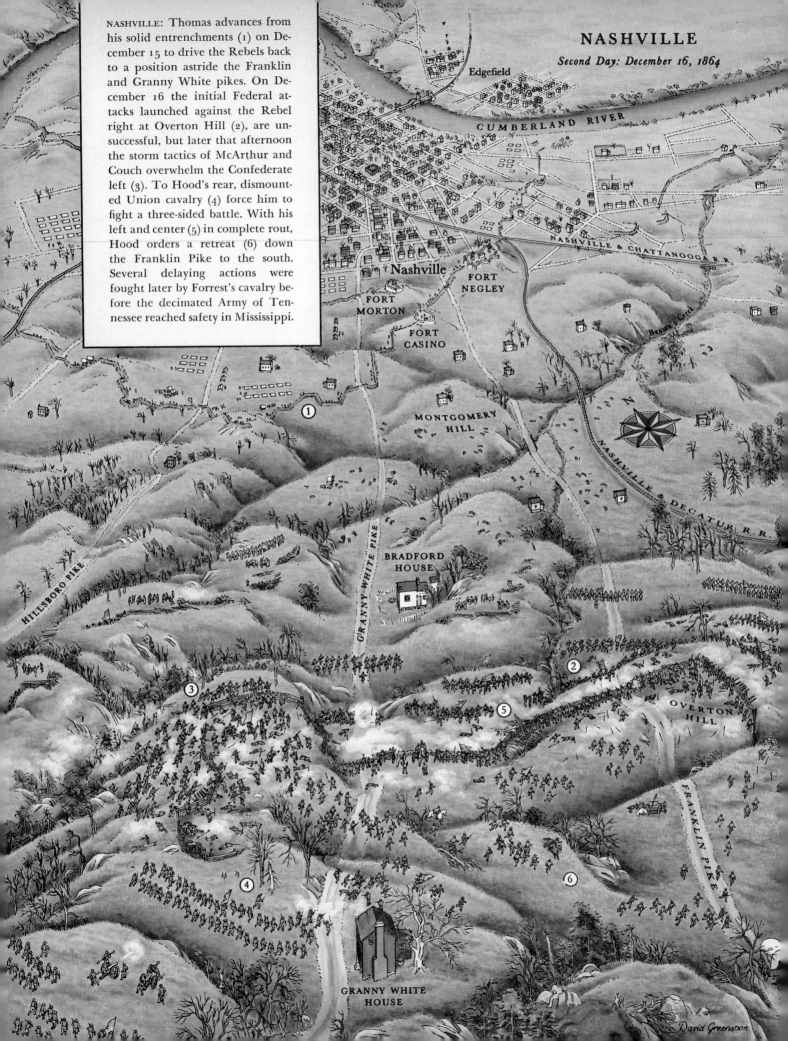

NASHVILLE: Thomas advances from his solid entrenchments (1) on December 15 to drive the Rebels back to a position astride the Franklin and Granny White pikes. On December 16 the initial Federal attacks launched against the Rebel right at Overton Hill (2), are unsuccessful, but later that afternoon the storm tactics of McArthur and Couch overwhelm the Confederate left (3). To Hood's rear, dismounted Union cavalry (4) force him to fight a three-sided battle. With his left and center (5) in complete rout, Hood orders a retreat (6) down the Franklin Pike to the south. Several delaying actions were fought later by Forrest's cavalry before the decimated Army of Tennessee reached safety in Mississippi.

NASHVILLE

Second Day: December 16, 1864

Edgefield

CUMBERLAND RIVER

NASHVILLE & CHATTANOOGA R.R.

Nashville

FORT NEGLEY

FORT MORTON

FORT CASINO

MONTGOMERY HILL

Brown Creek

NASHVILLE & DECATUR R.R.

HILLSBORO PIKE

GRANNY WHITE PIKE

BRADFORD HOUSE

OVERTON HILL

FRANKLIN PIKE

GRANNY WHITE HOUSE

David Greenspon

Hood's Invasion Ends in Rout

An endless line of Union tents, fading into the mist, confronted Hood at Nashville.

During the night of December 15, Hood reformed his lines along a shorter and much stronger perimeter about two miles to the rear of his original position. Meanwhile, Thomas determined to repeat the preceding day's successful strategy, hoping to bend back Hood's flanks and cut off a possible retreat south. This day, however, it seemed to take the Union soldiers longer to get into line—many had dropped in their tracks the night before and were separated from their units; and the secondary attack against the Rebel right on Overton Hill was thrown back.

Impatient at what they considered the long delay, two Union commanders; Darius Couch and John McArthur, almost simultaneously volunteered to storm the two steep slopes which comprised the Confed-

erate left. About 4 P.M. the assaults got under way. In the Federal rear, spectators held their breath as the tiny blue figures steadily mounted the slopes. In a matter of minutes the Stars and Stripes waved from the summit and an unmistakable cheer echoed across the valley—"the voice of the American people," Thomas called it. "It was more like a scene from a spectacular drama than a real incident of war," a Northerner wrote; ". . . so exciting was it all that the lookers-on instinctively clapped their hands . . ."

As Hood's left and then his center collapsed, Stephen Lee found himself holding an unprotected right. Seizing a flag from a color-bearer, he attempted to rally his men. "I doubt if any soldiers in the world ever needed so much cumulative evidence to convince them they were beaten,"

Schofield commented later. A heavy rain began to fall, and Hood ordered a retreat toward Franklin. "I beheld for the first and only time," he disconsolately admitted, "a Confederate Army abandon the field in confusion."

That night a Rebel private stumbled by error into Hood's tent. There sat the beaten commander, tears of disappointment coursing down his cheeks. Within a month he would resign his commission. His army had disintegrated, his career had ended in defeat, and the war in the West, for all practical purposes, was at an end. Out in the darkness, at that moment, George Thomas was riding with the Union cavalry in pursuit of stragglers. To anyone who would listen, he shouted heartily, "Didn't I tell you we could lick 'em? Didn't I tell you . . ."

Sherman's men specialized in railroad wrecking; the print above shows them at work during the march to the sea. Below is W. T. Crane's sketch of cotton captured at Savannah being shipped to New York.

The March to the Sea

A bummer, drawn by a Yankee soldier.

Sherman reviewing his army in Savannah, drawn by William Waud.

In mid-November, 1864, with Southern papers branding him "the spirit of a thousand fiends centered in one" and the "Attila of the west," Sherman led his army out of Atlanta toward the Atlantic port of Savannah. His 62,000 tough veterans fell on Georgia like a plague of locusts.

Marching at a leisurely pace on a wide front, the Federal army moved virtually unopposed. Thousands of Negroes followed the columns, delirious with joy. One, pointing to Sherman, cried, "Dar's de man dat rules the world!"—and as far as the part of the world that was Georgia was concerned, he was right.

If any of Sherman's men ate army rations it was only by choice. Each morning foraging details set out, returning at night with wagons groaning under the weight of booty. When army wagons were not sufficient, they showed up with "anything that had wheels, drawn by anything that could pull." Corncribs and smokehouses and barns were rifled and set afire; mills and railroads and bridges demolished; and, all too often, houses looted.

Soon the army trailed swarms of "bummers," men whose foraging was more pure banditry than anything else. Judson Kilpatrick's cavalrymen were particular offenders, but Georgians soon learned to fear even their own cavalry under Joe Wheeler.

At Milledgeville, Georgia's capital, the Yankees made their campfires of Confederate money, and repealed secession in a mock legislative session. Here, too, they found several Andersonville escapees, and an officer wrote that the sight of these living skeletons "sickened and infuriated the men who thought of them starving in the midst of plenty." Georgia began to howl even louder.

From Milledgeville they marched for Savannah, 175 miles away. The North waited impatiently for news; when Senator John Sherman asked Lincoln his brother's goal, the President replied, "I know the hole he went in at, but I can't tell you what hole he will come out of."

After a month of silence, the North learned that Sherman was at Savannah, his army intact. Hardee soon evacuated the city, and Sherman marched in on December 22. The spoils included 250 cannon and 40,000 bales of cotton. Instead of his earlier diet of "Beefsteak, porksteak, broiled chicken, sweet potatoes," a Yankee soldier enjoyed a new menu: "Oyster soup, oysters on the half shell, roast goose, fried oysters, rice, raisins, coffee, and roast oysters."

As he prepared to move north into the Carolinas, Sherman summed up the campaign. He estimated damages at one hundred million dollars, eighty million of which was "simply waste and destruction."

561

VICTORY

ON THE FIRST of February, 1865, Sherman and his army started north from Savannah, and the war shuddered toward its conclusion. Sherman had some 60,000 veterans, and when he reached North Carolina he would be reinforced by 21,000 more under Schofield. To oppose him, the Confederacy had the troops that had been pulled out of Savannah, some threadbare levies from the broken Army of Tennessee, and sundry home-guard and cavalry units—upwards of 30,000 men in all, many of them not first-line troops. There was not the slightest possibility that it could increase this number substantially; Joe Johnston, brought back from retirement and put in charge in the hope that he might somehow find a way to halt Sherman, confessed sadly: "I can do no more than annoy him."

Johnston's return was a sign of belated and unavailing effort to put new vigor into the defense of the dwindling Southern nation. Late in January the Congress at Richmond had passed an act providing for a general in chief for the armies of the Confederacy, and Robert E. Lee, inevitably, had been given this position. Lee restored Johnston to command in the Carolinas, but he could do very little to help him,

and there was not much Johnston himself could do. His chief immediate reliance would have to be on the weather and geography. Sherman's line of march would carry him through swampy lowland regions, cut by many rivers, and in rainy winter weather roads would be almost impassable and the streams would be swollen; all in all, it seemed improbable that he could make much progress during the winter months.

But Sherman's army had special qualities. Like the Confederate armies, it contained men who had lived close to the frontier, backwoods people who could use the axe and who could improvise their way through almost any obstacle, and these men came up through South Carolina as rapidly as they had gone across Georgia, corduroying roads, building bridges, and fording icy rivers as they came. Johnston, watching from afar, remarked afterward that there had been no such army since the days of Julius Caesar.

Sherman's men laid hard hands on South Carolina. They had been very much on their good behavior in Savannah, but they relapsed into their old habits once they left Georgia, burning and looting and destroying as they marched. There was a personal fury in their behavior now that had been missing in Georgia; to a man, they felt that South Carolina had

Still the proud, erect soldier, Robert E. Lee leaves the McLean House at Appomattox after surrendering to Grant.

started the war and that her people deserved rough treatment, and such treatment the unhappy South Carolinians assuredly got. The capital, Columbia, was burned after Sherman's men moved in, and although the Federals insisted that the burning had been accidental—a point which is in dispute to this day—most of the soldiers agreed that if the accident had not taken place they themselves would have burned the place anyway. As they came north their path was marked, Old Testament style, by a pillar of smoke by day and pillars of fire by night. South Carolina paid a fearful price for having led the way in secession.

In Richmond approaching doom was clearly visible, and the sight stirred men to consider doing what had previously been unthinkable—to lay hands on the institution of slavery itself. After much debate the Confederate Congress voted a bill to make soldiers out of Negro slaves. That this implied an end to slavery itself was obvious; to turn a slave into a soldier automatically brought freedom, and if part of the race lost its chains, all of the race must eventually be freed; and there was bitter opposition when the measure was first suggested. As recently as one year earlier the idea had been quite unthinkable. One of the best combat soldiers in the Army of Tennessee, Irish-born General Pat Cleburne, had proposed such a step at a conclave of generals, and the proposal had been hushed up immediately. But Cleburne was dead now, one of the generals killed at Franklin, and Lee himself was supporting the plan; and as spring came the Confederacy was taking halting steps to arm and train Negro troops.

At the same time Secretary of State Benjamin played a card which might have been very effective if it had been played two or three years earlier. To France and Great Britain he had the Confederacy's emissaries abroad offer the abolition of slavery in return for recognition. Neither London nor Paris was interested: the Confederacy was beyond recognition now, and nobody could mistake the fact, so the offer fell flat. If it had been made in 1862 or in the spring of 1863, it might possibly have bought what Richmond wanted, but like Confederate currency it had depreciated so badly by this time that it would buy nothing of any consequence.

If there was to be a negotiated peace, then, it would have to come from Washington, and in February the government at Richmond tried to find out if Washington cared to talk terms. It was encouraged to take this step by a recent visit paid to the Confederate capital by old Francis P. Blair, Sr., one of whose sons had been Postmaster General in Lincoln's cabinet, while the other was a corps commander in Sherman's army. Old man Blair was believed to be in Lincoln's confidence, and in January he came through the lines and went to the Confederate White House for a talk with Jefferson Davis; to Davis he suggested a reunion of the states and a concerted effort by the restored nation to drive the French out of Mexico. Davis refused to commit himself on this eccentric proposal, and it developed presently that Blair had made the trip on his own hook and definitely had not been speaking for Lincoln; but the mere fact that the feeler had been put out seemed to indicate that the Lincoln government might be willing to talk terms, and a semiformal conference was arranged for February 3 on a Federal steamer in Hampton Roads, Virginia. Representing the Confederacy were Vice-President Alexander Stephens, R. M. T. Hunter of Virginia, president pro tem of the Senate, and Judge John A. Campbell of Alabama, formerly of the United States Supreme Court. Speaking for the Union at this conference were President Lincoln and Secretary Seward.

The conferees seem to have had a pleasant chat, but they got nowhere. Lincoln was leading from strength, and he had no concessions to offer. It was told, later, as a pleasant myth, that he had taken a sheet of paper, had written "Reunion" at the top of it, and then had handed it to little Stephens with the remark that Stephens might fill in the rest of the terms to suit himself, but there was no truth in this tale. Lincoln's position was inflexible: there would be peace when the Confederate armies were disbanded and the national authority was recognized throughout the South, and there would be no peace until then. With acceptance of national authority, of course, would go acceptance of the abolition of slavery; the thirteenth amendment to the Constitution, ending slavery forever, had already been submitted to the states for ratification.

What this meant was that the Confederates must simply surrender unconditionally and rely on the liberality of the Federal administration for a reconstruction program that would make the lot of the Southland endurable. Of Lincoln's own liberality there was no question; he was even willing to try to get a Federal appropriation to pay slaveowners for the loss of their human property, and it was clear that he planned no proscription list or other punitive measures. But no Southerner could forget that what would finally happen would depend in large part on the Northern Congress, and such leaders as Thaddeus Stevens, Ben Wade, Zachariah Chandler, and Charles Sumner had ideas very different from Lincoln's. In the end the conference adjourned with nothing accomplished, the Southern delegates went back to Richmond, and Davis told his people that their only hope lay in war to the last ditch.

Sherman kept moving north, inexorably. As he came up through South Carolina his army sliced across the railroad lines that led to Charleston, and that famous city fell at last into Union hands. It had withstood the most violent attacks the Federal army and navy could make, but it had to be abandoned at last because the whole interior of the state was lost. The national flag went up on the rubble-heap that had been Fort Sumter, the Palmetto State was out of the war forever, and Sherman's hard-boiled soldiers tramped on into North Carolina. In this state they went on their good behavior, and the burning and devastation that had marked their path ever since they left Atlanta were held to a minimum. They did not feel the hatred for North Carolina that they had felt for her sister state; and, in point of fact, there was no military need for a policy of destruction now, because the war could not possibly last very much longer.

To the Confederacy there remained just one chance —a very slim chance, with heavy odds against it. In the lines at Petersburg, Lee faced double his own numbers; in North Carolina, Johnston was up against odds that were even longer. The one hope was that Lee might somehow give Grant the slip, get his army into North Carolina, join forces with Johnston, and defeat Sherman in pitched battle. This done, Lee and Johnston might turn back toward Virginia and meet Grant on something like even terms. It was most unlikely that all of this could be done, but it had to be tried because it was the only card that could be played. Lee would try it as soon as the arriving spring made the roads dry enough to permit his army to move.

The Federal army in Lee's front occupied a huge semicircle more than forty miles long, the northern tip of it opposite Richmond itself, the southern tip curling around southwest of Petersburg in an attempt to cut the railroads that led south. Lee proposed to form a striking force with troops pulled out of his attenuated lines and to make a sudden attack on the Federal center. If the striking force could punch a substantial hole and break the military railroad that supplied Grant's army, the Union left would have to be pulled back to avoid being cut off. That would make possible a Confederate march south and would pave the way for the combined attack on Sherman.

On March 25 the Army of Northern Virginia launched its last great counterpunch. Lee's striking force, led by the fiery young Georgian, General John B. Gordon, made a dawn attack on the Federal Fort Stedman; carried the fort, sent patrols back toward the railroad, seized a portion of the Federal trenches —and then ran out of steam, crumpled under a heavy Union fire, and at last had to confess failure. By noon the survivors of the attack were back in the Confederate lines. Lee's last expedient had misfired; now Grant would take and keep the initiative.

For many months Grant had refused to make frontal attacks on the Confederate fortifications. They were simply too strong to be taken by direct assault, so long as even a skeleton force remained to hold them, and the fearful losses of the first months of 1864 had taught the Federals the folly of trying to drive Lee's men out of prepared positions. Grant's tactics ever since had been to extend his lines to the west, using his superior manpower to compel Lee to stretch his own army past the breaking point. Sooner or later, Grant would be able to put a force out beyond Lee's flank and compel the Confederates to quit their position or fight a battle they could not win. The impassable roads of midwinter had caused a suspension of this movement, but after Fort Stedman it was resumed.

During the final days of March, Federal infantry tried to drive in past Lee's extreme right. The Confederate defenders were alert, and this infantry move was roughly handled; but Phil Sheridan, meanwhile, had brought his cavalry down from the Shenandoah Valley, after cleaning out the last pockets of Confederate resistance there, and with 12,000 mounted men he moved out to Dinwiddie Court House, south and west of the place where Union and Confederate infantry had been fighting for control of the flank. On the last day of the month Sheridan moved north from Dinwiddie Court House, aiming for a road junction known as Five Forks. This was well beyond Lee's lines; if the Federals could seize and hold it they could break Lee's railroad connections with the South, compel the evacuation of Petersburg and Richmond, and interpose themselves between Lee and Johnston. Lee sent a mixed force of cavalry and infantry out to hold Five Forks, and Sheridan called to his aid a veteran infantry corps from Grant's left flank.

On April 1 Sheridan and his powerful column routed the Confederate defenders at Five Forks. The Rebel force there was commanded by George Pickett, who would forever wear the glamour of that magnificent charge at Gettysburg, and Pickett was badly overmatched now. Sheridan had too many men and too much impetus, Pickett appears to have handled his own part of the assignment inexpertly, and as dusk came down on April 1 Pickett's column had been almost wiped out, with about 5,000 men taken prisoner, and most of the survivors fleeing without military formation or control.

Oddly enough, at the very moment that this sweeping victory was being won Sheridan removed Major General G. K. Warren from command of the Federal infantry involved, on the ground that Warren had been slow and inexpert in getting his men into action. Warren had brought the V Corps over from the left end of the Federal entrenched position; he had had a hard march in the darkness over bad roads, the orders he had been given were somewhat confusing, and the delay was not really his fault—and in any case the Union had won the battle and no real harm had been done. But Sheridan was a driver. At the very end of the war the Army of the Potomac was being given a sample of the pitiless insistence on flawless performance which it had never known before. Warren was treated unjustly, but the army might have been better off if similar treatment had been meted out to some of its generals two years earlier.

The way was clear now for Grant to get in behind the Army of Northern Virginia; to emphasize the extent of the Union victory, Grant ordered a blow at the center of the Petersburg lines for the early morning of April 2. The lines had been stretched so taut that this blow broke them once and for all. That evening the Confederates evacuated Richmond and Petersburg, the government headed for some Carolina haven where it might continue to function, and Lee put his tired army on the road and began a forced march to join forces with Johnston.

He was never able to make it. The Union advance, led by Sheridan, outpaced him, and instead of going south the Army of Northern Virginia was compelled to drift west, with Federals on its flank and following close in its rear. In the confusion that surrounded the evacuation of Richmond the Confederate government got its victualling arrangements into a tangle, and the rations which were supposed to meet Lee's almost exhausted army along the line of march did not appear. The army stumbled on, its march harassed by constant stabs from Yankee cavalry, its men hungry and worn out, staying with the colors only because of their unshakable confidence in Lee himself. At Sayler's Creek, Federal cavalry and infantry struck the Confederate rear, destroying a wagon train and taking thousands of prisoners. Witnessing the rout from high ground in the rear, Lee remarked grimly: "General, that half of our army is destroyed."

The end came on April 9, at a little town named Appomattox Court House. Federal cavalry and infantry had got across Lee's line of march, other powerful forces were on his flank, and a huge mass of infantry was pressing on his rear. He had no chance to get in touch with Johnston, no chance to continue his flight toward the west, no chance to put up a fight that would drive his foes out of the way; Lee had fewer than 30,000 soldiers with him by now, and not half of these were armed and in usable military formation. The rest were worn-out men who were pathetically doing their best to stay with the army, but who could not this day be used in battle.

The break came just as Federal infantry and cavalry were ready to make a final, crushing assault on the thin lines in Lee's front. Out between the lines came a Confederate horseman, a white flag fluttering at the end of a staff, and a sudden quiet descended on the the broad field. While the soldiers in both armies stared at one another, unable to believe that the fighting at last was over, the commanding generals made their separate ways into the little town to settle things for good.

So Lee met Grant in the bare parlor of a private home at Appomattox Court House and surrendered his army. For four long years that army had been unconquerable. Twice it had carried the war north of the Potomac. Time and again it had beaten back the strongest forces the North could send against it. It had given to the Confederate nation the only hope of growth and survival which that nation had ever had, and to the American nation of reunited North and South it gave a tradition of undying valor and constancy which would be a vibrant heritage for all generations. Not many armies in the world's history have done more. Now the Army of Northern Virginia had come to the end of the road, and it was time to quit.

One option Lee did have, that day, which—to the lasting good fortune of his countrymen—he did not exercise. Instead of surrendering he might simply have told his troops to disband, to take to the hills, and to carry on guerrilla warfare as long as there was a Yankee south of the Mason and Dixon Line. There were generals in his army who hoped he would do this, and Washington unquestionably would have had immense difficulty stamping out a rebellion of that nature. But the results of such a course would have been tragic beyond comprehension—tragic for Northerners and Southerners of that day and for their descendants forever after. There would have been a sharing in repeated atrocities, a mutual descent into brutality and bitterness and enduring hatred, which would have created a wound beyond healing. Neither as one nation nor as two could the people of America have gone on to any lofty destiny after that. All of this Lee realized, and he set his face against it. He and the men who followed him had been fighting for an accepted place in the family of nations. When the fight was finally lost, they would try to make the best of what remained to them.

In Grant, Lee met a man who was as anxious as himself to see this hardest of wars followed by a good peace. Grant believed that the whole point of the war had been the effort to prove that Northerners and Southerners were and always would be fellow citizens, and the moment the fighting stopped he believed that they ought to begin behaving that way. In effect, he told Lee to have his men lay down their arms and go home; and into the terms of surrender he wrote the binding pledge that if they did this, signing and then living up to the formal articles of parole, they would not at any time be disturbed by Federal authority. This pledge had far-reaching importance, because there were in the North many men who wanted to see leading Confederates hanged; but what Grant had written and signed made it impossible to hang Lee, and if Lee could not be hanged no lesser Confederates could be. If Lee's decision spared the country the horror of continued guerrilla warfare, Grant's decision ruled out the infamy that would have come with proscription lists and hangings. Between them, these rival soldiers served their country fairly well on April 9, 1865.

To all intents and purposes, Lee's surrender ended things. Johnston had fought his last fight—a valiant but unavailing blow at Sherman's army at Bentonville, North Carolina, late in March—and when the news of Lee's surrender reached him he knew better than to try to continue the fight. He would surrender, too, and nowhere in the Southland was there any other army that could hope to carry on. A ponderous Federal cavalry force was sweeping through Alabama, taking the last war-production center at Selma, and going on to occupy the onetime Confederate capital, Montgomery; and this force was so strong that even Bedford Forrest was unable to stop its progress. On the Gulf coast the city of Mobile was forced to surrender; and although there was still an army west of the Mississippi it no longer had any useful function, and it would eventually lay down its arms like all the rest. Lee and his army had been the keystone of the arch, and when the keystone was removed the arch was bound to collapse.

Amid the downfall President Davis and his cabinet moved across the Carolinas and into Georgia, hoping to reach the trans-Mississippi and find some way to continue the struggle. It could not be done, and the cabinet at last dispersed. Davis himself was captured by Federal cavalry, and the government of the Confederate States of America at last went out of existence. The war was over.

Davis went to a prison cell in Fort Monroe, and for two years furious bitter-enders in the North demanded that he be tried and hanged for treason. The demand was never granted; despite the furies that had been turned loose by four years of war, enough sanity and common decency remained to rule out anything like that. Davis' imprisonment, and the harsh treatment visited on him by his jailers, won him new sympathy in the South, where there had been many men who held him chiefly responsible for loss of the war, and he emerged from prison at last to become the embodiment of the Lost Cause, standing in the haunted sunset where the Confederate horizon ended.

He had done the best he could do in an impossible job, and if it is easy to show where he made grievous mistakes, it is difficult to show that any other man, given the materials available, could have done much better. He had great courage, integrity, tenacity, devotion to his cause, and like Old Testament Sisera the stars in their courses marched against him.

Above is George Barnard's photograph of fire-gutted Columbia, South Carolina. While denying they started the fire, Northern soldiers "smiled and felt glad" as they watched it.

Theodore R. Davis' pen-and-ink drawing (left) shows an advance element of Sherman's Army of the Tennessee, its tattered battle flag flying, toiling through a South Carolina swamp.

Lieutenant General Wade Hampton (right), Jeb Stuart's successor, led the Southern cavalry against Sherman. His handsome South Carolina mansion was destroyed by the invaders.

Sherman Invades the Carolinas

Watching Sherman's men strip his barn, a Georgian told them, "All I ask is that when you get to South Carolina you will treat them the same way." Moving north from Savannah in February, 1865, Sherman obliged him. His Yankees had a genuine hatred for the state they considered the "mother of secession." One wrote, "It seemed to be decreed that South Carolina, having sown the wind, should reap the whirlwind."

Lee sent Wade Hampton's cavalry to help out Joe Johnston's little force, but it was no use; nothing could stop Sherman, not armed Rebels, nor swamps, nor flooded rivers. Like a relentless blue tide, the army swept across some of the worst marching country in America. One private, struggling through a flooded lowland, remarked, "I guess Uncle Billy's struck this river endways." They made their roads as they went, leading a prisoner to complain, "If your army goes to hell, it will corduroy the road."

South Carolina became a "howling waste" where Sherman touched it. The capital, Columbia, was two-thirds destroyed by fire, and the state felt the bummers' heavy hand. The New York *Herald* reported: "The idea that Sherman is irresistible is at this moment a great demoralizing influence throughout the South . . ."

As the Federals swarmed into North Carolina hundreds of North Carolinians deserted Lee's army to protect their homesteads. On March 16 at Averasboro and on March 19 at Bentonville Johnston tried to stem the tide, without success. Sherman did not press his enemy; the end was obviously near.

569

The Second Inaugural

The day of Abraham Lincoln's second inauguration, March 4, 1865, began inauspiciously. In the morning it rained off and on; and at his oath-taking Vice-President-elect Andrew Johnson, numbed by whiskey taken to counter the aftereffects of typhoid fever, made an incoherent speech that mortified and shocked his audience.

But at 1 P.M., when the President rose to deliver his inaugural address outside the Capitol, the sun burst through the lowering clouds so suddenly that Lincoln later confessed, "It made my heart jump."

A crowd estimated at 30,000 listened attentively as Lincoln spoke of the conflict: "Both parties deprecated war; but one of them would make war rather than let the nation survive; and the other would accept war rather than let it perish. And the war came." Then, "Fondly do we hope—fervently do we pray—that this mighty scourge of war may speedily pass away." And as he spoke eloquently of the coming peace, reporters observed tears in many eyes.

"That rail-splitting lawyer is one of the wonders of the day," Charles Francis Adams, Jr., wrote his father. "This inaugural strikes me in its grand simplicity and directness as being for all time the historical keynote of this war . . ."

Lincoln (standing, center) delivers his second inaugural address. In Alexander Gardner's photograph John Wilkes Booth watches from the railed balcony at right center; the figure in the light, wide-brimmed hat below the President's lectern is Booth's fellow conspirator, Lewis Paine.

Lee's Last Attack

On the afternoon of January 31, 1865, a carriage from Petersburg came through the Rebel lines under a flag of truce. In it were commissioners on their way to discuss terms for a negotiated peace with Lincoln, and as they crossed no man's land men in blue and gray lined the parapets by the thousands and cast their votes. "Cheer upon cheer was given, extending for some distance to the right and left of the lines, each side trying to cheer the loudest."

But the conference came to nothing. The Civil War would continue until one of these cheering armies could fight no longer, and as the fourth year of the war neared its end

the odds against the South lengthened daily. The Confederacy had only Lee's army at Petersburg and Joe Johnston's in North Carolina, and to oppose these meager forces the North could bring to bear some 280,000 fighting men. Lee warned the Secretary of War, "You must not be surprised if calamity befalls us."

On March 2 Sheridan completely shattered the pitiful remnants of Early's Valley army at Waynesboro and started his two veteran cavalry divisions for Petersburg. Lee had to act quickly to prevent Sheridan's troopers from raiding his communication and supply lines and making it impossible for him to act at all. Typically, he chose to take the offensive.

Hoping to buy time to get his army away to join Johnston, Lee scheduled an attack on Grant's center. John B. Gordon, who had fought so well in the Wilderness and at Spotsylvania, was put in charge, and in the pre-dawn blackness of March 25 Gordon punched a gaping hole in the Union line at Fort Stedman.

The Federals were taken by surprise, but they rallied quickly; before Gordon could take the defending forts on each side of the break, he was hit hard by artillery fire and counterattacks. In less than four hours the Army of Northern Virginia's last offensive was broken. Before the month was out, Grant began his final campaign.

The winter of 1864–65 was a severe one for Petersburg's besiegers and defenders, and to the steady attrition caused by sniping, artillery fire, and patrol activity were added heavy losses from disease. At left is a barren Union cemetery at City Point, and at right, a Confederate soldier killed in one of the final Petersburg assaults. Below, the well-equipped Federals await Grant's spring offensive.

Breaking the Line at Petersburg

At the end of March, Grant began shifting his forces westward to turn the flank of Lee's Petersburg lines. The seemingly bottomless Virginia mud inspired the gagsters—"If ever anybody was to ask us if we'd ever been through Virginia we could say, 'Yes, sir! In a number of places'"—but Grant kept at it, and on March 31 and April 1 Phil Sheridan's troopers, supported by Yankee infantry, took on George Pickett's division at Five Forks.

This was a road center west of the Petersburg defenses, and if Lee lost it he also lost the Southside Railroad, his last rail connection with the rest of the shrinking Confederacy. Sheridan held off Pickett's attacks on the thirty-first; and the next day, braced by the Federal V Corps, smashed in Pickett's flank and rolled up his line.

Grant ordered a general assault on the main Petersburg lines for dawn on Sunday, April 2. The VI Corps broke through, collapsing the entire Confederate right, and only a gallant Rebel defense of Fort Gregg stemmed the rout. In the confusion Lee lost another great lieutenant, A. P. Hill.

When the news of Hill's death was brought to headquarters, an aide wrote, "I will never forget the expression on General Lee's face."

Jefferson Davis was attending church in Richmond when a courier brought a message from the War Department: "General Lee telegraphs he can hold his position no longer." Davis quietly left the church and set about removing what he could of his government from Richmond. That night Lee evacuated Petersburg; the Army of Northern Virginia had begun its last march.

Alfred Waud sketched the victorious charge of the Federal V Corps against Pickett's flank at Five Forks. Mounted on Rienzi and waving his personal battle flag, Sheridan (right center) led the attack.

Waud also drew the Yankee attack on Fort Gregg (above) during the Petersburg breakthrough. An eyewitness remembered "men struggling frantically to clamber up the high parapet . . . and only after 25 or 30 minutes of awful slaughter was that heroic garrison conquered." Below, the first Federal wagon train enters captured Petersburg.

The Fall of Richmond

As the Davis government and the army garrison evacuated Richmond its factories, arsenals, and mills were ordered destroyed, beginning the Southern capital's final ordeal.

Fires soon raged out of control; commissary depots were thrown open, setting off a wave of pillaging; whiskey stocks were broken into and "the streets ran with liquor." Through the night drunken mobs of civilians and deserters ranged through the stricken city, looting and burning. A Rebel gunner described the scene: ". . . an ocean of flame is dashing, as a tidal wave of destruction . . . from street to street. . . . Miles on miles of fire; mountain piled on mountain of black smoke . . . one ceaseless babel of human voices, crying, shouting, cursing; one mighty pandemonium of woe."

On the morning of April 3 a Richmond woman saw "a body of men in blue uniforms. . . . The Confederate flag that fluttered above the Capitol came down and the Stars and Stripes were run up . . . We covered our faces and cried aloud."

Federal troops got the fire under control and restored order, and the next day Lincoln himself toured the smoldering city. In the Confederate White House he sat for a moment, with "a serious, dreamy expression," at Jefferson Davis' desk.

As he watched Richmond ablaze and rocked by explosions, a Confederate soldier mused that "The old war-scarred city seemed to prefer annihilation to conquest." Below is a ruined locomotive amidst the charred debris of the Richmond and Petersburg depot.

Winslow Homer's "Prisoners from the Front" (above) symbolizes the war's last days when losses depleted Lee's army. Below, Denis Malone Carter exaggerated the welcome given Lincoln by Richmond's white population. Admiral David Porter rides with the President.

OVERLEAF: *the ruins of the great Gallego flour mills stand stark and grim on Richmond's waterfront. A Northern newspaperman found in the city "the stillness of a catacomb . . . far off into the gradual curtain of the night, stretches a vista of desolation."*

The Last Campaign:
Lee Heads
West from Petersburg

Above, Sheridan's cavalry bearing down on the Confederate rear guard at Amelia Court House is met with upraised rifles, the signal of surrender. At right, General George Custer receives a flag of truce from a Rebel officer at Appomattox Court House. Both these sketches are by Alfred R. Waud.

The Civil War's final, week-long campaign is outlined in the map below. Lee's flight from Petersburg and Richmond to Appomattox is shown in gray; Grant's pursuit is in black. Some units marched over forty miles in a day.

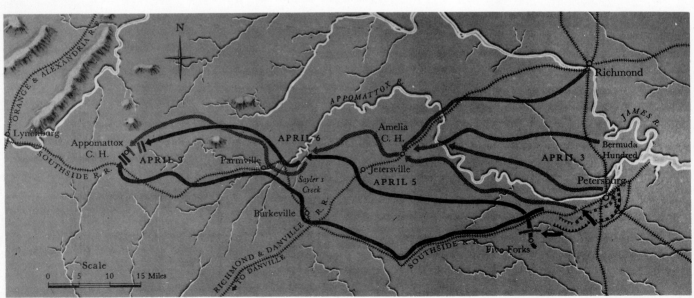

Lee's immediate objective, once his Petersburg lines were broken, was Amelia Court House on the Richmond and Danville Railroad. Here he hoped to pull together his troops from Petersburg and Richmond and move south via the railroad to join Joe Johnston.

Grant's pursuit, however, was swift and skillful. Sheridan blocked the railroad south of the Rebels, and Lee had to change his objective to Lynchburg, some sixty miles to the west. During the past year these two armies had raced each other to such strategically important places as Spotsylvania Court House and Cold Harbor and Petersburg; now the sol-

diers sensed that this was the final race. "We grew tired," a Yankee wrote, "but we wanted to be there when the rebels found the last ditch of which they had talked so much."

Sheridan's troopers constantly harried the Southern columns with quick sorties. On April 6 he cut out a Rebel wagon train and called up the VI Corps to attack Lee's rear guard at Sayler's Creek. The VI Corps had won under Sheridan in the Valley, and now it overwhelmed a sizable fraction of the mortally wounded Army of Northern Virginia. Over 6,000 Confederates were captured, including Dick Ewell.

On April 8 George Custer's Yankee

cavalry division seized four trains of supplies at Appomattox Station— west of Lee. Sheridan wrote Grant that if "the 5th Corps can get up tonight we will perhaps finish the job in the morning."

The next day Lee pushed aside Sheridan's cavalry blocking the road to Lynchburg near Appomattox Court House, only to meet solid lines of blue infantry. As the Federals prepared a final, massive attack, and the pitifully few Confederates waited quietly and defiantly under their ranked red battle flags, a horseman galloped out between the lines, waving a white flag, with a message from General Lee to General Grant.

Lee Surrenders His Army

Wilmer McLean had lived near Manassas Junction, where the war's first major battle had been fought in 1861. When his farm was overrun again during the Second Battle of Bull Run he moved his family out of danger to the quiet little village of Appomattox Court House. Now, after four years, the war had come full circle, to end in Wilmer McLean's parlor.

It was April 9—Palm Sunday— when Lee waited in the parlor to surrender his Army of Northern Virginia. Soon Grant rode up, looking, Lee's aide thought, "as though he had had a pretty hard time . . . dusty and a little soiled," and the two generals quickly agreed on terms. Confederate officers would retain their side arms and baggage; officers and men who claimed their own horses could keep them; and finally, in Grant's simple, magnanimous phrase, "each officer and man will be allowed to return to his home, not to be disturbed by the United States authorities . . ."

By 4 P.M. it was over, and Lee, "sad-faced and weary," mounted Traveller and rode slowly back to his Army of Northern Virginia. Union artillery began to fire salutes in celebration, but Grant stopped it. "We did not want to exult over their downfall," he wrote.

At left is the McLean House, scene of Lee's surrender, at Appomattox Court House. The original structure was dismantled in the 1890's; this one is a reconstruction on the original site.

The village of Appomattox Court House was built around a tavern and a county court house. The latter burned in 1892, but several old buildings survive today, including the brick jail (right).

Lee's veterans furl the Stars and Bars for the last time in Richard Brooke's painting below. Many of the Confederate units burned or buried their battle flags rather than surrender them.

A United Nation Welcomes Peace

Grant's official dispatch—"General Lee surrendered the Army of Northern Virginia this afternoon on terms proposed by myself"—triggered celebrations all over the North. This one was painted by an unknown artist.

SURRENDER OF GEN. LEE!

"The Year of Jubilee has come! Let all the People Rejoice!"

200 GUNS WILL BE FIRED

On the Campus Martius,
AT 3 O'CLOCK TO-DAY, APRIL 10,
To Celebrate the Victories of our Armies.

Every Man, Woman and Child is hereby ordered to be on hand prepared to Sing and Rejoice. The crowd are expected to join in singing Patriotic Songs.

ALL PLACES OF BUSINESS MUST BE CLOSED AT 2 O'CLOCK.

Hurrah for Grant and his noble Army.

By Order of the People.

The jubilant broadside above appeared in Detroit on the day following Lee's surrender. As Unionists rejoiced a Northern nurse in Richmond noted that "Flowers were blooming . . . in the desolate, dejected city."

OVERLEAF: Between Federal ranks Lee's army lays down its arms, drawn by J. R. Chapin. "On our part," wrote a Union officer, "not a sound of trumpet . . . nor roll of drum; not a cheer . . . but an awed stillness rather . . ."

Head Quarters Army of No: Virginia
10" April 1865

General Order }
No 9

After four years of arduous service marked by unsurpassed courage and fortitude the Army of Northern Virginia has been compelled to yield to overwhelming numbers and resources.

I need not tell the brave survivors of so many hard fought battles, who have remained steadfast to the last, that I have consented to this result from no distrust of them.

But feeling that valor and devotion could accomplish nothing that would compensate for the loss that must have attended the continuance of the contest I determined to avoid the useless sacrifice of those whose past services have endeared them to their countrymen.

By the terms of the agreement Officers and men can return to their homes and remain until exchanged. You will take with you the satisfaction that proceeds from the consciousness of duty faithfully performed, and I earnestly pray that a merciful God will extend to you His blessing and protection.

With an unceasing admiration of your constancy and devotion to your Country and a grateful remembrance of your kind and generous consideration for myself, I bid you all an affectionate farewell.

R E Lee
Genl

Brig. Genl. W. H. Stevens
Chief Engr. A. N. Va.

Lee Says Farewell

Through the sheets of rain that fell on the morning of April 15, 1865, a Baptist minister living on the outskirts of Richmond caught sight of a man on a gray horse. "His steed was bespattered with mud, and his head hung down as if worn by long travelling. The horseman himself sat his horse like a master; his face was ridged with self-respecting grief; his garments were worn in the service and stained with travel . . ." Robert E. Lee had returned at last from the wars.

Lee, a paroled prisoner, was indicted for treason but was never brought to trial; and on July 13 he applied for a Federal pardon—which was never granted. Courageous and resolute in war, Lee was never bitter in defeat. "The war being at an end . . ." he wrote in September, 1865, "I believe it to be the duty of every one to unite in the restoration of the country, and the establishment of peace and harmony . . ."

That month he became president of Washington College in Lexington, Virginia, a position which he held for the five remaining years of his life. On the morning of October 12, 1870, the old warrior lay dying. His former opponent, Ulysses S. Grant, was in the White House; but Robert E. Lee was once more on the battlefield. "Strike the tent," he murmured as he died.

This moving farewell order, written by Colonel Charles Marshall, was revised by General Lee. He signed several copies like the one at left.

Shortly after his return from Appomattox a stern, unbowed Lee reluctantly posed for Mathew Brady on the back porch of his home in Richmond.

END AND BEGINNING

THE WAR had lasted for four years and it had consumed hundreds of thousands of lives and billions of dollars in treasure. It had destroyed one of the two American ways of life forever, and it had changed the other almost beyond recognition; and it ended as it had begun, in a mystery of darkness and passion. If no one could say exactly why it had come about in the first place, no one could quite say what it meant now that it was finished. (A century of reflection has not wholly answered either riddle.) Things done by men born generations after Appomattox would continue to shed light on the significance of this greatest of all convulsions of the American spirit.

Of all men, Abraham Lincoln came the closest to understanding what had happened; yet even he, in his final backward glance, had to confess that something that went beyond words had been at work in the land. When he tried to sum it up, delivering his second inaugural address on March 4, 1865, he could do no more than remind his countrymen that they had somehow done more than they intended to do, as if without knowing it they had served a purpose that lay far beyond their comprehension.

"Neither party," he said, "expected for the war the magnitude or the duration which it has already attained. Neither anticipated that the cause of the conflict might cease with, or even before, the conflict itself should cease." (As he spoke, the Federal Congress had passed the thirteenth amendment and seventeen states had already ratified it; and in Richmond the Congress of the Confederacy was preparing to vote regiments of slaves into the Confederate service. Slavery was dead no matter how the war came out.) "Both read the same Bible and pray to the same God, and each invokes His aid against the other. . . . The prayers of both could not be answered; that of neither has been answered fully. The Almighty has His own purposes."

It was a thing to brood over, this war with its terrible cost and its veiled meanings, and the wisest man could perhaps do little more than ask searching questions about it. As he went on with his speech Lincoln was doing nothing less than remind the people of America that they could not hope to understand what they had done and what had been done to them without examining the central riddle of human existence. As the war storm slowly ebbed he left one of the great questions for all men to ponder:

On May 23 and 24, 1865, Union armies paraded up Washington's Pennsylvania Avenue in a final Grand Review.

"If we shall suppose that American slavery is one of those offenses which, in the providence of God, must needs come, but which, having continued through His appointed time, He now wills to remove, and that He gives to both North and South, this terrible war, as the woe due to those by whom the offense came, shall we discern therein any departure from those divine attributes which the believers in a living God always ascribe to Him?"

This question was propounded by a man who believed that both sides shared in the blame for the war, just as they had shared in the cost of it. Out of such a belief had to come a determination that both sections must also share in the victory. The peace that would come out of the war must, in Lincoln's view, be broad enough and humane enough to mean some sort of gain for everyone in the land—for the Northerner who had fought to reunite the country and to end slavery, for the Southerner who had fought against that goal, for the Negro who had humbly endured the struggle. In such a peace there could be no question of any punitive measures, any more than there could be any question of seeking to restore what the war had destroyed. If there was a triumph to celebrate, it was not the triumph of one set of men over another set, but of all men together over a common affliction.

To his great lieutenants, Grant and Sherman, Lincoln gave a glimpse of his policy in a meeting on board Lincoln's steamer *River Queen* at City Point, just before the beginning of the last campaign of the war. It was a policy rather than a detailed program, summarized in Lincoln's homely injunction: "Let 'em up easy." He wanted to see the Confederate armies disbanded and the men back at work on their farms and in the shops, and he wanted civil governments re-established in the secessionist states at the earliest possible moment. Sherman got the impression that Lincoln was perfectly willing to deal with the existing state governments in the South in order to maintain order, until Congress could provide for a more permanent arrangement. When Sherman returned to North Carolina to finish the job against Johnston, he took with him the conviction that Lincoln wanted a peace of reconciliation with no particular concern about formalities.

So when Johnston surrendered, Sherman was guided by what he thought Lincoln wanted. Two things, however, were wrong: Sherman appears to have gone beyond anything Lincoln was prepared to offer—and

when he and Johnston met to discuss surrender terms Lincoln was dead, and the atmosphere in which Northern politicians could be magnanimous and far-sighted had been fatally poisoned.

Johnston was brought to bay a few days after Lee surrendered. The Union army, more than 80,000 strong, was in camp around Raleigh, North Carolina. Johnston had fewer than half that many men, and not all of them were fully armed and organized. He and Sherman met near a place called Durham's Station, aware that Lee had given up and that the only task remaining was to get the Confederacy out of existence as smoothly as possible, and on April 18 they agreed on a document. Considering the fact that Sherman was looked upon as the South's most pitiless enemy, the hard man of war who struck without compassion and laid waste whole states without remorse, it was an amazing agreement.

To begin with, it covered not simply Johnston's army, but all of the remaining armed forces of the Confederacy. (Johnston had no authority over these, but he had with him the Confederate Secretary of War, General John C. Breckinridge, and Breckinridge's word would be binding.) It went far beyond the terms Grant had given Lee. Confederate regiments were to march to their respective state capitals, deposit their weapons there, and then disband, each man signing a pledge not to take up arms again. Each state government would be recognized as lawful once its officers had taken oath to support the Constitution of the United States. No one was to be punished for the part he had taken in bringing on or supporting secession, all political rights were to be guaranteed, and the rights of person and property as defined in the Federal Constitution were to be fully respected— which might, conceivably, give slavery a new lease on life. All in all, this treaty—for it was a treaty of peace, rather than a simple surrender document—gave all that any Southerner in this spring of 1865 could hope to ask; and by this time there was not a chance in the world that the government in Washington would ratify it.

Lincoln himself would almost certainly have modified it. From the moment when Confederate surrender became an imminent probability, he had insisted that generals in the field were not to concern themselves with political questions; they should give liberal terms to the surrendering armies, but all issues involving the readmission of the states to the Union, the restoration of civil and political rights, and the abolition of slavery, they were to leave in the President's hands. (Sherman apparently had missed this particular point.) To bring the seceded states back into full relationship with the rest of the Union would take the most delicate kind of political finesse, and Lincoln proposed to handle all of this himself. Congress would not be in session until late in the fall, and it was just possible that Lincoln could have his moderate reconstruction program well enough established by that time so that the bitter-enders in House and Senate could not upset it, but he never would have let any general set the pattern for him.

But an actor named John Wilkes Booth had chosen this moment to upset everything. On Good Friday evening, April 14—driven by an insane compulsion of hatred and perverted loyalty to a cause which he had never felt obliged to fight for as a soldier—Booth strode into the President's box at Ford's Theatre in Washington, fired a bullet into Lincoln's brain, vaulted from the box to the stage, and rode off desperately through the night, fancying that if he could just reach Confederate territory he would be hailed as a hero and a savior. His twisted, inadequate mind was never able to see that his trigger finger had done the South more harm than all the lawless bummers in Sherman's army.

In all American history there is no stranger story than the story of the plot that took Lincoln's life. Booth had been conspiring for months, doing it flamboyantly, dramatically, in a way that fairly invited detection. He had first nourished a crackbrained plan to kidnap Lincoln alive and take him down to Richmond, shifting to a scheme for wholesale murder after Lee surrendered and Richmond was captured. He planned to kill Lincoln, Grant, Vice-President Johnson, and Secretary of State Seward, and he conspired with a weird set of dimwitted incompetents who could hardly have carried out a plan to rob a corner newsstand. The odds that the whole scheme would fall of its own weight were fantastically long. And yet, somehow—the luck of the American people just then being out—the thing worked. Lincoln was assassinated; Seward barely escaped death when one of Booth's minions forced a way into his sickroom and slashed him with a knife. The plot to kill Grant and Johnson missed fire, but the central, disastrous feature of the plan worked. Lincoln died.

Lincoln died early on the morning of April 15, and his death left the Republican radicals—the men who hated the South and hoped to see stern punishment inflicted on it—in full control of the Federal government. Vice-President Andrew Johnson had demanded that treason be made odious: now he was President, with full power to make the peace as stern as anyone could wish, and although he would finally come to see that Lincoln's policy was the better one, and would wreck his career trying to put it into effect, he was surrounded by men of great force and determination who would put Lincoln's ideas into the grave along with Lincoln's lifeless body.

For the immediate present the Federal government would be effectively operated by Secretary of War Stanton, who made himself something very like a dictator during the first week or two of Johnson's regime.

Stanton was a man of immense drive; ruthless, often arrogant, of an incurably suspicious nature. The task of unraveling Booth's mad plot was in his hands, and as the details of the scheme came to light Stanton was convinced that Booth was no lone-wolf operator, but was in fact an agent for the Confederate government itself. In part this deduction came simply because Stanton was always ready to believe the worst, especially where his enemies were concerned; and in part it rested on the fact that the Confederate government had been operating that fifth-column business in the North, with agents trying to burn Northern cities, wreck railroads, seize military prison camps, and raid Yankee banks. The War Department had collected a great deal of information about this operation, some of it false, some of it true. It knew, among other things, that these operations had been directed by Confederate agents established in Canada, and it also knew that Booth himself had recently been in Canada. Under the circumstances it is hardly surprising that a man like Stanton should suspect that Booth might be a part of the Southern conspiracy which had been keeping Federal counterespionage operatives so busy.

Stanton did more than suspect: he informed the nation, without any qualifications, that Lincoln had been murdered by Jefferson Davis' agents, and that the whole tragedy was a direct part of the dying Confederate war effort. That he was never able to prove a word of this —it soon became clear that no one in Richmond had had anything at all to do with the murder, and that Booth had been as much an irresponsible fanatic as John Brown had been when he descended on Harpers Ferry—made no difference whatever. The damage was done; in the terrible revulsion of feeling that swept across the North few people would bother to speak out for the sort of peace Lincoln himself had wanted.

Stanton and the other bitter-enders saw to it that no one in the North was allowed to get over his grief quickly. Lincoln's body lay in state beneath the Capitol dome, and there was a state funeral in the White House. Then, in a special train, the body was taken back to Springfield, Illinois, for burial—taken there in the most roundabout way imaginable, put on display in New York and Chicago and in many other cities, made the occasion for the most elaborately contrived funeral procession in American history. Millions of Americans saw it. Those who could not file past the open casket, in places where it was on display, at least could gather by the railroad tracks and watch the train as it moved slowly past. Millions of people took part in this parade of sorrow. It lasted for two weeks, and although the grief which was expressed was undoubtedly sincere, the whole affair amounted to turning a knife in a wound—turning it again and again, so that the shock of sorrow and outraged indignation which had gone all across the North might continue to be felt.

In trying to capitalize on the nation's tragedy the radicals had something real and deep to work with. The millions who stood in silence to watch the funeral car, with its black bunting, drift past on its way to Illinois were the people who had supported Lincoln through thick and thin. They had provided the armies that he had called into being. They had sustained him at the polls when the issue was in doubt. He had spoken to their hearts, in a way no one else had ever done, when he explained the ultimate meaning of the war in his address at Gettysburg and groped for the unattainable truth in his second inaugural. He had expressed the best that was in them, speaking not so much to them as for them, and he had gone with them through four years of trial by doubt and fire. As the war ended they had come to understand his greatness: and now, when he was struck down at the very moment of his triumph, they felt an anger so black that Lincoln's own vision was blotted out.

The first step was to undo what Sherman had tried to do. His treaty with Johnston went first to Grant, who could see that Sherman had done much more than any general was authorized to do. Grant sent the papers on to Stanton and suggested that the whole cabinet might want to consider them. The cabinet did want to consider them, and it disapproved them in short order; Grant was ordered to go to Sherman at once, to cancel the armistice which was a part of the Sherman-Johnston agreement, and to resume hostilities. Grant obeyed and Johnston was notified that the deal was off. There was

no more fighting, as he promptly surrendered on terms identical with those Grant had given Lee.

None of this disturbed Sherman greatly. He could see that he had tried to exercise powers which belonged to the civil government, and when he was overruled he was ready to accept the fact quietly. What infuriated him was the way Stanton used the whole episode to inflame public opinion.

For Stanton made a public announcement concerning the Sherman-Johnston agreement in a way which strongly suggested that Sherman was disloyal or crazy. This agreement, Stanton declared, practically recognized the Confederacy, re-established the secessionist state governments, put arms and ammunition in the hands of Rebels, permitted the re-establishment of slavery, possibly made the Northern taxpayer responsible for debts run up by the Confederate government, and left the defeated Rebels in position to renew the rebellion whenever they saw fit.

An announcement of this kind, coming at the moment when the electorate was still in a state of shock because of Lincoln's assassination, and coming also at a time when the complicity of the Confederate government in Booth's murder plot was being proclaimed as an established fact, was a stunner. It raised Sherman to a high pitch of rage, and made him one of Stanton's most devout and enduring enemies; but this did no particular damage, since Sherman was a good hater and Stanton already had many enemies, and the public outcry that was raised against the general eventually subsided. In a few years no one in the North or the South would remember that Sherman had nearly wrecked his career in his attempt to befriend the South, and he would be enshrined as an unstained hero in the North and as an unmitigated villain in Southern memories. The real harm that was done was the mortal injury that was inflicted on the Lincolnian policy which Sherman, however clumsily, had tried to put into effect.

For the basis of Lincoln's whole approach to reconstruction was the belief that the broken halves of the Union could be fitted together without bitterness and in a spirit of mutual understanding and good will. The war was over, and there was no undoing of anything that had happened. No one had really intended that things should go as they had gone; the responsibility for it all was strangely divided, just as the almost unendurable suffering and heartache had been divided . . . the Almighty did indeed have His own purposes, and now it was up to the people of both sections to try to adjust themselves to those purposes and to work together in the adjustment. But by the time Lincoln's body had finished its long journey and lay in the tomb at Springfield, an atmosphere had been created in the North which put such an effort out of reach. President Johnson would try to make the effort, but he had not a fraction of Lincoln's political skill, and the job was too much for him. He was never able to use what might have been his greatest asset—the wholehearted support which the two most famous Northern generals, Grant and Sherman, would have given to an attempt to put Lincoln's policy into effect.

No one in the North, after Lincoln's death, had anything approaching the prestige which these two soldiers had, and Johnson could have used them if he had known how. But Sherman's experience following the rejection of his "treaty" left him embittered, deeply disgusted with anything smacking of politics; thereafter he would be nothing but the soldier, letting the people at Washington commit any folly they chose to commit, and President Johnson never understood how to soften him. And Grant before long became estranged, not because he opposed what Johnson wanted to do, but simply because Johnson could not handle him. In the end he would be counted among Johnson's enemies because the radicals were able to take advantage of Johnson's clumsiness and Grant's own political innocence.

So things happened in the familiar and imperfect way that every American knows about. The Union was reconstructed, at last, at the price of bitterness and injustice, with much work left for later generations to do. A measure of the amount of work bequeathed to those later generations is the fact that nearly a century after Appomattox the attempt to work out a solution for the race problem—that great untouchable which, many layers down, lay at the abyssal depth of the entire conflict—would still be looked upon as a sectional mat-ter and would still be productive of sectional discord. In the anger and suspicion of the reconstruction era the chance that the thing might be approached rationally, so that it could perhaps be solved rather than simply shoved aside and ignored, flickered out like a candle's flame in a gale of wind.

Nothing could be done rationally at that time because wars do not leave men in a rational mood. Bone-weary of fighting in 1865, the American people greatly desired magnanimity and understanding and a reasonable handling of vexing problems; but those virtues had gone out of fashion, and they could not immediately be re-established. What happened after the war ended grew out of the hot barren years when anger and suspicion went baying down the trail of violence: the years in which bitter appeals to unleashed emotion had made the fury of a few the common affliction of all . . . years of desperate battles, of guerrilla snipings and hangings, with a swinging torch for town and home place and the back of a hard hand to silence dissent. These had created the atmosphere in which men tried to put the Union back together, to turn enmity into friendship, and to open the door of freedom for a race that had lain in bondage. The wonder is not that the job was done so imperfectly, but that it was done at all.

For it was done, finally; if not finished, at least set on the road to completion. It may be many years before the job is really completed; generations before the real meaning and the ultimate consequences of the Civil War are fully comprehended. We understand today a little more than could be understood in 1865, but the whole truth remains dim.

Here was the greatest and most moving chapter in American history, a blending of meanness and greatness, an ending and a beginning. It came out of what men were, but it did not go as men had planned it. The Almighty had His own purposes.

On March 27 and 28, 1865, Sherman conferred with his superiors on board the steamer River Queen at City Point, Virginia. Pictured from left to right in G. P. A. Healy's "The Peace Makers" (above) are Sherman, Grant, Lincoln, and Admiral Porter, who later recalled that the President "wanted peace on almost any terms."

Less than a month later Sherman met Joe Johnston in this rude North Carolina farmhouse (right) to offer generous surrender terms, prompted by Lincoln's statements at City Point.

Sherman's Peace Terms Are Rejected

Near Raleigh, North Carolina, William Tecumseh Sherman met with Joseph E. Johnston on April 17 to discuss surrender terms and showed him a dispatch announcing Lincoln's assassination. "The perspiration came out in large drops on his forehead," Sherman recalled.

Against a background of this fearful news the two men went far beyond their own responsibility, took up the capitulation of all remaining Confederate forces, and the next day signed an armistice containing sweeping civil and political concessions. Sherman, who had talked with Lincoln at City Point, thought he knew what sort of peace the President wanted; but he reckoned without Secretary Stanton, who had assumed near-dictatorial powers, and who wanted harsh terms for the defeated South. Six days later Grant arrived to inform Sherman that his armistice had been summarily rejected. Grant urged his old friend to offer Johnston a more limited surrender proposal, and Johnston signed the revised agreement on April 26.

Traveling north, Sherman saw the uproar which Stanton's denunciation of his original terms to Johnston had created. Sherman's military strategy, his loyalty, even his sanity, were being questioned. "To say that I was merely angry . . ." he wrote later, "would hardly express the state of my feelings. I was outraged beyond measure."

But his gesture of offering the Rebels ten days' rations, Johnston wrote, "reconciles me to what I have previously regarded as the misfortune of my life, that of having you to encounter in the field." Twenty-six years later Joe Johnston died of pneumonia, contracted while he stood hatless in the rain at William T. Sherman's funeral.

Sherman's original terms (above), granting a general amnesty, were too sweeping, and he was forced to replace them with the more modest agreement (below), signed on April 26.

598   The Mark of War

At left, Abraham Lincoln in Springfield, June 3, 1860; above, five years later in Washington, April 10, 1865.

An Assassin Strikes at Ford's Theatre

FORD'S THEATRE

TENTH STREET, ABOVE E.

SEASON II —— WEEK XXXI —— NIGHT 196
WHOLE NUMBER OF NIGHTS, 40 5

JOHN T. FORD .... PROPRIETOR AND MANAGER
(Also of Holliday St. Theatre, Baltimore, and Academy of Music, Phil'a.)
Stage Manager .... J. B. WRIGHT
Treasurer .... H. CLAY FORD

Friday Evening, April 14th, 1865

BENEFIT!
—AND—
LAST NIGHT
OF MISS
LAURA KEENE

THE DISTINGUISHED MANAGERESS, AUTHORESS AND ACTRESS,
Supported by
JOHN DYOTT and HARRY HAWK.

TOM TAYLOR'S CELEBRATED ECCENTRIC COMEDY,

As originally produced in America by Miss Keene, and performed by her upwards of

ONE THOUSAND NIGHTS,
ENTITLED
OUR AMERICAN
COUSIN

FLORENCE TRENCHARD .... MISS LAURA KEENE
(Her original character.)

Abel Murcott, Clerk to Attorney	John Dyott
Asa Trenchard	Harry Hawk
Sir Edward Trenchard	T. C. GOURLAY
Lord Dundreary	E. A. EMERSON
Mr. Coyle, Attorney	J. MATTHEWS
Lieutenant Vernon, R. N.	W. J. FERGUSON
Captain De Boots	C. BYRNES
Binny	G. SPEAR
Buddicomb, a valet	J. L. EVANS
John Whicker, a gardener	J. L. De BONAY
Bailiffs	G. A. PARKHURST and L. JOHNSON
Mary Trenchard	Miss J. GOURLAY
Mrs. Mountchessington	Mrs. H. MUZZY
Augusta	Miss. H. TRUEMAN
Georgiana	Miss M. HART
Sharpe	Mrs. J. H. EVANS
Skillet	Miss M. GOURLAY

PATRIOTIC SONG AND CHORUS
"HONOR TO OUR SOLDIERS."

"Honor to our soldiers,
Our nation's greatest pride,
Who, 'neath our Starry Banner's folds,
Have fought, have bled and died;
They're nature's noblest handiwork—
No King so proud as they.
God bless the heroes of the land,
And cheer them on their way."

Words by H. B. Phillips; Music Composed and Arranged by Prof. William
Withers, Jr.; Solos by Miss M. Hart, H. B. Phillips and George M. Arth
and the Ladies and Gentlemen of the Company.

SATURDAY EVENING, APRIL 15,

BENEFIT of Miss JENNIE GOURLAY

When will be presented BOURCICAULT'S Great Sensation Drama,

THE OCTOROON

Easter Monday, April 17, Engagement of the YOUNG AMERICAN TRAGEDIAN,

EDWIN ADAMS

John Wilkes Booth (above) never quite achieved the fame of his father, Junius Brutus, or his brother, Edwin, both distinguished tragedians. He openly espoused the Southern cause and, in the Washington boardinghouse of Mrs. Mary Surratt, hatched a wild scheme to abduct Lincoln. Samuel Arnold, a Confederate veteran, and Michael O'Laughlin, a Baltimore clerk, backed out of the conspiracy when assassination became the goal. On the fatal night Booth sent a 23-year-old drifter, David Herold, to direct muscular, witless Lewis Paine to Seward's house to murder the Secretary of State. George Atzerodt, an uneducated immigrant, did not even attempt his mission of killing Andrew Johnson. Mrs. Surratt's son, John, may have been directed to attack Grant, but he claimed that he was in Canada on April 14. Edward Spangler, a stage carpenter, apparently helped Booth escape.

This playbill announced the fateful performance.

Lewis Paine

George Atzerodt

Mary Surratt

David Herold

Samuel Arnold

Michael O'Laughlin

John Surratt

Edward Spangler

On the afternoon of April 14, 1865, Lincoln, speaking to a friend, alluded wearily to a theatre party planned for that evening: "It has been advertised that we will be there, and I cannot disappoint the people. Otherwise I would not go. I do not want to go."

At 7 P.M. a slender young actor left Washington's National Hotel and asked the desk clerk if he were going to Ford's Theatre. "There will be some fine acting there tonight," John Wilkes Booth commented.

The President and Mrs. Lincoln, accompanied by a young officer and his fiancée who had substituted at the last minute for General and Mrs. Grant, entered the theatre about 9:00. After receiving an ovation from the crowd, the Presidential party was shown to a flag-draped box, where the exhausted Lincoln eased himself into an upholstered rocking chair.

A half hour later Booth arrived at Ford's Theatre. Lincoln's unreliable guard had left his post, and the entrance to the Presidential box was unguarded. Booth slipped along a back corridor, sighted his victim through a tiny peephole he had drilled in the door to the box that morning, and silently entered. He leveled his six-inch brass derringer at the back of Lincoln's head and fired. After grappling briefly with the young officer, Booth jumped from the box, catching his spur as he leaped, and broke his leg as he fell onto the stage. In an instant, however, he was out through the wings and making his escape on a horse waiting in the alley.

Across town, at that very hour, one of Booth's accomplices, Lewis Paine, was making an unsuccessful attempt on the life of Secretary of State Seward. Fear and hysteria gripped Washington as Lincoln was removed to a house across the street from the theatre. Through the night doctors did what they could to save the President's life, but at 7:22 the following morning Abraham Lincoln died.

601

The Nation Mourns the President's Death

Hermann Faber based this sketch of Lincoln's death on eyewitness testimony. Bearded Gideon Welles dozes at left as a physician takes the President's pulse. At the moment of death Stanton, standing at right, reportedly said: "Now he belongs to the ages." Below is Lincoln's funeral train on a Lake Michigan pier at Chicago.

After a funeral service in the White House on April 19, Lincoln's body lay in state in the rotunda of the Capitol and, two days later, was placed aboard the seven-car funeral train. The 1,700-mile journey, virtually retracing the route he had taken four years earlier to his first inauguration, had begun.

As the train passed Lancaster, Pennsylvania, a tired old man in a carriage watched from the edge of the crowd; it was James Buchanan. The coffin was taken to Philadelphia's Independence Hall, where Lincoln had once raised the 34-star flag, and in New York 100,000 hushed mourners accompanied the cortege through the streets. Since no building in Cleveland was large enough to accommodate the expected crowds, a special pagoda was erected in a city park. Bonfires illuminated the route to Chicago; along the way thousands stood all night in the rain for a glimpse of the passing train.

On February 11, 1861, in bidding an affectionate farewell to his home town, Lincoln had said: "I now leave, not knowing when or whether ever I may return . . ." On May 4, 1865, he was laid to rest in Springfield.

Above is a poster offering a reward for Booth, who was trapped in a burning barn in Virginia and shot on April 26. A military tribunal sentenced Herold, Atzerodt, Paine, and Mrs. Surratt to be hanged. John Surratt escaped; the other conspirators, as well as Dr. Samuel Mudd, who set Booth's leg, received prison sentences.

The Lincoln Legend

To the poet Walt Whitman, Lincoln's death came as a personal tragedy, and from the depths of his grief he composed a timeless elegy for the tall, homely man who had come out of the Illinois plains to save the Union. Lincoln the man was to become Lincoln the legend.

"When lilacs last
   in the dooryard bloom'd,
And the great star early droop'd
   in the western sky in the night,
I mourn'd, and yet shall mourn
   with ever-returning spring.
Ever-returning spring,
   trinity sure to me you bring,
Lilac blooming perennial
   and drooping star in the west,
And thought of him I love. . . .
With the tolling tolling bells'
   perpetual clang,
Here, coffin that slowly passes,
I give you my sprig of lilac."

Abraham Lincoln is virtually a living presence in his Springfield home. His shawl and stovepipe hat hang in the hall; his desk and the shadowed door above might have been photographed in 1861. Millions of Americans make the pilgrimage to the Lincoln Memorial in Washington (right).

A SOUND
OF DISTANT
DRUMS

The Civil War left America with a legend and a haunting memory. These had to do less with things that remained than with the things that had been lost. What had been won would not be entirely visible for many years to come, and most people were too war-weary to look at it anyway, but what had been lost could not be forgotten. The men who had marched gaily off in new uniforms and who had not come back; the dreams that had brought fire and a great wind down on a land that meant to be happy and easygoing; the buildings the war had wrecked, the countryside it had scarred, the whole network of habits and hopes and attitudes of mind it had ground to fragments—these were remembered with proud devotion by a nation which had paid an unimaginable price for an experience compounded of suffering and loss and ending in stunned bewilderment.

North and South together shared in this, for if the consciousness of defeat afflicted only one of the two sections, both knew that something greatly cherished was gone forever, whether that something was only a remembered smile on the face of a boy who had died or was the great shadow of a way of life that had been destroyed. People clung to the memory of what was gone. Knowing the cruelty and insane destructiveness of war as well as any people who ever lived, they nevertheless kept looking backward, and they put a strange gloss of romance on what they saw, cherishing the haunted overtones it had left.

As the postwar years passed the remembrances became formalized. In cities and in small towns the Decoration Day parade became a ritual; rank after rank of men who unaccountably kept on growing older and less military-looking would tramp down dusty streets, bands playing, flags flying, ranks growing thinner year by year until finally nobody remained to march at all. In the South the same ceremonial was performed, although the date on the calendar was different; and in both sections orators spoke at vast length, reciting deeds of bravery and devotion which somehow, considered from the increasing distance, had the power to knit the country together again. Their stereotyped speeches were oddly made significant by the deeds which they commemorated.

The South had the bitterer memories, and it wrapped them in a heavier trapping of nostalgia. Decaying plantation buildings, with empty verandas slowly falling apart under porticoes upheld by insecure wooden pillars, became shrines simply because they somehow spoke for the dream that had died, the vitality of the dream gaining in strength as the physical embodiment of it drifted off into ruin. There were cemeteries for both sections—quiet, peaceful fields where soldiers who had never cared about military formality lay in the last sleep, precisely ranked in rows of white headstones which bespoke personal tragedies blunted at last by time. There were statues, too, with great men frozen in cold marble, presiding over drowsy battlefields which would never again know violence or bloodshed.

And, finally, there was the simple memory of personal valor—the enduring realization that when the great challenge comes, the most ordinary people can show that they value something more than they value their own lives. When the last of the veterans had gone, and the sorrows and bitternesses which the war created had at last worn away, this memory remained. The men who fought in the Civil War, speaking for all Americans, had said something the country could never forget.

606

*Union veterans march in a Decoration Day parade in Boston in 1890,
as painted by Henry Sandham. The officers in the front rank include
Generals Schofield and Howard (extreme left) and Sherman (right).*

The Lost Cause

A symbol of the ruined antebellum South is Bellechasse (opposite), once the lovely Louisiana mansion of Confederate cabinet member Judah Benjamin. Above is Virginia's monument "to her sons" at Gettysburg. The statue of Robert E. Lee looks across the mile-wide valley toward Cemetery Ridge.

Monuments to the Heroic Dead

*This weathered stone, one of several score like it, marks
the grave of an unknown Rebel who fought and died
for Bedford Forrest at the Battle of Brice's Crossroads.*

Typical of Civil War battlefield monuments is this tribute in stone to a Federal regiment that stood, bloodied but firm, with Thomas, "The Rock of Chickamauga."

OVERLEAF: *In rank upon orderly rank lie the dead of Antietam. Of the young men interred in this century-old national cemetery, nearly 40 per cent are unknown.*

With malice toward none; with charity for all; with firmness in the right, as God gives us to see the right, let us strive on to finish the work we are in; to bind up the nation's wounds; to care for him who shall have borne the battle, and for his widow, and his orphan —to do all which may achieve and cherish a just, and a lasting peace, among ourselves, and with all nations.

ABRAHAM LINCOLN, *Second Inaugural Address*

ACKNOWLEDGMENTS
AND
INDEX

ACKNOWLEDGMENTS

The Editors are especially grateful to the following individuals and organizations for their generous assistance, and for their co-operation in making available pictorial materials in their collections:

Abby Aldrich Rockefeller Folk Art Collection, Williamsburg, Va.—Mrs. Mary C. Black

Ansco Corp., Binghamton, N.Y.—Philip M. Mikoda

Department of the Army, Office of Military History, Washington—Mrs. Marian McNaughton

City of Atlanta, Department of Parks—George I. Simons

Mrs. Anita Barer, Bronxville, N.Y.

Berry-Hill Galleries, New York—Henry Hill

Boston Museum of Fine Arts—Elizabeth P. Riegel, Mrs. Anne Blake Freedberg

Mrs. John Nicholas Brown, Providence, R.I., and the Brown Collection librarian, Richard B. Harrington

Le Duc de Castries, Paris

Chicago Historical Society—Mrs. Mary Frances Rhymer, Joseph B. Zywicki

Mrs. Arthur Ben Chitty, Sewanee, Tenn.

Cincinnati Public Library—Yeatman Anderson III

Mrs. Frank J. Coleman, New York

Confederate Museum, Richmond—India W. Thomas

Cooper Union Museum, New York—Richard P. Wunder

Corcoran Gallery of Art, Washington—Hermann Warner Williams, Jr.

Alexander McCook Craighead, Dayton, Ohio

Dayton (Ohio) Art Institute—Charles H. Elam

Eli Whitney Debevoise, New York

Detroit Public Library, Burton Historical Collection—James M. Babcock

Fairfax Downey, West Springfield, N.H.

George Eastman House, Rochester, N.Y.—Beaumont Newhall

Edward Eberstadt & Sons, New York—Charles and Lindley Eberstadt

Eleutherian Mills-Hagley Foundation, Wilmington, Del.—Joseph P. Monigle

Henry Ford Museum, Dearborn, Mich.—M. W. Thomas, Jr.

Frick Art Reference Library, New York—Mrs. Henry W. Howell, Jr.

Edgar William and Bernice Chrysler Garbisch, New York

U. I. Harris, St. Louis

Robert E. Harwell, Nashville

Historical Society of Pennsylvania, Philadelphia—Nicholas B. Wainwright

Stanley F. Horn, Nashville

Houghton Library, Harvard University, Cambridge, Mass.—Carolyn Jakeman

Illinois State Historical Library, Springfield—Margaret A. Flint

Iowa State Department of History and Archives, Des Moines—Fleming Fraker, Jr.

S. W. Jackman, Bates College, Lewiston, Me.

Richard M. Kain, Louisville, Ky.

Kansas State Historical Society, Topeka—Robert W. Richmond

Kean Archives, Philadelphia—Manuel Kean

William R. Kelly, Watkins Glen, N.Y.

Mrs. Katharine McCook Knox, Washington

Mrs. Dorothy Meserve Kunhardt, Morristown, N.J.

Halleck Lefferts, South Royalton, Vt.

Lester S. Levy, Pikesville, Md.

Library of Congress, Washington—Milton Kaplan, Virginia Daiker, Hirst D. Milhollen, Carl Stang, David C. Mearns, Donald C. Holmes

Lincoln Memorial University, Harrogate, Tenn.—Wayne C. Temple

E. B. Long, Oak Park, Ill.

Pierre Longone, Paris

Louisiana Historical Association, New Orleans—Kenneth Trist Urquhart

Ian W. McLaughlin, Yonkers, N.Y.

Mrs. Alice Reed McWilliams, Dwight, Ill.

Mariners Museum, Newport News, Va.—Mrs. Agnes Brabrand

Maryland Historical Society, Baltimore—James W. Foster, Eugenia Calvert Holland

Frederick Hill Meserve, New York

N. S. Meyer, Inc., New York—Abner A. Raeburn, Betty Arbitter

Missouri Historical Society, St. Louis—Mrs. Ruth K. Field, Marjory Douglas

Museum of the City of New York—Henriette Beal

National Archives, Washington—Josephine Cobb, Victor Gondos, Jr., Forest L. Williams

National Broadcasting Company, Project Twenty, New York—Daniel W. Jones

National Gallery of Art, Washington—William P. Campbell, Huntington Cairns

National Library of Medicine, Washington—Sheila M. Parker

National Maritime Museum, Greenwich, England—A. H. Waite

National Park Service—Herbert E. Kahler, Chester L. Brooks, Bernard T. Campbell, Joseph P. Cullen, Albert Dillahunty, Harry W. Doust, Charles S. Dunn, Ralph Happel, James N. Haskett, Charles E. Hatch, James B. Myers, O. F. Northington, Jr., Raymond K. Rundell, Wallace T. Stephens, Frederick H. Tilberg, John T. Willett, Francis F. Wilshin

New Hampshire Historical Society, Concord—Philip N. Guyol

New-York Historical Society—Arthur B. Carlson, Betty J. Ezequelle, the late Bella C. Landauer

New York Public Library—Elizabeth E. Roth, Wilson G. Duprey

North Carolina Department of Archives and History, Raleigh—W. S. Tarlton

Ohio Historical Society, Columbus—Robert S. Harper

The Old Print Shop, New York—Robert L. Harley

Lloyd Ostendorf, Dayton, Ohio

Le Comte de Paris, Paris

Peabody Museum, Salem, Mass.—M. V. Brewington

Harold L. Peterson, Arlington, Va.

Joseph Verner Reed, Paris

Franklin D. Roosevelt Library, Hyde Park, N.Y.—Herman Kahn

Margaret Ruckert, New Orleans

Seventh Regiment Armory, New York—Major Kenneth C. Miller

Nathan Shaye, Detroit

Mrs. Charles J. Sinnott, New Orleans

South Carolina Historical Society, Charleston—Mrs. Granville T. Prior

Southern Historical Collection, University of North Carolina Library, Chapel Hill—Anna Brooke Allan

Victor D. Spark, New York

Sir Stanley Spurling, St. George, Bermuda

D. H. Strother, Milwaukee

Tennessee State Library and Archives, Nashville—Dan M. Robison

Time, Inc., New York—Dorothy L. Smith

C. C. Travis, Grand Rapids, Mich.

Union League Club, New York—Edward P. Newton

Union League of Philadelphia—Daniel M. Layman

United States Military Academy, West Point, N.Y.—Colonel Vincent J. Esposito, Richard E. Kuehne

United States National Museum, Washington—Edgar M. Howell, Wilcomb E. Washburn

Valentine Museum, Richmond—Elizabeth J. Dance

Virginia Cavalcade, Richmond—Mrs. Ulrich Troubetzkoy

General Lew Wallace Study, Crawfordsville, Ind.—Mrs. Inez Cunningham

Western Reserve Historical Society, Cleveland—Mrs. Alene Lowe White

Mrs. W. M. Williams, Denver, Colo.

Wisconsin State Historical Society, Madison—Paul Vanderbilt, Cheryle Hughes

W. E. S. Zuill, Hamilton, Bermuda

Color photography of paintings: New York—Herbert Loebel, Geoffrey Clements, John D. Schiff; Richmond—A. L. Dementi; Philadelphia—Charles P. Mills and Son; Washington—Henry B. Beville, Stanley T. Manzer

INDEX